EUROPEAN WEAPONS
AND ARMOUR

EUROPEAN WEAPONS AND ARMOUR

From the Renaissance
to the Industrial Revolution

EWART OAKESHOTT

F.S.A.

*With line illustrations
by the author*

THE BOYDELL PRESS

First published 1980
The Lutterworth Press

Reissued 2000
The Boydell Press, Woodbridge
Reprinted in paperback 2012, 2016, 2018, 2019

ISBN 978-0-85115-789-4 hardback
ISBN 978-1-84383-720-6 paperback

The Boydell Press is an imprint of Boydell & Brewer Ltd
PO Box 9, Woodbridge, Suffolk IP12 3DF, UK
and of Boydell & Brewer Inc.
668 Mt Hope Avenue, Rochester, NY 14620, USA
website: www.boydellandbrewer.com

A CiP catalogue record for this book is available
from the British Library

For

SYBIL

without whom

this

would have been

impossible

Contents

CONTENTS

Brief bibliographies appear at the end of relevant chapters

List of Illustrations

MONOCHROME PLATES

NOTE A list of photographic acknowledgments appears on page 268.

LINE DRAWINGS

LIST OF ILLUSTRATIONS

LIST OF ILLUSTRATIONS

Abbreviations

References in the text to *A of W* and *S in A of C* are to the author's earlier works, *The Archaeology of Weapons* and *The Sword in the Age of Chivalry*.

Weight and measurement are expressed in imperial terms, the closest metrical equivalents being given in parentheses, with the abbreviations mm for millimetre, cm for centimetre, m for metre (usually, however, spelt out in full), g for gramme (again, usually spelt out in full), and kg for kilogramme.

Conventional abbreviations, such as p for page, Fig. for Figure, *q.v.* for *quod vide*, and so on, are employed throughout, and are not glossed here.

Note

There is one further point that should be mentioned. In order to emphasise the cross-fertilisation between European states and cities in the manufacture and trading of arms and armour, foreign names, such as *flamberge* or *schiavona*, are given in italic type. A fair proportion of these names are German and according to correct German usage should have a capital letter (for example, *Landsknecht*). However, as the terms are used frequently in this book, and appear alongside French, Italian and Spanish names, they have been treated as if integrated into English, and appear without capitals.

Author's Acknowledgments

So many people have given encouragement and support to my research during the past thirty-five years, and to my efforts to prepare this book in the last ten of them, that to name them all would be impossible. My formal thanks to certain museums for the use of photographs are given at the end of this book, but to the officials whose main concern is with arms in these museums, and to many others, who have all helped to forward my work, thanks of a less impersonal nature are due. There are many private individuals too, collectors and amateurs of arms who have generously made pieces in their collections available to me for study or for inclusion here among the illustrations. They prefer to remain anonymous, but I would like to think they know how much I appreciate their interest.

However, in any Acknowledgment of this kind it cannot be amiss to name those who are one's friends as well as one's mentors. Mr A. V. B. Norman, BA, FSA, Master of the Armouries at the Tower of London, and Mr Claude Blair, MA, FSA, of the Victoria and Albert Museum, have for decades guided my sometimes errant enthusiasms along the path of academic rectitude, as well as giving unstintingly of their profound knowledge and experience of the subject of arms and all others relating to it. So too have Mr William Reid of the National Army Museum and Mr J. Scott, MA, SMA, FSA Scot., of the Art Gallery and Museum, Glasgow. But my first introduction to them and to the late Sir James Mann, I owe to Mr H. Russell Robinson of the Armouries at the Tower of London. When on a winter morning of 1946 we fell into talk across a case full of gauntlets in the old Horse Armoury, I could never have imagined what wealth of knowledge and unending interest would grow from that meeting, or that I should be privileged to benefit as I have from his incomparable flair for the whole touch and taste and smell of the more practical approaches to the study of armour, as well as its academic aspects. His recent untimely death is a personal grief to many, but a loss beyond measure to the study of military archaeology.

It is with regret that I have also learned, since this book reached proof stage, of the sad deaths of Mr E. A. Christensen and Mr Harold Peterson whose collections are cited in these pages.

I owe, too, far more than a few words can express to Mr R. T. Gwynn, Mr Howard Blackmore, FSA, FGA, Mr Evan Perry and Mr David Jeffcoat. To the firm of Peter Dale Ltd, I owe formal thanks for the readiness with which, on request, they have caused countless swords to be photographed for inclusion here, and less formal and most sincere ones to Mr Peter Dale, Mr Derek Spalding and Mr Robin Dale, for their generosity in giving me access to all the high-quality armour and arms continually passing through their hands.

AUTHOR'S ACKNOWLEDGMENTS

I do not use a typewriter. Every word has gone down on paper in a vile, tiny, cramped handwriting; and the original version of this book was some 10,000 words longer than it is now. All of it has been typed for me with patience and good humour beyond belief by Mrs Kay Rees. What can an author say about such things? And then the whole typescript, cut, amended and extended by interpolations on odd pieces of paper, was put into order by Miss Jenny Overton and her colleagues at Lutterworth Press, creating sanity out of a Pandemonium of line drawings, and for the third time in eighteen years producing a book from my labours. So to say that I thank them is feeble, but it is all I can do.

Ewart Oakeshott

Cwmystwyth, 1977

PREFACE

The aim of this book is to present a sketch—space forbids its being more than that—of the development of weapons, from the end of the ·fifteenth century until the end of the eighteenth, in much the same way as in a previous volume, *The Archaeology of Weapons*, I attempted to present the story of military hardware from the Bronze Age to the Renaissance. So this, though in a different form, is really no more than a continuation of that attempt, taking it from the Renaissance towards the present day. However, as we get nearer to our own time the material becomes harder to present. On the one hand, wars become more complex and arms show greater variation in style and purpose according to nationality, even to regional locality, and fashion alters their forms much oftener than it did in earlier centuries. Many more arms are produced too, and an infinitely greater number has survived. On the other hand, as the centuries pass we find that there are fewer and fewer *types* of weapons in use: the mace, the axe, the hammer, the pike, the halberd and bill, the bow and crossbow, even the dagger, go out of use in Europe until by the middle of the seventeenth century the only weapons left to describe are the gun and the sword—though, of course, daggers and knives were still used to some extent, as were bows and crossbows (for hunting mainly, though the Scots carried bows at the battle of Tippermuir in 1644). In the same way, armour, growing to a peak of perfection in the first half of the sixteenth century, declines in quality and effectiveness (in direct ratio to the increase in the quality and effectiveness of firearms) until by 1650 it is well on its way to the museum.

But if the field is narrowed to the study of the sword and the gun, the task is not made any easier. The mutations and variations of sword types steadily grow until by the start of the nineteenth century the task of classification and analysis would call for a specialised work with one volume for each nation in Europe and one for America. Fortunately when it comes to the study of firearms the job is done, for the huge mass of material has been accurately presented in meticulous detail by many specialist authorities of the first rank; it is not in my brief.

To the reader's first glance it may seem that this book is very much biased in favour of the sword. It has to be, for the reasons given above and because so far only comparatively scant attention has been given to the study of swords.

Owing to inescapable limitations, I have to present my sketch in as clear and direct a manner as possible. The emphasis has to be upon clarity, so there will be many illustrations but few footnotes. I write for the student of arms whose interest is not academic but practical, be he writer, actor, collector, artist or—perhaps best of all—mere amateur. What I mean by a mere amateur (and what would instantly have been understood by it half a century ago) is one whose interest is inspired not by the purity of scholarship or by academic professionalism, but by love. If anything should be found in the following pages to appease the scholar or satisfy the academic, so much the better; but it should be made plain before I set out upon such a hazardous enterprise as this attempt, with so vast a mass of material crammed into so small a compass of paper and ink, that there will be shortcomings. To avoid them I should need three more volumes, not one. These inevitable *lacunae* may offend the scholar but will not, I believe, affect the amateur for whom I write. My choice is clear: if I sacrifice clarity for pedantry, illustration for footnotes, I shall produce a book whose fate will be to moulder in quiet, undisturbed respectability on library shelves. It is not for this that I have undertaken a lifetime of research.

INTRODUCTION

With the last decade of the fifteenth century, military history enters a new epoch. One cannot say that any particular date or decade marks the end of the Middle Ages or the beginning of the Renaissance, for in some parts of Europe society remained firmly medieval until well into the sixteenth century, while in Italy the Renaissance began before the end of the fourteenth. When it comes to the art of war and the history of arms, however, we can be positive: the decade 1490—1500 marks a definite turning-point and ushers in the era of musket and pike in much the same way at the Visigoths' crossing of the Danube in AD 376 and the battle of Adrianople in AD 378 ushered in the era of the armoured knight. The latter lasted more than a thousand years, whereas musket and pike only dominated the fields of war for two centuries, for the introduction of the socket bayonet in the 1690s brought it to an end when the musketeer became his own pikeman. Thus began the supremacy of bayonet and cannon, in its turn to be swept away in 1914—1918.

September 12 1494 is a date full of significance in the history of arms. On that day Charles VIII of France gave grudging and discourteous audience to Ludovico Sforza, Duke of Milan, in an intolerably hot hotel overcrowded with soldiers, *aides de camp*, councillors, priests and hangers-on. This was in the town of Asti in Savoy, the property of Charles's cousin, Louis d'Orléans, who had inherited it from his mother. For this reason it had been chosen as the mustering-place for a great army of invasion which France was about to loose upon Italy with the purpose of seizing the kingdom of Naples for the French crown. On that same day, far away at Cognac, a baby was born to Louise de Savoie, wife of the Comte d'Angoulême. Charles's invasion was to begin a war which would last for sixty-six years; and the baby was to inherit it. He grew up to become François de Valois, Duc d'Angoulême, and, at the age of twenty, François I, King of France. Once he was safely on the throne he threw himself with tremendous verve into the war, obsessively seeking the paths of glory, thereby ensuring that it lasted for the rest of his life and enabling himself to hand it on, in good going order, to his successors.

Up to the last decade of the fifteenth century, war had been an occupation in which feudal chivalry found its glory, and efficiency in it was the attribute of a class. After about 1490, this efficiency became the attribute of a profession, the subject of careful study and much experiment. The vigorous, questing, scientific spirit of the sixteenth century added many new forms to the art of war which made medieval martial concepts seem more remote from modern warfare than were those of the great days of Rome.

The army mustering at Asti was the finest Europe had seen since the days of Imperial Rome—better financed, better organised, better armed and trained and fed than any army had been since Diocletian reorganised the legions in AD 289. It fairly crackled with enthusiasm, fiery and confident in its efficiency and strength and in the strategic plan which had brought it into being. The idea was excellent, curiously modern: an exuberant enterprise of aggression, carried out with a compact army of 40,000 men, a swift *blitzkrieg* down a prostrate Italy cowed with terror of the French arms, and an easy dashing victory at the end of it.

The meeting between Charles and Sforza provides intriguing contrasts: the King, heir to all the greatness of the noblest royal house in Europe, behaved with unmannerly boorishness, while Sforza, heir to a soldier of fortune whose forefathers had been peasants, bore himself with princely dignity and exquisite good taste. But Charles for all his kingship was a boor, and with such a force behind him could afford to treat like a lackey the second-generation ruler of a duchy which had the anatomy of a pancake, with no defensible frontiers. France itself was arrogant and brash in its newly-found mightiness (such a contrast to its abject condition only forty years before at the end of the Hundred Years War), while Italy, like Sforza, was rich in ancient culture as in material wealth, but lacked any real military power. France now needed Milan's support; Milan was terrified of the French, and so the support was given, and an enormous loan with it.

Charles owed his power to his father, Louis XI; God knew to what he owed his misshapen body and feeble mind, but in 1494 his big head was stuffed with romantic ideas of a crusade to free the Holy Land from the Turk, taking in the conquest of Naples *en route* for Jerusalem. *He* may have dreamed of Charlemagne and Godfrey de Bouillon and St Louis, but his advisers—political, military and religious—did nothing of the kind. Their interest was practical. Some fifty years earlier, in 1442, the kingdom of Naples and Sicily, which had been ruled for almost two hundred years by a cadet branch of the French royal house, had fallen into the power of Aragon; the merging of Aragon and Castile in 1469 had meant that it was now controlled by the far more dangerous power of a united Spain. Charles's advisers saw this glittering *chevauchée* for what it was (after all, they had created and organised it), a venture of political aggression designed to secure France against the growing nationhood of her neighbours. The practical and sensible aim of the invasion was the acquisition of power, with as much plunder thrown in for individuals as could be got. It was Europe's first essay in raw nationalism. Hence the army at Asti, bent on getting in the first blow and showing what France was capable of.

It certainly was impressive, however futile the Royal youth who was carried along with it like a leaf on a mountain stream. Its leaders were young men '*as full of spirit as the month of May, and gorgeous as the sun at Midsummer*' who were soon to show their mettle and blazon their names across the pages of history and romance in countless battles, sieges, onfalls and forays for half a century. They gathered in great state around Asti: the gleaming *gens d'armes* of the *Compagnies d'Ordonnance*, a permanent standing force of the finest cavalry in Europe; the columns of mercenary Swiss pikemen fresh from their triumphs over Charles *Le Téméraire*, 'the Rash', of Burgundy; and the train of artillery built up in France over the last half-century and now without equal anywhere in the world. The very best war material available was poised to sweep through Italy and take Europe by the nose.

Europe, of course, retaliated, and Charles's dream of becoming a second Charlemagne turned into a nightmare which grew more appalling as the decades passed. His initial invasion succeeded, but no sooner was he master of Naples than all the states of Italy, whose timid neutrality had let him through, united behind him in passionate hostility and cut him off from his homeland. He had to bring what was left of his army—disease and desertion had almost halved it—racing back to fight its way past a great confederate host in the dry mountain valley of the Taro near the village of Fornovo on July 6 1495. The Italian army, composed mostly of the mercenary armies of the *Condottieri*, was decisively beaten though it out-numbered the French by two to one. But for two centuries the Italian style of war had been to avoid actual fighting; after all, the men-at-arms of a *condottiere* were his stock-in-trade, he was not going to risk losing them or getting them damaged, so if two armies were unfortunate enough actually to confront one another, they engaged in a chessboard series of manoeuvres and feints until one side agreed that it had been out-matched by the other. Not so on the Taro: the French meant business, and the Italians were horrified. Many of them fought bravely enough, but the greater part rode off the field in disgust at this unsporting behaviour on the part of an army which by all the rules of (Italian) war was beaten before its men drew blade.

So Charles got by—he bore himself well too, fighting valiantly when for a while he was cut off by a group of Italian knights: but it was a near-run thing.

He had not long to enjoy his success, such as it was; three years later he died in a silly domestic accident. He left no son, so his cousin, Louis d'Orléans, succeeded him as Louis XII, and thus inherited the Royal claim to Naples as well as his own family claim to Milan (he was the grandson of Valentina Visconti, heiress to the Duchy which a generation earlier had been taken over by the adventurer Francesco Sforza, father of the magnificent Ludovico). So the war was resumed with even greater vigour—Louis not only had a good claim to Milan, but was a good soldier as well. No support was asked of Sforza this time. The French crossed the Alps and simply annexed Milan. Ludovico tried to escape among the retiring columns of his defeated mercenaries, dressed as a humble pikeman, but someone gave him away, and Louis had him carted off and shut up in the castle of Loches, where he died nine years later.

Louis went on to capture Naples, but he did not hold it long; in 1502 his army of the south was beaten at Seminara by a Spanish force under Gonzalo de Córdoba. Now the war clarified into its true colours as a struggle between France and Spain for domination in Italy: it went on that way for two centuries (with a forty-year break in the middle when France went out of the game, preoccupied with her own civil wars). Louis XII lost Naples in 1503, and Milan ten years later. In 1515 he died; and François d'Angoulême, the child born with the war, succeeded him.

From the very start of his reign François I flung himself into the war with romantic zest. He took yet another army across the Alps—this time adventurously, by a little-known pass, which enabled him to catch his opponents on the farther side completely off-guard—and in a confused battle, much of it fought in dim moonlight, outside Milan, by the village of Marignano (Melegnano) he won a decisive victory over the Milanese hireling Swiss. This was on September 13 1515.

The victory was not only decisive in regaining Milan, it was also decisive in convincing François that he was indeed what he had always wanted to be, a great war leader. His army had won him a splendid battle, but he personally had fought with great bravery and distinction, getting stunned twice, slightly wounded, and having the beautiful new German armour which he had put on that day for the first time battered and spoiled. Not just a warlord, then. A most gallant chevalier! The ideal of his own ambition, the accolade of knighthood conferred upon him after the battle by the finest knight of them all, the incomparable Bayard!

All this boded ill for Europe. From now until his death, François would pursue this will-of-the-wisp of personal glory, which ever after eluded him—indeed in 1525 it landed him a prisoner-of-war in a Spanish gaol after the most dreadful defeat his arms ever suffered.

But in spite of this, for twenty-two years more he persisted in sending army after army to destruction in Italy. He never gave up, and bequeathed the war which had started on the day he was born to his son, and to the whole of Europe for generation after generation, for every European war since then has stemmed from that.

Why in the face of repeated disaster the people of France were willing, and her kings eager, to persist in this futile adventure is one of the wonders of history. It made certain that almost ceaseless nationalistic wars would ravage Europe for four centuries, wars which by the seventeenth century had spread to the Americas, by the eighteenth to India, by the nineteenth to Africa, and by the twentieth were to engulf the entire globe.

Or was it really so? Those 'devastated' nations, 'bled white by war', produced unimaginable accumulations of wealth and prestige, and splendours of creative art. No, it is a gross misrepresentation to say that these wars ravaged all Europe—they ravaged little bits from time to time, much as a particular kind of wood-boring grub covers a dry piece of timber with a pattern of tortuous little channels, leaving large areas of the surface untouched. But it is certainly true that the wars grew more terrible as time passed, partly by reason of the constantly increasing efficiency of firearms, partly because greater numbers of people were involved. In the early sixteenth century an army of 50,000 men would be regarded as a big one; in the wars of Louis XIV, a century and a half later, we read of armies of up to 90,000 or 100,000; while in the Napoleonic wars, armies of up to 200,000 conscripted men are common. And of course in our own time tens of millions have been involved. The concept of total war now affects whole peoples, whereas four centuries ago (and in 1540 war could be just as 'total' as it was in 1940) comparatively insignificant numbers were directly affected and relatively small regional areas were devastated.

Whatever else the Italian wars of the early sixteenth century may have done, one thing is certain: they started the biggest boom in armaments that Europe had ever known. Never before had such quantities of arms and fine armour been needed; and just as the political weather of the war had been brewing all through the fifteenth century, so the arms trade— the great workshops of Milan and Brescia, Augsburg and Innsbruck, Nuremberg and Landshut—had been growing in manufacturing capacity, and by the time the demand came in the late 1490s, the business was ready for it. Never before had so many fine craftsmen and artists been engaged in the making and decorating of arms, and they were there to match the exacting demands of all the youthful nobility of Europe.

Of course, great quantities of more ordinary arms, munition stuff, were made as well, but at this period—and consider what a period it is in the history of art and culture!— there seems to have been a spirit abroad among the warriors which demanded the best. Even the most down-at-heel *landsknecht* demanded the handsomest arms he could lay his hands on—often literally, for he would be a poor soldier indeed if after surviving an engagement or two he had not managed to acquire something of quality. And, of course, very many serving infantrymen were in fact gentlemen of blood and coat-armour, younger sons, social misfits, criminals and well-born drop-outs who found in the infantry units a chance of employment, enjoyment and possible advancement.

So, huge quantities of fine arms were produced between about 1490 and 1550, and plenty of them survive in good condition; and when we consider them, we must be struck by the excellent quality of even the plainest piece, whether it be defensive armour or offensive weapon. Never had armour been so efficient, so handsome in form or so fine in decoration as at this period; and after it, the quality declined. As for arms, the sword was still the queen of weapons as it had been since the Bronze Age: endowed with an ancient mystique and much religious symbolism, both pagan and Christian. It was by far the most useful fighting weapon too, and as such retained its pride of place until the middle of the nineteenth century, after which its practical uses waned. Its mystique, however, remained; and still remains vestigially to this day.

New methods of using the sword which had developed in about 1475—1500 had brought new complexities to its hilt; never before had these weapons been so effective in use, so elegant in appearance and so fine in workmanship. Certainly with their more complex guards they lacked the clean austere beauty of proportion which dignified their medieval predecessors, but even so they were aesthetically as pleasing, if in a different way. The period from about 1500 to about 1620 was the greatest for the sword as a weapon for Everyman: no longer was its use a privilege confined to the knightly class. During this time the most beautiful of swords were possessed by men whose social position would not have permitted them such ownership during the Middle Ages.

The basic styles developed between 1480 and 1520 remained in use until the 1630s, when all kinds of new transitional and experimental types appeared: these experiments were a manifestation of the questing scientific spirit of that century, in transition from the medieval to the modern world. Between about 1675 and 1700, these weapons began to give way to the more or less standardised form of the so-called 'smallsword', the most elegant and deadly hand-weapon ever devised by Man. It is a strange paradox that these swords, so much more efficient as killing instruments than any other type ever made, were rarely used for fighting (in spite of the countless duels recounted by the romantic novelists) and were carried more as exquisite pieces of masculine jewellery than as weapons of offence.

With the triumph of the smallsword as the weapon *par excellence* of the non-military gentleman, a clear break was made between swords meant for town-wear and swords meant for war. Now began the development of national and regional types of heavy cavalry sword, of light cavalry sabres, of infantry swords—the list is endless and the material overwhelming, but during the eighteenth century the nations of Europe began to produce standard patterns of sword for all purposes; this attempt at standardisation (and its corollary, mass production) was only sporadic until the very end of the century. After this, classification becomes possible once more, and swords as handsome and well-made as those of the sixteenth century begin again to be produced.

* * * * *

The period in the history of arms with which this book begins comes at the start of a great upsurge of European art—not just a matter of the production of great works by great artists, but an expression of appreciation by the ordinary people. In the taverns of Rome or Florence the merits of the artists of the day were discussed as today the merits or shortcomings of football clubs and baseball teams may be argued in the pubs of Barnsley or the bars of the Bowery.

At the very summit of the appreciation of art during this period, when it was flourishing like the flowers in May, stood that enigmatic potentate, Maximilian, successor of the great Dukes of Burgundy and ruler of the Holy Roman Empire, in theory the chief among all the monarchs of Europe, though in real fact an impoverished, perpetually overdrawn, desperately unlucky, engaging and frivolous nobleman, with superb good taste and an enthusiasm for art which led him into boundless extravagances. But what we, the amateurs of arms of the twentieth century, owe to this taste, this passion for quality (which he bequeathed to his successors and rivals), is as boundless, for though he encouraged artists of every kind, it was to the armourer and the weaponsmith that he seems to have given his heart. He once said, 'A man who isn't remembered while he's alive won't be remembered after he's dead; he'll be forgotten as soon as the bells toll.' On that precept he certainly acted, for few of his contemporaries left such monuments, both great and small, behind them, or have been better remembered. His constant political disasters have not affected his fame as a patron of the arts. 'What greater thing can a prince own,' he used often to say, 'than the armour which protects his body in battle?' To this passion of his we owe not only the experimental engineering of master-armourers like the Helmschmieds or Seusenhofers, but also that wonderful sculptural quality we so admire in the armour they made, produced in response to his insistence upon excellence of form.

At the same time, his delight in the 'minor arts' of the etcher and the engraver, his encouragement of their practitioners, and his vision of the glories which would stem from their alliance with the armourer and the swordsmith, gave us the lovely decorated armours which survive, so many and yet, when we think of the numbers actually built, so pitifully few, in the great armour collections of the world.

The true warrior always went to a fight as to a festival, and attired himself accordingly. When Maximilian and his contemporaries and successors went on campaign, very often they would have armours or garnitures made specially for the occasion. In the same way they, and the lesser nobles of their Courts, would commission armour and arms for the tournaments and festivities attendant upon such functions as meetings of the Imperial Diet or great dynastic weddings. Their war armour was as fine, and as elegantly decorated, as that which was made mainly for 'parade', but princes, like the warriors they led, made a festival of battle. Nor were they like the Duke of Plaza Toro who led his regiment from behind—he found it less exciting—no, like François I at Marignano, they put their beautiful armours at risk by getting into the thick of it.

The art of the armourer and the weaponsmith was greatly affected by changes in fashion: fashion in costume, fashion in architecture, fashion in the minor decorative arts. There was much overlapping of styles as outworn modes yielded to new, particularly in architecture (Henry VII's Chapel at Westminster, for instance, was built in the 1530s in a purely Gothic style), and everyday items, such as furniture, wall-hangings, and household goods, continued to be used long after they had become outmoded—continued, even, to be *made* in outmoded styles, for change spreads slowly, and while Italy, for instance, was by 1450 in the full tide of the classical Renaissance, the nations of the North were still living in a world entirely Gothic, and the inhabitants of the Western Isles and Ireland, in surroundings unaltered since Hadrian's Wall was new. But when it comes to arms, we are in the realms of fashion: changes in style applied as much to the armour worn and the weapons carried as they did to the clothes a man put on and the accessories chosen to set them off.

In the period from about 1475 to 1500, the old styles were putting up their last stand against what Ruskin called 'the foul tide of the Renaissance', producing in that last twenty-five years the style of armour which Rubens, early in the seventeenth century, dubbed 'Gothic'. In men's garments and armour (very much the same thing), this resulted in those slender, exaggeratedly-pointed forms, a sort of *dernier cri* of the age-old fashion style based on the slim-fitting doublet and hose, with long-toed shoes and a mantle, either long or short. This style, varying only in detail, had served men in Europe since the Dark Ages. Then, round about 1495, for reasons which we shall never fully know, there came about a change so swift and so radical that it seems to be unique in the history of fashion. Within half a decade, all over Europe, the old style had gone, replaced by something absolutely and fundamentally different. The silhouette, for ten centuries elegantly slender, became stout, burly and rounded. The long, pointed shoe gave place to one with a broad, square toe: the tall, thimble-shaped hat was replaced by a flat, broad cap like a plate: almost every garment assumed a shape directly opposite to that which had preceded it. These changes were immediately reflected in the outline of armour, and the style of weapons conformed, much as today the accessories to women's clothes conform to the general trend of a fashion style.

And yet as late as 1520 men were still occasionally wearing out-of-date Gothic armour and using old-fashioned weapons; and more than this, such outmoded things were still being made and *sold*. It seems very strange. Many middle-aged men might not have been able to replace the armour and weapons of their youth merely at the dictate of Fashion, but it is hard to accept that makers of fine arms indulged in deliberate archaism, for this change was so positive that even in Germany and England the old Gothic forms were quite *démodé* by 1510. In Highland Scotland and Ireland, of course, as in the wilder parts of Wales, things were as they had always been, a century or so behind the current trend.

Why then was it that by 1530, when the 'new look' was not only well-rooted but had become overblown, arms should still be made and marketed in a style so utterly out of fashion? Who would buy them? They were the products of industry and trade, subject to market trends like everything else. But the study of arms concerns men, and is about things intensely personal to them. While a Renaissance gentleman might be content to go on sitting in an old chair, with Gothic tapestries on his walls and a Gothic goblet in his hand—even to pay for the building of a chapel in a Gothic style—one would expect him to think twice before going out clad in an out-of-date costume, and four times before he would allow his arms, those most intensely personal symbols of his status and dignity, sanctified by heroic tradition, to be in a style suitable only for his poor relations.

And yet the personal element in arms should never be disregarded. They were made for, and used by, people—and many of those people, however cultured in some ways, were only semi-literate by modern standards, subject to much superstition, and readily influenced by religious or political slogans. The inscriptions, heraldic devices, mottoes and decorative subjects which adorn fine arms testify to the fact that their makers and owners were not twentieth-century scholars but sentimental, silly, ordinary people. This we tend to forget.

CHAPTER ONE

THE DEVELOPING POWER
OF THE HANDGUN

'Would to God,' wrote Blaise de Montluc in 1523, 'that this unhappy weapon had never been invented, and that so many brave and valiant men had not died by the hands of those who are often cowards and shirkers who would never dare to look in the face of those whom they lay low with their wretched bullets. They are tools invented by the Devil to make it easier for us to kill each other.'

They are indeed, but so have missile weapons always been regarded. Not so very many years earlier, the great Bayard (who was himself killed by a bullet in 1524) had much the same to say about crossbowmen. He wanted to hang them all. They were cowards, he said, striking from safe distances with no respect for the old rules and courtesies of elegant combat. The same sentiments have been expressed by aristocratic warriors back into the dawn of military history—we find them in the Sagas, the Bible and the Iliad. The introduction of effective firearms into war must have been a traumatic experience for the knighthood of Europe. It had been possible to respect a bowman—even a crossbowman— for it was accepted that however safe the distance from which he might shoot, he was always ready to engage hand-to-hand; and anyway his arrow was a clean thing of wood and steel which flew, like the angels, by means of feathers. Besides, he needed great skill and a lifetime of training to master his weapon. But any clod could become a usable gunman after only a few hours of training, shooting pellets of dolorous lead out of his filthy little pipe with flash and thunder and brimstone stink. He was truly devilish; for many decades after his first introduction into the noble game of war it was believed that a demon bestrode each flying ball—did it not shriek and howl as it passed, to prove it? In 1439 in a battle, begun in the time-honoured *condottiere* manner of move and counter-move and no real fighting, between the mercenary forces of Bologna and Venice, the Bolognese used handgunmen and actually killed some Venetian men-at-arms. This was infuriating; the Venetians dispensed with the rule-book and went to it in earnest, defeated the Bolognese and massacred every gunman, for they said if people continued to use this devilish innovation, war would become really dangerous. Later in the century the *Condottiere* Vitellozzo Vitelli caused it to be given out that he, at least, would give no quarter to any soldier caught with a gun.

We can appreciate this point of view, though it is clear that the military mind of Europe had not yet come to terms with the fact that the power of armoured chivalry had already received its death-blow at the hands of Flemish burghers at Courtrai in 1302, of

Swiss peasants at Morgarten in 1315, and of English ones at Crécy in 1346, and in even worse disasters at Sempach in 1386 and Agincourt in 1415. Even after this, it seemed as if the armoured knight would have a new era of success opening before him. The armourers (particularly those of Milan) had devised armour which was very nearly proof against arrow or bolt; it was lighter and more flexible, harder and far handsomer than what had preceded it. The man-at-arms looked magnificent, and knew it. Clad from head to foot in darkly-gleaming iron, each piece of his harness a work of art in itself, though the visual effect of the whole was far greater than the sum of its parts, he must have felt like one of the very gods of war. Beautiful as Apollo, terrible as Mars, he was the master of any infantryman who might come against him. But he had not reckoned with the powers of Hell. In engagements small or large in Italy and Bohemia, he began to find that it only needed a demon-ridden little leaden ball to punch a ragged hole in his beautiful armour and lay him in the dust. No magnificent aspect, however godlike, could protect him; his chivalrous pride and courage were no proof against the lowly pellet; and the bang and the stink frightened his horse, which in normal circumstances feared nothing. Maybe there were occasional compensations, as when the little iron tube failed to contain the force of the charge and blew the face off the gunman; but it was poor consolation. Even to see a row of tatterdemalion corpses swing from the branches of a tree was little better.

However, the earliest appearances of handguns in the field had small effect upon military thinking, for the occasions of their use were few and confined to regions of Europe which by the nature of things were cut off from the mainstream of tactical development. Cannon, which had been used very successfully since about 1340 in battering and siege work, were not the same, did not pose the same problems. They had been tried in the field with very little success. Their day was to come, but in the 1420s it was over half a century away.

In the earlier Middle Ages in Europe, the art of war, and the hardware used to develop it, had varied little from Finland to Spain and from Wales to the Caucasus. With the accelerating decline of the unifying concept of 'Christendom' and the first stirrings of nationalism in the late fourteenth century, we find that wars were being fought all over Europe in complete isolation from one another, each body of combatants creating their own tactical ideas and developing their own weapons. The great wars between England and France, the non-events on the battlefields of Italy, the struggle of Aragon and Castile to clear the Arabs out of Spain, the endemic war between the Balkan lands and the Turks, the fight of the Swiss to enlarge their newly-freed Confederation at the expense of its neighbours, and the ferocious wars of those pre-Luther Protestants, the Hussite rebels of Bohemia: their participants produced divergent methods of dealing with their problems, and specialised weapons to put them into effect. When at the very end of the century Charles VIII's adventure began the first pan-European war, all these different weapons and tactical skills were brought together. It was inevitable that progress in the art of war had to be rapid and far-reaching.

Of the new weapons, two were of overriding importance; not now weapons for individual use, but for mass combat, they were to transform the whole scene, setting the stage for all the horrors of the twentieth century. The first was the handgun and the second was the pike. In this chapter I shall briefly trace the progress of the gun, from 'handgonne' to arquebus to musket; and in the next I shall attend to the pike and its predecessor and contemporary, the halberd, as well as all those other varied weapons which together are referred to as 'staff-weapons'.

EARLY HANDGUNS

The question of the date and place of the origins of gunpowder has no relevance here, neither does the development of artillery, for although artillery on the field of battle had become a common phenomenon by the end of the fifteenth century, there was nothing the individual soldier could do in the way of developing defences against it, he could only endure it or try to get out of its way; but, very early on, the handgun provided a fine new stimulus to the armour trade, driving its professionals to make even more improvements upon the defences they had devised to counter the problem of the English arrow. So for a hundred years, between about 1430 and 1530, the design and technical quality of armour continued to advance while the quantities called for increased.

Cannon were actually being used during the 1320s, not very effectively. They were at that time regarded more as a bad joke than a terrible portent; the handgun followed very soon and seems to have been in use, if not widely, by the 1370s. A list of arms supplied by John Halton, Keeper of the Tower of London, to the Chamberlain of Berwick in 1371 includes

> '*iii cannones parvos vocatus handgonnes*'

and an entry in the Wardrobe Accounts in 1375 lists expenditure for

> '*helvynge viii gunnorum et x hachettos de stauro antiquo ad modum pycoys*'

That eight guns and ten hatchets should be hafted with parts of an old pole in the manner of pikes is significant, for it clearly indicates 'handgonnes', not cannon; but Chaucer's reference in The House of Fame—

> '*As swifte as pellet out of gonne*
> *When fyre is through the poudre ronne*'

—might refer to either. (The poem was probably written between 1374 and 1382.)

The earliest handguns were short tubes, forged in iron or cast in bronze or latten, between about eight inches and eighteen inches long (20 cm and 45 cm), fastened to 'helves' either by having the breech-ends formed as sockets which, like spear-heads, fitted over the ends of the hafts, or simply being bound to the ends of the helves by iron straps. There are many representations in art of such guns in use; some show the end of the helve resting on the ground while the gunman supports the thing with his right hand and applies the fire to a touch-hole in the breech-end of the tube with his left, while others (generally later) show a helve which is a bit shorter and held under the right armpit. Both kinds of gun are invariably shown pointing upwards at an angle of about 45° to the ground. There could have been little prospect of actually hitting a specific target by such means.

'Handgonnes' were fired off by the same method as large cannon, by the application of a light to a touch-hole in the breech of the barrel. Again the Wardrobe Accounts provide evidence of the various instruments needed for the firing of guns. Throughout the second half of the fourteenth century and the first half of the fifteenth, we find entries for expenditure upon 'drivells' and 'tampions', 'touches' and 'fyrepannes'. The gunner loaded his piece by shovelling a charge of powder down the muzzle and ramming it home (if it was a cannon) or by pouring a small charge down the upturned barrel (if it was a handgun). In both cases the charge was followed by a 'tampion', a disc maybe of wood or leather or cloth or old parchment—anything to hold the powder in. Then the ball went down, rammed home with the 'drivell'. Ready now to give fire, the gunner pointed his piece in the general direction of his target and applied the 'touche' to the hole, and the ball screeched off on its way. Gunners firing a large cannon always had a 'fyrepanne', some sort of a brazier from which they could take a glowing coal in a long pair of tongs, or a red-hot wire or a small torch—a bit of oil-soaked rag or tow—in the end of a long stick. By about 1500 this had become the usual instrument, already known as a linstock:

> '. . . and the nimble gunner
> With linstock now the devilish cannon touches,
>   (Alarum, and chambers go off, within)
> And down goes all before them!'

as we find in the Prologue to Act III of Shakespeare's *Henry V*. I remember forty or so years ago when I first read this play wondering why the gunner should be nimble. This betrayed not only an ignorance of Shakespeare's masterly use of language but of medieval gunnery as well. When fire was put to the touch-hole of a gun, the great fountain of flame which back-fired out of the hole called for very great nimbleness if the gunner were to avoid getting burned. The same method was used to fire the tiny charge in a handgun but the use of a 'fyrepanne' was clearly not appropriate to the mobile gunman. We do not know precisely what the 'touche' was, except that it was almost certainly some kind of cord which when lit would maintain a slow-burning, glowing end. In the many pictures showing handguns, we can see small thin objects in the gunmen's hands like bits of wire or string. This 'touche' was the forerunner of the later and far more efficient 'match', a flaxen cord impregnated with a solution of saltpetre and spirits of wine.

DEVELOPMENT OF THE STOCK

By the middle of the fifteenth century the crude early handgun had been succeeded by something a good deal better, for the pole-like stock had been improved by shortening it and making it to a flat oblong section, more like a modern gunstock. Later the barrel was made with three or four small lugs projecting downwards from its underside. In each lug was a hole, and in the hollow trough cut in the top of the stock were openings into which the lugs would fit; then holes were bored in the stock, crosswise, to correspond with the holes in the lugs on the barrel. Pegs were driven through these holes from side to side, and the barrel was not only held securely, it could easily be dismounted if the stock got broken. In some guns, probably a majority of those made, there was another, much bigger, lug forged under the barrel, more like a large hook, projecting downward about a third of the way along the gun from the muzzle. This was to hook over any support that offered (as a parapet or a stand or the branch of a tree would do), to steady the gun against

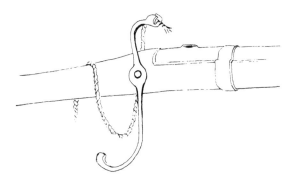

FIGURE 1   The primitive firing mechanism

the recoil. By the 1450s this recoil had become significant, owing to the very great improvements in gunbarrels and in gunpowder.

Many gunstocks now began to be made with a rudimentary butt, either a broadening-out of the end of the stock, cut off flat to rest against the shooter's chest, or a sharp downward curve. Because of this fashion of holding the gun against the chest (*la poitrine* in French) the handgun acquired the sobriquet of 'petronel'. Because of the hook below the barrel, in German-speaking lands it had begun to be called a *hakenbüchse*, 'hookgun', by the 1550s.

To improvements in the form of gunstocks came an enormous advance in the efficiency of the process of firing. While the shooter had to hold his touche in his hand, he could not steady or aim his gun. So a simple device was added: to the right-hand side of the stock, just behind the breech and touch-hole, a long Z-shaped arm was fixed upon a pivot. One end extended back along the underside of the stock where the shooter held it with his right hand; the other, shorter, end stood up above the top of the barrel. To the top of this extension of the arm (very soon to be called the 'cock' by reason of its cockerel-like shape) was fixed a clamp, into which the glowing end of the touche could be fixed (Fig. 1). When he wanted to shoot, the gunman simply squeezed the long end of the arm upward, thus bringing the short arm down upon the touch-hole.

Thus by 1450 or so we have the handgun, called variously 'petronel' or '*hakenbüchse*'. But no Frenchman could, or would, pronounce so German a word as *hakenbüchse* correctly. Its mutation seems to have been as instant as it was complete. By 1470 we find the French firmly saying 'arquebus'. Being of Germanic stock, the English were not so drastic; they merely altered it to 'hackbut'. As we follow the progress of weapons from age to age, we shall find the name 'arquebus' coming more and more to apply to the ordinary handgun, and 'petronel' to a shorter version of it (not a pistol—that had yet to make its debut) used by horsemen, while the names 'serpentine' and 'culverin' were applied to small cannon.

IMPROVEMENTS IN FIRING MECHANISMS

The simple firing mechanism very soon became more sophisticated. The long Z-shaped arm was cut in two, and the upper end, the cock, was turned around, separated and pivoted to the side of the stock with a short crank fixed to the pivot end. The cut-off long

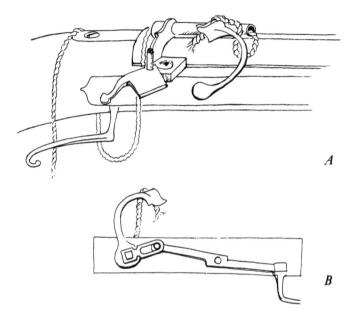

FIGURE 2 *The basic firing mechanism of the matchlock from*
about 1520 to about 1650, seen from the outside in
Illustration A and from the inside in Illustration B

end of the serpentine was fixed to a hole in this crank by a rivet, the whole thing moving freely. Now when the long end of the arm was squeezed up towards the underside of the stock, the cock came down against the touch-hole. Soon, in better models, the crank became a long lever, called the 'sear', pivoted in the middle and fixed at one end to the pivot of the cock and at the other to the 'tricker', as the long end of the old serpentine arm began to be called. Next a stiff spring was added below or above the sear which held the cock up, for safety, only allowing it to come to the touch-hole when the tricker was pulled up. Then an opening was cut in the side of the stock; the sear and tricker and spring were pivoted to the inside of a flat metal plate, with the cock on the outside, and the whole thing was screwed against the side of the stock, the opening accommodating the working parts. The touch-hole was moved from the top of the breech to the right-hand side, a pan with a hinged cover was provided for the touch-powder, and the tricker, still the old cut-off serpentine arm, was improved into a proper trigger. With this development there appeared a true gunlock (Fig. 2), one which was to remain in use practically unchanged until the end of the seventeenth century in Europe and until the late nineteenth in Asia.

IMPROVEMENTS IN GUNPOWDER

Another factor which influenced improvements in gunnery was the quality of gunpowder. In its earlier forms it was composed of saltpetre, sulphur and charcoal roughly in the proportions of 80, 13 and 7 parts, mixed and ground to a very light powder which had severe disadvantages. It was so light that the wind blew it away, so fine that it caked easily and required great care, skill even, in loading it into the gun, for if it was rammed in too tightly, it would not explode but merely burned and fizzled ineffectually, but if too loose, it would only produce a feeble belch just powerful enough to trundle the ball out of the muzzle. It had to be just right. In transport, the joggling it received in its tubs caused the constituents to separate according to their specific gravities—sulphur at the bottom of the tub, saltpetre in the middle and charcoal on the top. So it all had to be mixed again before any gun could be fired. After firing four or five charges, every gun had to be scraped out, because the bore got clogged with a thick coky deposit.

Some time between about 1425 and 1450, an improvement was effected by the introduction of 'corned' powder. This was made by wetting the loose powder with a mixture of alcohol and water. One is lured down fascinating paths of speculation as to the empirical means by which this discovery was probably made, particularly when we learn that urine was considered to be a better mix than mere water—more, that a wine-drinker's urine was better than a beer-drinker's, and a wine-drinking bishop's best of all. This last must have been a rare and valuable commodity, though we do hear of its being bestowed upon princely arsenals as a mark of episcopal favour.

Corned powder was made by mixing the loose powder to a paste, allowing it almost (but not quite) to dry out and then compressing it into a hard cake. The cake was then broken into bits and ground up in a mortar. Speculation is endless: could this have been the origin of the mortar as a projectile-throwing weapon, when some unrecorded disaster befell a powderer's assistant? This corned powder was very much more forcible than the old stuff, with the result that the old style of cannon, made of staves of iron welded together side by side round a wooden core and reinforced with hoops, was too weak to contain it; even good cast cannon could not cope with the big charges that were needed, so for many decades more, until much better cannon could be made, the old loose powder was continued in use for artillery. But for the tiny charges (only about an ounce and a half, or 40 grammes) used in a handgun, corned powder was excellent.

HANDGUNS IN ACTION: THE HUSSITE WARS (1421—1434)

So with the development of corned powder, a manageable gunstock and an efficient firing mechanism, a workable handgun had come into being. By the period 1480 to 1500 it was pretty universally known as the arquebus, and would soon dominate the fields of war as once the armoured knight had done.

The first really serious encounters which medieval chivalry had with the handgun took place in Italy (where gun-making experiments were more prevalent) and in Bohemia—but especially in Bohemia.

In 1420 the Czechs had risen in arms against the Emperor Sigismund in a fury of outraged nationalism and reforming spiritual zeal. They were determined to drive the intruding Germans back beyond the Erz Gebirge mountains and to avenge their martyred prophet, John Huss. It would have been hopeless to set against the Germans the lances of the Czech nobles, for there were very few of them and they were politically divided; the undisciplined and unarmed masses of farmers and workers who were left to fight it out risked being trampled down by the armoured might of the feudal *noblesse*, so unless the problem could be solved there seemed to be little future for Czech patriotism. It was solved in a most effective way by an experienced warrior, John Zizka of Trocnov, who had learned much of the art of war while campaigning with the Poles against the Teutonic knights of Prussia. He saw clearly enough that the only strength of the peasant forces lay in their fierce patriotism and religious zeal. Even in this there were hazards, for while half of the 'Hussites', as they called themselves, were reforming zealots, the other half were only quiet folk who hated the Germans. Zizka saw that until some tactical system was worked out and some sort of unifying discipline acquired by the rebels, nothing but a cautious defensive policy would do. So, towns were put into a state of defence and earthworks thrown up wherever necessary. In the first year of their revolt, 1420, the Czechs were helped enormously by the utterly ineffectual military capabilities of Sigismund's nobles, and the total absence of cohesion between the multitude of small regional units of which his forces were composed. The Germans were held at bay with very little trouble, for they made very little effort.

During the respite gained by this policy, Zizka was putting into effect ideas he had got while campaigning in the east of Europe, a system of tactics which could be developed and turned to account by an army of infantry forced to take the defensive against an enemy whose only strength lay in an overwhelming feudal *noblesse*. For more than a century there had been prevalent in Russia a method of coping with cavalry attacks by means of drawing up a quantity of carts and wagons into a square or a circle to form a defensive position. Specially-made pavises were carried in the wagons as well as chains and poles to fill the gaps between them when drawn up into the *gulaigorod*, 'moving town'.

Except that the defenders were armed with bows and crossbows instead of Colt revolvers and Winchester rifles, they fought like the pioneers in the American West, or the Boer settlers in South Africa, a century ago. It was of great antiquity, too, for the ancient Scythians had used it, as did the Goths—indeed all the wandering peoples of the Migration period and pretty nearly every army since.

But the Russians, and Zizka's Czechs after them, made a highly-specialised thing out of the *wagenburg*. Whereas the wandering barbarians made use of their baggage wagons as a defensive overnight camp, and medieval armies drew them up as a defence for the baggage itself, the Russians and Czechs used them as a weapon. True, they carried the army's supplies, but they constituted as well the elements of a moving fortress and were in fact archetypal Armoured Fighting Vehicles. The disadvantage was that once formed up, this fortress had to stay where it was, and could only be truly effective if the enemy could be persuaded to attack it. If he preferred to sit down and starve the defenders out, the *wagenburg* would become a trap. However, in this particular war, that never happened. The men who used it were good psychologists; they knew that their opponents would be feudal nobles who could be relied upon to learn nothing, even after the most fearful experiences—they would always attack, full of confidence and pride and contempt for a pedestrian enemy. The sort of thing which had happened in the West at Bannockburn, Morgarten, Crécy, Poitiers, Nájera, Aljubarrota, Sempach, Agincourt—the list is endless—would happen in the East.

So Zizka built up a wagon-train and went out to war with it in 1421, and defeated the Germans at Luditz and Kuttenberg. In each case, having found a good position he drew up his wagons, closing the side-gaps with chains and poles and pavises or anything else handy, and arranging the wagons so that there was a large gap at the front of the *laager* and another at the back, each being blocked with easily-removable posts and chains so that when the enemy was beaten back, his own men could dash out to finish the thing off. They were divided into squads, ten or twenty men to a wagon according to its capacity. Half of each squad had staff weapons—pikes, spears, scythes, flails, anything; the other half had crossbows or handguns. He had some cannon too, mounted on special carts. When the German horse charged, the Hussites would wait until they were at point-blank range and then let drive all together with everything they had. The effect was shattering. At that range the balls smashed through plate armour as if it were paper, and the men no more than the horses could face the fearful flash and thunder of the discharge right in their faces. In this first campaign the Germans tried gallantly enough to penetrate the wall of wagons while the gunners were reloading, hacking at the spearmen in the gaps and trying to get at the gunmen through the woodwork of the wagons; but all the time the crossbow-men shot at them, and they could see the gunners getting ready to fire again. A second volley scattered them; then the Hussites snatched aside the chains and posts in the gaps and rushed out among the demoralised horsemen.

After this first campaign the Germans would never face more than one volley, if they could be persuaded to attack the *wagenburg* at all. Soon it was not even necessary for the Czechs to shelter behind the wagons. They came out into the open against the Germans, who still refused to face them. They became so exalted with the extraordinary moral effects of their tactics that they carried out many slow, lumbering *blitzkriege*, sending out 'armoured columns' deep into German territory, the long dreadful wagon-trains plodding at some two miles an hour across Bavaria or Hungary or Silesia without hindrance, leaving trails of desolation behind them, and returning, year after year, laden with the spoils of eastern Europe. All this was achieved, as the remarkable successes of the English longbow had been achieved, by the skilful use by one side of an effective, demoralising missile weapon used in a well-chosen defensive position, and by the lack on the other side of any trace of common sense or tactical ability to balance a demented passion of pride and absurd heroism. The Germans could have over-run the Hussites any time they wanted if they had not been so frightened of them. When the long war was brought to a close in 1434, it was not done by the Germans; the two Czech factions finally turned upon each other and met in battle at Lipan on May 30 1434. The zealots (Taborites, they called themselves) fought in the time-honoured way in the *wagenburg*. The moderates (called Calixtines) played the attacking role, and got the treatment they had so often meted out to the Germans. Like the Germans, they fell back—and out came the Taborites, just like old times. But they forgot they were chasing men who only the year before had been their own comrades, and who were made of sterner stuff than the German knights. Once the Taborites were well clear of the *wagenburg*, the Calixtines turned, regardless of handgun or crossbow, and destroyed them.

Thus a challenge to feudal chivalry was offered in the East every bit as deadly as the one the English had offered in the West; and the military leaders of Europe took as little notice of the one as of the other. While the making of war was still the privilege of a noble class, it would be made as that class wanted it, regardless of any opposition to the rules of elegant combat. By 1450 the armoured knight might be as obsolete as the charioteer, but he was not going to admit it. Nor would he for another seventy-five years. It was not until the splendid *gens d'armes* of François I's *Compagnies* were mown down by the Spanish arquebusiers at Pavia in 1525 that he finally accepted the end of his long supremacy.

HUNTING GUNS

We are not concerned here with detailed examination of the ways in which technical development improved the gunlock. It was the matchlock arquebus of the sixteenth century which reduced the validity of defensive armour, and the matchlock musket of the seventeenth which brought about its final abandonment. It caused changes in weapons too, by reducing the number of types of weapon in use. When the prime arm of the infantryman was either musket or pike, such weapons as halberds, gisarmes, bills, axes, hammers and flails became obsolete.

No. The mechanical improvements to the gun were produced not by the pressures of war but by the exigencies of the chase. When it became obvious that a gun was a better game-shooting weapon than a bow, a reliable firing mechanism was needed. The cumbersome and unreliable processes of loading and firing matchlock guns were acceptable, within limits, for squads of soldiers shooting together; but it was no use trying to keep a match glowing while stalking game, even less use to rekindle it once the game was in range—about seventy-five yards (70 metres) for a matchlock gun in 1500. By the time the gun was ready, the birds would have flown, the deer or bear would be well on its way to cover. It was essential to have a gun which could be brought into the presence of one's quarry in a state of instant readiness to fire.

THE WHEEL-LOCK GUN

From the earliest days of *Homo Sapiens* it has been known that a piece of pyrites or flint struck against iron will produce sparks. All that was needed to fire a gun was to produce a mechanism which would cause a bit of pyrites to strike a piece of iron at a point where it could fire the priming powder. By applying a principle akin to clockwork to this primeval function, a remarkably efficient lock was produced late in the fifteenth century. There is no means of knowing where this came about, or exactly when; but in one of Leonardo da Vinci's notebooks (now called *Il Codex Atlantico*) are some sketches for parts of wheel-lock mechanisms and a drawing of a completed one and a tinder-lighter. Most of the sketches on one folio are of methods of attaching a short chain to a V-shaped spring, which is the essential mechanism of a wheel-lock. Recent research seems to show pretty clearly that these sketches (made perhaps around the turn of the fifteenth/sixteenth centuries) are the genesis of the design of this mechanism, and that Leonardo was its inventor.

The earliest literary references to wheel-locks are first, a reference in a book of accounts for the year 1507 of the steward of Cardinal Ippolito d'Este, Archbishop of Zagreb, which relates how a servant called Caspar the Bohemian, going on a pilgrimage to Germany, was commissioned to buy for the Archbishop 'a gun, of that kind which is fired by a stone' (*unam piscidem de illis qua incenduntur cum lapide*); and secondly, a story told by the Augsburg chronicler Wilhelm Rem in his *Cronaca Newer Geschichten* of 1512—1527: 'How Laux Pfister shot a whore in Constance.'

'In the year of Our Lord 1515, on the day of the Three Holy Kings [January 6] there was in Constance a young citizen of Augsburg who had engaged a handsome whore; and when she was with him in a little room he took up a loaded gun in his hand, the lock of which functioned in such a way that when the firing mechanism was pressed, it ignited itself [*so schlug es selb feur auff*]. He was playing about with this when he pressed the trigger and shot the whore. The bullet hit her chin and passed out through the back of her neck. So he had to compensate her and give her 40 florins, and another 20 florins per annum for life. He had to pay the doctor 37 florins too, as well as other costs amounting to some 30 or 40 florins.'

A costly evening's entertainment for Pfister (frustrating too) but it has given posterity another definite date by which wheel-locks were in use, for no other firing mechanism at that date ignited itself.

The principle upon which a wheel-lock works is simple; its basic element is a wheel or disc working on a spindle on the outside of the lockplate: to the spindle, on the inside, is fastened one end of a small chain whose other end is fixed to a strong V-shaped spring. The edge of the wheel is grooved and toothed, and it intrudes into the bottom of the flashpan through a slot. Just in front of the wheel is the cock; no longer, as in a match-lock, holding in its jaws a piece of match, but instead a piece of iron pyrites. The pan is covered by a sliding lid. To load, the wheel is wound up—the other end of its spindle is square and protrudes about an eighth of an inch (3 mm) clear of the outer face of the wheel, and it is wound with a key like a clock-key, or a spanner. This wraps the chain about a turn round the spindle against the pull of the spring. The priming powder is put into the pan and securely covered by the lid. When the trigger is pressed, the wheel spins, the lid of the pan moves away and the lock comes down, bringing the pyrites hard against the whizzing wheel, and a big spark is generated right in the middle of the priming, to send the flash through the touch-hole to the charge in the barrel. However simple the idea might be, a wheel-lock is a most complex piece of machinery, some having as many as fifty parts (Fig. 3).

It was soon found that this kind of lock could be fitted to very small guns, some no more than nine or ten inches long (23 to 25 cm). It has been said that the pistol was named

FIGURE 3   The wheel-lock, c. 1520—1620

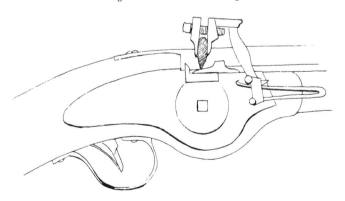

after the Italian town of Pistoia, an early gun-making centre; but it has also been asserted that the name comes from a Czech word, *pist'ala*, meaning a small Bohemian handgun. But whatever its derivation, the pistol was the first gun that could be concealed upon the person and fired with one hand. It was very soon in widespread popular use for purposes of intimidation, armed robbery, murder and assassination. The advent of self-igniting guns, such as the one the luckless Augsburger played with, had from the start produced edicts against their use. In 1518 we find Maximilian I prohibiting the manufacture and use of such things throughout the Holy Roman Empire; in 1523 the city of Ferrara issued an ordinance forbidding the carrying of 'an especially dangerous kind of firearms, vulgarly called Stone-guns' without licence, upon pain of the public chopping-off of a hand. Other European cities followed suit, with as little effect. The wheel-lock gun had come to stay. Its use, however, was limited to those who could afford a big price for a gun, for it was very expensive. Even so, by the middle of the sixteenth century we find large bodies of horsemen armed with wheel-lock pistols. The little murderous 'pocket' pistols, some of which survive, were generally made entirely of steel (the most notable is one made for the Emperor Charles V in 1547) but the horseman's pistol was bigger and heavier, sometimes nearly three feet long (90 cm). A rider could carry three—one on his right boot-top or in his belt, and the others in holsters, one on each side of his saddle. Such a weapon also made a very serviceable club after it had been fired.

RIFLING

The use of rifling in gunbarrels began probably late in the fifteenth century, improving the power and accuracy of a gun, but it was no use for bird-shot (so smooth-bore guns continued in use as fowling-pieces), and it made loading difficult, too. The ball had to fit exactly and very tightly; the only way to achieve the proper result was to hammer the ball down into the barrel with an iron ramrod struck with a mallet so that the grooves were actually filled by the lead; this prevented the gas from seeping out of the grooves round the ball, with consequent loss of force. This was a lengthy and noisy performance, so found little favour with hunters, and was well-nigh impossible in battle conditions. The answer to that problem still lay in the future.

Not so far ahead lay the invention of a gunlock much simpler and cheaper to produce than the wheel-lock, and very nearly as efficient. The principle was the same, except that flint was more ordinarily used than pyrites, but its application was different. The flintlock had been invented well before the sixteenth century ended; in its earliest form it was simple and effective, but it was not until about the middle of the seventeenth century that its final form was perfected. From about 1650 until the 1850s in Europe (and almost to the present in parts of Asia and Africa) it was in use—not just by wealthy sportsmen or princely bodyguards but by the average bandit, highwayman, assassin or infantryman all over Europe and America.

The variations of mechanical detail which differentiate one of these locks from another are of infinite complexity and have no place here. Figure 4 may suffice to give the reader some idea of the basic construction of the flintlock mechanism. If a deeper study of these matters is sought, any or all of the admirable books listed at the end of this chapter will provide it.

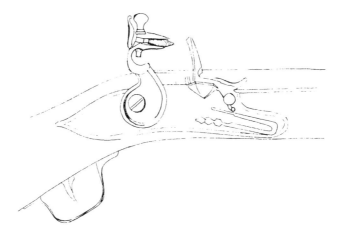

FIGURE 4   The basic construction of the flintlock mechanism

THE MATCHLOCK ARQUEBUS AND MUSKET

While all these new inventions were being exquisitely wrought and developed by the gunsmiths of Europe for the benefit of the wealthy, the armies went on using the old matchlock. Cumbersome, inefficient and dangerous it might be, but it was cheap. As the sixteenth century wore on, larger and larger grew the numbers of arquebusiers required by the armies. In a few places princely bodyguards might be armed with expensive wheel-locks, but the ordinary infantryman continued to run the risk of being blown up by his own bandolier—a broad leather shoulder-belt upon the front of which were hung a number of small cylindrical containers, each holding a charge of black powder; if a spark from the match touched off one of these, the whole series would explode with unfortunate results.

Late in the sixteenth century, the term 'arquebus' began to be more and more confined to the weapon of the murderer or the gentlemanly sportsman. The gun of the infantryman was called a 'caliver' by the end of that century and a 'musket' by the beginning of the next. The caliver was a rather longer gun than the arquebus, firing a heavier ball; otherwise it was much the same, and could be fired without its muzzle-end having to be supported in a forked rest. Not so its successor. This seems to have had a Spanish origin, for it was first called a *moschetto*, though why it should bear the Spanish name for a sparrowhawk is not clear. At first it was probably a wall-piece, for it was too long and too heavy—its barrel was some fifty to fifty-five inches in length (125 to 140 cm) and it weighed up to twenty pounds (9 kg)—to be held and fired unsupported like the caliver and the arquebus. But it was very effective; its long barrel gave it range and accuracy and its heavy ball would go through the best armour at 120 paces. By the first decade of the seventeenth century, it had become the weapon *par excellence* of the armies of Europe, all of which rapidly organised regiments of musketeers. Since the musketeer had not only to carry this great gun about, but also a long forked rest to support it with, as well as his bandolier of cartridges, his two powder flasks (a big one for the coarse propellant powder and a little one for the finer priming), his bag of leaden balls, his pouch or box for the wads he needed to separate ball from powder in the barrel of his gun, his lengths of match (each some four feet [1 metre] long) *and* a sword and dagger, he must rank as the most heavily encumbered infantryman the armies of Europe have ever employed.

The process of loading and firing his piece among all this dangling paraphernalia involved very carefully worked out drill movements, which in imagination or in contemporary illustrations look almost impossible to perform. This drill is clearly shown in the admirable illustrations to a Dutch drill manual commissioned by Maurice, Prince of Orange, in about 1606 and published in The Hague in 1607; it is by one Jacob de Gheyn, entitled *The exercise of Armes for calivver, Muskettes and Pikes*, and it very clearly shows how all these arms are to be managed. If one drapes oneself with all a musketeer carried, takes a matchlock gun and its rest, and carefully follows de Gheyn's movements, it is surprising how practical in fact it is. The great danger, of course, comes from the burning match which the musketeer must carry, both ends aglow in case one goes out, between the fingers of his left hand. If he carelessly allows it to come against the charges of his bandolier, he blows up. In loading, he would pour one of these charges down his gun, following it with a wad which he tamped down with his ramrod. On top of the wad went a ball which he had been holding in his mouth (for instant readiness) along with half a dozen others. He then tamped another wad down on top, to prevent the ball's rolling away from the powder, replaced his ramrod in its socket below the stock of his musket, adjusted the forked rest so that it took the weight of the gun just forward of the lock, blew on his match, fastened it into the clamp at the end of the cock and was ready to fire if he had been able to survive the hazards attendant upon him while he loaded.

CARTRIDGES

Cartridges pre-loaded with powder and ball, the whole contained in a wrapper of stiff paper (hence the name 'cartridge paper'), had been in use since about 1550 (though Leonardo da Vinci refers to cartridges forty or more years earlier) but these were more for the benefit of wealthy owners of wheel-lock or flintlock guns. The ordinary musketeer (who incidentally was often of noble birth) had to be content for the most part with his bandolier and bullet-bag for many decades more, though occasionally he had the benefit of pre-packaged powder and ball. Did not that old war-dog Sir John Smyth write in 1590 of 'cartages with which musketeers charge theyr peeces both with Poudre and Ball at 1 tyme'?

By the middle of the seventeenth century, muskets were being made ten inches or so shorter than previously (about 25 cm) and consequently lighter and more manageable, and we hear no more of the caliver; and by the 1670s they had become smaller still.

Ordinary military guns of the sixteenth and seventeenth centuries had none of the elaborate decoration which graced the stocks and locks and even the barrels of most good-quality civilian firearms, both long-guns and pistols, making of them works of art in their own right, some of absolutely outstanding beauty. These guns combined the skills and craftsmanship of the specialists who wrought lock, stock and barrel, and the artists (goldsmiths and silversmiths, steel engravers, sculptors and inlayers of precious metals or bone or wood or ivory) who decorated them. The reader is again referred to the list of specialised books at the end of this chapter.

There is a wealth of written evidence of the power and effectiveness of firearms (as well as the diatribes against them) and much interesting material can be found in inventories, accounts, wills and the like. Even muster-rolls yield the occasional gem: in German rolls of the early sixteenth century we find evidence of the roaring trade done by quacks of all kinds who sold protective charms and amulets to soldiers, in entries such as: 'Herman Winkelbaum, Q.D.I.G. [*Quem Dicetur Impenetrabilis Glandibus*]' 'Who is said to be bullet-proof.'

BIBLIOGRAPHY

Blackmore, H., *Guns and Rifles of the World*, London, 1965

Blair, Claude, *Pistols of the World*, London, 1968

George, John Nigel, *English Guns and Rifles*, South Carolina, 1947

   and also .... *English Pistols and Revolvers*, London, 1938

Hayward, J. F., *The Art of the Gunmaker* (2 volumes), London, 1962, 1963

CHAPTER TWO

STAFF-WEAPONS

The handgun man could never have become the arbiter of battle on his own; no kind of military unit has ever been so vulnerable, particularly to cavalry attack, as an unsupported body of musketeers. When it was only possible to give fire once in three minutes, in the best conditions, a steady charge of cavalry could always break up and ride down any such body. But if the musketeers had pikemen to hold cavalry off while they reloaded, they presented a formidable problem. It was this combination of gun and pike in the sixteenth and seventeenth centuries and the ultimate invention of the socket bayonet (which turned every musket into a combination pike-cum-musket) which gave the handgun its domination until the entire concept of war changed after 1914.

THE RISE OF SWISS POWER
IN THE FOURTEENTH CENTURY

The principal exponents of pike-fighting during the sixteenth and seventeenth centuries were the Swiss, but their particular method of waging war took a long time to come to perfection. To find the origins of the pike we have to look back at least as far as the early fourteenth century—if we are to be pedantic about it, we can gaze down the long gallery of the centuries to the all-conquering phalanx of Philip II of Macedon and his successor Alexander the Great. These Macedonian spearmen of the third century BC used the same weapon and tactical formation as the sixteenth-century Swiss—so indeed did the armies of the Pharoahs—though it is unlikely that the Swiss pike column was any sort of descendant of the Macedonian phalanx. Its origins were much nearer home, both in place and time.

Its most notable predecessor was perhaps the 'schiltron' of the Scots in their wars of independence, under Wallace and Robert Bruce, against the English. At Stirling Bridge (1297), Falkirk (1298) and Bannockburn (1314), they used very Swiss-like tactics. At Falkirk they were beaten because Edward I at once saw that the first charges of his feudal cavalry failed to make any impression on the Scots schiltrons—deep solid columns of men armed with long spears drawn up in a formation which could rapidly change from a column to a bristling square or circle. He drew his cavalry off and brought his Welsh longbowmen into play, ordering them to shoot together at the schiltrons, concentrating their shot at specified points. A few minutes of this caused great slaughter, making gaps into which the next charges could penetrate; the schiltrons were rapidly broken up after that and the Scots army dispersed.

Not so at Bannockburn. Here Bruce used the same formations as his predecessor, Wallace, but Edward II made little attempt to follow his father's example. All he, or his captains, did was to send in wave after wave of England's chivalry to die upon the spears.

This was not the first overwhelming defeat suffered by feudal chivalry at the hands of largely peasant armies. Twelve years before Bannockburn, in 1302, a large French army was devastatingly defeated outside Courtrai by a Flemish army of townsmen and peasants armed not with spears, like the Scots, but with a fearful slashing and stabbing weapon which they called a godendac, and which seems to have been a kind of archetypal halberd.

These crushing defeats of feudal chivalry by peasant armies must have shocked the European military mind, but however deep an impression they may have made, little practical effect resulted from it. This impression was strengthened when, a year after Bannockburn, the Swiss first appeared upon the scene of European warfare. Their swift, savage annihilation of an Austrian army at Morgarten on the shore of the lake of Aegeri was a portent of things to come. Their weapon at Morgarten was the halberd, one which seems to have been similar to the Flemish godendac, and they used it again with even greater significance at Laupen near Berne in 1339, where they defeated a well-organised Austrian host without the advantages of terrain and surprise which had benefited them so much at Morgarten. They did it on an open hillside in a straightforward slogging match between armoured cavalry and halberd-wielding infantrymen. Forty-eight years later, in 1386, when the Austrians again had cause to take the field against Swiss expansionist aggression, they were better prepared and seem to have taken the lesson of Laupen to heart. Like the King of France at Poitiers, Duke Leopold of Austria at Sempach met the threat by dismounting his vaward of men-at-arms, deeming that a solid column of fully-armoured knights, advancing in close order with their long lances levelled, ought to be able to roll over the unarmoured Swiss, halberds or no. When the battle began, only part of the Swiss force was on the field; Leopold's first column met them front to front, and for some minutes the fight wavered to and fro. Then the banner of Lucerne went down and it looked as if Austria had the field, but the main body of Swiss, led by the Canton of Uri, came up and the tide turned against the Austrians. The Austrian chronicler Hagen tells how a cry for help ran down the disordered ranks:

Darnach hort der edel Furst agin chleglicke geschray, 'O retta, Oesterreich, retta,' und sah die Bannyr swehen, gleichsam sie wolbe undergehn. Do ruft er an all sein Ritter und Knecht das sie mit samst tretten von der Rossen, und retteten Ritter und Knecht.

'Then the noble prince heard a terrible cry, "Oh rescue, Austria, rescue," and he saw the banners waver as if they were going to fall. Then he called on his knights and followers to dismount in haste and thus to come to the help of their brothers in arms.'

Leopold leaped down from his horse and led his second corps on foot into the fight; but they were in too much of a hurry and could not get into proper array; and the broken first wave falling back upon them disordered their ranks still further. The Swiss now had the moral advantage as well as the advantage of impetus. The third column of Austria, led by the Count of Hohenzollern and the Baron of Oberkirch, still mounted, assumed that the battle was lost and the field of Sempach no place for them; so they turned and rode off. The Duke and the few who were left standing were hewn down after an heroic resistance, though some of their comrades managed to get off.

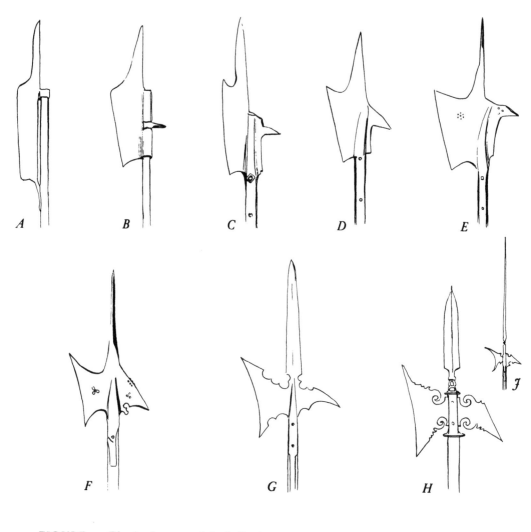

FIGURE 5   *The development of the halberd*

Illustration A and Illustration B relate to the period . . . . c. *1380—1420*
Illustration C relates to the period . . . . c. *1420—1450*
Illustration D relates to the period . . . . c. *1450—1500*
Illustration E relates to the period . . . . c. *1480—1520*
Illustration F relates to the period . . . . c. *1520—1570*
Illustration G relates to the period . . . . c. *1560—1620*
Illustration H relates to the period . . . . c. *1750—1800*
Illustration J relates to the period . . . . c. *1680—1750*

Duke Leopold and twenty-six of his noble companions were buried in the Abbey of Königsfeld; in 1898 their tombs were opened and it was found that most of the skulls were dreadfully split by halberd-strokes. Two splendid swords were found as well (*A of W*, pp. 312—313, and *S in A of C*, pp. 66, 105) in the graves of Frederiks von Tarant and Friedrich von Griffenstein.

So Laupen had proved that the Swiss method could beat the knight on his horse; now Sempach proved that it could beat him dismounted too, on good ground and with fairly equal numbers. From now on the Swiss were masters of the Alps and went out to sweep all before them for the next century and a quarter.

DEVELOPMENT OF THE HALBERD

The term 'halberd', like the weapon, is Swiss in origin; it is first found as *hellembart* in a poem by Konrad von Würzburg, who died in 1287. It is perhaps tempting to see the halberd as a cross-breed produced by a spear out of a billhook, but it seems fairly certain that it was a development of the long-handled 'Danish' axe, of the type shown, for instance, in the Bayeux Tapestry. In some later forms, this big-headed, five-foot-hafted axe (called in England a sparth) had the lower extremity of its edge prolonged and curled around the haft to produce what was in effect a secondary, reinforcing socket. In that passage in Chaucer's *The Knight's Tale* where the spectators at Theseus of Athens's tournament are

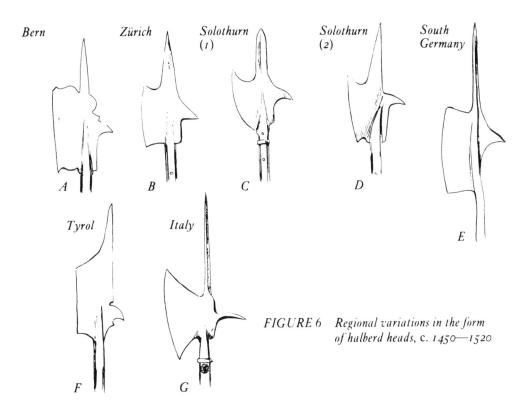

FIGURE 6   *Regional variations in the form of halberd heads, c. 1450—1520*

47

commenting upon the form of the contesting knights, we read (among much other grossly-misunderstood military terminology):

> '*Somme seyden thus, somme seyde it shal be so;*
> *Somme helden with hym with the blake berd,*
> *Somme with the balled, some with the thikke-herd;*
> *Somme sayde, he loked grim and he wolde fighte;*
> *He hath a sparth of twenty pound of wighte.*'

To follow the development of the halberd would occupy far too much text space, so I refer the reader to the illustrations (Fig. 5) which show how the halberd changed from the mid-fourteenth century until the late eighteenth, by which time it had become entirely a ceremonial weapon, used occasionally as a leading-staff (*q.v.*, p. 55).

It has been possible recently to identify and isolate certain regional variations in the shape of halberd heads, which differ from Canton to Canton in much the same way as in contemporary England the form of the ordinary bill-hook differs from county to county. These variants are shown in Figure 6.

THE BARDICHE

Before leaving the descendants of the Danish axe, there are two more to be noted. One is another localised (though very widely localised) development of the sparth, in use in

FIGURE 7   The bardiche, c. 1600

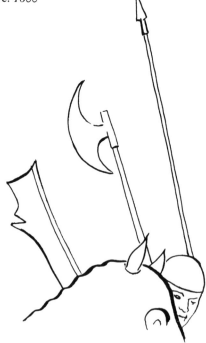

FIGURE 8   Part of a miniature from the Maciejowski Bible (c. 1250), showing staff-weapons

Scandinavia, Russia and eastern Europe, mostly in the sixteenth and seventeenth centuries. Known at that time as a bardiche, it differs from the halberd in neither having a lug or hook at the back nor a spear-like point ahead of the top of the haft; instead the blade is narrow and much longer than that of a halberd, its upper part curving back above the end of the haft and being cut off square instead of drawn into a point (Fig. 7). Although it seems fairly certain that the true bardiche of this form was not in use before 1500, there are numerous medieval manuscript pictures which show weapons of a very similar kind as early as about 1250 (Fig. 8).

THE POLE-AXE

That most knightly of weapons, the pole-axe of the fifteenth century, is another collateral of the halberd, also descended from the sparth. Until the late fourteenth century, it seems to have been just another infantry weapon, but with the more or less universal use by the European man-at-arms of a complete armour of plate during the second half of the fourteenth century, combined with the fact that he so often fought on foot, weapons capable of crushing armour or hacking through it became most desirable. One could batter an armoured opponent with a sword all day without making the least impression on him, but with axe or hammer or pick it was possible to cripple him. A good example of this is an eye-witness account of an incident in the battle of Fornovo in 1495, from the *Mémoires* of Philippe de Commynes*. He tells how he saw one of the companies of *condottieri* routed and pursued; many dismounted, assuming that in the time-honoured Italian way they would be held for ransom. But it was not to be:

'We had a great number of grooms and servants with our wagons, who flocked around the Italian men-at-arms when they were dismounted and knocked most of them on the head. The greatest part of our men had their hatchets (which they carry to cut their firewood with) in their hands and with them they broke up the Italians' head-pieces and then bashed out their brains; otherwise they could not easily have killed them, they were so very well armed.'

Since the ordinary pole-axe combined these three offensive elements, the axe and hammer and pick, it became the arm *par excellence* of the knight fighting on foot—though this statement needs some qualification: one popular usage of it was in the 'peaceful' fights at tournaments or in the processes of legal duels. For combat in war, either mounted or on foot, a short version of the same weapon was very much in favour between about 1370 and 1550; but I shall deal with these short-hafted knightly weapons—axe, hammer, pick and mace—on their own in a separate chapter.

The true pole-axe had a long haft; some are no more than about five and a half feet in length (1·675 metres), some have hafts of nearly seven feet (2·1 metres). This must have been a matter of personal choice. The head generally consisted of an axe-blade, never as large as a halberd blade, balanced at the back by a hammer-head with a dentated face; and

* Philippe de Commynes, Lord of Argenton, *c.*1447—1511. Chamberlain to Charles *Le Téméraire*, Duke of Burgundy, from 1464 until in 1472 he went into the service of Louis XI of France. For a long time he was very close to the king, and though he fell somewhat from favour in the last years of Louis' life, he served his son Charles VIII and was with him in his extraordinary campaign in Italy of 1494—1495.

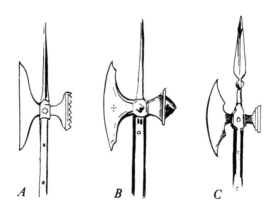

FIGURE 9   Various forms of the pole-axe, c. 1450—1520

at the top of the haft, a strong spike of rectangular section. In rarer cases, the pole-axe had a curved pick at the back instead of a hammer, and of course, as with all weapons, there were infinite variations of detail (Fig. 9). One thing all pole-axes had in common, as indeed did all staff-weapons. Forged in one with the head were two (sometimes four) long steel straps ('langets') which ran down the haft, often as far as three feet (900 cm). This was to prevent the staff from being cut through and the head cut off.

The name, by the way, derives not from the word 'pole' but 'poll' ('head'). In some Scottish texts of the sixteenth century we find the weapon being referred to as a 'pow axe'.

A variant of the pole-axe is the long-hafted hammer (Fig. 10). Here there is a hammer-head instead of an axe-blade, balanced by a pick at the back. In England such weapons too were called pole-axes, but on the Continent they were given the French names of *bec de*

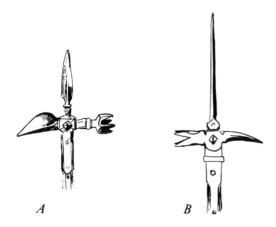

FIGURE 10   Two long-hafted war-hammers, c. 1480—1520

faucon, bec de corbin, martel and *marteau*. These weapons seem to have been very popular with some of the Canton levies of Switzerland from the fifteenth century to the seventeenth, particularly those of Lucerne. In the old Zeughaus there, many of these hammers are preserved; late examples are rather feeble things, with long, slim spikes and picks, and frail, little hammer-heads drawn out into four long spikes. Such hammers are generally known today as Lucerne hammers.

As well as being splendid weapons for fighting on foot, pole-axes had more domestic uses; it seems that in the fifteenth and sixteenth centuries, three or four pole-axes were often kept in a rack just inside the house door, for defence should a caller prove to be hostile. An extract from one of the Paston letters shows this very clearly:

Right Worshipful husband, I recommend me to you, and pray you to get some Cross Bows and Wyndacs to bend them and quarrels, for your houses here be so low that there may none man shoot out with no long bow, though we had never so much need. I suppose ye should have such things of Sir John Fastolf, if ye would send to him; and I also would ye would get two or three short pole-axes to keep with doors, and as many Jacks as ye may.

Margaret Paston to her husband John Paston, 1449

Halberds and bills (*q.v.*) were used in the same way.

I have treated the halberd at some length since it is a staff-weapon which not only developed within the Middle Ages and survived until modern times, but had perhaps more effect than any other upon the continued improvement of armour. It was also the means by which the Swiss came to be so prominent on the battlefields of Europe towards the end of the fourteenth century; a prominence which, coupled with their passion for aggressive expansion, led them in the fifteenth century to adopt the pike, whereby for half a century they dominated the battlegrounds. The pike itself as a weapon has little to recommend it, showing simply a rather boring variety of slightly differing spearheads on long hafts which, a spearhead being just a spearhead whether it is of the fifteenth century BC or AD, is not a very fascinating subject for study; but the methods, martial customs, political or military ethics, villainy, heroism, triumphs and disasters of the Swiss who used it most certainly are. Alas that there is no space here to examine these things; may I refer the reader again to the list of books at the end of this chapter.

GLOSSARY OF STAFF-WEAPONS

To examine the other staff-weapons in use by infantry during the sixteenth century (Fig. 11, p. 54—5), it will again be necessary, as it was with the halberd, to look back into the Middle Ages to trace their origins. Ever since Viking times there have been weapons which in translation from Old Norse are generally called 'hewing spears' (*A of W*, pp. 160—161). *Hoggspjot* is a word often used (*A of W*, p. 119). These may have been a sort of ancestral bill; descriptions of their use are in fact very similar to contemporary comments upon the godendac, but so far archaeology has not produced any literal confirmation of this. By the twelfth century, we begin to find miniatures in manuscripts which show clearly some interesting staff-weapons. These are all variants either of spear or axe, or of agricultural implements—scythe, billhook, flail, sledgehammer and pitchfork. These are often clearly shown to be no more than scythe-blades or billhooks mounted on long straight hafts, while flails and pitchforks needed no alteration—a sharp pitchfork is still one of the most effective weapons one could wish for. It is interesting, too, to observe in these manuscript paintings that the shape of a billhook was the same in 1977 as in 1177. In spite of the fact that most medieval illuminations were in no way concerned with showing mere foot-soldiers among the knights and barons and kings and saints who composed the personnel of their pictures, we do often see, very accurately rendered, their staff-weapons sticking up above or over the shoulders of the principal characters.

Staff-weapons in medieval and Renaissance England were all lumped together under the generic term of 'staves', but when dealing with them in detail we are faced with great terminological difficulty. There never seems to have been any clear definition of what was what; there were apparently far fewer staff-weapons in use than there were names to call them by; and contemporary writers up to the seventeenth century use these names with abandon, calling different weapons by the same name and similar weapons by different names. To add to this, we have various nineteenth-century terminologies used by different scholars. We must remember too that any particular kind of weapon, though in itself exactly the same in form and usage whether it was used in Spain or Sweden or anywhere else in Europe, had everywhere a different name. However, this confusion has now been rationalised and I shall use here the terminology Claude Blair presented in *European and American Arms* (London, 1961).

Since verbal description of these weapons is confusing and lengthy—tedious too—I shall present here a list in alphabetical order showing the origin, development and mutation of the principal 'staves' in use in Europe from the twelfth century until the eighteenth, omitting those which I have already described. Figure 11 (p. 54—5) illustrates a number of those discussed.

Ahlspiess   Called in France the *lance à pousser*, this was a thrusting weapon with a long quadrangular spike mounted on a haft some four feet long (1·2 metres). It had a rondel at the base of the head to protect the user's hands. Used sometimes by foot-soldiers, it was most popular for foot-combats in the lists (Fig. 11 A).

Axe   This basic tool/weapon is the ancestor of most of the cutting staff-weapons, halberd, bill, gisarme, bardiche and vouge (*q.v.*). Early forms depicted in manuscript illustrations show how, by fixing the blade of the axe to the haft by a socket at either end, the archetype of these weapons was formed. Axes of this shape were also used in ancient Egypt.

Bardiche   See page 48 and Figure 7.

Bill   Derived from the common billhook. Was used all over Europe from the tenth century until late in the sixteenth. The various spikes and lugs protruding from the blade to either side made the bill a very effective parrying weapon (Figs. 11 B, C).

Chauve-Souris   This is a modern French term, fairly widely used, for a form of couseque (*q.v.*) with large angular side blades somewhat resembling a bat's wings (Fig. 11 D).

Couseque   Derived probably from the earlier medieval winged spear. Most popular in France and Italy (Fig. 11 E).

Flail   Basically the agricultural implement pressed into warlike use. In some examples, a large spiked wooden or iron ball was attached to the haft by a length of chain.

Fork   Basically and sometimes actually a pitchfork, though by the fifteenth century, military forks were being specially made, most with downcurved hooks as well as the two, or sometimes three, tines (Fig. 11 F¹, F²). These hooks were used in siege-work for pulling down fascines or gabions or for scaling walls. Forks had mostly gone out of use by the mid-eighteenth century, but in France sergeants in the *Regiment Dauphin* continued to carry forks instead of halberds as leading-staffs.

Gisarme   First mentioned in texts of the twelfth century and continuing in use up to the seventeenth. Often identified with the bill, it seems to have had a totally different origin and to be an offspring of the axe, not the billhook, and may be identified with the crescent-shaped double-socketed axe. In the English poem *Sir Gawaine and the Green Knight*, written between 1360 and 1400, it is referred to as a 'giserne', this name being applied to the Green Knight's weapon, which is also called a sparth and an axe. To clinch this, an illustration to the poem in a late-fourteenth-century manuscript (B.M. Cott. Nero A, x) shows that the 'giserne' in the text was this type of long-handled crescentic axe.

Glaive   A term first recorded in the thirteenth century, used at that time as an alternative to lance, but from the fifteenth century onwards it is used as a synonym for sword and dagger; at this time also it may have been applied to a large, sharply-pointed, back-edged blade shaped like a modern kitchen knife, sometimes with a short false edge near the point. Such (or similar) weapons are very occasionally shown in thirteenth- or fourteenth-century manuscript pictures wielded two-handed by horsemen. The notable example is the Maciejowski Bible in the Pierpont Morgan Library, New York (*A of W*, Pl. 11a). Shown in Figures 11 G¹, G².

Godendac   See page 45.

Halberd   See pages 47—8.

Hammer   In manuscript pictures from about 1200 up to the mid-fifteenth century, we find representations of enormous mallet-shaped weapons on long hafts, usually with large pyramidal spikes springing from each face of the head. In England such a weapon was called a 'maul'.

Holy-Water Sprinkler   A slang term found in English texts of the sixteenth and seventeenth centuries to describe a long-hafted spiked club, of varied form. The best-known is one in the Armouries of the Tower of London, known as 'Henry VIII's Walking-Staff'.

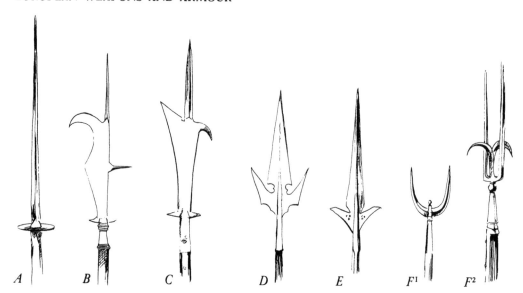

FIGURE 11   A selection from the staff-weapons described on pages 52—6

> *Illustration A shows an Ahlspiess*
> *Illustration B shows a Bill, and C a variant form of Bill*
> *Illustration D shows the Chauvre-Souris*
> *Illustration E shows the Couseque*
> *Illustration F¹ shows a Fork, and F² an elaborated form for siege work*

Javelin   In sixteenth- and seventeenth-century English texts, the word seems to have been used to denote an ordinary boar spear, a specifically throwing-spear being called a 'dart'. A light horseman's spear usually with a leaf-shaped head.

Jedburgh (or Jeddart) Staff   Referred to in Scottish sixteenth- and seventeenth-century texts, but its form is uncertain. There is no evidence that it was a long-handled axe (Fig. 11 H).

Lance   Once used synonymously with 'spear', but now exclusively denotes the horseman's spear—which, up to the fourteenth century, was always called a 'spear'. The first use in English texts was in the mid-sixteenth century as 'demi-lance', a term denoting a light spear carried by medium cavalry as distinct from the fully-armoured men-at-arms. It was also used to denote the horseman himself. Up to about 1400—1450 the war-lance was a spear some fourteen feet long (4·25 metres) made of a tough wood such as ash, with a small leaf-shaped or lozenge-shaped head. As early as the 1320s, a hand-defence of steel, called a vamplate, was sometimes fixed over the haft in front of the hand, though it was more usual on the jousting-lance until about 1450—1500. From the early fifteenth century the wood of the haft of the war-lance was thickened in front of the hand and behind it, forming a grip. The jousting-lance followed the development of the war-lance, except that

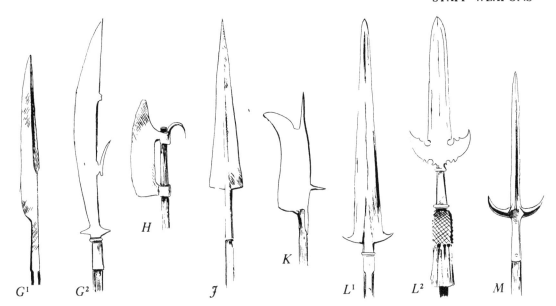

FIGURE 11   Illustration G¹ shows an early Glaive, and G² a later form, or Gisarme
(Cont.)   Illustration H shows a Jedburgh Staff
              Illustration J shows a Langdebeve
              Illustration K shows a Lochaber Axe
              Illustration L¹ shows a fighting Partisan, and L² a ceremonial Partisan
              Illustration M shows a Rawcon

it was sometimes fitted with a rebated head for the *joust à plaisance*. As early as the 1280s we find this kind of lance described as a 'lance of courtesy' (*A of W*, p. 192). From about 1490 some jousting-lances were made hollow, so that although they looked very massive they were in fact light and broke up easily on impact.

Lancegay   A light throwing-spear, referred to in texts from the fourteenth century to the seventeenth. The term probably derives from the same root as the Near Eastern *zagayah*—hence *assegai*.

Langdebeve (*Langue de Boeuf, Langue de Beve*)   A spear with a very large, broad blade, rather like a partisan (*q.v.*) without lugs at the base of the blade (Fig. 11 J).

Leading-Staff   A light staff with an ornamental head, used from the later sixteenth century to the eighteenth by captains of infantry companies to give signals when leading their men. (A modern equivalent is the staff of the drum-major of a military band.) The small, ornamental head might be in the form of halberd, bill or fork.

Lochaber Axe   A Scottish halberd-like weapon, more nearly resembling in shape the basic billhook (Fig. 11 K).

55

Morgenstern   A German term used for the so-called Holy-Water Sprinkler.

Partisan   This seems to have developed during the fifteenth century from the winged spear. It had a very long, two-edged blade, often some twenty-eight inches (70 cm) in length, broad at the base, from which sprang two small upturned lugs. Very effective as a fighting weapon, it soon became the most popular form of ceremonial or parade staff-weapon, remaining in widespread use for this purpose until the nineteenth century, and is still retained by the Yeoman Warders of the Tower of London, the Yeomen of the Guard, and the Papal Guard in the Vatican. In later examples the lugs, originally used for parrying, were cut into complex shapes. See Figures 11 L^1, L^2.

Pike   The term was often used for any kind of foot-soldier's spear, but its specific use is applied to the long pike which is described on page 57 below. The half-pike, a short pike about six feet long (1·9 metres), was used at sea ('boarding-pike') up to the late nineteenth century, and sometimes in the sixteenth and seventeenth centuries as a leading-staff.

Plançon à Picot   A five-foot-long wooden truncheon (1·5 metres), thickened at the top where it is bound about with iron, with a long spike protruding from the end. This is the weapon so clearly shown on the oak chest of early-fourteenth-century date preserved at New College, Oxford, carved with scenes showing the battle of Courtrai (1302). This has caused it to be confused with the godendac. Sometimes called also a *chandelier* or *plançon à broche*.

Rawcon (Ranseur, Rancoon, Ronka)   A weapon with a three-pronged head, having a narrow, central, two-edged blade with a long upcurved one on either side of it. *But* in sixteenth- and seventeenth-century Italy, a bill was often called a *roncone* (Fig. 11 M).

Spontoon   Term derived from the French *esponton*, sometimes used in the Middle Ages to denote a dagger. From about 1550 it appears as *spontone* in Italian texts, referring to some kind of spear, and in seventeenth-century France it was applied to the half-pike. In its final form in the eighteenth century, a small triangular blade with a short bar protruding horizontally from the socket below it, it was used as a leading-staff, in England by officers until 1786 and by sergeants from 1792 until 1830.

Vouge   This term is perhaps the most vague of all. Medieval French texts suggest that it denotes what in England was called a bill, and several of them use it for a tool for hedging or cutting brushwood—*i.e.*, a billhook. Martin du Bellay in his *Mémoires* (1582) implies that it was a characteristically English weapon—*i.e.* a bill; but modern writers have used it to denote a glaive (*vouge français*) or an early halberd (Swiss *vouge*).

DEVELOPMENT OF SWISS PIKEMEN

In 1422 the Swiss suffered their first real defeat. They had been for many years annexing small pieces of territory south of the Alps, and in 1422 they made an incursion in some strength into the territories of Filippo Maria Visconti of Milan, near Bellinzona. This was too much for Visconti, who sent a strong mercenary force out against them under the famous *Condottiere* Carmagnola and his colleague Angelo de la Pergola. Battle was joined at Arbedo on June 30, and like Edward I at Falkirk, Carmagnola saw after his first frontal cavalry attack that such tactics were useless against the Swiss column. So he sent his crossbowmen in to shoot gaps in the mass of halberdiers while he dismounted his men-at-arms. He had some three times as many men as the Swiss, all of them fully armoured. Now the tactic which Leopold of Austria had tried without success at Sempach in 1386 was vindicated; the Italians rolled into the mass of the Swiss, who fought desperately to hold their ground. Just as the Italians were beginning to push the Swiss back, a new Swiss force was seen to come into the field. Carmagnola believed this force to be the men of the Cantons of Zürich, Schwyz, Glarus and Appenzell, whom he knew to be in the neighbourhood; so he withdrew his attack. When his men were disengaged, he saw that in fact the new arrivals were no more than a group of foraging parties, too weak in numbers to make any attack. The main body of the Swiss took this opportunity to retire in good order; their defeat had not been decisive, but it was significant.

During the heat of the fighting, the Swiss leaders had actually been contemplating surrender. The *Schultheiss* of Lucerne stuck his halberd upright into the ground in token of submission, but Carmagnola would not accept it. He yelled out that men who gave no quarter would get none, and urged his men on. It was just at this point that the new force appeared and ended the battle.

Arbedo showed clearly the superiority of the long spear; properly deployed in a massive formation, it was far more effective than the shorter halberd. The Swiss had always used a weapon they called a *spiess* among the halberds, but only in small numbers. This seems not to have been the long, eighteen-foot pike (5·5 metres long) of later years but a shorter weapon more like the *ahlspiess* (q.v.). At Arbedo there had been only (roughly) one *spiess* to three halberds. The serried mass of the men-at-arms of Carmagnola rolling down upon them bristling with spearpoints seems to have made the Swiss think. After 1422 we find many documents relating to organisation which make the same point over and over again: there are too few pikes. Every man who is able to carry a pike ought to do so: *Welcher ein Spiess trägen könn, einen Spiess trägen sollte*, 'Whoever can carry a pike, ought to carry a pike'.

This referred to the true pike, a ten-inch steel head (25 cm) upon an eighteen-foot haft (15·5 metres) of ash. It was not a weapon to be used by single men or in open order, for one's opponent had to be at least twelve feet (3·65 metres) away if one was to be able to harm him. Once he came nearer, the long pike became an encumbrance; but when used at the proper distance, in close order, it was deadly. It was grasped with both hands, widely extended, and poised at shoulder level with the point inclining a little downward. In front of the columns of pikemen projected not only the pikes of the first rank but of the second, third and fourth, as well; a bristling, impenetrable hedge. The men in the interior of the column held their pikes upright, ready to step forward to take the places of those who fell in the front ranks. With their points twelve feet (3·65 metres) above the heads of the men, the pikes made the charging column look like a moving wood. Above it always waved countless flags; the pennons of districts, towns and guilds, and the banners of the Cantons. The common expression 'to trail a pike' refers to the usual manner of carrying this cumbersome weapon from place to place, held more or less at mid-point and at arm's length, with the spearpoint in the air and the butt-end trailing on the ground behind. Until recently, an infantryman carried his rifle 'at the trail' when he held it with his arm down by his side and the weapon parallel with the ground.

The rapidity with which the Swiss moved their forces, marching from mustering-place to battlefield and charging upon their foes when they got there, added greatly to the fear inspired by their solid unbreakable formations. The normal order of battle which they employed, however large or small their numbers might be, was to advance in three divisions, deployed in echelon. The leading division (the *vorhut*—what would have been called the vaward in a medieval army) made straight for a given point in the enemy's line while the main-battle (the *gewaltshaufen*) came on parallel with it but a little to its rear, on the right or left. The rearward (the *nachhut*) advanced even farther back, often halting until the results of the first clash could be seen; acting in fact as a reserve.

By using this tactic, room was left at the rear of each column to allow it to retire if necessary without running back into and breaking up the following column (as had happened to the French at Poitiers and the Austrians at Sempach, for example). It also prevented the enemy from wheeling inwards and taking the columns in flank—always there was the second column ready to move in and outflank the outflankers. It depended upon the ground and the conditions to determine whether the right or left column should attack first; but whatever the conditions it seems that even small bodies of pikemen could take care of themselves. This was shown, for instance, in the Swabian war, in 1499, when six hundred men of Zürich, caught in open country by a thousand Austrian men-at-arms, 'formed the hedgehog [the *igel*] and broke off the enemy with ease and much jesting'. During the same year the whole Swiss army, being forced to offer battle in the open, went out to meet the Imperialist cavalry in three great hollow squares with the Cantonal banners and their guards in the middle; but as in the Hussite wars of fifty years before, the German cavalry knew what they were up against and would not face the squares.

One of the last medieval potentates to try conclusions with the Swiss on their home ground was Charles *Le Téméraire*, Duke of Burgundy. He was defeated twice, in March 1476 and June of the same year, by the new pike-tactics, and once again at Nancy in the winter of early 1477. In this battle Charles himself, fighting heroically to cover the retreat of his broken army, was cut down by a halberd, cleft through helmet and skull by a tremendous blow which split his head from temple to chin.

The actual manner of Charles's death is obscure, but it seems fairly certain that when he was cut down in the confusion of flight nobody knew who he was. His stripped body was identified next day in a ditch. Commynes says very little about the fight because he was not there. A knight named Claude de Bausmont claimed to have killed the Duke; he told how he saw a rider trying to get his horse across a little stream; the horse threw the man and he tried to get away on foot. When he saw de Bausmont pursuing him he cried out for quarter, saying who he was; but de Bausmont was deaf and couldn't hear, so he cut him down. This claim rather fails to tally with the account in the *Annales Burgundiae* which mentions the great wound which cleft the side of Charles's armet and split his head from brow to chin, and two other wounds as well, a thrust in the groin and another 'near the fundament'. Only a weapon like a halberd could have broken through his helmet, and the wounds in his crutch, the only unarmoured part of a fully-armed man's body, are entirely consistent with the way halberds were used. A blow to the head would unhorse a man, or drive him forward over saddle-bow so that his unarmoured rear rose out of the protection of the saddle, when the spear-like point of the halberd could be put to good use.

The very last attempt of the Germanic Emperors to regain the territories lost to the Swiss in the early fifteenth century was Maximilian's effort in the Swabian war of 1498—1499. During this war the Swiss showed to perfection that characteristic of theirs which was to be so important during the great wars in Italy. This was the most unflinching courage allied to a total lack of imagination or real military skill. They never produced a real 'General'; all their commanders were simply veterans, long service with the pikes being more important to promotion than tactical skill. Their leaders were always men of the same sort of calibre as a good R.S.M. The one idea of these leaders was to bring their force into the presence of the enemy and send it in straight at him. At Frastenz in 1490 the battle was won by a charge straight up the face of a cliff, and at Dornach—the last battle fought by the Swiss on their home ground until the eighteenth century—the fortune of the day depended upon a slogging match between the Swiss and Swabian pikemen; and the Swiss stuck it best, and won.

They never entirely abandoned the halberd; it was used to arm the picked guards of the Cantonal banners, who marched in the middle of the columns; and if the column was brought to a stand, these halberdiers would often emerge from their place and coming out through the disengaged rear or side ranks would fall upon the enemy's flank. Occasionally in the fifteenth century, and frequently in the sixteenth, these banners were guarded by men with large two-hand swords instead of halberds; but these will be dealt with in their proper place (p. 146).

Two things combined to ruin the Swiss: their refusal to learn anything from the tactical and technological improvements in the art of war, and their absurd 'democratic' method of conducting their mercenary business. After their resounding successes over Charles of Burgundy and in the Swabian war, other national armies developed methods which were to prove the undoing of the hitherto invincible pikeman.

The great struggle just beginning in Italy served as a school for the captains in other European nations, who began to co-ordinate the military theories of the ancients with hard-won practical experience, developing an art of war far better than anything since Roman times. New forms of professional efficiency were emerging and new tactical weapons being developed: the sword-and-buckler men of Spain, for instance, the arquebusiers of Germany, and the 'stradiots' (light cavalry) of France and Italy. All threatened the Swiss and were ignored by them. However, they continued to go from success to success. As Machiavelli said, they could 'march with ten to fifteen thousand pikemen against any number of horse, and win a general opinion of their excellence from the many remarkable services they performed'. They certainly left their mark on the military history of every nation of Europe and set the mind of every capable officer to work devising methods whereby they might be defeated.

THE *LANDSKNECHTE*

One factor which helped the process of reducing Swiss power was the fact that Europe's captains were no longer handling indisciplined feudal armies but trained bodies of professional soldiers who were capable of coherent action and steadiness in the face even of an onrushing column of pikemen.

The Germans, inspired in this, as in so many military matters, by their Emperor, Maximilian I, raised forces of '*landsknechte*' which were directly based upon the Swiss model. They used (at first) the same weapons—pikes with a small contingent of halberdiers—but long before the Swiss were forced to admit the pike's deficiencies and introduce handguns, the *landsknechte* took to the arquebus.

Spain seems to have looked to *El Gran Capitan* as they called him, Gonzalo de Córdoba, to produce a tactical weapon. This took the form of well-trained and highly-disciplined corps of hardy fighters well (though lightly) armoured and armed with short swords and small light bucklers. In this they were to some extent based (to the obvious approval of Machiavelli, who is unstinted in his praises of them) upon the ancient Roman legionary with his *lorica*, shield and short stabbing sword. When the Swiss and these swordsmen first met in 1502 under the walls of Barletta, the Spaniards had the best of it:

'When they came to engage, the Swiss at first pressed so hard upon their enemy with the pike that they opened up their ranks: but the Spaniards, under the cover of their bucklers, nimbly rushed in upon them with their swords, and laid about them so furiously that they made a great slaughter of the Swiss, and gained a complete victory,' recorded Machiavelli.

The bearer of the shorter weapon always had the advantage at close quarters, as the Austrians had found at Sempach. The long pikes were useless once the Spanish were into the column; and in a hand-to-hand fight with swords, the unarmoured Swiss were at a disadvantage. At Ravenna in 1512 the same thing happened; with the Spaniards 'rushing at the Pikes, or throwing themselves on the ground and slipping below the points, so that they darted in among the legs of the pikemen' just as the Sudanese Arabs did at El Teb in 1884 when they broke up a British square.

At Marignano in 1515, the Swiss employed by Massimiliano Sforza of Milan were defeated by François I of France by a combined use of cavalry and artillery. The cavalry made charge after charge at the Swiss columns, quite ineffectually because they got nowhere near the pikemen, but they did force the columns to halt, and stay halted, thus offering the very efficient batteries of Galiot de Genouillac's cannon perfect targets. Immediately the cavalry drew off, the artillery fired devastating salvoes at the Swiss. As soon as the pikemen moved forward against the guns, the cavalry went at them from all sides and brought them to a stand. This process was repeated until it became too dark to see; and when the Swiss supply organisation lit fires to cook some food for the famished pikemen, de Genouillac fired again upon the tall forests of pikes standing up there against the glow of the fires. As soon as it was light, the battle began afresh, but the same thing happened; when after several more hours a new force of Italian cavalry appeared on the field in rear of the Swiss, they drew off in good order.

At Marignano the Swiss were held, but at Bicocca seven years later, in 1522, they were almost annihilated, for they tried to storm across a deep ditch with a high steep bank topped by a wall on the farther side; this wall was strongly held by *landsknechte*, a great proportion of whom were using the arquebus. The Swiss attacked in their usual impetuous (and indeed, in this case, foolhardy) way, and were mown down by the guns, while the *landsknecht* pikemen and halberdiers behind the wall skewered or hewed apart any who survived the shot.

This was virtually the end of the Swiss as a military force of pikemen only. For nearly three centuries more, Switzerland continued to provide the best mercenary soldiers in Europe, but they were no longer all pikemen. After Bicocca, the Swiss, like the *landsknechte*, turned more and more to the handgun, at first the arquebus, then the caliver and finally the musket.

So we have seen the two principal weapons which changed the whole face of war in their early days, each, handgun and pike, acting on its own. When the two were combined in equal proportions of guns and pikes in the same force, a new tactical weapon had been forged. If the Swiss at Marignano had had as many 'shot' as they had pikes, the French cavalry could not have survived long enough to give their artillery its chance—nor, indeed, could the gunners have loaded and fired undisturbed at their sitting target. By about 1550 the concept of 'modern' warfare was thoroughly established.

BIBLIOGRAPHY

Blair, Claude, *European and American Arms*, London, 1962

Boissonas, Charles, *Armes Anciennes de la Suisse*, Paris, 1910

Buttin, C., *Les Armes d'Hast*, Bulletin de la Societé des Amis du Musée de l'Armée, Paris, 1936, *et seq.*

Carpegna, Nolfo di (Ed.), *Armi Antiche dal Sec. IX al XVIII gia Collezione Odelscalchi*, Rome, 1969

Laking, Sir Guy, *A Record of European Armour and Arms Through Seven Centuries*, London, 1920—1922

Oman, Sir Charles, *The Art of War in the Middle Ages* (Volume II), London, 1928

and also . . . . . *The Art of War in the XVI Century*, London, 1928

Zeitz, Heribert, *Blankwaffen* (Volume I, Volume II), Braunschweig, 1968

The Kretzschmar von Kienbusch Collection of Armour and Arms, Princeton, 1963

The Wallace Collection Catalogue (Volume II), London, 1962

CHAPTER THREE

MACE, WAR-HAMMER AND HORSEMAN'S AXE

Aesthetically the short-hafted staff-weapons used by the mounted men-at-arms can be as satisfying as that most elegant of weapons, the sword. Most of them have the same qualities of line and proportion, and many have been decorated with great skill and good taste by the artists who showed so much technical brilliance in the decoration of sword-hilts and fine armour.

There are only three basic types of these knightly staff-weapons: the mace, the war-hammer and the horseman's axe. The flail (a squalid weapon) was often adapted in a short-hafted version, and 'knights' are much given to the use of it—knights, that is, in modern films or television 'historical' productions; in fact flails were rarely used except by infantry or rebellious peasants. These crude weapons lack any kind of aesthetic appeal, and in close combat they must have been as much of a threat to one's friends as a menace to one's enemies.

THE MACE

In its basic forms, the mace was as crude an instrument as the flail; its congeners may be found in any war-club or kerrie or shillelagh, and it was used in the same way, as a club. But as it developed in the later Middle Ages, it became very sophisticated, and in its final forms, in the late fifteenth century and all through the sixteenth, it was never clumsy, and often exceedingly handsome; as handsome as it had been in its earliest civilised form in Ancient Egypt. The beautiful stone mace-heads found in pre-dynastic and early dynastic contexts are splendid weapons, their craftsmanship often attaining the status of works of art in the sculptural qualities of the stone—basalt, alabaster, obsidian or diorite—out of which they were made. As well as being very effective as weapons, they were endowed with very definite attributes as symbols of power and leadership; though which was their primary function and which secondary is open to conjecture. In both they seem to join hands across the centuries with the finely-wrought steel maces of the Renaissance and the elaborate silver and gold ceremonial civic maces of today.

There is a persistent legend that in western Europe during the Middle Ages the mace was a favourite—many would say it was the sole—weapon of fighting churchmen. 'All they,' says Holy Writ, 'that take the sword shall perish with the sword' [Matt. 26, 52]. Can we really believe that medieval prelates were so simple-minded (or imagined their contemporaries to be) that they sought to avoid the wrath of God by so childish an evasion? Evidence for this belief is extremely slender; Sir Walter Scott undoubtedly had much to do with it, reinforced perhaps by the figure of Bishop Odo of Bayeux in the Bayeux tapestry, who is shown wielding a club—not a mace, a kind of rugged shillelagh. *Hic Odo Eps* runs the stitched caption above his head, so there shall be no mistake. 'This is Odo the Bishop.' He wields a mace: *ergo*, bishops used maces in battle. Why? To avoid the effusion of Christian blood. But there is in this document one other figure wielding a club similar to Odo's. If we are to accept Odo's 'mace' as evidence for one myth, then we must accept that of the second figure as evidence for another myth—that conquerors, or Dukes of Normandy, or monarchs, or commanders-in-chief, always used 'maces' in battle, for the second figure with a mace is Duke William. There are other maces or clubs shown in the Tapestry, but none in anyone's hand; all are flying through the air. They are quite unlike the clubs of William and his half-brother, too, for they have short stalks with curious trilobed 'clover-leaf' heads to them, like the Clubs on a playing card. Maybe they were not so much clubs as some kind of missile weapon. Exactly similar weapons were in use as missiles in New Guinea up to modern times.

There is a far better (and entirely credible) story about warrior-bishops which concerns these two half-brothers. In 1072 William had occasion to take the field against Odo, who had risen in arms against him. In a skirmish he captured Odo, fully-armed, and very properly locked him up. Whereupon the Pope wrote sternly to William, demanding to know by what right he dared imprison a bishop, who was to him as a son in Christ. William replied characteristically by sending Odo's mail hauberk to the Pope, with a terse reference to the story of Joseph in Genesis: 'Is not this thy son's coat?'

Throughout the Middle Ages, bishops were great landowners, rulers of cities, and statesmen, often with very wide princely powers. They were always leading their troops into battle, armed to the teeth like any secular prince, and using whatever knightly weapon suited them best, as did the warriors of the monastic orders who fought with lance and sword, axe, mace or hammer like everyone else. (Until the French Revolution the Bishop of Cahors, for example, had the right to lay his helmet, shield and sword upon the altar when he celebrated High Mass.) The mace myth, though like so many other romantic medieval nonsenses a gift to the historical novelist, should be regarded with reserve by serious students of arms.

If we may legitimately reject the 'evidence' of the tapestry to uphold the theory that bishops only fought with maces, there is nonetheless something of interest in this which we may accept. Here we see the Generalissimo of the invading force and his second-in-command armed, not with spear or sword or axe like every other one of the tapestry figures, but with staffs, batons, sticks. Not weapons at all, perhaps? We find the same thing, four centuries later, in many Italian paintings of battles; the frescoes in the Church of S. Francesco at Arezzo by Piero della Francesca (painted 1452—1466) and the three pictures of the Battle of San Romano by Paolo Uccello (*c.* 1462), for instance. The leaders—Cyrus, King of Persia, Heraclius, Nicolo da Tolentino the *Condottiere*—carry batons, in the same way as British infantry officers tended to go 'over the top' in the Great War with walking-sticks. There are countless examples in prose, poetry and picture of officers riding or walking about in battles armed only with sticks, like Caesar in the battle against the Nervii; when things got desperate, he grabbed a sword and a shield from an infantryman and weighed in himself. Was not a vinestock walking-stick the prime symbol of a centurion's office?

A great many more maces seem to have survived than either hammers or axes. This may seem to indicate that the mace was a more popular weapon, more widely in use than the others, but maybe it is not so. Where an old, outmoded hammer or axe might usefully be handed down to the servants when the master had no further use for it, to finish its days as a tool about the manor, there was no domestic future for an unwanted mace. So it is reasonable, perhaps, to suppose that the rarity today of war-hammers, or horseman's axes, indicates not that fewer were made but that most of them were used about the house till they wore out and were then thrown away, while the maces were preserved in the armoury.

In ancient times, maces (as distinct from clubs) seem to have been used by the ordinary Egyptian warrior only until the XIIth dynasty (*c.* 1990—1780 BC) though right up to Roman times we find wall-paintings and reliefs showing Pharaohs ritually slaying captives with maces—more evidence here, maybe, of the mace being a ritual object. They seem to have been used occasionally in war by all the other peoples of the eastern Mediterranean except the Greeks. The Romans did not use them at all, and there is no hard evidence that their Celtic and Teutonic adversaries did either. Many mace-heads cast in bronze have been recovered from the earth, some of which are considered to have been found in Late Bronze Age contexts (notably one in the Blackmore collection of Bronze Age weapons and tools in the Salisbury Museum, Wiltshire, England). However, doubt is cast upon this attribution because similar mace-heads of bronze have been found in Russia, said to have come from medieval contexts. We have seen often enough how a form of weapon can survive the millennia, or return to regular usage after a lapse of many centuries—the Early Bronze Age rapier of Ireland and the eighteenth-century smallsword, for example, or to take a valid parallel, the smiths' marks stamped upon Celtic iron blades of the fourth century BC reappearing on German blades in the seventeenth century AD, almost unaltered. So maybe the Salisbury mace does date *c.* 800 BC and the Russian ones *c.* AD 1250. After all, modern craftsmen, such as carpenters or stonemasons or jewellers, use the same techniques and tools as their fore-runners did three thousand years ago.

The short final phase of the mace's existence as a weapon saw much development of these primeval forms, which had remained almost unchanged at least from the twelfth century until about 1470. The basic shape remained, the elaboration only affecting detail and ornament. While the old maces consisted mainly of two elements, the cast, or occasionally forged, head and the plain wooden haft, in the latest ones each of these elements might consist of as many as four parts. The head was made up of a number of flanges, which might be quite plainly shaped, or formed with a great elaboration of angles and curves, projections and indentations. There were generally seven of these, all brazed together round a central tubular core, the base of each flange separated from its neighbour by a little billet of steel. Each flange was set as the continuation of a radius of the circle formed by the diameter of the tubular core. At the top of the head there was a little detachable finial, and at its base generally (not always) a little collar. These finials came in a great variety of shapes: there were spikes, long or short; knops variously decorated with flutings, straight or spiral, or with mouldings, and of spherical, pear or acorn shape; there were pyramids, with straight sides or curved, decorated or plain; little castellated fillets with graceful turrets rising from the centre; in some cases, the finial was even made in the shape of a tiny crown. Most of them were detachable, fitted with a little threaded shank to screw into a corresponding hole in the top of the mace-head. Because of this, many finials have been lost and a number of beautiful maces now have a vaguely unbalanced look for the lack of them—like the beautiful mace in the Bargello Museum, Florence, where only the threaded hole remains to show where the finial was fitted.

The haft might be in two parts; some had a steel section fitted into the head, with a wooden section fitted below it, though after the 1470s most mace-hafts were entirely of steel or iron. Even some of these were made in two parts, screwed or brazed together. On the haft itself were other fittings, mostly in the form of variously decorated collars; there was often a collar, moulded or roped, to mark off the upper end of the grip from the haft, and another larger one at the bottom of the grip serving the office of a pommel. A ring was frequently fixed into the bottom of the haft to take a wrist-thong. If there was not such a ring, a hole was bored through the haft just above the grip.

Maces during their final century fall into four main types, each according to the shape of the head—though of course there was almost infinite variation of detail within the basic form. It is plain to see, too, from which of the primal forms each took its origin. In Figure 12, I have shown these basic forms, old and new: Types M 1, M 2, M 3 and M 4.

Type M 1 (Figs. 12 A^1, 12 A^2) is always referred to as the 'Gothic' mace, and never was the adjective, in its architectural sense, more aptly applied to anything. Among all the host of so-called 'Gothic' arms, from armour to swords, from staff-weapons to horse-armour, nothing is so like a bit of detached Gothic architecture as a mace. These maces tended to be a good deal smaller and lighter than their forerunners—some 18 inches long (45 cm) and some 45 ounces in weight (1275 g) on average. Illustrations in Plate 4 and Figure 12 show a few of these lovely little weapons. Characteristic is the acutely-pointed shape of the flanges of the head, the distinct grip, often thicker than the haft and bound with fabric, thonging or wire, like a sword-grip with a 'pommel' at the bottom, and a feature more like a guard than a decorative collar at the top. These guards were generally flat discs cut to a hexagonal or octagonal shape, with each facet filed to a deep concavity.

Decoration was kept as a rule to a minimum, and was entirely architectural; on the head, openings cut in the flat sides of each flange like stone tracery in windows; little 'crockets' at each end of the edges of the flanges, and sometimes all along the edges as well; moulded collars on hafts which were as often of hexagonal as of circular section, looking like slender stone columns; and more rarely, lines or very simple patterns of latten inlaid in the steel. A very few maces of this period are covered all over with intricate carving in relief, again in just the same manner, and to the same designs, as decorated 'flamboyant' Gothic architecture (these last tend to be quite hideous, their graceful forms ruined by over-elaboration).

Around 1500, this light, elegant form of mace began to go out of fashion, to be replaced by a heavier, larger weapon of a bolder design—Type M 2, Figure 12 B^1. It is plain to see where the differences of form lie, and there is no possibility of mistaking one type for the other. Owing perhaps to the greater length of the flange edges, there was plenty of scope for elaboration. There are a few maces, notably one in the Stibbert collection in Florence, which are almost transitional in form between the M 1 and M 2 types. The Stibbert example (Fig. 12B¹) is of the same size as an M 2 and has the same long flanges, but the edges of these are cut to a distinctly 'Gothic' shape.

There are far more maces of the M 2 type surviving than of any other kind, some of them having belonged to well-known personages. At the head of this group is the mace of Charles V in the Royal Armoury, Madrid. This retains its original wrist-thong, a rather dainty cord of silk finished off with a handsome tassel. The flanges here are each drawn to an acute spike; there is a mace almost exactly the same, wrist-thong, tassel and all, in the Metropolitan Museum of Art, New York.

In maces of this type the flanges are thinner than in the Gothic ones, about an eighth of an inch (3 mm) as against three-sixteenths of an inch, or rather less (4—5 mm). The greater size of the head makes these edges look even thinner than they are, and they seem to be set more widely apart. The average length of these Type M 2 maces was between 24 and 26 inches (60 and 70 cm) and they weighed between 80 and 110 ounces (2 and 3 kg).

Type M 3 (Fig. 12 C) is of a form loved by romantic writers and illustrators and

FIGURE 12   *Illustrations A¹ and A² show late-fifteenth-century forms of the 'Gothic' mace, Type M 1*
                    Illustrations B¹ and B² show early-sixteenth-century forms of Type M 2
                    Illustration C shows a form dating from the early to mid-sixteenth century, Type M 3
                    Illustration D, dating c. 1550—1700, is an eastern-European form, called a 'bulawa', Type M 4

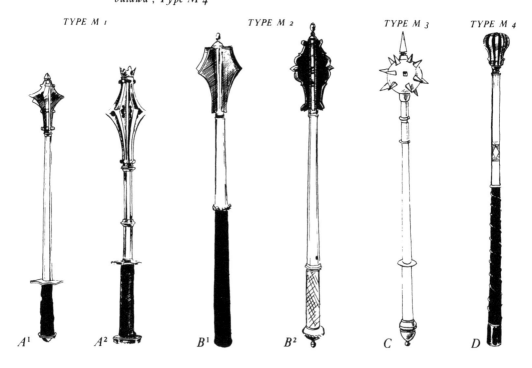

TYPE M 1   TYPE M 2   TYPE M 3   TYPE M 4

A¹   A²   B¹   B²   C   D

television designers, but it was in fact rarely used. It consists of a steel globe bristling with spikes, looking very like a sea-mine of the Great War. There are very few survivors, though let it at once be said that I mean western European survivors, for this type of mace was popular in Persia, and particularly in India, well into the nineteenth century. The two most notable surviving ones are perhaps those which are in the Wallace Collection, London, and in the Musée de l'Armée, Paris. Maybe they were not popular because when used against armour—and after all the main purpose of a mace, as of a hammer or an axe, was to crack armour open where a sword blade could not penetrate—the spikes would punch neat holes into which they would stick. Maybe. There is no evidence for this, only a practical application of the imagination. These probably derived from smaller, but similarly shaped, cast bronze heads. There is a large, handsome, spiked early example, in the shape of a truncated cone made of cast iron, in the Van Zuylen Collection.

Type M 4 (Fig. 12 D) is of eastern European—possibly Polish—origin, and is known as a bulawa. Characteristic is the onion-shaped head, the multiplicity of thick flanges, and the absence of any kind of angle or spike. Like so many other eastern European weapons, it is very close in design to the maces of Turkey and Persia. Some surviving ones have been dated as late as the mid-nineteenth century. A fine early example, though almost impossible to date accurately, is in the Bavarian National Museum, Munich, together with a fine example of another eastern type, called a buzdigan. This has the characteristics of a western mace, with the usual seven-flanged head, but all the striking edges are rounded, almost semi-circular, giving it a very oriental aspect. In Stockholm there is a mace which is actually of Turkish workmanship, yet looks more western than the one just described, for the flanges are of typical angular western shape. It was given by the Hungarian Bethlen Gabor to Gustavus Adolphus of Sweden early in the seventeenth century. This is clearly not a fighting mace, for its head is very heavily inlaid with roses of gold and rubies, and its haft with gilding, *niello* and coloured enamels. It is a clear example of a decorated mace firmly on the far side of that very blurred line which distinguishes the sixteenth-century fighting mace from the mace used purely as a *bastone di comando*.

There is in the Odescalci Collection in Rome a most interesting mace of aberrant form, like a rather graceful club forged in steel with a little finial at its head shaped as a truncated cone reversed, and a small spherical button at the end of the narrow, shaped grip, illustrated in Figure 13. This is a rare example of such a mace, though several are to be seen in Italian paintings of the fourteenth century—notably a fresco by Giotto in the Cappella della Scrovegni, Padua (c. 1303—1305), and a predella by Giovanni di Bartolomeo Christiani (c. 1367—1393) in the Metropolitan Museum, New York. It seems to have been a type of weapon confined to Italy, used probably only during the fourteenth century since no representations of it exist later than Christiani's predella.

Surviving from this period, 1475—1580, are mostly fine-quality maces; even if they are not decorated, they are all well-proportioned and well-made; nothing crude about them. This makes the occasional rough-looking survivor seem odd. There are two maces in the Castel Sant' Angelo in Rome which, though the museum has them dated in the first half of the fifteenth century, could equally well have belonged to the thirteenth, or, in Poland, to the seventeenth. One has a small, rectangular, flanged head, very crudely forged, set on a short wooden haft, rather the shape of a policeman's truncheon. The

FIGURE 13   An unusual form of iron mace, of uncertain date but probably fifteenth century, now in the Odescalchi Collection, Rome

other, a little bigger, with a rather less insignificant head of seven flanges, is mounted on a haft roughly cut to a hexagonal section and studded with pyramidal nail-heads, finished off at the bottom with a ferrule, like an umbrella.

The next stage in the mace's development, a final one, was its total mutation to a cult object, surviving in full flower to this day. When the bodyguards of civic dignitaries carried real maces in the fifteenth century, it had become correct form to carry them with the heads downward. So, when special maces of silver or silver-gilt were made for Corporations in the last part of the seventeenth century, the head (at the bottom) atrophied to a small ornamental knop, while, the pommel (at the top) was promoted to the great ornamental 'head' of the latter-day civic mace. So it ended, in the Speaker's Mace in England, as it had begun in ancient Egypt four thousand years earlier, as the symbol *par excellence* of ultimate authority.

Its role as a commander's baton, already referred to on page 63, was always nebulous, for such batons were indeed 'weapons' made specifically for that purpose. Countless portraits of military leaders, from monarchs to field-officers, show them holding batons; eighty per cent of them being plain straight objects like short lengths of gas-pipe, though a few show mace-like *bastoni* or war-hammers, or in even fewer instances, actual maces. A number of these batons survive (not including the countless Marshals' batons of the last three centuries), perhaps the earliest being a decorated and inscribed ivory example found in a grave in the Cathedral of Urbino, once having belonged to the *Condottiere* Nicolo Trinci. This is of the gas-pipe genre, though it is more shapely. Donatello's great equestrian statue of Gattamelata outside the church of S. Antonio in Padua shows him holding a straight, plain baton; but inside the Church is preserved the actual silver *bastone di comando* presented to him by the Venetians when he became Captain-General of the Republic in 1438. This is shaped like a mace, with an apple-shaped, smooth head surmounted by a little moulded button upon a straight, tapering haft; the decoration (very lavish) is of Venetian style; but the shape of the thing itself is purely oriental. There are two similar *bastoni* in the Palazzo Ducale, Venice, one having belonged to the Conte di Pitigliano when he was Captain-General from 1488 to 1514, and in Stockholm is a third which was made for Charles IX of Sweden, *c.* 1600. Here the shape is the same as that of the others but the haft is of Augsburg work and the silver head is Persian. These *bastoni*, which one could be tempted to call Venetian were it not for the hybrid Stockholm one, are of exactly the same shape as those with which Pharaoh after Pharaoh is shown clubbing captives on countless temple reliefs from the first Dynasty to the Ptolemys.

FIGURE 14   *A hammer shown in a painted Spanish retable at Rubio,
dating c. 1365—1370*

THE WAR-HAMMER

The earliest representation in art of a short-hafted war-hammer is in the hand of an unnamed knightly effigy, *c.* 1250, in Malvern Priory Church, Worcestershire. This is shaped rather like a small, compact, ice-axe, with a square hammer-head on one side and a short, slightly curved pick on the other. A hundred years or so later, several are shown in Spanish paintings dating *c.* 1350—1400; two of these, however, have long hafts. Both the latter are carried by standing figures, one in a retable in the Church of the Abbey of La Conea painted before 1394, and another in a retable in the Church of Rubio painted between 1365 and 1370 (Fig. 14). A short-hafted hammer is held by one of the sleeping guards at the Holy Sepulchre on a retable painting in the Museum of Art, Catalunya, but the best-known representation of one of these hammers is perhaps that in the first of the 'Battle of San Romano' paintings by Uccello, now in the National Gallery, London, dated *c.* 1462 (Fig. 15).

Whether this kind of hammer had a long haft or a short one appears to have been a matter of taste, or depended on the purpose required of it by the user—long haft for fighting on foot, short for fighting on horseback. The size and form of the head seem to have been the same, in any case. Of surviving examples there are very few earlier than about 1500, a fair number datable to the first half of the sixteenth century, and many dating between about 1580 and 1700. During this period the actual form changed a good deal, seemingly regardless of place of origin. The early hammers were primarily just that, hammers, the pick being no more important in size or shape than the hammer-head; but after about 1550 the pick becomes primary, and in the seventeenth-century examples it

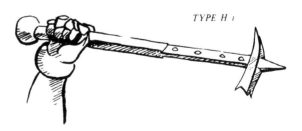

TYPE H 1

FIGURE 15   *Hammer shown in one of
Uccello's 'Battle of San
Romano' paintings, c. 1462*
(National Gallery, London)

TYPE H 1

FIGURE 16   Hammer, Type H 1, c. 1450 (Wallace Collection, London)

would be far more realistic to refer to them as war-picks than war-hammers, for the pick is long and stout while the hammer-head has shrunk to a quite insignificant size.

These hammers may be classified into three basic types, the H 1, H 2, and H 3. Type H 1 could be called the primal form, exemplified by the Malvern example, the Uccello example, and a third, an actual survivor, *c.* 1450, in the Wallace Collection, London (Fig. 16). In the latter, the head is square in section, but set at an angle of 45° to the section of the haft, giving it a diamond-shaped section; the face of the head is not flat, but forged to a very flattened pyramid. The pick is short and slightly curved, of a similar section to the hammer; a short square/diamond-section spike projects in front, with a slight moulding at its root joining it to a cubical box of steel which fits over the junction of haft, beak and hammer. The haft, in this case, is modern, so there is no knowing how long it should have been, or what form of ferrule or pommel it had at the end. The hammer in Uccello's painting, very like this one in the shape of its head, has a large spherical pommel at the end of its haft. A similar hammer in the Wallace collection, half a century later in date, is built up in much the same way, but is much more elaborate in its details and the head is secured to the haft by long langets. The haft is original, the grip covered with red velvet, but it has been shortened and a modern ferrule fitted. The metal parts are of gilded iron, lightly etched in the manner popular in Italy between 1480 and 1520 with floral scrolls, a coat of arms, a badge and portrait medallions.

TYPE H 2

Later in the sixteenth century the pick became more prominent, as in Type H 2. There are many surviving hammers of this type: for instance, one in the State Museum, Brunswick, which belonged in the mid-sixteenth century to Duke Henry II, the Younger, and another in the Kunsthistorisches Museum, Vienna, which was once the property of Francesco Maria della Rovere, Duke of Urbino, and which is of about the same period (Fig. 17).

FIGURE 17   Hammer, Type H 2 c. 1550, belonging to Francesco Maria della Rovere, Duke of Urbino (Kunsthistorisches Museum, Vienna)

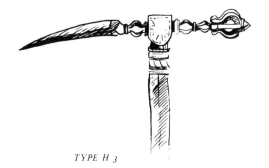

FIGURE 18   Hammer, Type H 3, from a
                portrait of Count Pio Capodilista,
                dated 1617
                (Museo Civico, Padua)   TYPE H 3

Another very similar was in the Saxon royal collection at Dresden, sold at Sotheby's (Lot 24) on March 23 1970, though this one dated from some seventy-five years later. Like most other hammers of the seventeenth century, it has a long belt-hook at the side of the head.

Type H 3 is individual and specialised, confined apparently in date to about 1575—1600, and owing much of its distinctive form to the maces and hammers of India and the Middle East (Fig. 18). The haft is quite long, some 32 inches (80 cm) as against the average twenty-one to twenty-four inches (53—60 cm) of the Type H 2 examples. The pick is very long and slender, and the hammer is formed as a mace-head of the flanged, onion-shaped bulawa type. Surviving examples tend to be very elaborately decorated and suggest a *bastone* rather than a weapon—an assumption rather borne out by a portrait in the Museo Civico, Padua, dated 1617, of Count Pio Capodilista. He stands fully armoured with a wide, knee-length, lavishly-embroidered, frock-like surcoat over his harness; his elaborately-plumed close helmet and his gauntlets lie on a table beside him; his sword hangs at his side; and in his right hand he holds one of these hammers. There is an example in the Kienbusch Collection in Philadelphia very similar to this, and another in the Odescalchi Collection in Rome.

Type H 4 is a rare form which seems to have been of Flemish or West German origin, from the period between about 1480 and 1525. It has a head of cast bronze in the form of a hand holding a dagger, which is of steel; the blade forms the pick and the pommel the hammer. Similar weapons are found in Mughal India, used either as weapons or elephant-goads (*ankus*).

Among the group of *bastoni di comando* in the Palazzo Ducale, Venice, is one in the form of a hammer. The gilded head is of curious form, for the pick is curved right round, almost into a spiral. An exactly similar Persian hammer, dated with dubious accuracy to the eighteenth century, is in the Rijksmuseum voor Volkenkunde, Leiden.

There can be no denying that from the fifteenth century onwards there must have been a great deal of cross-fertilisation between East and West in the design of weapons other than swords, for again and again we find exactly similar maces and axes used in Europe, Persia and India, and in some case in Turkey and the Middle East. European maces take oriental forms while oriental ones are often of pure western form. These eastern weapons

FIGURE 19   Axe-head, c. 1450

are almost invariably dated, for lack of any precise knowledge of them, to the eighteenth or nineteenth centuries—so much so that a seeker after information searching through any publication on Indian arms, or looking at specimens in a museum, must be brought to the conclusion that from ancient times until about 1700 no arms at all were made or used east of a line from Istanbul to Cairo. There are, of course, countless very detailed paintings dated firmly enough from the fifteenth century to show that not only were there in fact plenty of weapons but also that their form changed not at all until they were abandoned in the twentieth century.

THE HORSEMAN'S AXE

For the origins of the light horseman's axe we can go back to the ancient world, particularly to Egypt, as in the case of maces. This was another kind of weapon which does not seem to have been used at all by the classical Greeks, Etruscans or Romans, though it appears to have been fairly common in Mycenean and Cretan contexts. The barbarian adversaries of the Roman world used all kinds of battle-axes, large and small, but it is not possible to distinguish any specific kind which could be called a horseman's axe. In medieval times we find numerous manuscript paintings showing axes wielded by horsemen, some quite small, others (as in the Maciejowski Bible) like the old English foot-soldier's sparth.

In the later fourteenth century, some rather distinctive kinds of axe-cum-hammer appeared (Fig. 19), but on the whole it is safe to say that until about 1510 an axe was simply an axe, to be used indiscriminately for felling trees, chopping up kindling, fighting on foot or on horseback. It is an accepted fact, based upon literary evidence, that in the fourteenth and fifteenth centuries English archers carried small axes or hammers—mauls—at their belts. One such would be indistinguishable from a horseman's axe. Perhaps the best-known literary or historical mention of one of these axes is in the descriptions of Robert Bruce's feat of arms on the day before the battle of Bannockburn: the English knight, Henry de Bohun, seeing the Scottish king riding a palfry, and without a sword, rode at him, and was killed by Bruce's axe.

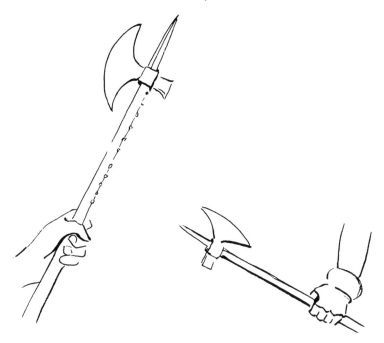

FIGURE 20 (left) *and FIGURE 21* (right)

Two 'Resurrection' axes:
the one shown in Figure 20, on the left, is taken from a painting in the
Art Museum of Catalunya and dates c. 1370;
the one on the right, in Figure 21, is taken from a painting in the Provincial
Museum of Saragossa, also c. 1370

When we come to the undeniably knightly axes of the late fifteenth century, and of the sixteenth, there is no confusion. They seem mostly to have been of the same shapes as knightly pole-axes, only a good deal smaller and lighter. One of the most prolific sources of information for these axes in the fifteenth century is Spanish painting. It seems to have been customary with painters and sculptors (not only in Spain) to depict the Roman guards sleeping outside the Holy Sepulchre as armed with short axes, or maces. In several Resurrection pictures from the mid-fourteenth century onwards (for example, one in the Art Museum, Catalunya) we find axes with small curved blades balanced by small hammers at the back and finished with long spikes in front (Fig. 20). Another is in the Provincial Museum of Saragossa (Fig. 21); and it is interesting to see how little the form changed in nearly two centuries if we compare these with an extremely fine little axe of gilded iron, from the early sixteenth century (Plate 4). This belonged to Giovanni Giacomo Medici di Marignano; it is thickly gilded and etched with floral designs and the

FIGURE 22   Axe c. 1520 (Historisches Museum, Frankfurt)

Medici arms, with Latin inscriptions engraved around the edges:

[on one side]
BENEFICIUM. DANDO. ACCEPIT.
CUI. DIGNO. DEDIT

[on the other]
FALLENT. SEMEL. NON. FACILE.
RURSUS. FID. S. ADHIBENDA. EST

An axe with a head almost identical in shape, though it may be some three decades later, is in the Tower of London.

An axe with a different form of head (Fig. 22) is in the Historisches Museum, Frankfurt. This is more akin to the earlier small axes than the Medici one, which is of the same general form as most pole-axes.

Most of these axes of the Medici form were balanced by a hammer, while the others generally had a pick at the back. In these axes we again find a very close similarity between the European and the oriental ones.

BIBLIOGRAPHY

See the list of material given at the end of Chapter 2.

CHAPTER FOUR

ARMOUR: 1400—1525

The study of armour is a subject of limitless range in the field of war's archaeology and has been dealt with very fully in specialised publications. The scope of this book being limited, and its main subject weapons, there is room only for a relatively brief discussion of armour. A study of weapons, however, which ignored the parallel development of defence would be inadequate, so I shall try to present as clear a sketch as possible of the way change, improvement and decline affected armour from the 1450s until the early seventeenth century. In order to do this briefly, I shall concentrate upon the basic forms, or outlines, of complete armours, leaving out questions of changing detail.

The years between the fall of the Plantagenet dynasty at Bosworth in 1485 and the deaths of Henry VIII of England and François I of France in 1547 were the last in which complete armour was worn as a matter of course upon the fields of war. During this time the whole of European society was being subjected to the upheavals caused by the effects of the High Renaissance in Italy and the Reformation in Germany, which had destroyed the age-old stability of medieval civilisation. This was a period of intense creative turmoil in thought and action, in the arts of war as well as in the arts of peace. To incubate and spread the former there was the great pan-European struggle which brought pretty well every fighting man in Europe into contact with the exuberance of Italian culture; but over and above this was the direct influence of the rulers of Europe—the Emperor Maximilian I, his grandson and successor Charles of Spain (later the Emperor Charles V), Henry VIII of England and François I of France, brother-monarchs who vied with one another in improving the design and efficiency of all the 'materiel' of war. Maximilian was as interested in the design of a cuirass as the Prince Regent was later to be in the frogging of a hussar's tunic and the cut of his dolman; and his influence upon the armourers of Innsbruck and Landshut was as great as that of Prinny and Brummel upon the fashionable tailors of London and Bath. Henry of England set up his own workshops in the Palace of Greenwich, staffed with master-armourers imported from Germany. François was more concerned with art—*he* imported Leonardo—and with the business of making war itself; while Charles V was perhaps the first collector of armour. (He collected clocks as well; when in 1557 he retired to spend the last two years of his life in the bleak monastery of San Juste, he took with him his clocks, one fine armour, and one sword.) Charles was once heard to say that he would go ten miles on foot to see a fine armour—a remark which Shakespeare appropriated in *Measure for Measure*.

TYPOLOGICAL SCHEME

This period of its greatness is of extreme significance in the history of armour, as well as that of civilisation itself. In describing it, I have relied for the sake of clarity upon illustrations of armours, each one of which is a good surviving example of a particular type. Linked with these illustrations I submit a typological code for ease of reference. Where a style already has an accepted title, as, for example, 'High Gothic' (HG) or 'Maximilian' (M), I have retained it; where it does not, I have suggested one, based either upon a characteristic of the style itself or upon the name of the original owner of the prototype. This code is set out, with diagrams, on pages 82—4 (Fig. 24).

In working out this scheme, it has seemed reasonable to base it upon the form of the body armour, not upon varying details of pauldron, vambrace or legharness. In the body armour, the elements which mark the fashion are the 'cut', the shape and position of the neckline, the fullness or tightness of the 'bodice', the height of the waist, the length of the skirt—precisely the same things which determine women's fashion today.

Never before the Italian wars had so many fine armours been demanded, but there was an even greater demand for 'munition' armours, workaday harnesses consisting mostly of cuirass, tassets, and open helmet, for the use of infantry or light cavalry. Judging by works of art of this period, it seems possible that often only parts of a complete armour were worn in the field, or even (as in a portrait by Dosso Dossi of Alfonso d'Este, see Figure 26, below) elements of two different armours worn together—and this not by some impoverished *landsknecht* but by one of the great princes of Italy. It was at this time, too, that armour for the tournament began to take on its own highly specialised forms, here quite clearly under the hand of Maximilian (not for nothing did he style himself *Der Letzte Ritter*, for he strove always to keep alive the old ways of knightly prowess) who devised some of the courses, each demanding a particular kind of armour (p. 262).

THE GARNITURE

Intensified activity both in making armour for war and for the tournament led in the last decade of the fifteenth century to the practice of building 'garnitures'. One of the earliest of these to survive is the armour of Andreas, Graf von Sonnenberg, made between 1505 and 1510 by Lorenz Helmschmied of Augsburg, and now in the Kunsthistorisches Museum, Vienna. Here the basic field armour (or 'hosting harness') has an alternative, heavier helmet which if worn with other reinforcing pieces for tassets, breastplate, bevor, left shoulder, left elbow and left hand, turns it all into an armour for the tournament. These extra pieces were called in England 'pieces of advantage', 'pieces of exchange' or 'double pieces'. This practice reached its peak in the 1540s and 1550s when great garnitures were made consisting of fifty of sixty extra and alternative pieces, whereby an armour could be adapted for fighting on foot over barriers, jousting, fighting on foot with pole-axe or hammer, light cavalry work, and so on. The famous *Adlergarnitur* (p. 101) made in 1547 by Jörg Seusenhofer for Archduke Ferdinand of the Tyrol, also now in Vienna, consisted of over sixty separate pieces, all decorated *en suite* with the eagle motif which gave the garniture its name; with these could be assembled three types of tournament armour and five types of field armour with variations.

THE DESIGN OF ARMOUR

It could be assumed that plate armour evolved, developed, matured and declined over the centuries as a biological species might across millennia. The development, however, was so rapid and the changes so frequent that we must look for forces other than purely empirical or natural ones to explain it—after all, the whole process from inception through maturity to decline and extinction took some three hundred and fifty years, a time span which compels the belief that whatever evolution there may have been was helped along by deliberate processes of design and invention.

Of these forces, no doubt the most important was the inter-relation of the warrior's experience in the field with the technological skill of the armourer to bring about evolutions in design. I believe we ought to accept the supposition that each new style in armour was designed, deliberately, before it was hammered out. Such a piece of craftsmanship as a fine armour was not built by taking a pair of shears and half a dozen sheets of iron, and simply cutting it out. Because no true working drawings of armour have survived (or have so far been found—though designs for decoration certainly exist), it is possible to declare that there were none; there is no academically acceptable evidence, let alone proof, that there were. I can only suggest a thoughtful examination of a good armour. Surely in the ingenuity and homogeneity of its construction, in its form and sheer sculptural quality, there is evidence enough that some kind of drawing or model must have preceded the cutting out.

There *are* a few drawings, dating roughly within the period 1480—1525, of pieces of armour, but these are more in the nature of armourers' advertisements than working drawings or blueprints. This is not to assume that each individual armour had its own drawing (though why should it not?), but before a change in form or style was hammered out on the anvil, it was probably first worked out on the drawing-board. Once a general shape had been designed, armour after armour could be built to suit all shapes and sizes of men, and minor modifications of detail might come into being on the bench. Another force to be considered is the inescapable fact that once a piece of mechanism is invented, whether a ship or a gun or an engine or an armour, man's ingenuity and curiosity will make constant improvements to it, and go on doing so for as long as any demand for it persists.

ARMOUR AND FASHION

Armour cannot be studied in isolation from its historical and cultural context; being an intensely social thing, its development has to be studied along with movements in art, literature and philosophy, with the ideas in men's heads as well as the clothes on their backs. Simultaneous social upheavals as powerful as the classical Renaissance in Italy and the Reformation in Germany changed the outward appearance of men as much as their culture and social *mores*.

Before considering the actual changes in the style of armour, we should look for their possible origins. These changes were initiated by German, not Italian, armourers. (The splendid harnesses produced by the workshops of Milan and Brescia all through the fifteenth century and into the first quarter of the sixteenth show no evidence at all that they were affected by fashion; but then, in Italy the style of men's wear itself changed very little during this period, never reaching the extremes of the northern fashions.) All through the fifteenth century, the Franco-Germanic court of the Dukes of Burgundy was the home of fashion. The arbiters of fashion were in Bruges and Antwerp, Ghent and Tournai and Dijon, not in Florence or Milan. It is not that the Italians were not interested in fashion, but that the Italian tendency was to graft Greek and Roman elements upon existing style; this applied also to armour.

It was probably not from the extraordinarily rich and cultured Burgundian society that the practice of wearing armour as ceremonial dress originated, though the custom of wearing black for formal occasions did—it was Duke Philip the Good, not Beau Brummel, who started that. Up to the 1450s there is little to show that armour was considered to be (as the most striking symbol of a man's wealth and prestige) the wear for ceremonial occasions such as weddings, political alliances, treaty-signings and civic functions, but after that, particularly in Germany, there is evidence to suggest that it had become accepted as the correct attire. German nobles, for instance, attended the Imperial Diet in armour. This may well have been one of the reasons why German armour held so closely in outline to the current style in dress.

Philip the Good and his son Charles the Rash ruled as Dukes of Burgundy, the richest and most powerful monarchs in Europe, from 1419 until 1477. Charles over-reached his power and was decisively checked by Louis XI of France and destroyed by the Swiss Confederation, but shortly after his death his daughter Marie, 'Mary of Burgundy', married the Archduke of Austria—Maximilian, later to be the Emperor: he thus became Duke of Burgundy in right of his wife. So from 1477 this fashion-conscious society was headed by the intensely armour-conscious Maximilian, who in 1493 became head of the Holy Roman Empire, with excellent opportunities for spreading the Burgundian fashionable taste and his own enthusiasm for armour. In so far as it was undoubtedly his interest and patronage which brought forward the houses of Helmschmied, Seusenhofer and Treytz, as well as many other families, the giving of his name to the armour of the period is undoubtedly fully justified.

PUFFS AND SLASHES: THE 'NEW LOOK'

It may be reasonable to suppose that it was this feeling for the fashionable aspect of armour that caused it so swiftly and completely to follow the strange turnabout in style of the 1490s (discussed on pp. 27—28); and contemporary writers at the end of the century stated quite clearly what they believed to be the cause of the change itself*.

When the Swiss Confederates beat Charles the Rash so completely in those two battles of Granson and Morat in May and June of 1476, they took from Charles's camp an enormous booty, all of Charles's personal effects and a great hoard of stuff belonging to his

---

* In *Modes and Manners*, 1932, Max von Boehlen wrote that contemporaries unanimously ascribed this style to the Swiss. Pellicanus (quoted on page 79) is quite specific. Rabelais called it a Swiss fancy. In England it was also known as 'blistered' clothing.

nobles. Among this was a lot of armour and innumerable clothes made of the richest and most beautiful materials. The Burgundian nobles were born and brought up in the saddle, with the slender, wiry legs of horsemen; besides, they were highly bred, with small, elegant bones. The Swiss were tough, rugged mountaineers, walkers to a man, burly and large-boned, with the muscles of peasants. The Burgundian armour was no use to them, so they hung it up in their Cantonal churches and town halls as trophies, or sold it off; but the clothes! Of course they could not get into them; even the original owners had had to be stuffed into those clothes like sausages into their skins or British cavalry officers of a century ago into their overalls.

So the Swiss pikemen went roaring victorious home to their villages, lugging wagon-loads of fabulous clothes which they could not wear. Some time afterwards, an ingenious soul found the answer. Where the material fitted most tightly, at knee and elbow and shoulder and across the chest, cut it into ribbons, then fill in the gaps with lighter fabric. So were born 'puffs and slashes', and when the Swiss went to war again they sported a new fashion; soon every mercenary soldier in Europe was puffed and slashed at every point. In the *Chronicon* of Konrad Pellicanus of Ruffach is an entry under the year 1490:

'Up to this time nobody had ever seen bright-coloured puffed and slashed clothing, but now the tailors have had to set about learning this art of slashing, for these paid-off soldiers bring endless novelties home.'

A sartorial novelty only needs to be outrageous to be an assured success, and once the *landsknechte* took it up, the thing was launched. Everything was slashed—doublet, hose, sleeves, gloves, hats, shoes; and of course extravagances soon appeared. So much so that some of Maximilian's lords tried to persuade him to prohibit such follies by law. But Maximilian stuck up for his soldiers: 'Let them be,' he said, 'for they lead such miserable, stunted lives that one can't grudge them a pastime.'

Slashes were in, and by the early sixteenth century had spread into high society. Soon the armourers were copying the style in steel, and the fashion lasted late into the century. This was the factor that brought about a literal bursting out from the narrowness of the late Gothic style and introduced the New Look, broad and muscular. Another fashion, originating probably in the north-west, when added to the slashes completed the change.

Characteristic of the High Gothic dress of the 1470s and 1480s was a very short, high-waisted, high-necked, tight-fitting jacket, with an abbreviated skirt showing the buttocks and making the most of the front flap of the hose—not yet a codpiece, but very prominent. This costume is shown in countless paintings of the period. In pictures painted two decades later, on either side of the Alps, we find that the jacket has been discarded and its place taken by a shirt, occasionally with a waistcoat and a short cloak worn over it. It is worn short, the bottom cut off at the waist and either tucked into the top of the hose or fastened to it with points; but the significant thing from our point of view is the neckline. This is cut straight across the top of the chest below the collar-bones. The sleeves may be part of the shirt, or separate ones fastened to the armholes, but in most cases they are full—very full over the shoulders—giving a very wide look to the figure. This costume showed off to perfection the essential maleness of the wearer. If we examine carefully the pictures on which it is shown, we see that it was worn by young men: either soldiers, tearaways, or just young men-about-town. The sober citizen preferred a doublet—not a short jacket in the Gothic mode but a rather full, pleated garment with a kilt-like skirt and sleeves either simply cut (but quite full) or elaborately padded on the shoulders, and slashed. At first the neckline of this doublet was high and close to the neck, but by about 1495 it seems to have been adapted to go with the new shirt-wearing mode: the doublet's neckline was cut low and square to show the upper part of the shirt. All this helped the broadened appearance of the costume. At the same time the shoes, after some three centuries of being narrow with long, pointed toes, suddenly became comfortably shaped with rounded toes, soon to acquire an exaggerated breadth, perhaps due to the fashion of slashing the toes. A legend that the broad shoe (and hence the rounded sabaton) became fashionable because Charles VIII of France had eight toes on one foot is intriguing, but suspect.

So now in fashionable male costume all the elements of the 'New Look' in armour were present: full, rounded front to the body, neckline cut low and straight across between the points of the shoulders, and broad-toed shoes. The theory that the new style was a product of a fusion between the 'rounded, burly Italian style' and the 'rippled' decoration of the German style has to accommodate two facts: first, that by the late 1480s Italian armour was not nearly as rounded and burly in outline as it had been in the 1440s and 1450s (it was in fact getting quite slim, with very long, high-necked breastplates, a style which continued in Italian-made armour up to at least 1510, whereas it had been abandoned by the German masters twenty years before); and secondly, that in Germany the complex rippling of the Gothic style was often abandoned, to be replaced by, first, a very restrained system of a kind of elongated dog-tooth ridging embossed upon the principal plates (a rarely-used decoration only found on German armours), and then, perhaps as early as the 1490s, by the true 'fluted' style of covering the main plates with close-set flutings, a decorative treatment which was only taken up round about 1510 by the Italians, and then only tentatively.

These fashionable manifestations are visible only in the cuirass, for limb armours gave no scope for niceties—they had to conform to the shape of arm and leg, and moreover, had to be mobile and comfortable—whereas the more or less rigid large plates of the breast and back could be shaped like cloth doublets.

RIPPLED AND CRESTED DECORATION

So the last decade of the fifteenth century saw the old styles of the German High Gothic and what, for convenience, has been (with dubious relevance) called the 'Italian Gothic', in use together side by side with new styles based upon a rigid design scheme of vertical and horizontal lines (see Fig. 24, pp. 82—84), and the first years of the sixteenth century saw the introduction of fluting to decorate the surfaces.

Before going further, it is necessary to define the terms used to denote the various means of decorating armour. The term 'fluting' may itself be confusing. In fifteenth- and sixteenth-century Germany this kind of decoration, as applied to the Gothic as well as the Maximilian style was called *geriffelt*, 'rippled', and rippled it certainly was. In England, later in the sixteenth century, they called it 'cresting'. Modern scholars do not, however, use the latter term, which tends to be confusing; 'fluting', by some seventy years of usage, has become customary, while 'rippled' is most appropriate when applied to the High Gothic.

The rippled decoration on High Gothic armour was based upon sprays radiating outward from the main constructional axes of the various plates, while in the later style the flutings ran parallel to them. The term 'fluting' should not be applied to the radiating ridges, like pleats, which were embossed upon some mid-fifteenth-century German armours as well as a few early-sixteenth-century ones; nor to the gadrooning used occasionally on Italian breastplates, *c.* 1500—1505. Fluting is a term borrowed from architecture (as the fluting on an Ionic column), and gadrooning from the eighteenth-century decorative arts as applied to furniture, but each defines the result of a different technical process. The ridging upon cuirasses is, in section, as shown in Figure 23 A, while true fluting has been shown in section in Figure 23 B, and gadrooning in section in Figure 23 C.

All through the fourteenth century, plate armour, having superseded mail, had been steadily maturing in technical quality and functional design. By the 1370s the practice of covering most of the plates with fabric (probably to prevent the metal rusting, or, if it did so, to prevent the rust from showing) had been abandoned, and a full harness of plate had become the standard equipment of the man-at-arms all over Europe. This 'International' style, fully developed by about 1380—1400, showed only minor regional variations and

FIGURE 23 *Illustration A shows ridging*
Illustration B shows fluting
Illustration C shows gadrooning

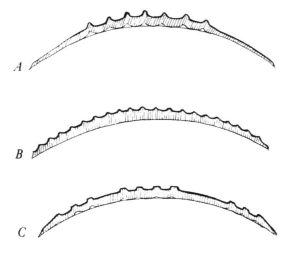

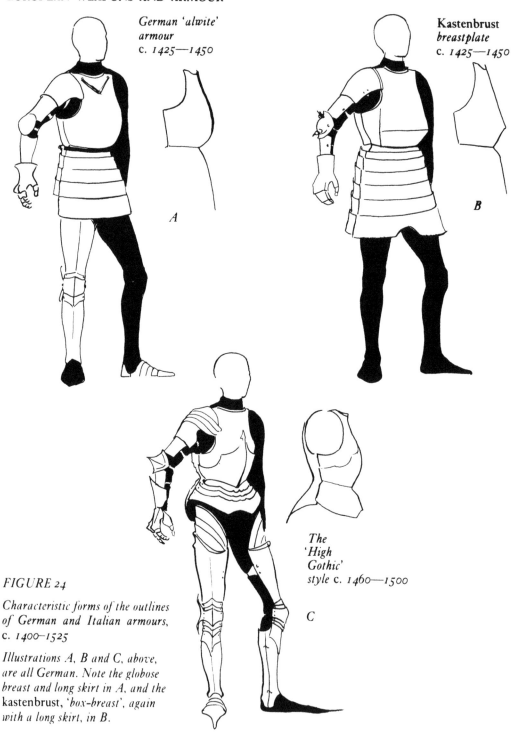

German 'alwite'
armour
c. 1425—1450

A

Kastenbrust
breastplate
c. 1425—1450

B

The
'High
Gothic'
style c. 1460—1500

C

FIGURE 24

Characteristic forms of the outlines
of German and Italian armours,
c. 1400–1525

Illustrations A, B and C, above,
are all German. Note the globose
breast and long skirt in A, and the
kastenbrust, 'box-breast', again
with a long skirt, in B.

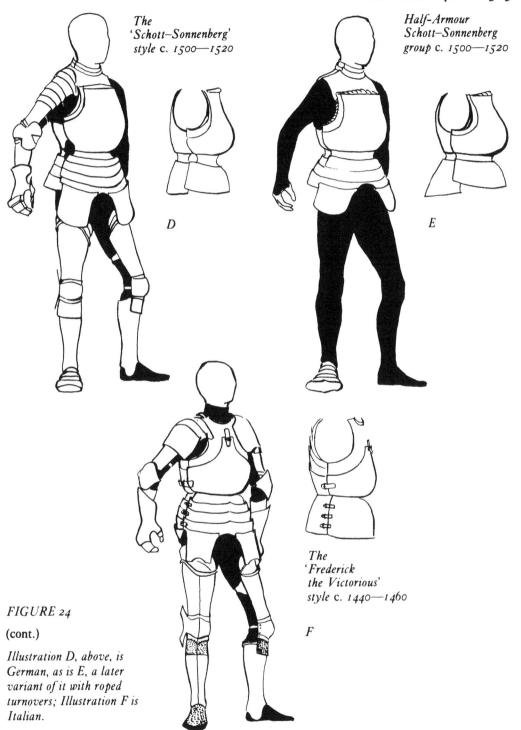

The
'Schott–Sonnenberg'
style c. 1500—1520

Half-Armour
Schott–Sonnenberg
group c. 1500—1520

D

E

The
'Frederick
the Victorious'
style c. 1440—1460

F

FIGURE 24

(cont.)

Illustration D, above, is
German, as is E, a later
variant of it with roped
turnovers; Illustration F is
Italian.

83

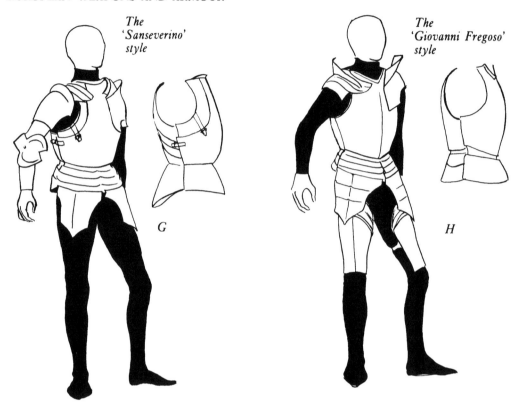

The
'Sanseverino'
style

The
'Giovanni Fregoso'
style

G

H

FIGURE 24   Two further characteristic Italian armour outlines
(Cont.)   Illustration G shows the 'Sanseverino' group (S), dating c. 1480—1500
                Illustration H shows the 'Giovanni Fregoso' group (CF),
                dating c. 1490—1520

these mainly affected the kind of surcoat, or decoration, which might have been worn with the armour, not the shape of the armour itself.*

After about 1425, however, the armourers of Germany began to introduce very distinctive variations upon the old style, mostly affecting the form of the cuirass, and their products began to show marked individuality. We have to rely upon painting and sculpture for our information about these, for very little actual armour survives from the first half of the century. Because of this, it is not possible to attribute any particular idiosyncrasy to any particular armourer, or even to any particular armour-producing centre, as we can do with the armours of the next two hundred years. Figure 24 A shows one possible 'outline'.

* It is an interesting reflection that this so-called 'International' style in armour was exactly contemporary with what art historians call the period of the 'International Style' in painting and sculpture.

Italian armour, too, began at this period to show its own strong characteristics. These, and the specially styled export armours produced in Milan, will be treated separately. The German style had many more variants and needs to be dealt with first.

The variations of detail—regional, constructional or simply personal—which affected armour for the limbs is almost infinite, while helmets (totally unaffected by costume fashion) will be discussed later. As for the decorative objects with which the knight, particularly the fashion-conscious man, bedizened himself—bells on chains, or balls, immense hanging sleeves, collars, belts, armorial gee-gaws, surcoats—these are fascinating but beyond the scope of this chapter.

CUIRASS AND SKIRT

Many works of art made in about 1425—1450 suggest that some German armourers were trying to imitate in steel the cut and hang of a civilian doublet. The globose cuirass of the period 1360—1420, so often hidden beneath the tight-fitting fabric jupon, came out into the open, as it were, in the 1420s, and at once developed fabric-suggesting forms. The surfaces of breastplates and backplates were decorated with embossed radiating ridges, like pleats, and the breast was made to 'hang' at an angle from the shoulders, sometimes quite flat down to a point just above the waist, then turning abruptly inwards at a sharp angle like a loose-fitting doublet. (This style of breastplate (Fig. 24 B) has been called *Kastenbrust*, 'box-breast', by the Germans.) Sometimes the box-like effect was combined with pleats, and sometimes the breastplate was not flat and angular but rounded and pouched. If one compares the doublet of a figure on a French tapestry dating *c.* 1440, now in the Metropolitan Museum, New York, for instance, or many on the great Hardwick tapestries in the Victoria and Albert Museum, London, with the tomb-effigy of Konrad von Weinsberg (1446) at Schontal an der Jagst or with the famous picture in Basel by Konrad Witz (*c.* 1400—*c.* 1445) of Sabothai bringing water to David, it is plain that the cut of the doublet influenced the design of the breastplate and the long, deep skirt below it.

Effigies and pictures of the next decade show how the skirt becomes shorter and the front of the breastplate loses its box-like form to become rounded (though the lower part still bags out); it now begins to develop a keel-like ridge down the front, like the breastbone of a fowl. One of the very rare surviving pieces of armour from this period is a breastplate in the Rathaus, Vienna, with this feature, which appears again in a statue of the Emperor Frederick III (Maximilian's father and predecessor) dated 1453, but here the whole of the front is covered with a broad spray of closely-set ridges, so close that they look like tucks rather than pleats.

In the 1460s, the German High Gothic style (Fig. 24 C) came into fashion, following the Burgundian fashion trend (or did it, perhaps, lead it?). The style's popularity was short, for though in a few cases it seems to have lingered on into the 1520s, it was generally *démodé* by 1500. It is described in greater detail on pages 88—89.

VAMBRACES AND PAULDRONS: LEGHARNESS: GAUNTLETS: COLLARS

During this period there was much diversity of detail in limb armour, the most noticeable being in the development and variation of the pauldrons and of the upstanding 'haute-pieces' (once known as pike guards) upon them, and the change in the shape of the sabatons, parallel with the changing fashion in footwear.

During the period 1425—1450, two distinctive kinds of vambrace were in use, one in Italy and one in Germany. The Italian style was a direct continuation of the late-fourteenth–century vambrace in the 'International' manner (*A of W*, p. 287) characterised by the couters being attached to the upper and lower cannons of the vambrace by one or more small lames above and below the couter, fastened by rivets. These vambraces were always worn with large pauldrons, which tended to increase in size as the century wore on. The German vambrace was a simpler affair, basically differing little from the earliest plate vambraces of the early fourteenth century. The fore and upper arms were protected by single gutter-shaped plates, laced to the mail sleeve with arming-points with very simple, shell-shaped couters between, also tied with points to the sleeve or to the plates above and below. Pauldrons were not worn with this type of vambrace until late in the fifteenth century; instead there was a small spaudler, consisting of a single plate shaped closely to the point of the shoulder with three or four narrow lames below enclosing the outside of the top of the arm. These were secured by laces at the top and a strap at the bottom encircling the upper arm. This vambrace continued in use with German armours well into the sixteenth century, the only developments being that in some cases the lower cannon was made of two plates enclosing the forearm, and generally the couters became bigger and more efficient. Often the gaps at the front of the armpits were protected by circular or rectangular besagews.

FIGURE 25   On the left, in Illustration A, a German vambrace, of the style common
c. 1350—1500, and on the right, in Illustration B, an Italian vambrace,
c. 1350—1520

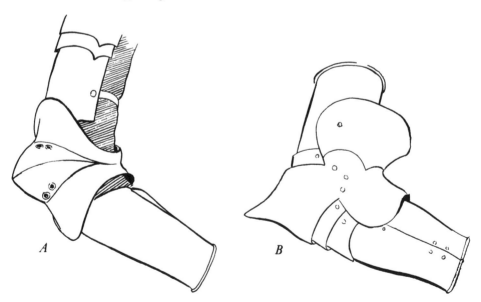

A   B

The International legharness was improved by an enlarging of the sideplates of the poleyns and the extending of them round towards the back of the knee by a wide V-shaped pucker, while extra plates, normally one but sometimes two, were added to the sides of each cuish to extend protection further round the back of the leg. At the same time, in Italy, plate sabatons were abandoned in favour of flaps of mail fastened at the ankle to the lower edge of the front plate of the greave, and at the top by a lace in the upper of a stout shoe, and pendant fringes of mail began to hang from a special lame below the poleyn. The actual forms of German and Italian legs (not surprisingly) differed little, except perhaps that all surviving Italian greaves seem to have been made to fit calves much stouter than those enclosed by surviving German greaves, but this is because most of such survivors were made to fit the slender calves of Maximilian I.

Towards the end of the century, the ridge or stop-rib at first riveted upon the top of the left pauldon, later embossed on it, and finally forged integrally with the plate, grew very large, standing vertically like part of a high collar protecting the front and left side of the neck and the weak spot where helmet and collar joined.

After about 1470 a similar, though smaller, haute-piece was built into the right pauldron. The front of this pauldron, too, was generally cut at the armpit to allow the lance to be couched properly and fitted to the 'arrest', or lance rest, on the right side of the breastplate.

Gauntlets differed, too, during this period. The bell-cuffed, fingered glove of the International style was replaced, round about 1425, by mittens, the German style tending to be squarer in shape than the Italian, which by the 1440s had developed a long, sharply-pointed cuff. During the High Gothic period, the German armourers reverted to fingered gauntlets and long pointed cuffs, producing some of the most elegant pieces of armour ever made. In the same period the Italians stuck to their very simple mittens. With the change in fashion of the 1490s, short-cuffed gauntlets came into use north of the Alps, though not for another twenty-five years in Italy. They had infinite variations which were personal to armourer or customer rather than regional. Fingered gloves did not come in again until the late 1530s.

Until quite late in the fifteenth century, Italian and German necks were usually protected by high mail collars (made exactly like the polo necks of knitted sweaters) and by whatever defence hung from the lower rim of the helmet, if it was a closed one, or by a chinpiece, or 'bevor', if it was an open one. (The word 'bevor' or 'beaver' is derived from the old French word *baver*, 'to slobber', 'to dribble': when a man is breathing heavily with his face enclosed by thickly-lined plates in the heat of conflict, he is bound to dribble lavishly.) The Germans occasionally used plate collars in the fifteenth century, though breastplates continued to be cut very high and close against the throat; but when in the 1490s the German armourers adopted the low-necked globose breastplate, the plate collar became essential and noticeable. However, the Italians continued to use the very high, close neckline and the mail roll-neck for another twenty years, only adopting the German collar round about 1510.

THE HIGH GOTHIC STYLE

The High Gothic style has already been referred to on page 85, but reappears here to give proper context to the transitional armours.

Much High Gothic armour survives, in composed harnesses, in partial ones, in countless isolated pieces and in a mountain of imitations. Owing to its extremely romantic aspect, it has been imitated by the faker and the theatrical costumier more than any other sort of armour; and of course it received an enormous vogue in the last decades of the nineteenth century when it was taken up so enthusiastically by the pre-Raphaelite painters in England.

If the pre-Raphaelites enjoyed painting it, so quite obviously did the German and Flemish artists of the late fifteenth century, for there are great numbers of paintings and drawings which show High Gothic armour in careful detail. The list of them is immense —far too long to deal with here; let it suffice to say that while armour with exaggerated decoration is shown usually in clearly non-combatant contexts, tomb effigies and pictures —particularly drawings—tend on the whole to show practical armours of a kind such as, for instance, the mounted Gothic armour (A 20) in the Wallace Collection in London which, though highly composite, shows a characteristic warharness.

By the end of the 1480s, the rippled decoration had either become extreme or been abandoned altogether. There is in the Kunsthistorisches Museum, Vienna, an armour made in 1490 by Lorenz Helmschmied of Augsburg for Maximilian I, where all the external *lines* of the High Gothic are present but none of the rippled decoration, only 'pleats' on backplate and culet. In one or two ways this armour foreshadows the next development, a transition from a vertical to a horizontal emphasis. If tassets were worn at all with the High Gothic style, they were of one piece and of a spiky, pointed shape, fastened to the lowest plate of the skirt by buckles and straps, but in this armour they are made of three overlapping lames riveted to the lower plate of the skirt, and are cut off square at the bottom, foreshadowing the 'new' style of the later 1490s.

Another transitional armour is that extremely well-known one shown in Albrecht Dürer's drawing of a man-at-arms for his print 'The Knight, Death and the Devil'. It is dated 1498, and he has written on it: *This is the armour worn in Germany at this time.* This may be the most interesting document we have relating to the armour of this region and period, for here is a drawing, presumably from life, of an ordinary man-at-arms; maybe a knight, maybe not; his armour is as workaday and practical as his horse, or the fox's brush hung below his lancepoint, instead of a pennon, or the twig of oak leaves bound into his horse's docked tail. The first impression one gets of this armour is that it is of the usual Gothic form (probably because Dürer's model wears a sallet on his head), but closer inspection makes it clear that this is nearer in feeling and form to the true 'Maximilian' armour than the Gothic. The sallet is a very graceful one with a movable visor. The interesting thing it is that it is covered with leather (except the visor) tooled with the initials *W. A.* The man wears no bevor but has the ends of a hood knotted under his chin; over his breastplate, which we are unable to see, he wears a kind of leather tabard. This consists of a short garment shaped at the back like a jacket but having only two broad crossed straps over the chest. The pauldrons are of almost pure 'Maximilian' form in this 'Dürer' armour with an upstanding haute-piece on the upper plate, fluting in the Maximilian manner decorating the principal lames. There is no vambrace in the accepted sense; the forearm is protected by the elbow-length cuff of the Gothic-style gauntlet and the upper arm by a deep plate fixed to the lowest lame of the pauldron; the couter appears to be fastened to the sleeve of the arming-doublet, not to the plate above it, for we can see the sleeve pouched out above and below the couter. The tassets are just visible, of the same squared-off shape as in Maximilian's armour of 1490; the cuishes are typically Gothic in shape, as are the poleyns and the deep plate below them drawn down into a sharp point over the shinbone. There are neither greaves nor sabatons, only the hose over the calf and a long soft boot which is folded down around the ankle. The main plates of this armour are decorated with ridges which look at first glance like the usual Gothic sprays, but they are in fact neither these nor 'Maximilian' flutings, but long, curved isosceles triangles of the pattern the Germans call *wolfzähne*, 'wolf's teeth'.

THE SCHOTT–SONNENBERG STYLE (Fig. 24 D)

The wolf's-teeth pattern appears again on the cuishes of an armour worn by St Maurice in a picture painted by Hans Baldung Grien in 1507 and showing the 'new' style of armour which had by then been in use for some fifteen years. An existing armour of this pattern in the collection of Mr R. T. Gwynn was built before 1497. It was made in Nuremberg for Kunz Schott von Hellingen, a colourful character who, like many of his noble German contemporaries, was captain of a small army of mercenaries and lived the life of a robber baron. His little force (some eighty knights and four hundred men-at-arms) was based upon the town and castle of Rothenburg. Schott was *burggraf* (military governor) of this town which controlled one of the main roads into Nuremberg. He sold the services of his band to anyone who could pay them and worked a sort of medieval protection racket in his own neighbourhood, and in 1497 he began a nastily savage war with the city of Nuremberg which went on for years and made him Nuremberg's Public Enemy Number 1 for the rest of his life. His armour bears the marks of the Armourers' Guild of Nuremberg, so he must have had it made before his war began in 1497.

This is perhaps the earliest clearly-datable armour of the new transitional style, shown in Fig. 24 D. The breastplate is high-waisted and very rounded, while the three-lame skirt springs out below the waistplate in a corresponding curve. The tassets are short and square, riveted to the lower lame of the fauld. The culet is short, cut off square over the bottom, not drawn down into an elegant point as in the late Gothic armours. There is no decoration at all except Schott's arms engraved at the top of the breastplate. The vambraces are of the German fashion, except that an Italian technical element has been adopted and the couters are fixed by narrow lames, two above and two below, to the upper and lower cannons and not tied with points. The armpits, where they are left exposed by the small spaudlers, are protected by besagews. The mitten gauntlets are contemporary but do not belong to this armour. The helmet is a rather Italianate visored sallet (to be discussed later). The legharness is simple, the lower plate of the poleyn being cut off square instead of pointed over the shin as in earlier armours. Again, adopting an Italian practice, there are no sabatons but a mail flap over the shoe.

In Glasgow is a half-armour, once in the Tower of London, (probably once a complete armour but now lacking its legharness) which except for a minor detail is remarkably similar in shape to the Schott armour (Fig. 24 E). Helmet, collar, vambrace and spaudler, breast and back, skirt and culet, are the same in form. The differences are that the turnovers at the neck of the breastplate and the armholes are strongly roped, and the tassets, though of the same shape, are made each of a single plate. This half-armour also was made in Nuremberg; the roping of the turnovers suggests a date rather later than the Schott armour, and the remarkable similarity of the two rather unusual helmets suggests perhaps a Nuremberg style.

In the Kienbusch Collection in Philadelphia is another armour which by its general form ought to be included in this group, though it differs in detail from the preceding two. The helmet is an armet of Italianate style (*q.v.*), the neckline is curved, not straight across, while the tassets retain Gothic characteristics, for their lower edges are pointed (albeit bluntly) and each bears an embossed spray. The vambraces are of Italian style, and there are large pauldrons with haute-pieces; each pauldron is joined to the tubular upper cannon by a turning-joint—an embossed horizontal flange round the upper part of the vambrace is enclosed by a corresponding ridge embossed in the lower lame of the pauldron. The legharness is similar to that of the Schott armour, but large splayed sabatons are worn. The gauntlets are short-cuffed mittens. This armour originally came from the armoury of the Counts Barfus of Brandenburg and is intriguing because of its very large size; its owner was of much the same build as Henry VIII in his later years.

The finest armour in this group is in the Waffensammlung, Vienna. It was built between 1505 and 1510, another of Lorenz Helmschmied's masterpieces. It belonged to Andreas, Herzog von Sonnenberg, one of Maximilian I's ministers, though it may not have been made *ab initio* for him, but rather for his master who made him a present of it in recognition of his services. Sonnenberg did not have long to enjoy his gift, for he was assassinated in 1511 by Felix von Werdenberg, a rival for the Emperor's favour. The armour is one of the earliest surviving garnitures—a basic field armour with an alternative helmet, heavier than the one for field use, and reinforcing pieces for bevor, breastplate, tassets, left shoulder, elbow and hand. These effectively convert it to an armour for the joust.

In its outward form this looks very like the Schott armour, the main differences being that it has large pauldrons with haute-pieces and that its helmets are armets in the German style. In the Wallace Collection is an armour (A 22) which is not unlike it in outline, once thought because of its similarity to be another work of Helmschmied's; but though it is of the same style and of superb workmanship, there are too many constructional differences for it to have been a Helmschmied armour. Etched on the breastplate is a crowned *W*, which leads to the belief that it may have been made for Wladislaus, King of Bohemia from 1471 until his death in 1516 (and from 1490 to 1516, King of Hungary as well).

These armours form a distinctive group, which I have called the SS (Schott-Sonnenberg) group (Fig. 24 D); and though these are the only complete armours in it (or rather almost complete, for the Wallace armour's greaves and sabatons are restorations), there are a great many cuirasses which clearly belong to it. I have described these armours to an extent I cannot afford with most subsequent ones, because it seems important at this point to emphasise the amount of variation of detail which may be found in armours of

FIGURE 26   Portrait by Dosso Dossi of Alfonso d'Este,
Duke of Ferrara, c. 1510 (Brera Gallery,
Milan)

the same basic type, and also to show how, though the fashion of the cuirass is German in origin, many of the technical practices of the Italian armourers have been adopted by the Germans, such as the visored sallets of the first two, and the pauldrons, vambraces and armets of the others. These armets are fitted with strong, circular, turned-over rims at the bottom of the cheek-pieces which turn upon the upper lames of the collars, an entirely German innovation.

Many of these SS armours are shown in paintings executed round about 1500, both Italian and German. There is in the Villa Borghese, Rome, a picture by Dosso Dossi, 'Saul with the Head of Goliath', showing the King of Judah wearing an armour extraordinarily like Schott's, though he wears no helmet; by the same artist is a portrait in the Brera Gallery, Milan, of Alfonso d'Este, Duke of Ferrara, as St George. The Duke wears a breast-plate of the SS type, with knee-length tassets and a collar, pauldrons and vambraces of true 'Maximilian' style— an interesting combination of two entirely different armours (Fig. 26). A 'St George' by Paris Bordone shows a fine armour like Sonnenberg's, with pauldrons, but here again there is no helmet; Baldung Grien's 'St Maurice' in Berlin is the same—an armour like Sonnenberg's with high haute-pieces; the helmet lies at his feet.

Dossi's 'Alfonso d'Este' shows a tendency which was greatly increasing at this time, for a nobleman to wear infantry armour, sometimes with, but more often without, a backplate, and with long, loose-hanging tassets reaching to a point just above the knee. Armour of this sort was sometimes worn over a mail shirt, sometimes simply over a puffed and slashed (maybe padded) doublet, with a light, open helmet (*q.v.* below). Many such breast-and-tassets in the SS style were made in about 1500—1515 by the Milanese armourers for the German market—or rather, since in these years between Fornovo and Marignano Italy was overrun with the soldiers of every nation in Europe, they worked not for a German market but rather *alla Tedescha*, 'in the German style'.

It is interesting to find that the cuirass-shape of the Schott–Sonnenberg style was foreshadowed in Germany half a century before it finally appeared. Several tomb effigies and paintings of 1400—1450 show extremely rounded, bulbous breastplates—as I have said (page 82), this was often an alternative to the boxed *Kastenbrust* style; but there is one in particular which is interesting in this connection. The effigy on the tomb of Peter von Stettenberg in the church at Brombach (erected *c.* 1440) wears a cuirass of a distinctly

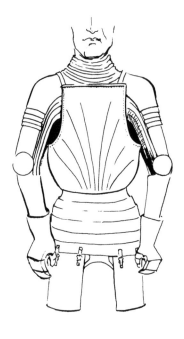

sixteenth-century style (Fig. 27). The skirt is longer—
six lames instead of four—but the breastplate is cut
straight across the top, low in the neck between the
points of the shoulders; the lower part is globose, the
skirt springs sharply out in a reflected curve from the
waist, and the short tassets are cut square at the bottom. It is worn over a mail-reinforced arming-doublet,
and the arm defences are as old-fashioned, typical
of the period round about 1350, as the cuirass is advanced. It is a point worth noting that these German
cuirasses antedate the Italian mid-century globose
ones by at least a decade.

During the period 1490—1510, the German and
Italian armourers borrowed technical elements freely
from each other, but these borrowings were more
noticeable in helmets and in armour for the limbs; for
while the German cuirass became rounded and Ger-
man gauntlet cuffs were cut off square, as were the lames below the poleyns, in Italy the
cuirass became long and slender, often with a distinct keel down the middle like the German High Gothic breasts; and tassets remained sharply pointed, as did the long cuffs of
gauntlets. It seems that while the Germans borrowed many technical details from Italy,
the Italians began to design the outlines of their armours in the slender lines of Germany's High Gothic.

ITALIAN ARMOURS OF THE FIFTEENTH CENTURY

Italian armour (which we must now turn back to consider) can also be separated into
distinct stylistic groups, and until at least 1510 shows no sign that its design owes anything
to changes in civilian fashion. We can trace an uninterrupted progression from the 'International' forms until about 1510 when the Italian armourers finally merged their styles
with those originated in Germany twenty years earlier.

There are a few pieces of Italian armour surviving from the 'International' period,
notably a cuirass, vambraces, gauntlets and bascinet in the armoury at Schloss Churburg in the Tyrol, and a series of associated pieces in the Metropolitan Museum, New
York, which make up a complete harness of *c.* 1400. Both of these show the high-waisted
globose breastplate so typical of this period. The next armour in date, *c.* 1420, is also at
Churburg; here the cuirass first shows a design which was to be characteristic of Italian
Gothic armours up to the end of the century. The breast is made in two pieces; the
breastplate proper, still rounded but not so much so as the earlier ones, cut straight
above the waist, and a second plate which overlaps the main plate in a shallow point,
where it is fastened by three vertical straps and buckles. It curves in slightly at the waist

and carries a skirt of three upward-lapping lames joined by rivets and internal leathers. The back is made in similar fashion with a culet of (originally) three lames.

This is an isolated example, but dating from the mid-century is a group of six armours all showing very similar characteristics. At their head is an armour in the Kunsthistorisches Museum made *c.* 1455 in the Missaglia workshops in Milan for Friedrich *Der Siegreiche*, 'Frederick the Victorious', Count Palatine of the Rhine.

THE 'FREDERICK THE VICTORIOUS' STYLE (Fig. 24 F)

The Missaglia armour of *c.* 1455 is a very fine one, both in its quality and its perfect state of preservation. Its helmet is a late form of the great bascinet (p. 118), and unlike most Italian armours of this period it appears to be fitted with sabatons, queer-shaped steel slippers, not covering the heel, with long, straight, tubular points sticking out in front; they are, in fact, stirrups. Its forms are smooth and rounded, but showing none of that emphasis upon horizontals so characteristic of the armour of the Maximilian period. This armour gives its name to the FV group in my code (Frederick the Victorious), as shown in Figure 24 F. The earliest of the group, dating *c.* 1435—1440, is in the Metropolitan Museum, New York, and is composed of parts of several armours; but the cuirass is characteristic of the period. The outer breastplate is larger than that in the preceding style, reaching in a high point halfway up the chest, and the deep skirt, unlike the others in the groups, has no tassets.

Two of the others in this group are at Churburg, not quite complete. The armour of Galeazzo de Arco lacks a right arm, and that of the giant Ulrich von Matsch, Captain-General of the Tyrol (whose helmet is in the armouries of the Tower of London), lacks vambraces and one tasset: but both show the characteristic form. The tassets, however, differ from Frederick's, for instead of coming to a point at the bottom, each is cut out in a shallow arch. A fifth in the group, once at Churburg, is in the Museum and Art Gallery, Glasgow. Though maybe not so fine, nor so nearly complete (it lacks its helmet and tassets) as Count Frederick's, it is the handsomest of the group—indeed, many hold it to be the handsomest armour of any kind in existence. A sixth composite one is in the Historical Museum at Berne (probably part of the Swiss loot from Morat in 1476); like Frederick's, it has an associated great bascinet. A cuirass of this type is among the armour found in 1929 in the Sanctuary of the Madonna delle Grazie at Mantua.

The backplates of these armours are very complex and flexible. Like the breasts, they are made in two parts, a lower reinforcing backplate cut to a point reaching up between the shoulderplates, and the backplate proper made up of four large plates, each cut to an acute point, overlapping upwards. This is the direct opposite of the German Gothic backs dating a little later, which are made of a single main plate shaped to the waist with two overlapping plates across the shoulders, overlapping *downwards* (Fig. 28). The culets in this group conform in shape and depth to the faulds. This kind of armour is very clearly shown in Paolo Uccello's three pictures, 'The Battle of San Romano'.

THE 'SANSEVERINO' STYLE (Fig. 24 G)

There are two excellent survivors of the 'Sanseverino' group, both in Vienna. The more important is the complete armour made in Milan, *c.* 1480, for Ferdinand of Aragon, who by

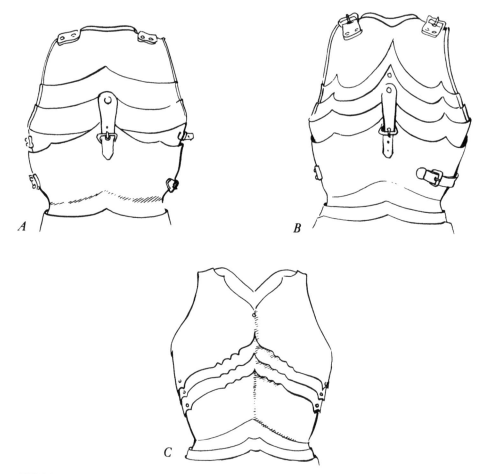

FIGURE 28   Illustration A, an Italian backplate c. 1440—1460, and Illustration B, also
Italian, c. 1470—1490, are here contrasted with a German backplate, c. 1480,
shown in Illustration C.

his marriage in 1469 to Isabella of Castile had united those two royal houses and laid the
foundations for Spain's rise to European pre-eminence in the sixteenth century under his
grandson, Charles I of Castile and Aragon and Charles V, head of the Holy Roman
Empire. Ferdinand's armour shows certain modifications of form upon the purely
Milanese style, so ought not to give its name to this group. The armour which can rightly
do so was made, also in Milan, at about the same date, for the Venetian *Condottiere*
Roberto di Sanseverino, who was killed in battle in 1487.

There are also two cuirasses in this Sanseverino group from Delle Grazie. Characteristic
is the narrower breast, cut high in the neck, in a curve fitting right up against the throat;
the outer plate covers almost the entire surface of the inner plate, reaching right up to the

turnover at the neck. The skirts are very short, like the contemporary German ones, and the tassets are longer and more pointed than in the preceding type. The backplates are simpler, and more elegant. The outer, reinforcing plate is dispensed with, and the culet now dips downward over the bottom in a graceful curve. The pauldrons, which in the FV group had grown very large, in the Sanseverino group (Fig. 24 G) become enormous, actually overlapping at the back.

'ENGLISH' MILANESE ARMOURS

Ferdinand of Aragon's armour, of the Sanseverino group, is an example of an armour made for export. According to the *Chronicon Extravagans* of Galvano Fiamma, written early in the fourteenth century, Milan had already become a great centre for the manufacture and export of armour by the end of the thirteenth century. In England the travelling salesmen of these export houses, the Milaners, gave a word to the language, 'milliner'. That they must have done good business with the knighthood of England is indicated by the many monuments there showing armour of Milanese style decorated with a little Germanesque rippling and variations of detail which demonstrate an identifiable English fashion for which the Milaners catered, as they did similarly for their customers in Germany and Spain.

English monuments after about 1475, as well as showing a very marked falling-off in artistic quality, indicate a definite change of fashion: at first leaning more towards German Gothic forms, though never very far, by about 1490 they begin to present a very distinctive style of their own, matched only by similar monuments and other works of art emanating from the Low Countries, which, together with certain documented evidence to be discussed later, points clearly to a marked Flemish style during the period 1490—1520.

It would be pleasant to be able to believe that these English monuments define an English style produced by native English armourers—after all, the Armourers Company of London was inaugurated in 1346 and is still extant; but by about 1512 Henry VIII found it essential to import master armourers from Italy, the Low Countries and Germany in order to produce at home the quantities of armour he needed for his forces and the quality he demanded for himself and his Court, so it does not seem likely that any native armourers of the required competence existed.

The finest of the English effigies showing Milanese armour is the bronze-gilt figure of Richard Beauchamp, Earl of Warwick, in St Mary's, Warwick. He died in France in 1439, but his tomb and effigy were not ordered until 1454. It shows an armour basically of the FV style, but with minor German decorative elements; each side of the breastplate is decorated with a broad shallow trough running parallel with the armholes; the tassets also have similar curving channels, and each cuish has four horizontal ridges in the German manner. The legharness in outline is purely Milanese, but there are no mail fringes below the poleyns and the feet are covered with plate sabatons. The vambraces and large pauldrons are similar to the other FV armours. The figure for this effigy, which is as complete at the back as at the front, down to the last strap and buckle, was carved by John Massingham of London and cast in bronze by William Austin, in consultation with William Webb, Master of the Worshipful Company of Barber-Surgeons (an office which corresponds with the present-day Master of the Royal College of Surgeons) who advised on matters of anatomy. The effigy they produced is the finest of its kind (*pace* the Black Prince in Canterbury Cathedral) in existence. Much of Massingham's work survives, enough to give him a place as one of the great sculptors of his time, a worthy contemporary of Donatello.

ITALIAN ARMOURS IN GERMANY

A good deal of Milanese armour was exported to Spain. Very little of it survives other than the armour of Ferdinand the Catholic, but there is a great wealth of fifteenth-century painting in Spain which shows almost exclusively Italian or Flemish armour. The main regional characteristics here are that the top of the outer breastplate has a distinctive fishtail form and the mitten gauntlets have strongly-flared cuffs.

There are quite a number of German effigies of the 1450s and 1460s which show Italian armour, and several of actual pieces of Milanese armour made to the German taste survive. There is even a complete armour (probably composite) in the Church of the Holy Cross at Schwäbisch Gmünd, of the FV style with several Milanese marks. Concessions to German fashion are that the tassets have curving channels in them (of precisely the same shape as Richard Beauchamp's) and the breastplate and fauld have a strong vertical keel down the middle. Also in the German manner, the outer plate is fixed at the top to the breastplate with a rivet, not a strap or buckle. An almost exactly similar armour is shown in the effigy of Ulrich von Hohenrechburg (*c.* 1460) at Donzdorf in Wurtemburg. In the Kunsthistorisches Museum, Vienna, is a breastplate of typical German High Gothic form, by tradition having belonged to Bartolomeo Colleoni. It has elegant ripplings round the inner edges of the armholes and along the upper edges of the outer plate, which is finished at the top with an elaborate finial; it is, however, Milanese. Its most interesting features are that the turnovers at the neck and armholes are roped (the earliest example of this feature so far known), and that round the armholes and neck, alongside the turns, is a band of etched decoration—again, perhaps the earliest example of etching upon armour, though there is a beautiful etched design, now much corroded, in the fuller of the blade of the sword of Sancho IV, *El Bravo*, of Castile. This sword was found in his tomb, opened in 1943, and since he died in 1295, it is of an earlier date than that—indeed, it has been suggested that it possibly belonged to his father, Alfonso X, *El Sabio* (1252—1284). This puts the art of etching upon metal firmly into the late thirteenth century.

ITALIAN ARMOUR IN ART

There are a great many Italian paintings of the period 1410—1525 which show in excellent detail these Milanese armours, far too many to discuss in detail; Gentile da Fabriano's 'St George' of 1425 in his altarpiece in the Uffizi, Florence, for instance, shows an armour of the same form as the early-fifteenth-century one at Churburg, and there is a statue, made *c.* 1420, of the Paladin Roland in the town square at Dubrovnik in Jugoslavia which shows a good example of the style. There are countless paintings and drawings too which show the FV style, like Uccello's 'San Romano' pictures; one should note Mantegna's 'St George' in the Accademia, Venice, painted between 1459 and 1462. Here is an armour which has the FV form but is in detail almost exactly like the Schwäbisch Gmünd armour, with its keel down the breast and skirt, and 'crested' tassets. These and the sideplates of

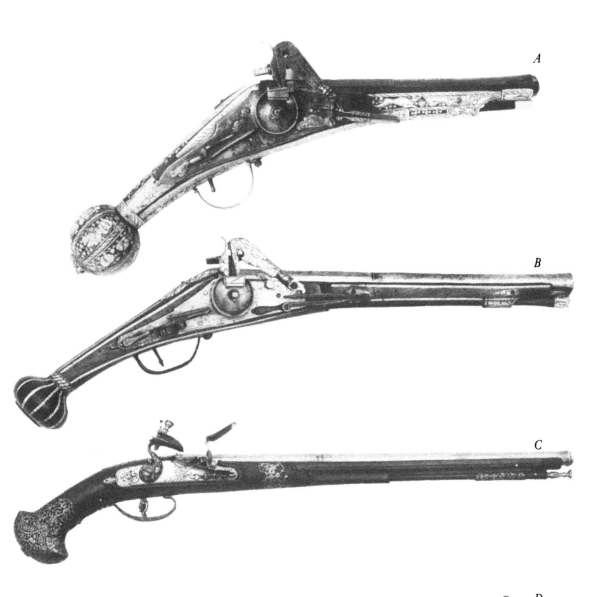

Plate 1

A Wheel-lock pistol, German, *c.* 1575
B Wheel-lock pistol, German, *c.* 1575
C Flintlock pistol, Italian (Brescian),
   c. 1660
D Detached wheel-lock pistol, German
   (Suhl), *c.* 1660

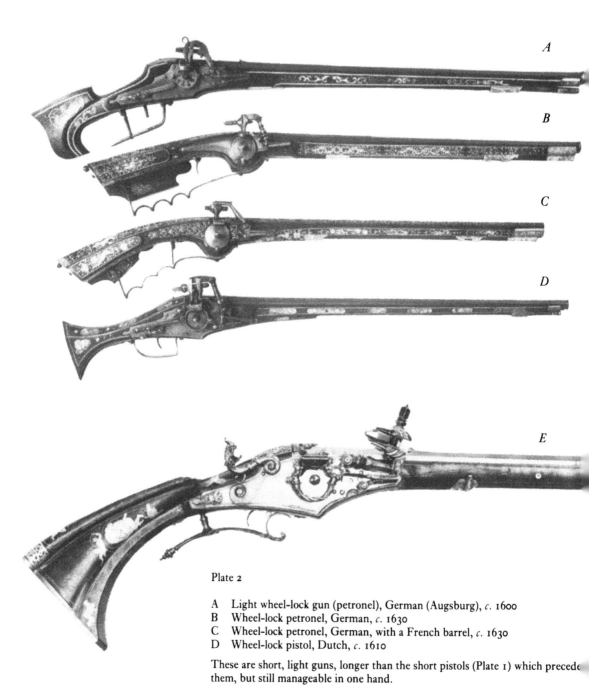

Plate 2

A   Light wheel-lock gun (petronel), German (Augsburg), *c.* 1600
B   Wheel-lock petronel, German, *c.* 1630
C   Wheel-lock petronel, German, with a French barrel, *c.* 1630
D   Wheel-lock pistol, Dutch, *c.* 1610

These are short, light guns, longer than the short pistols (Plate 1) which precede
them, but still manageable in one hand.

E   Gun with combination match- and wheel-lock: thought to be one of the
many superb guns which belonged to Louis XIII: Italian, *c.* 1620

Plate 3

A Bill, Italian, *c.* 1525–1550
B Pole-Axe, German, *c.* 1520
C Halberd, Swiss, *c.* 1450–1500 (Zürich style)
D Halberd, Swiss, *c.* 1500 (*cf* Italian style, Fig. 6)

A   *B*   *C*   *D*

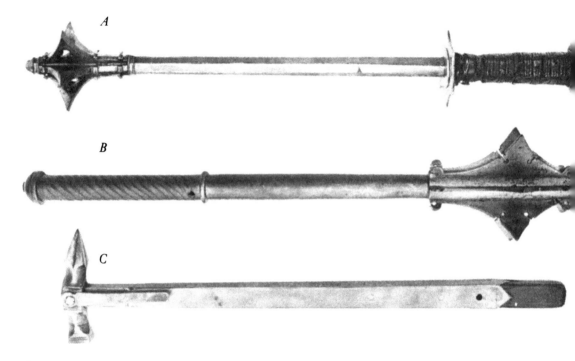

A

B

C

Plate 4

A   Type M 1 mace, German, *c.* 1460–1490: of pure
    'Gothic' form with six acutely-pointed flanges,
    each pierced with a trefoil, surmounted by a
    cap of brass. The haft is hexagonal, of steel, each
    face inlaid with a strip of brass. The grip is
    round in section bound with thongs of cord and
    leather. There is a small guard of flat hexagonal
    shape at the forward end of the grip and a flat
    disc secured by a brass rosette at the other end.
B   Type M 2 mace, German, *c.* 1520
C   Type H 1 horseman's hammer, German,
    c. 1550

Plate 4 (*cont.*)

D   Horseman's axe of Giovanni Giacomo Medici
    di Marignano: Italian, *c.* 1525: gilded and
    etched with floral designs and the Medici arms

D

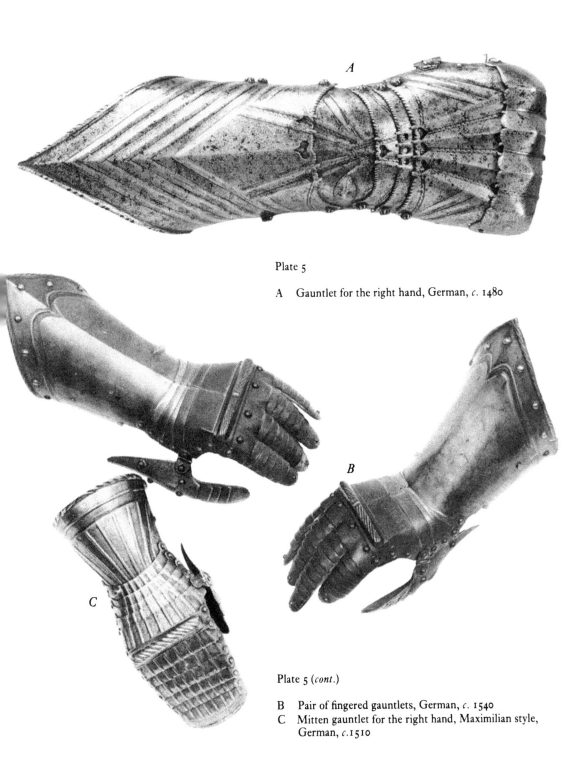

Plate 5

A   Gauntlet for the right hand, German, *c.* 1480

Plate 5 (*cont.*)

B   Pair of fingered gauntlets, German, *c.* 1540
C   Mitten gauntlet for the right hand, Maximilian style,
     German, *c.*1510

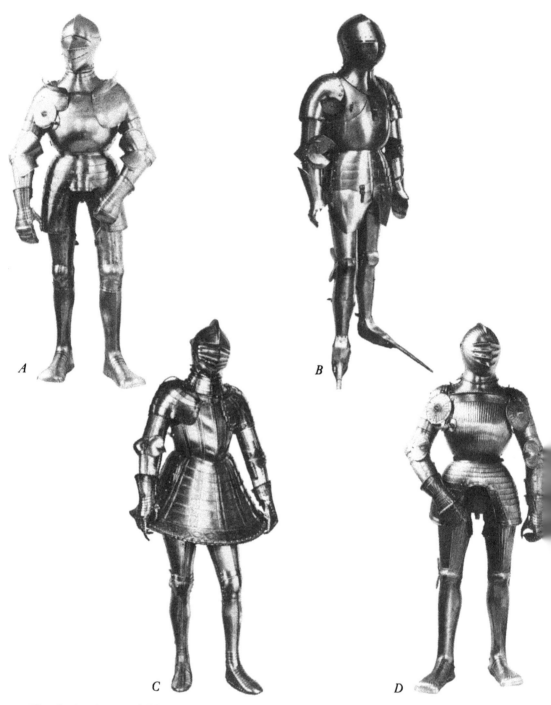

Plate 6 A Armour of 'SS' style, German, c. 1510: on the evidence of the etching on the breastplate, this may have belonged to Wladislaus of Bohemia and Hungary (died 1516)
   B Milanese armour made for Frederick I, Elector Palatine, c. 1451
   C The Roseleaf garniture made by Franz Grossschedel for the Emperor Maximilian II, c. 1571
   D Armour of fluted 'Maximilian' style, German, c. 1515–1525

Plate 7

A Barbuta, Italian, c. 1425–1450
B Sallet, German, c. 1460–1480
C English close helmet, c. 1510: in profile this looks like the
   German armet of the same period (D), but the method
   of opening the bevor is different
D Armet, German, c. 1510–1520

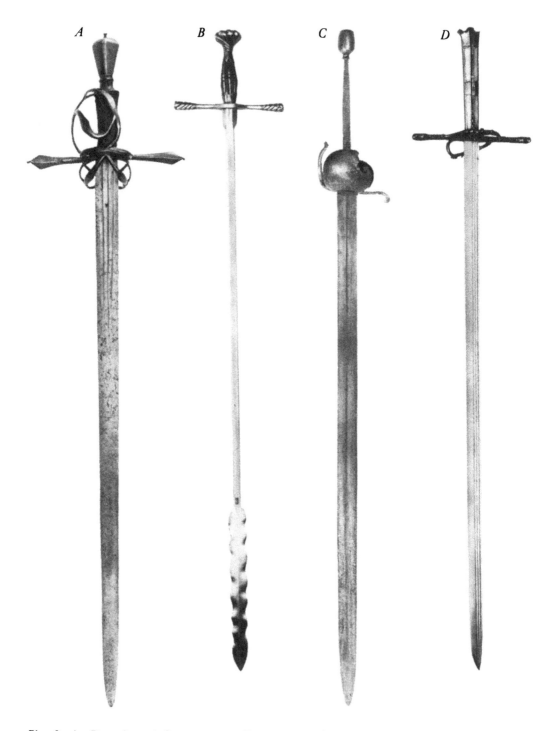

Plate 8 A Bastard sword, German, *c.* 1520: Saxon-type guards and quillons
           B Boar-sword, German, *c.* 1530: the short bar, or toggle, which crosses the plane of the
               blade where it broadens to the wave-edged portion is missing, but the hole through
               which it was fixed is visible
           C 'Twahandit' sword of 'Lowland' Type B, Scottish, *c.* 1600–1650
           D Back-edged sword of 'Grosze Messer' type, German/Swiss, *c.* 1530

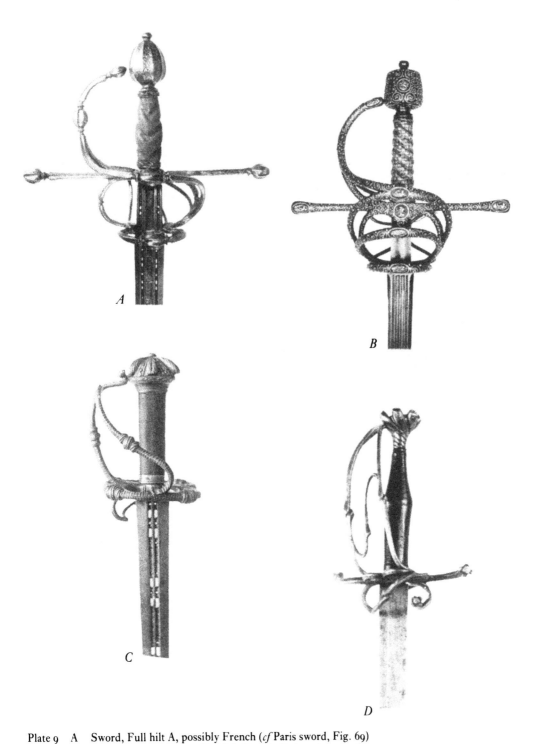

Plate 9   A   Sword, Full hilt A, possibly French (*cf* Paris sword, Fig. 69)

B   Sword, Italian, *c.* 1600: Full hilt D, chiselled steel decoration

C   Late form of *landsknecht* sword with knuckle guard and loop guards, German, *c.* 1540: unusually elaborate, both as to hilt and blade, for this type of weapon

D   Sabre, Swiss, *c.* 1530 with semi-basket knuckle guards: this form of hilt was also used on bastard swords (*cf* Plate 8)

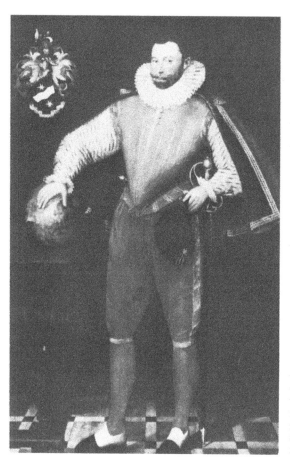

A

B

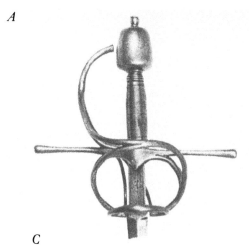

C

D

Plate 10 A Sir Francis Drake: artist unknown, *c.* 1585: compare simple outline with——
            B Henry Rich, 1st Earl of Holland: Mytens, 1632–1633: note the lacy collar, wider
                breeches, and flamboyant boots

            C Rapier, *c.* 1580: a classic example of Full hilt A: compare with——
            D Rapier, Italian, *c.* 1620: Full hilt D 2 with chiselled steel decoration

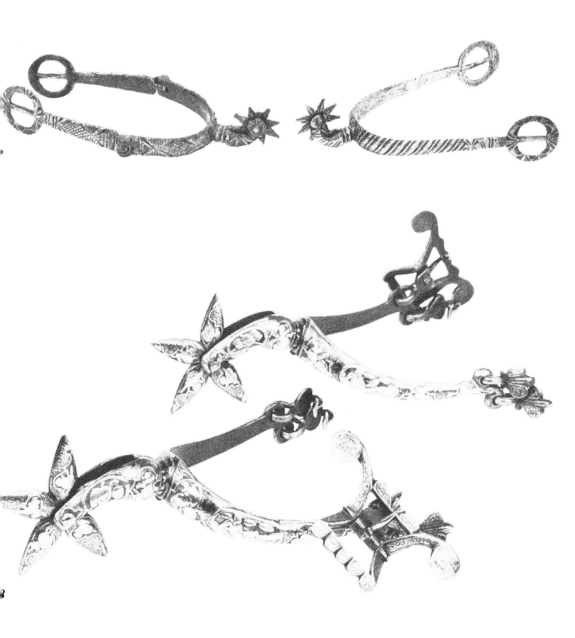

Plate 11 A   Two spurs, late sixteenth-century: compare with——
         B   Spurs, English, *c.* 1625: iron encrusted with silver decoration, and gold damascening

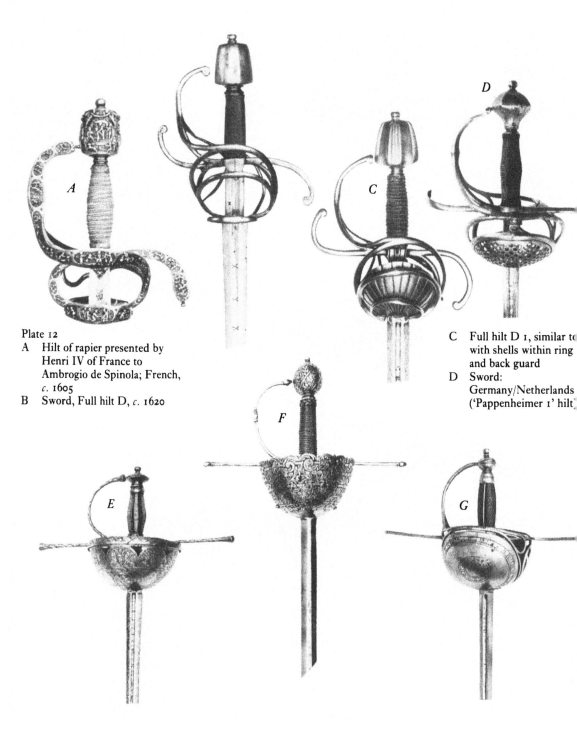

Plate 12
A   Hilt of rapier presented by
    Henri IV of France to
    Ambrogio de Spinola; French,
    c. 1605
B   Sword, Full hilt D, *c*. 1620

C   Full hilt D 1, similar to
    with shells within ring
    and back guard
D   Sword:
    Germany/Netherlands
    ('Pappenheimer 1' hilt)

Plate 12   E   Spanish cup-hilt rapier, *c*. 1660
(*cont*.)   F   Italian cup-hilt rapier, *c*. 1660; note the deeper cup and large pommel
            G   Spanish Bilbo, *c*. 1660

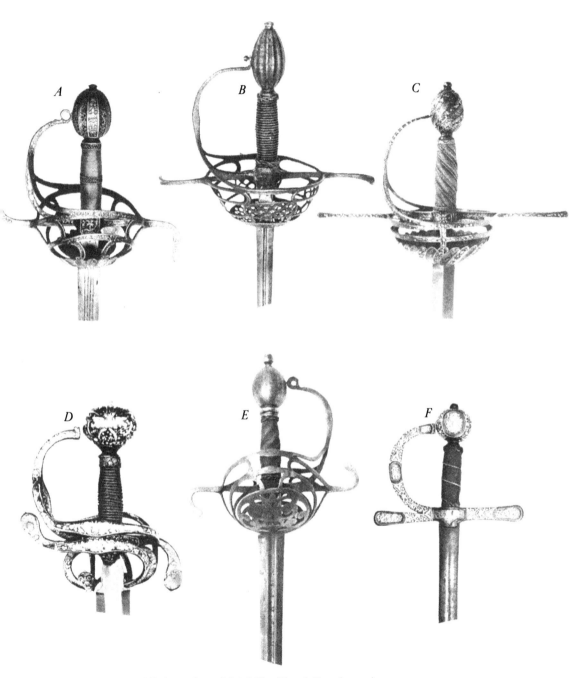

Plate 13 A English hilt A, *c*. 1620: with inlaid gold and silver decoration
           B English hilt B
           C English hilt B, with silver and gold damascening
           D Sword: English hilt D, heavily encrusted with silver decoration
           E English hilt A: rapier, *c*. 1630
           F Sword: English, *c*. 1630: the very simple hilt is encrusted with silver decoration
              (*cf* Pl. 14B)

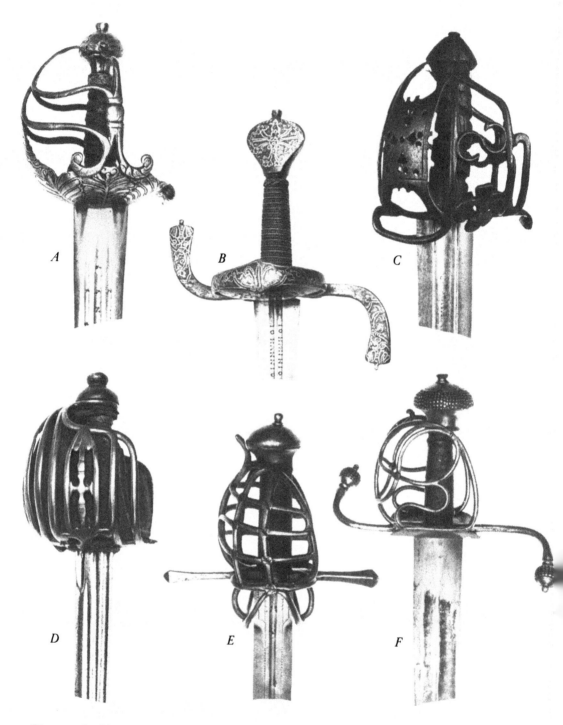

Plate 14 A   Mortuary sword, English, *c*. 1640–1650: note feather-like pattern
              B   Broadsword, Swedish/Netherlands, *c*. 1650: 'Sinclair 2' type, silver decoration
              C   Claymore with Stirling hilt incorporating the letter S in the side guards: retains its
                   original browning
              D   English cavalry sword with basket hilt, *c*. 1760
   E and F   Two broadswords, South German, hilts of pre-Schiavona (?) basket form, *c*. 1600

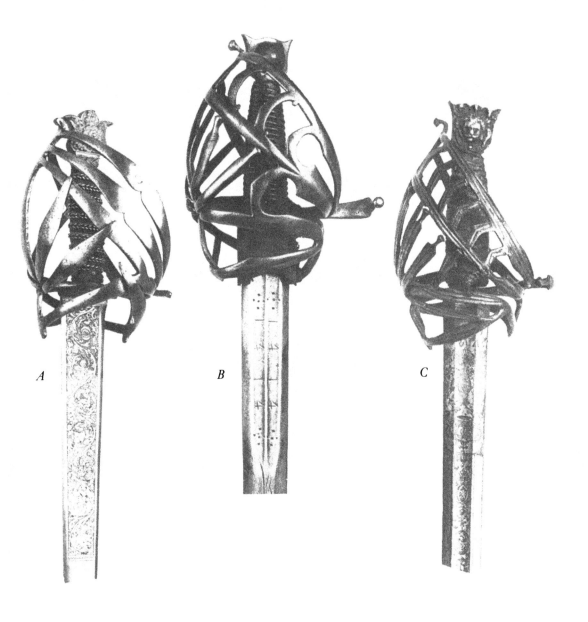

Plate 15   A   Sword of 'Schiavona 1' type: re-used back-edged sword-blade, finely etched (once gilt) at the forte: Italian, *c.* 1500: hilt with Venetian mark, possibly dating *c.* 1650

            B   Sword of 'Schiavona 2' type: broad two-edged blade marked 1414, retains its original leather sheath cover: South German (?), *c.* 1630–1660

            C   Sword of 'Schiavona 2' type: hilt of iron gilded, pommel of bronze with a fiercely moustached mask: blade etched with decorative designs and gilded, the decoration incorporating the arms of the Empire and the name of the Emperor Charles VI (1711–1740). This dates the sword; it is interesting to compare it with the type 2 hilt above, in which is mounted a blade stamped with (?) cabalistic numerals in the fullers and thus probably dating 1600–1650. Is this an old seventeenth-century blade in an eighteenth-century hilt, or is the Charles VI example an eighteenth-century blade in a seventeenth-century hilt?

Plate 16   Field armour made in 1546, by Desiderius Kolman Helmschmied of
            Augsburg, for Philip II, of Spain, then Crown Prince; later sent by him
            to the Heroes Armoury at Ambras, in memory of his father, Charles V:
            figure completed by silver portrait head painted in oils, *c.* 1556, by
            Pompeo Leoni of Milan, royal sculptor in Madrid

the poleyns and the couters are exactly similar to those on the Beauchamp effigy too; but the top of the outer breastplate is fastened with a strap and buckle.

There are even more pictures showing the Sanseverino style; an interesting one is by Luca Signorelli, painted c. 1503, of the Damned being driven into Hell by three armed angels; two wear beautiful Milanese armours of the Sanseverino group, one with a curious angelic winged hat and the other with a light, open, cap-shaped helmet (q.v. below), but the third is most interestingly attired in the same sort of steel cap, with pauldrons, vambraces, cuishes and poleyns of the Sanseverino form; there are no greaves or shoes, just the angel's stockinged feet, and his cuirass is of antique Roman form, breastplate and backplate moulded to the muscles of the torso, and a skirt of pendant strips instead of a plate skirt and tassets. This is one of the frescoes in the Chapel of St Brizio in Orvieto Cathedral. There are many other paintings of even earlier date which show similar 'Romanised' armour, or armour which is entirely Roman. Even Donatello's statue of Gattamelata (made c. 1443—1453) has long pendant strips of fabric or leather hanging down under the pauldrons and the skirt in the Classic manner. No actual armour made à l'antique survives from the fifteenth century, but there is a wealth of it dating from the 1520s onwards.

THE 'GIOVANNI FREGOSO' STYLE (Fig. 24 H)

There are three armours in the next group (Fig. 24 H), the final expression of the Milanese style developed from the 'International' patterns. One is in the Kunsthistorisches Museum, Vienna, and two are in the Musée de l'Armée, Paris; with the group, but not of it, are a cuirass and pauldrons in the Hungarian National Museum, Budapest, and an extremely important armour in England. The earliest of these armours was made for Giovanni Fregoso, Doge of Genoa, so I shall call the group GF. Made c. 1505, this armour shows all the characteristics of the group: a long, slim breastplate, now made in one piece instead of with an inner and an outer plate, ridged down the middle, high in the neck, noticeably lower in the waist than the armours in the Sanseverino group, and large pauldrons with, perhaps for the first time in Italy (though they had been in use in Germany earlier), tall haute-pieces, the left higher than the right. In this armour there are no tassets. The two armours in Paris were both made by the same master, Nicolo de Silva of Milan, and are dated around 1510—though the cuirassses of both are still uncompromisingly Gothic. They have the typical Italian high neck, cut in a shallow V-shape, the breast is ridged, and the three-lame tassets, vertically ridged and pointed at the bottom, hang by straps and buckles from the lowest lame of the skirt. The legs too are in the Milanese tradition, but there are typically German broad-toed sabatons. Also borrowed from the German SS style is the high collar, the tall haute-pieces forged in one with the main plates of the pauldrons, and the helmet, fitting over and revolving upon the top lame of the collar. The mitten gauntlets have long, Gothic, sharply-pointed cuffs.

Again, there are many Italian paintings showing this kind of armour with its low waist and high neck, the very opposite of contemporary German armours with high waists and low necks; good examples being a 'St William' in a 'Virgin and Child' by Ercole Grandi in the National Gallery, London, and a 'St Quentin' in a similar picture by Bianchi Ferrari in the Louvre, Paris. Neither of these saintly warriors wears a complete harness: Grandi's St

FIGURE 29   *Armour of Flemish/English style, from a tapestry c. 1510* (Musée de Cluny, Paris)

William has neither helmet nor pauldrons, while Ferrari's St Quentin has no greaves, sabatons or helmet. In each case the long, low-waisted breastplate is very clearly depicted.

The part-armour in Budapest has much in common with other armours of the group, particularly in the shape of the cuirass and pauldrons. It was once thought to be Milanese like the others, but by comparing the mark upon it, a Roman *M* surmounted by a crescent, with other pieces of armour stamped with the same mark, Claude Blair has established that it was in fact, like the other pieces, made by an armourer working in the Low Countries, though probably of Italian origin. At this period, around the turn of the century, *c.* 1500, many Milanese armourers were established under royal patronage at centres such as Arbois in Burgundy, Tours in France, and London in England. The English and Flemish brasses and effigies of this period show, as I have said, a distinctive English/Flemish style.

Basically, this is the same as these armours of de Silva's; even more like them are the armoured figures in a series of tapestries showing episodes in the story of David and Bath-sheba. These are in the Musée de Cluny, Paris, and were probably made in Brussels in 1517 (Fig. 29).

Other armours with the mark of the *M* and crescent are two bards (horse armours) in the Royal Armoury, Madrid, an armet in New York, and the bard of the engraved and silvered armour of Henry VIII in the Tower of London, which was once thought to have been given to Henry by Maximilian in 1515. Claude Blair has now established that Maximilian's gift was in fact a costume armour similar to the one Seusenhofer made for the Archduke Charles (*q.v.*, p. 101), not the engraved and silvered armour at all, which is of Milanese GF style and in every way but one closely akin to de Silva's armours in Paris. The armour for the man was in fact made in England by two armourers, Filippo de Grampis and Giovanni Angelo de Littis, Milanese craftsmen who, on the evidence of several documents, were relatives of Nicolo de Silva, and probably worked with him before coming to England. Hence the close similarity in the style of this armour and the Paris ones. The bard, on the other hand, bearing the same mark as the armour in Budapest, is known to have been made in the Low Countries to match the man's armour,

FIGURE 30   Bases of Henry VIII's
                silvered armour, c. 1515
                (Tower of London)

and when it was completed, was sent over to be decorated, silvered and finally gilded, together with the man's armour, by Paul van Vrelant, a Flemish artist working in London, employed as the King's harness-gilder.

This armour differs from the others in that instead of having an ordinary skirt and tassets, it is furnished with a long, flared and pleated skirt of steel, reaching to a point just below the knee. This is a feature which had a brief spell of popularity between about 1510 and 1520, a direct imitation of the long pleated skirts to the fashionable doublet, called 'bases', and it deserves a section of its own.

BASES

Cloth bases were sometimes worn, like the lower half of a surcoat, with armour, over the skirt and tassets—in fact, judging by the great number of battle-pictures and 'St Georges' showing these colourful bases being worn, it must have been a fashion with a very wide popularity.

There are few armours with steel bases (Fig. 30) surviving, only the one of Henry VIII's mentioned above and a little *Kostümharnisch* which Konrad Seusenhofer made in 1511—1512 for the young Archduke Charles (later the Emperor Charles V), to the order of Charles's grandfather, Maximilian*. Made at the same time, and very similar (it seems) in form, was another costume armour with bases and silver-gilt decoration which Maximilian ordered from Seusenhofer as a gift for Henry VIII of England. Charles's survives intact in Vienna but Henry's has almost all vanished—except for the helmet, which will be dealt with later. It was delivered to the King in 1515 and is listed in the inventories of the armouries made in 1547 and 1561, but in the next, made in 1611, only the helmet appears. This omission is explained by a letter which Sir Henry Lee, Master of the Armouries at the Tower, wrote on July 29 1601 to Sir John Stanhope, in which he complains that Henry VIII's armours at Greenwich had been 'taken from their place of so longe contynuance' and 'thrown appon hepes'. The very last record of this armour is contained in an inventory of goods belonging to Charles I, sold by Order of the Council of

* In the Metropolitan Museum, New York, is an isolated pair of bases, formed very like the ones on Henry VIII's engraved and silvered armour, etched and gilded in imitation of damask.

State, 1649—1652. Among entries recording objects 'in the Tower Jewel House' is the following:

> 70   Twenty six peices of Broken Armour and Buckles
> Steel and Silver Gilt Valued at £1.15s
> Sold to Saml. Edwards the 27th Decr 1649 for £2.7s

Bases should not be confused with tonnlets, which are described in the following section.

TONNLETS

The tonnlet is a steel kilt worn with a particular kind of tournament armour, especially designed for fighting on foot. Bases are made like the skirts of a coat, cut away in front and behind to accommodate the saddle-steels when mounted; tonnlets are complete kilts, falling to just above the knee as a rule (Fig. 31). There are several armours of this kind, the earliest being made c. 1490 for Claude de Vaudrey, Grand Chamberlain of Burgundy, by two Italian armourers, Damiano Missaglia and Giovan Marco Meraviglia, working at

Arbois in Maximilian's workshop there. In this armour the tonnlet is comparatively short, about the same size and shape as the deep fauld on the FV armour in New York. The de Vaudrey armour is now in the Kunsthistorisches Museum, Vienna. A very similar armour was made by Francesco da Merate, also at Arbois, for Maximilian, between 1500 and 1508. In the Tower of London is a tonnlet armour in the Italian style made for Henry VIII, c. 1512, by Italian armourers working in England, though the helmet bears the mark of the Missaglia factory in Milan. The skirt of this armour is much longer and wider than the skirts of the preceding two. In the Waffensammlung, Vienna, is a remarkable tonnlet armour which, except that it is fitted with a tonnlet instead of bases, is of the same genre as Seusenhofer's costume armours made for Charles V and Henry VIII. It may also be the work of Konrad Seusenhofer; the tight-fitting, puffed vambraces, the short, sleeve-like 'pauldrons', the puffed cuishes, are all similar in appearance to the Archduke Charles's, but the tonnlet is a vast flared and pleated skirt with an arch-shaped section in the

FIGURE 31   *Tonnlet on Henry VIII's Italian foot-combat armour, c. 1530* (Tower of London)

front which can be removed. The close helmet is a fantastic affair, with its visor embossed in the likeness of a cockerel's head (W.S.V. A 78).

Three other notable tonnlet armours—*kempfküriss*, as the style began to be called at about this time—survive from the middle years of the sixteenth century. All three belonged to garnitures built for specific State occasions. The first two, made in Innsbruck and Augsburg respectively, were made to the order of the Emperor Ferdinand I, King of the Romans, and younger brother of Charles V. After the battle of Mühlberg in 1547, when these two monarchs broke the power of the Protestant princes of the Schmalkdic League, they summoned the princes and nobles of all Germany to attend the Imperial Diet. Ferdinand had his armourer, Jörg Seusenhofer of Innsbruck, make a garniture for his younger son, the Archduke Ferdinand, Lord of the Tyrol, for this occasion; and when a little later he obtained the promise of the crown of Bohemia for his eldest son, Maximilian, he had a second garniture made for him, this time by Matthäus Frauenpreiss of Augsburg. Both garnitures included pieces to make a *kempfküriss*. Seusenhofer's tonnlet was knee-length and flared to a bell-shape at the bottom, while Frauenpreiss's was slightly shorter and fell in a straight line from the waist. Seusenhofer's garniture was decorated with etched and gilded bands by the Innsbruck engraver, Hans Sumersperger; these included among the decorative motifs the Eagle of ancient Austria, because of which it has been called the *Adlergarnitur* ever since. Frauenpreiss's was decorated by Jörg Sorg of Augsburg and has acquired no specific name, but the date '1550' is incorporated in the decoration on the tonnlet.

Twenty-one years later, in 1571, Maximilian, now Emperor in his turn as well as King of Hungary and Bohemia, had a garniture made by Hans Grosschedel of Landshut. This was for his use in the tournaments and festivities which attended the wedding of his brother, Charles of Styria. Many other fine armours still surviving are now known to have been made for different potentates on this occasion, one of the most important political and social events of the century. This rather late garniture differed from the earlier ones in that instead of being a basic field armour with extra pieces to make up into some twelve different complete armours, it now consisted of five complete armours and a horse armour. Its tonnlet was bell-shaped, as that of the *Adlergarnitur*. This garniture is known as the 'Roseleaf' by reason of the roseleaves incorporated in the design of the etched decoration. It is interesting that Maximilian raised his armourer Hans Grossschedel to the nobility in recognition of his artistic achievement, in the same way as Charles V ennobled Titian.

All these garnitures are now in the Kunsthistorisches Museum, Vienna.

'COSTUME' ARMOUR

The fashion of making armour to follow the trend for puffs and slashes produced a number of costume armours (*Kostümharnisch*) which show great skill on the part of the armourers who built them. The richest survivor is the little armour with bases, now in Vienna, which Konrad Seusenhofer made for the Archduke Charles in 1511—1512, a deliberate imitation of the fashionable wide-skirted doublet and puffed hose, sleeves and shoes of the period. Instead of pauldrons there are wide, short sleeves, formed of a series

FIGURE 32 *'Vambrace', or sleeve, of a costume armour belonging to Wilhelm, Graf von Rogendorf, c. 1515*

of concentric overlapping lames, which widen out to cover the gap under the arm. The vambraces are imitations of the fashionable close-fitting sleeve, with small couters without side-wings, and the bend inside the elbow is protected by a series of small overlapping lames, similar to the vambraces on Lorenz Helmschmied's Gothic armour of 1490, made for Maximilian, and another which he made some fifteen years later and which came into the possession of the Duke of Sonnenberg. This was a technical *tour de force* much in use on fine armours about 1490—1530, going out of use for some ninety years and coming into favour again about 1620—1650.

In 1511, when the Archduke Charles was twelve years old, the Innsbruck armourer Hans Rabeiler made a little costume armour for him which was totally different in style from the one Seusenhofer made a year later, for it was in form a conventional armour, but each piece was heavily embossed with simulated puffs and slashes. This too is now preserved in the Kunsthistorisches Museum, Vienna.

Another very striking costume armour of rather similar form is in the Metropolitan Museum, New York. Until recently this was considered to be the work of Koloman Helmschmied, the son of Lorenz Helmschmied, and its ownership was attributed to the Elector Frederick III of Saxony, Grand Master of the Teutonic Order. Unfortunately, it has now been established that very little of this armour is genuine, the bulk being the work of a nineteenth-century 'restorer', of a skill almost worthy of the Helmschmied workshop.

However, in Vienna there is a genuine work of Koloman Helmschmied's, which might be called the costume armour to end all costume armours. It is a foot-combat armour in a style different from the tonnlet-fitted *kempfküriss*, for it has long articulated cuishes fixed to the lower lame of a short skirt fitting close around the hips, the gap between the upper inner edges of the cuishes and the lower edge of the skirt being filled in with a great codpiece. The culet is shaped to conform to the curves of the bottom, affording very considerable all-round protection. There are no vambraces in the accepted sense, but instead vast puffed sleeves (Fig. 32). The surface of this armour is covered with small simulated S-shaped slashes set in vertical rows. It is known to have belonged to Wilhelm von Rogendorf, one of Charles V's most trusted councillors, Captain of his Guard, Commander-in-Chief in Spain, and one who carried out several confidential diplomatic missions for the Emperor as well as his military functions. The armour is part of a garniture, some of which survives, parts of it being in Vienna, parts in Madrid, parts in London. It seems that it was originally made for Charles V himself, who at some time gave

FIGURE 33   *Portrait of Guidobaldo II
della Rovere, Duke of
Urbino, by Agnolo
Bronzino, c. 1531*

this foot-combat arrangement of it to Rogendorf, much as Maximilian gave his own armour to Sonnenberg.*

As a fashion, slash decoration was short-lived, although armour decorated in this way went on being made until late in the century. After about 1525, the build on the whole is conventional, the slashes small, and the puffs non-existent, the decorative emphasis now being directed more towards etched and engraved all-over patterns simulating brocades or damasks. A late example of a cuirass made to imitate a doublet is to be seen in a portrait by Agnolo Bronzino, painted *c.* 1531, of Guidobaldo II della Rovere, Duke of Urbino. He wears a half-armour of an intriguing green colour whose cuirass is made with the collar and spaudlers in one with it, in cut as well as surface decoration looking exactly like a slashed brocade doublet (Fig. 33). The vambraces and tassets are conventional, and the armour is worn over a scarlet arming-doublet and a pair of scarlet hose which are elaborately embroidered in gold thread, as is the splendidly arrogant scarlet codpiece. There are many armours decorated in this way, dating up to the last decades of the century.

THE 'MAXIMILIAN' STYLE

The armours described above were *prunkharnisch*, 'parade harness'. The ordinary field armour of this period, about 1515—1525, was basically similar in shape to the SS group, except that the fauld tended to spring more robustly out below the waist, the couters were bigger, and the haute-pieces upon the pauldrons rose less vertically, flaring outwards a good deal to give the whole armour a more flamboyant outline. Whether the surfaces were fluted or not (many Maximilian armours were quite plain), the edges of the plates almost invariably had turnovers strongly roped. There are many different ways in which

---

* Among the items of the garniture was a pair of conventional vambraces, puffed and slashed to match. Part of the left vambrace is in the Wallace Collection, London (A 245), and part of the right one, and the gauntlets, are in Vienna. The helmet is associated.

flutings—or ridges or gadrooning—were applied to the surfaces. Gadrooning was only suitable for the decoration of the large areas of breastplates, whereas fluting could be applied to the smallest surfaces, like those of short cuffs on gauntlets. Sprays of ridging too were mostly confined to the large plates, though very often faulds and tassets as well as vambraces which appear at first glance to be fluted are, if one is to be pedantic, ridged. The first usage of the typical close-set fluting was probably in the 1490s, though there is no precisely datable 'Maximilian' armour as early as this; there are, however, several rather later representations of it such as Hans Burgkmair's drawing of Maximilian himself, dated 1508, in the *Weisskönig*.

So many Maximilian armours survive that it is impossible to do more than merely mention their existence. There were many variations, but on the whole they all more or less followed the same design. An early and particularly fine example which I would nominate to illustrate the style is one from the Kunsthistorisches Museum, Vienna, and was made for Eitel Friedrich, Graf von Zollern, a man who has a claim on our interest partly as an ancestor of Kaiser Wilhelm II, partly as a friend and comrade in arms of Edward IV of England, beside whom he fought on and off during the Wars of the Roses. The Graf died in 1512 at the age of sixty; the slender waist and general form of the armour might tempt one to date it to his younger days, but this is impossible. We must instead assume that he did not thicken with age like, for example, Johann Friedrich, Elector of Saxony, whose stout, middle-aged, fluted armour is dated 1530.

After about 1530, fluting becomes very rare, though there are a few armours which still have it, for example one in Vienna which by its form cannot be dated earlier than *c.* 1550. After 1530, however, where 'flutes' do appear they are generally rather feeble, not well-formed, and somewhat ineptly set out on the plates.

The armourers of Milan, whose work until the very end of the fifteenth century had been uncompromisingly free of any kind of decorated surface, began to introduce flutes and gadroons into some of their *alla Tedesca* work. There are a number of Italian cuirasses, which can generally be dated between 1500 and 1510, all in the SS German form, whose surfaces are decorated, mostly with flutes, a rare few, such as a beautiful etched breastplate in the Musée de l'Armée, Paris, with gadroon, and some—not many— with embossed sprays of ridges. It is possible to suggest that Italian fluting, not in its technical formation but in the manner of its disposition upon the plate, has certain characteristics which distinguish it from similar German armour. First, the flutes tend to be applied in groups separated by plain areas; secondly, these groups of flutes are disposed at a graceful angle across the plate—not parallel with its axis, like true 'Maximilian' fluting, nor yet at right-angles to it like Gothic rippling, but something between the two, set through angles between thirty degrees near the middle of the plate and seventy towards the armholes. Another point about these *alla Tedesca* armours is that the tassets are generally quite long, of up to ten lames, vertically fluted and very rectangular in shape. Good examples of Italian cuirasses decorated with sprays of ridges are a breastplate and a backplate in the Wallace Collection, London, of *c.* 1500 (A 215), and a 'St Sebastian' by Rondani in St Peter's, Modena, painted at about the same date.

Another typical Italian adaptation of the Maximilian pattern, applied only to extremely *bombé* breastplates, was to hammer the surface into a series of parallel, deep, embossed ridges, arranged like flutes but deeper and more angular in section. A portrait by Titian of the Venetian Admiral Giovanni Moro, *c.* 1520, formerly in the Kaiser Friedrichs Museum, Berlin, presented one; and there is an actual example in the Armouries of the Tower of London.

It is interesting to compare the appearance of an ordinary fluted breastplate of the early 1520s with pictures showing Italian male costume in the 1460s. During the fifteenth century the Italians seemed not to favour either the short tight jacket of the Gothic style or the knee-length, full-skirted doublet. Instead we see them wearing a sort of tight-fitting tunic with a loose, sleeveless surcoat or over-tunic above it, made like a poncho from a long piece of material, with a hole to put the head through; it falls loosely before and behind, and is clipped in at the waist by a belt or cord. These over-tunics were pleated, the pleats at front and back being gathered at the top into a straight yoke. The pictures in which this garment is to be seen are without number; in practically any painting from 1440 to 1520, it may be found. When the warriors of the Gothic world irrupted into Italy after 1494, they came into contact with examples of this style, not only walking about, as it were, but portrayed in the paintings and frescoes of artists like Piero della Francesca, Botticelli, Mantegna, Verrocchio and countless others, which met them and compelled their admiration at every turn. Not only that. We know that during these years there was a liaison between artist and armourer such as had not existed before—Lucas Cranach, for instance, lived for years in Koloman Helmschmied's house at Augsburg, and Daniel Hopfer was Desiderius Helmschmied's brother-in-law, to name two cases. Nor before had there ever been so great or so universal an appreciation of works of art for their own sake. Maybe we should add, to the influences brought to bear upon developments in armour design, the growing influence of the artist.

THE CLASSICAL INFLUENCE

Later in the fifteenth century we can see the impact of the newly-discovered works of art of the ancient world, not only upon painting but upon fashion itself. The short over-tunic I have just mentioned lent itself to this, for by very little change in shape, it became exactly the same in appearance as the garment worn by most men in the late Roman Empire. Even the flat cap, so very typical of High Renaissance male dress, is only an ancient Greek one reworked. The silver tetradrachm of Antimachus of Bactria, *c.* 175 BC, for instance, at first sight could unhesitatingly be taken for a Renaissance medal or coin. There can be little doubt that the rediscovery of the works of art of the ancients had as much influence upon fashion as their philosophies did upon contemporary thought. We shall see how in the mid-sixteenth century that influence produced quantities of the finest—though the most useless—armour in a purely Antique style.

It can be no accident of circumstance that the master armourers of the cities of northern Italy and southern Germany were producing the noblest creations of their art at a time when some of the finest works of sculpture the world has ever known were in the making. It is not inappropriate to set the names of Missaglia, Seusenhofer and Helmschmied beside those of Della Francesca, Massingham, Donatello and Verrocchio. The sculptor hewed the creations of his genius from unaccommodating stone, but the armourer hammered the no less shapely products of *his* genius from dull sheets of inelastic iron. The sculptor's work had no other function than to exist—to ravish the eye and uplift the soul, maybe, but it was static, immovable. When the armourer's finished creation was assembled upon a living man, its aesthetic impact was in no way less than the sculptor's; and in addition, it had to be an efficient piece of machinery, durable enough to survive a lifetime of destructive wear; it had to fit its wearer like a second skin, move with him with the ease and smoothness of silk, be not too heavy for him to bear its weight, yet hard and tough enough to protect him in the utmost rigours of the battlefield. Well might a modern writer dub the work of the great masters 'sculpture in steel', for it is that and much more, equal for aesthetic quality with the greatest sculpture in stone, as well as with superb machinery, and far superior in sheer glamour. No sculpture could ever match the visual impact of a fine armour worn by a well-set-up young man, mounted in glittering motion upon a spirited horse. The warriors who wore these armours were perfectly aware of the splendours of their appearance, a feeling expressed, as always, with dazzling effect by Shakespeare, in *Henry IV* (Part I, Act 4, Scene i):

> '*All furnish'd, all in arms;*
> *All plum'd like estridges that wing the wind;*
> *Bating like eagles having lately bath'd;*
> *Glittering in golden coats like images;*
> *As full of spirit as the month of May,*
> *And gorgeous as the sun at midsummer.*'

Youth, colour, glamour, life—a whole picture in six lines; but above all, a real awareness of these things. Armour, though fallen from its high estate of a century before, was still a living thing in Shakespeare's time. A much more down-to-earth example is to be found in a comment Philippe de Commynes made upon that *louche* young monarch, Charles VIII of France, on the day of the battle of Fornovo, in 1495. Here we can see the effect a fine armour and a good horse had even upon the personality of a very thick-witted and uncouth young man, as seen through the eyes of a hardened and cynical courtier:

'The next morning, the 6th July 1495, being a Monday, by seven o'clock the King mounted, and called for me. I came to him and found him fully armed and mounted upon the best horse I ever saw in my life. The horse was called Savoy, a present from Charles, Duke of Savoy. It was a black horse, not very tall, with only one eye, but big enough for him that rode him. This young prince seemed that day quite another thing than what one would normally expect him to be; he was very *louche*, especially in conversation, and still is so; and no wonder, for he had been brought up in the company of inferior people. But now being mounted on his horse and armed, his eye sparkled with fire, his look was fresh and lively, and his words showed wisdom and discretion.'

There is more of interest, too, in Vernon's speech in *Henry IV*; Shakespeare follows up the description of the glittering, spirited young knights with these lines describing how Prince Hal mounted his horse:

> '*I saw young Harry,—with his bevor on,*
> *His cuisses on his thighs, gallantly arm'd,—*
> *Rise from the ground like feather'd Mercury,*
> *And vaulted with such ease into his seat,*
> *As if an angel dropp'd down from the clouds,*
> *To turn and wind a fiery Pegasus,*
> *And witch the world with noble horsemanship.*'

Here is no fooling by a playwright with the nonsensical notion of an armoured man being hoisted into his saddle with a crane. Henry of Monmouth, on the eve of the battle of Shrewsbury in 1403, leaps fully armed into his saddle without touching stirrup, a feat taken as a matter of course by any properly trained and fit man-at-arms then and for two centuries after. The crane business was a gag invented to get a laugh by the producer of a farce called *When Knights Were Bold* which first saw the lights of the Lyceum Theatre, London, in the 1890s. It is sad that the English-speaking world still has to be dogged by this idiotic brain-child of the long-forgotten producer of a Victorian farce, and that writers, directors and producers, illustrators and teachers, still perpetuate it as truth, instead of condemning it for the futile nonsense that it manifestly is.

BIBLIOGRAPHY

Blair, Claude, *European Armour*, London, 1958

 and also ... *Maximilian I's Gift of Armour to King Henry VIII*, Archaeologia, 1965

Boccia, C. G., and Coelho, E. T., *L'Arte dell' Armatura in Italia*, Milan, 1967

 and also .... *Armi Bianchi Italiane*, Milan, 1975

Carpegna, Nolfo di (Ed.), *Armi Antiche dal Sec. IX al XVIII gia Collezione Odescalchi*, Rome, 1969

Gamber, Ortwin, *Armour Made in the Royal Workshops at Greenwich*, Scottish Art Review, Vol. XII, No. 2, Glasgow, 1969

Mann, Sir J. G., *The Sanctuary of the Madonna Della Grazie, Mantua*, Archaeologia, 1930

  and also . . . . . *A Further Account of the Madonna Della Grazie, Mantua*, Archaeologia, 1938

  . . . . *Notes on the Armour of the Maximilian Period*, Archaeologia, 1929

  . . . . *The Lost Armoury of the Gonzagas*, R. Archaeological Journal, 1939

  . . . . *The Etched Decoration of Armour*, Proc. British Academy, 1942

Norman, A. V. B., *Arms and Armour*, London, 1964

Norman, A. V. B., and Pottinger, D., *Warrior to Soldier, 449—1660*, London, 1966

Ross, Francesco—Carpegna, Nolfo di (Ed.), *Armi Antiche dal Museo Civico L. Marzoli*, Brescia, 1969

Thomas, Bruno, and Gamber, Ortwin, *L'Arte Milanese dell'Armatura*, Storia di Milano, Parte XIII, Milan, 1958

Thomas, Bruno, Gamber, Ortwin, and Schedelmann, Hans, *Arms and Armour*, London, 1964

Trapp, O., and Mann, Sir J. G., *Catalogue of the Armoury of the Castle of Churburg*, London, 1929

The Kretzschmar von Kienbusch Collection of Armour and Arms, Princeton, 1963

CHAPTER FIVE

HELMETS: 1400–1525

Helmets were practical things and their evolution was functional, not fashionable. There were two basic kinds in use during the fifteenth and sixteenth centuries: open hat-like ones and closed visored ones.

THE *CELATA* AND THE *BARBUTA*

In late-fourteenth-century Italy two forms of open helmet were coming into use to rival the old, popular, wide-brimmed steel hat, the helmet which the English called a 'kettle hat' in the thirteenth century and a 'tin hat' in the twentieth. The new Italian types were called the '*celata*' and the '*barbuta*'. Both terms are first noted in an inventory of the Gonzaga family's armour, taken in 1407; and though two distinct forms of helmet are indicated, it is difficult to differentiate between them. However, there are many pictures made between about 1370 and 1425 which show two types of helmet, each with a different shape to its face-opening, and because one of these was adopted in western Europe and called 'salade', there is little doubt as to which was which. One of the earliest of these artefacts is a silver altarpiece in Pistoia Cathedral, completed in 1376, which shows the two types (Fig. 34). From other sources we gather that the *celata* was like a bascinet with

FIGURE 34   Representation of figures on a silver altarpiece, c. 1370, in Pistoia Cathedral, showing the celata *and the* barbuta

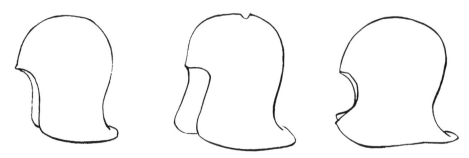

FIGURE 35   Forms of the celata, 1400—1440

neither aventail nor visor, and with the sides drawn forward at the bottom to protect the cheeks and chin and outward over the nape of the neck in a short upturned tail (Fig. 35). Over the eyes was a pointed peak, either forged in one with the skull or pivoted to it at the sides. If this was the *celata*, by inference the *barbuta* was the other, where the face-opening is narrower, shaped like a ⊤ and formed by the sides being drawn even farther forward almost to enclose the face (Fig. 36).

There is a tendency among modern scholars to use the term *barbuta* for both of these helmet types, reserving *celata* for the style into which the early type developed late in the century, for while the true *barbuta* went out of fashion by about 1470, the other form—the *celata* of the Gonzaga inventory and of such pictures as the Pistoia altarpiece—remained in use side by side with the developed form.

Many fine-quality *barbute* survive, all probably dating *c.* 1440—1470, and some are identical in form and construction with the Corinthian helmet of the ancient Greeks

FIGURE 36   Forms of the barbuta, 1400—1480

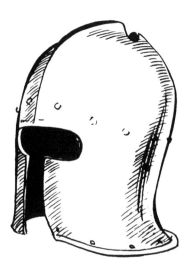 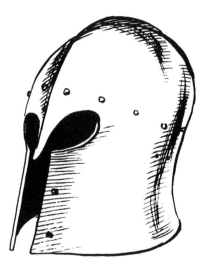

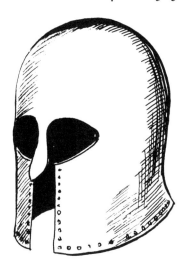

FIGURE 37 Bronze 'Corinthian' helmet, from the fourth century BC.

(Fig. 37), except that they are made of iron and not of bronze. This similarity is so close that it is hard to accept that it was coincidental and that the form was no more than a logical mutation of the bascinet, owing nothing to the influence of ancient exemplars. It is curious to be told that at a time when in Italy every cultured person was afire with enthusiasm for the rediscovered glories of Greek art, the sudden appearance of a purely Grecian helmet-design had nothing to do with this. When every artist and every patron of artists (the latter were also the patrons and customers of armourers) strove to introduce classical elements into everything, it seems incredible that the master armourers of Milan should have stood aloof, and by doing so allowed a classical design to creep unnoticed into existence as a mere logical development of a traditional style, not an adaptation of a classical one such as might be demanded by popular taste. Being the craftsmen, practical and war-wise, that they were at this time, they would have had nothing to do with a design that was not functional, however much popular demand called for it; but the Corinthian helmet was a gift to them, for a more functional headpiece has seldom been devised, nor a handsomer one. Of course *barbute* had the shape of bascinets. So did the ancient Corinthian helmets, yet they were no logical development of anything. However, argument is pointless. There can be no final proof.

THE SALLET AND THE BEVOR

The *barbuta* seems never to have become fashionable in western Europe or Germany. But the celata was adopted in France early in the fifteenth century (and called the *salade*), while, partly because of cross-fertilisation brought about by the Hundred Years War with England, and partly because of the English going to Italy and importing much Italian armour into England, it became popular with the English too. It soon spread to Germany, so much so that, having almost entirely superseded the old bascinet, it became in its turn almost an international style. Nearly every manuscript picture or painting showing men-at-arms in the period 1420—1470 arms them with this style of *celata*, *salade*, or—to use the English name—sallet. By the mid-century a characteristic English–Burgundian style had evolved (Fig. 38 A), while in Germany in the 1460s a very striking mutation had taken place. Its early history in Germany is obscure. There are two references in the archives of Innsbruck, one dated 1425, the other 1426; the first refers to *drei tscheleren* and the second to *drei tscheleden. Tschelede* is clearly a corruption of *celata*, so it probably applies to the exported products of Milan; later in the century we find the words *schaller* and *schallern*, and by the 1460s the distinctive German sou'-wester shape with its long pointed tail had appeared (Fig. 38 B). This style was probably evolved by the crossing of the developed

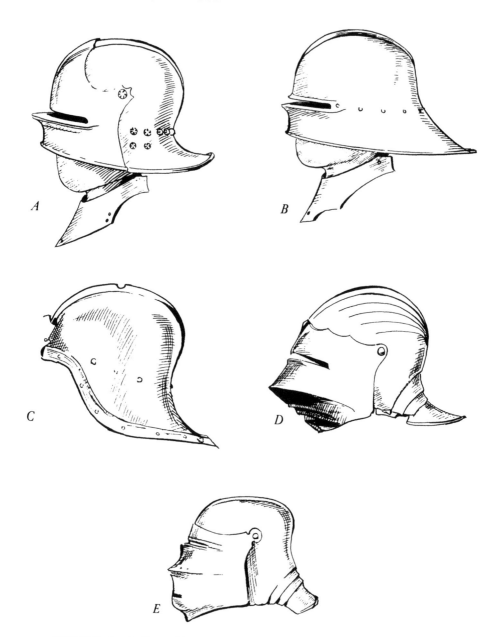

FIGURE 38   Sallet and bevor

Illustration A shows an English/Burgundian style, c. 1450—1475
Illustration B shows a German style, c. 1450—1490
Illustration C shows an Italian style, c. 1490
Ilustrations D and E show later German styles, c. 1500—1510

FIGURE 39   German kettle hat and bevor, c. 1480

German form of kettle hat (Fig. 39) and the *celata*. It remained in use as a tournament helm right into the middle of the sixteenth century, and even later at Dresden.

All these sallets were worn with scoop-shaped bevors to protect the chin. They were fastened round the neck with a strap and the lowest point of the front plate was often fixed to the breastplate by a bolt or a strap or sometimes an arming-point. Some were simply made of two plates, a bevor proper and a gorgetplate, but some had an extra plate at the top which, pivoted at the sides, could fall down to free the mouth. The bevor reached up to the nose, fitting deep inside the front of the sallet, which came down level with the mouth; there was in some a simple slit for vision, but many had movable half-visors, the sight being formed by a gap between the upper edge of the visor and the lower edge of the brow of the helmet. A few had complete visors, mostly after about 1480, with a horizontal slit for vision, a cusped extension above forming a reinforce to the brow. In Philippe de Commynes's description of the confused battle of Montlhery on July 16 1465, between the forces of Louis XI of France and the Lords of the League of the Public Weal, led by Charles, Count of Charolais (soon to become Charles the Rash, Duke of Burgundy), he tells how Charles was wounded in the neck because his bevor fell off:

'Fifteen or sixteen men-at-arms fell on him, just when a party of his own troops had left him. Right away they killed the squire who carved for him, Philip d'Oignies, who was carrying a pennant bearing the Count's arms. Charles was in very great danger and received several blows, amongst them a sword-cut in the throat, the scar of which remained with him for the rest of his life. This happened because he was not wearing his bevor which had been carelessly fastened in the morning and, as I saw myself, fell off.'

In Spain (and probably in the Low Countries as well) the kettle hat evolved an equally distinctive form, though totally different from the others. Called the *cabacete*, its skull was tall and pointed, shaped like an almond-shell cut in half crosswise, and drawn out to a little stalk on top. There was a narrow, downturned brim coming to a sharp point fore and aft (Fig. 40). This became one of the most universally-used open helmets all over Europe until late in the seventeenth century.

In Italy the *celata* developed a new and more shapely form late in the century. The sides became less deep and were swept back gracefully from the face into a long tail over

FIGURE 40   Spanish form of the celata, *known as the* cabacete, *c. 1460*

the neck, often made of three or four lames, and the brow was reinforced by a cusped plate, reminiscent of the brow-reinforce upon Attic helmets (Fig. 38 C). Early in the sixteenth century, some were fitted with large visors which completely covered the face and fitted round under the chin (Fig. 38 D). Some of these began to show a feature which was becoming popular in Spain and the Low Countries, a series of horizontal ridges across the visor below the sights. They could be very handsome, but mostly they were bold and bluff. In Germany a similar headpiece was adopted, but here the back of the skull was moulded closely to the head while a little flat duckbill tail swept out over the neck, made of three or four lames. The helmet of Schott von Hellingen is of this type, as is the helmet of the similar Nuremberg armour in the Glasgow Museum. These are handsome, but most of the German visored sallets are hideous. One in the Wallace Collection (Fig. 38 E) is one of the ugliest pieces of armour in existence. There is another, of rather crude make, in the same collection, which is painted with a tusked monster's mask, more comical than fearsome.

Many of these *celate*, *barbute* and sallets were covered with fabric for funerary purposes; where this survives, it is generally velvet, and is held in place round the rim of the headpiece by a decorative band which might be of gilded copper or silver gilt—or, no doubt, in some cases which naturally enough have not survived, of pure silver or gold; and often the entire surface was covered with beautifully-fashioned leaf or scroll motifs cut out in the same sort of metal. Several survive, notably a splendid one in the Bargello Museum, Florence, which retains its crest of a demi-lion rampant. No typically German sallet survives with a fabric covering, but Dürer's man-at-arms (1498) wears one which by the look of its pale tan colour is covered with leather.

This warrior of Dürer's has a sallet of another distinctive German form, albeit a well-made one. Such sallets were sometimes crude, made for munition purposes to arm the lesser breeds of the military hierarchy. 'Black sallets' they were called, because their surfaces were left rough from the hammer and not glazed; often they were painted with fanciful designs or heraldic charges.

THE BURGONET OR BURGUNDIAN SALLET

In Italy another kind of open helmet appeared early in the sixteenth century. The skull was low and rounded, deep at the back and turned outward like a small brim running

FIGURE 41 *Two burgonets: the one shown in Illustration A is the burgonet of Guidobaldo I of Urbino, dating c. 1505, and the one in Illustration B is worn by an angel in Signorelli's mural, 'The Damned', c. 1500, in Orvieto Cathedral*

round the back of the neck to below the ears. The cheeks were left unprotected, for the sides of the helmet were cut off vertically just by the earlobe. Some protection for the eyes was given by a projecting peak, forged in one with the skull or pivoted at the sides. There is a good example made *c.* 1505 for Guidobaldo I da Montefeltro of Urbino, in the Wallace Collection (Fig. 41 A). This is similar to those worn by the angels in Signorelli's picture at Orvieto, 'The Damned' (Fig. 41 B). Another, of a rather different shape, is in

FIGURE 42 *The burgonet from the Metropolitan Museum, New York, dating c. 1510, shown in A, may be compared with the silver stater of Eucratides of Bactria, 180—150 BC, which is shown in Illustration B*

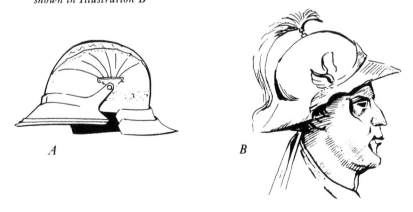

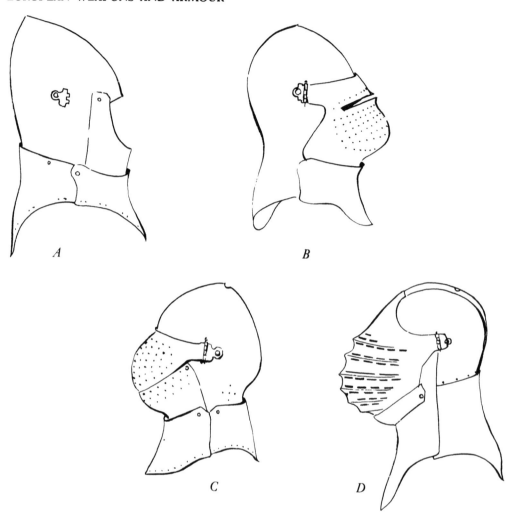

FIGURE 43   The great bascinet
Illustration A, 1390—1410; Illustration B, 1420—1430;
Illustration C, 1430—1460; Illustration D, 1490—1540

the Metropolitan, New York (Fig. 42 A). The skull is cut straight across above the ears; there is a downturned brim extending back to a point above the ears, and a little lower, behind the ears, is a downturned half-brim formed of two overlapping lames. The same thing is to be seen in the silver stater struck for Eucratides I of Bactria c. 180—c. 150 BC (Fig. 42 B). In the Metropolitan example, there is no surviving crest, but the hole to which one was originally fixed is there, as in every other helmet of this period.

These light helmets, called burgonets, later acquired large earflaps hinged to the front edge of the rear part of the skull, and the face was protected by a sort of enlarged bevor, called a 'buffe', which was fastened by a strap round the neck.

THE BASCINET AND THE GREAT BASCINET

The closed bascinet and its successors also stemmed from a primal form of helmet in use at least as early as the Hallstatt period, and possibly earlier. At a point early in the fifteenth century, the mail aventail of the bascinet was replaced by plates. This produced a helmet known to its contemporaries as a great bascinet; it is possible, though by no means certain, that the term *bicoquet* (in England, bycocket) was also applied to it. The great bascinet remained in use until about 1450 when it was almost entirely superseded by the armet, except for foot combat. Figure 43 sets out the evolving forms.

In the period from about 1390—1410, the tall profile of the bascinet (Fig. 43 A) had its apex at the back, with the rear of the skull falling in almost a straight line vertically to the shoulders. Ten years later (Fig. 43 B) it began to curve inwards at the neck, conforming to the shape of the head, and soon the entire helmet had become more close-fitting. At the same time the visor, which had attained a quite exaggerated pointed snout, became rounded, until by about 1430 (Fig. 43 C) it had an ape-like aspect, and by the 1450s had become almost globular. The great bascinet went out of fashion for field use after 1450, but continued as the regular helmet for foot-combat tournament armour well into the sixteenth century (Fig. 43 D).

Many representations occur in art: English brasses of the period 1400—1430 show them (without visors), and they are even more clearly shown in sculptures. Examples of brasses are those of Thomas, Lord Camoys, dated 1419, at Trotton in Sussex, and of Sir John Leventhorpe (1433) at Sawbridgeworth in Herts. Among sculptures, there is a fine effigy, *c.* 1440, in Hoveringham Church in Lincolnshire, and a monument in Arundel Church, Sussex, to John FitzAlan, seventh Earl of Arundel, who died in 1435. The Hoveringham effigy shows the rather earlier form, the FitzAlan one the more close-fitting style (Fig. 44).

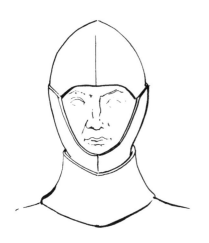

In the earlier ones, the plates which replaced the aventail reproduced its cape-like shape, so that the opening was wide enough to go easily over the head, but once the helmet began to be narrowed by the closer fit, it became necessary to pivot at the sides the front gorgetplate and the bevor which fitted inside it to narrow the face-opening, so that by pulling the front and back plates apart, the opening could be made big enough to allow the head to pass through. In many great bascinets, the rear gorget plate was forged in one with the skull, and they were generally fastened to the breastplate and backplate by straps or staples, and did not turn; the head moved inside the helmet.

FIGURE 44   *The great bascinet from the effigy of John FitzAlan, seventh Earl of Arundel, c. 1435* (Arundel, Sussex)

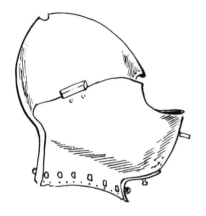

FIGURE 45   Early form of the armet, Milanese,
c. 1420 (The Armoury, Churburg)

THE ARMET

The term 'armet' was used in the fifteenth and early sixteenth centuries to denote any kind of closed helmet, but modern scholars have applied it to a particular type of headpiece, originating in Italy, which was constructed upon a different principle from the great bascinet.

Both the armet and the bascinet were used side by side until the 1450s, when the bascinet went out of popular favour.

The earliest surviving armet, which is now in Mr Gwynn's collection, but was once in the Churburg armoury, is Milanese, and dates c. 1420 (Fig. 45). At a glance, the profile of this looks not unlike that of a close-fitting great bascinet. The apex of the skull is towards the middle of the head, and the rear line conforms with the contours of head and neck in a manner not followed by the bascinet until some time later. The mechanics of this helmet are such that we must assume that it was not so much a chance development from an existing helmet type as a positive invention on the part of an armourer or a fighting man. The skull was cut off horizontally above the ears, leaving only a very narrow, tail-like piece following the line of the back of the head. To the lower rim of the skull were hinged two deep cheekplates which met edge to edge across the 'tail' at the back, and were drawn well forward in front of the face to overlap at the chin, where they were held in position by a spring-pin engaging in a hole. No visor has survived—indeed, it is possible that it never had one.

These helmets have often been referred to in modern times as armets à rondelle, by reason of a strange feature: a little stalk projecting from the lower part of the 'tail' where it curves in to the neck, upon the end of which is fixed, mushroom-like, a little flat disc. This is too flimsy a construction to have been intended as reinforcement for the point where cheekplates and tail overlapped; its use is connected with another piece of armour worn with the armet as a reinforce for the front of it. This, now referred to as a 'wrapper', was a tall plate standing up in front of the visor, completely covering it on the left side. (An opponent's lance, couched under the right arm, was pointed forward at an angle across the horse's neck so that it struck upon the left side, and for this reason all the extra reinforcing pieces so popular in the sixteenth century were made to cover the left hand, arm, and shoulder, and the left side of the head. The armet's wrapper was not the earliest of such extra pieces; reinforcing 'barbers' were used on joust helms during the fourteenth century.) The wrapper covered the left of the visor back to the ear, and curved a little round to the right side; below the chin were two overlapped gorgetplates projecting downward over the cheek. This wrapper was attached by passing a strap round the neck of the armet, fastened with a buckle at the side. It has been suggested that the stalk-and-disc was a

*FIGURE 46   The method of attaching an armet's
visor to the helmet-skull*

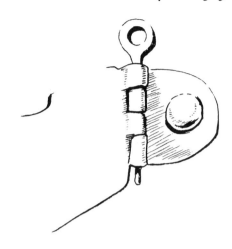

protection for the strap, and that the stalk
served to prevent its riding downward.

The armet's visor was still fixed by the same
method as the bascinet's, by means of two
pieces of metal pivoted to the skull above the
ears, their leading edges formed as half of a
hinge. The backward-reaching arms of the
visor had their rear edges formed as the other
half-hinge. When the visor was put on, the
hinges engaged, and were secured by pins, held
to the pivot-pieces by small chains (Fig. 46).
This method remained in use upon armets
until the 1520s, and was rarely used for tilt helms or for the later close helmets which
succeeded the armet. The early example from Churburg, however, had its problematical
visor attached by a staple and pin at the front of the chin, a method not so far found
elsewhere.

This kind of armet, with its wrapper, can be seen in Uccello's
three pictures, 'The Battle of San Romano'. Many of the armets here show a feature which, until it was recently matched
by the discovery of an actual example, had been regarded as
something of the artist's fancy: the forward lower edge of the
brow, which formed the upper edge of the sight, was cut upward in two shallow arches over the eyes. There is now, in
the collection of the *Cavalliere* Luigi Marzoli at Brescia, an armet with this feature.

The Uccello pictures also show the tall, elaborate crests
worn by many of the men-at-arms on top of their helmets. A
good number of crests survive, some upon decorated *celate* and
some detached, but none upon an armet, though at Churburg one of the armets retains the fitting to which a crest, probably made of some light stuff such as buckram or leather, or
even paper, could be attached. It is in the form of a steel stem
made of three flat lengths of spring steel, which are welded at
the top and splay out loose at the bottom, the end of each
spring-leaf being here finished with a slot, with a projection below it (Fig. 47). When the loose ends of the springs were

*FIGURE 47   The fitment for attaching a crest to the skull of an
armet*

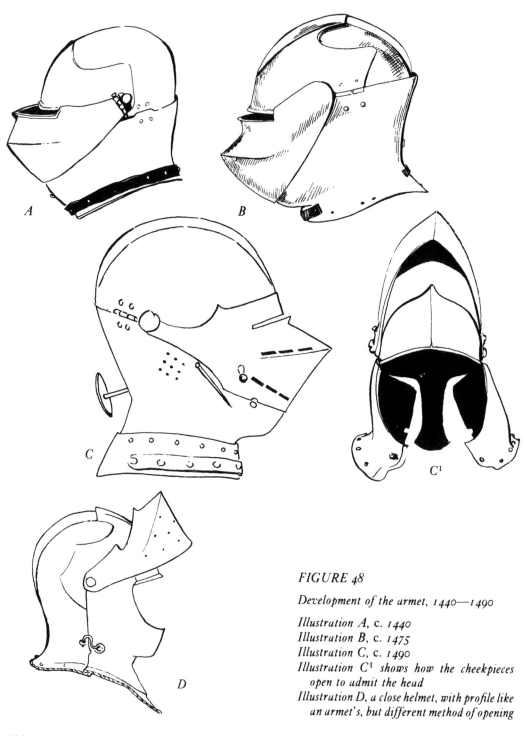

FIGURE 48

Development of the armet, 1440—1490

Illustration A, c. 1440
Illustration B, c. 1475
Illustration C, c. 1490
Illustration C¹ shows how the cheekpieces
    open to admit the head
Illustration D, a close helmet, with profile like
    an armet's, but different method of opening

FIGURE 49   A German variant of the armet, c. 1440

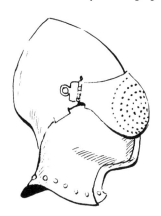

FIGURE 49   A German variant of the armet, c. 1440

pressed together, the stem could be inserted into a hole in the crown of the helmet-skull; when released, the leaves would spread out, allowing the slots to engage with the edges of the hole, and holding the stem firmly in place.

The armet carried a rudimentary aventail. A piece of mail, fastened to a strip of leather, was secured along the whole length of the bottom of each cheekplate by being sandwiched between the plate itself and a strip of metal, the whole being fixed by small rivets. The hinges of the cheekplates were put inside the helmet to protect them from damage and to obviate their presenting a lodgement for the bite of a blade. All that is visible from the outside are the heads of the rivets which secured the hinges; in many cases, these were filed flush with the surface. In a few examples there is a small flange, forged out of the rim of the skull, projecting at a downward angle over the hinge as an added protection.

While in the 1430s and 1440s the great bascinet in Germany and in western Europe was becoming more closely shaped to the head and neck, in Italy the armet, which had begun by being shaped like this, now grew more and more like the old bascinet, the line of the chin and the back of the head becoming straight, almost vertical (Fig. 48 A). It was not until the 1460s that the definite form of chin and neck began to reappear. Figures 48 B and C show later developments.

In Germany the armet was not, apparently, very popular. An early example, not unlike the early one in the Gwynn collection, is in Berlin (illustrated above, Fig. 49). This is shaped very closely round the neck, and the upper edges of the cheekplates are not cut straight across, but instead curve and sweep down to the nape. The small visor is still in position, secured by the traditional pivot-hinge-and-pin method, but it is a rather shapeless saucer-like affair, just covering the small face-opening; both sight and breath are supplied by numerous small holes.

THE CLOSE HELMET

Late in the fifteenth century, an earlier mechanical system was revived to enclose the head, producing what is now always known as the close helmet. In the sixteenth century it was known by many names, 'armet' among them.

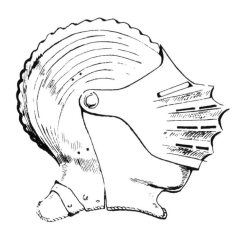

FIGURE 50   An early form of the close helmet, German, c. 1510

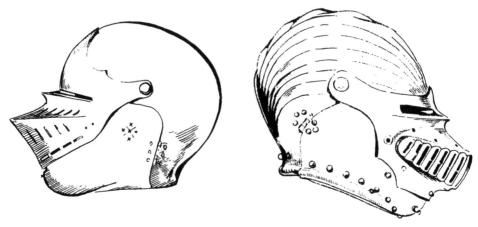

FIGURE 51 (Left)   A Germany armet, c. 1510; note how the cheekpieces are hinged at the
                    side behind the ears, not, as in Italian armets, at the top above them

FIGURE 52 (Right)   A 'Maximilian' armet of 'Augsburg' form, c. 1520; this may be
                    compared with the 'Nuremberg' form in Figure 50

The skull was built like that of a great bascinet, but now it was small and close-fitting, carried down almost to the shoulders at the back and cut off vertically in the front, level with the ears. Chin and cheeks were protected by a close-fitting bevor pivoted at the sides of the skull above the ears. To this same pivot was attached the visor (Fig. 50).

Between 1500 and 1530 a bewildering variety of close helmets was produced, as well as armets and visored sallets which were, in many cases, almost exactly the same shape (Figs 51, 52). The difference lay in the method of opening the helmet. Some of the earliest and most confusing close helmets are a group of Anglo-Flemish ones, which have the same profile as the later Italian armets, the only difference being in construction (Fig. 48 D).

Perhaps the most familiar close helmet of this period is the so-called 'Maximilian' form which 'went with' Maximilian armour. Like the armour, some of these helmets had skulls decorated with fluting, while others were quite plain. They generally had skulls of a pronouncedly globular shape, finished across the top with a low comb, generally roped (in a few cases there are three such combs). The skull fitted closely at the back, and three—sometimes four—overlapping lames projected abruptly outward in the form of a short, square tail to protect the nape and the atlas bone. The visor was quite large, coming upward over the brow and overlapping the bevor in front to a depth of about half an inch (some 10 mm); sight was provided by two horizontal slits in front of the eyes, and the 'snout' of the visor was in many cases furnished with deep horizontal ridges, varying in number from three to six, giving it a bellows-like shape (see Figure 50, above). The profiles of these bellows visors vary strongly, some being handsome and well-formed, but a great many, often of excellent quality, ill-shaped and ugly. Another form popular in the 'Maximilian' style had instead of bellows-like ridges, a flat pug-nosed snout, more or less rectangular, projecting a little way outward from the profile-line of the visor, and carried backward on both sides almost as far as the trailing edges (see Fig. 52, above). These snouts were almost invariably vertically-fluted and pierced with slots for breathing—as of course were the indentations upon a bellows visor. A few of these helmets had visors of the sparrow's-beak form, but with eye-slits cut in the front, and some were beaten into the form of grotesque masks, with human, animal, or bird faces.

The Germans produced a modified form of the armet after about 1515, where the cheekplates, instead of being hinged by their horizontal upper edges to the lower edge of the skull, were now hinged by their vertical rear edges, cut short just behind the ears, to the front edges of a greatly broadened tail. This form of helmet went on being used until the 1560s. In profile it was exactly the same as the contemporary close helmet; only the method of opening differed. A very rare form had the entire bevor made in one, hinged by a rear edge to the tail and closing across the face like a gate, being secured by a spring-pin to the opposite edge of the tail.

There was another general difference between Maximilian close helmets and the very similar armets: the close helmet, until perhaps 1520 or thereabouts, nearly always had its short flat tail and the lower rims of its skull piece and bevor splayed out to project downward over the rim of the collar, while the armet had its corresponding lower edge strongly turned over inwards to form a hollow rim which, when the helmet was shut, fitted closely over the turned-over rim of the collar, thus forming a fairly impenetrable joint. By 1525 it seems to have become a matter of personal choice whether a close helmet had this kind of fitting or an 'open' one; but the armets always had the closed rim.

GROTESQUE VISORS

There are many helmets surviving with 'grotesque' visors which were probably worn with 'costume' armours, though of the ones described earlier (pp. 101—2), two have no visors (these being Charles V's little ones) and another, Wilhelm von Rogendorf's, has an ordinary helmet, though it is etched and gilded *en suite* with the decoration on his enormously-puffed armour. The dubious costume armour in the Metropolitan, New York, has a most elegant helmet, the skull fluted and etched, with a hideous, hook-nosed, middle-aged face, fat and moustached and sour. In the Kienbusch collection there is a similar helmet whose visor is formed of a kind of half-man's, half-lion's face, but with an entirely human mouth stretched in a huge, toothy grin, suggesting infinite *bonhomie*. The most notable example is on a helmet in the Tower of London, all that survives of the armour made by Konrad Seusenhofer for Henry VIII, by Maximilian's order, at the same time as he was making the little harness for the Emperor's grandson (p. 99). It is in the shape of a mask, just filling the face-opening and fastening upon the forehead, and this mask is in the form of a slightly caricatured portrait of Maximilian himself. It seems as if he enjoyed letting his armourer beat out his long hooked nose and wolfish smile, with an addition which was obviously an unfortunate characteristic of this unconventional prince —a dewdrop hanging from the tip of the nose, faithfully preserved for us in Seusenhofer's iron.

HELMET LININGS

All of these helmets, whether open or closed, were of course fitted with linings. Many tomb effigies show the linings inside the great helms upon which the stone warriors' heads rest, but from the end of the fourteenth century onward, many linings from ordinary helmets have survived more or less intact. They were made of fabric—canvas, linen, soft leather—cut into a series of triangles, with the bases sewn to a stout strap which ran round the inside of the helmet at hat-band level and was fixed to the skull by rivets, and the apices, at the crown of the skull, joined by a drawstring which could be tightened or loosened as required. These linings were made double, so that they could be stuffed. Hay, horsehair, wool, straw, have all been found in surviving linings. The wearer's own long hair, bunched up into an arming-cap, gave added protection. The bevors worn with sallets, as well as the integral bevors of close helmets, were often padded as well, though sometimes the chin was protected not by a lining in the bevor, but by a thick rolled bandage round the chin and jaw.

Open helmets were made fast to the head, then as now, by chinstraps fixed to the lining-strap just forward of the ears and fastened under the chin by a buckle; and probably so too were armets and close helmets.

BIBLIOGRAPHY

See the list of material given at the end of Chapter 4.

CHAPTER SIX

SWORDS OF THE SIXTEENTH CENTURY

'The shorte Sword,' wrote George Silver, Gentleman, 'and Sword and Dagger are perfect good weapons, and especially in service of the Prince. What a brave weapon is a short sharpe light Sword, to carie, to draw, to be nimble withall, to strike, to cut, to thrust both strong and quicke. And what a goodly defence is a strong single hilt, when men are clustering and hurling together, especially where varietie of weapons be, in their motions to defend the hand, head, face, and bodies, from blowes, that shalbe given sometimes with Swordes, sometimes with two handed Swordes, Battell Axe, Halbardes, or blacke Billes, and sometimes men shalbe so neare together that they shall have no space, scarce to use the blades of their Swordes belowe their wastes, then their hilts (their handes being aloft) defendeth from the blowes, their handes, armes, heads, faces and bodies: then they lay on, having the use of blowes and Gripes, and manie times in hurling together, scope is given to turne downe their points, with violent thrusts at their faces, and bodies, by reason of the shortnesses of their blades, to the mightie annoyance, discomfort and great destruction of their enimies. One valiant man with a Sword in his hand, will doe better service then ten Italians, or Italienated with the Rapiers.'

George Silver's *Paradoxes of Defence*, quoted above, was published in London in 1599, a perfect example of the conservative, gentlemanly fighting man trying his best to set back the clock. His treatise is 'an Admonition to the noble, ancient, victorious, valiant and most brave nation of Englishmen to beware of false teachers of defence', and it epitomises, with all the prejudices of the conservative Englishman, the conflict of opinion which surged around the forms and usage of the sword during the sixteenth century. With the development in the last decades of the preceding century of the *espada ropera*, the sword worn with the civilian gown as distinct from the arming-sword worn with military harness, and the establishment early in the sixteenth century of Schools of Fence which began to organise and develop formalised swordplay where the weapon itself served for defence as well as attack, the controversy was launched. One of the principal tenets of this new philosophy of the sword was that a thrust was more effective, swifter and more lethal, than any cut. It was also more difficult to perform; a man with a sword in his hand will slash instinctively, whereas to make a timed, accurate and powerful thrust calls for a degree of control which can only be attained through training. Silver deplores this:

'They teach men to butcher one another here at home, wherewith they cannot hurt their enimies abroad in warre. For when battells are ioyned, and come to the charge, there is no roome for them to draw their bird-spits; and when they have them, what can they doe with them? Can they pierce his corslet with the pointe? Can they unlace his helmet, unbuckle his armour, hew asunder their pikes with a Stocata, a Riversa, a Dritta, a Stramasone or such like tempestuous terms? No, these toyes are fit for children, not for men, for stragling boyes of the camps to murder poultrie, not for men of honour to try the battell with their foes. This I have for the trial of the truth, betweene the short Sworde and the long Rapier for the saving of the life of our English gallants who are sent to certayne death by their uncertaine fights and for abandoning of that mischievous and imperfect weapon, which serves to kill our friends in peace, but cannot much hurt our foes in warre.'

He does not mince his words. Further on, he sets himself to prove that a cut reaches its target, by going round an arc, more quickly than a thrust, which has to go along its chord. He is at pains to demonstrate that the arc is shorter. But the rapier had come to stay, in spite of reactionary Englishmen.

FOUR FAMILIES OF SWORDS

During the sixteenth century and the first quarter of the seventeenth (which have to be taken together as a single period in studying the development of the sword) there were four principal families of long sword in use.

First was the old knightly war sword which became the 'Bastard' or 'Hand-and-a-Half' sword round about 1500 and remained almost unaltered in its simple form until about 1520, after which it acquired a more complex hilt; towards the end of the century it mutated into the proto-typical forms of the regional types of broadsword of the seventeenth and eighteenth centuries.

Secondly there was the '*Estoc*', so popular in the last half of the fifteenth century for single-fights in the *champ clos*, which lasted on into the sixteenth, becoming by the end of the century a specialised weapon for use on horseback.

Third is the weapon which Silver calls the 'shorte Sword', though he makes it plain that he means a weapon with a blade some thirty-eight inches long (95 cm). This kind of sword (of which there are countless survivors) is generally lumped together with the rapier, which is misleading, for it is a far less specialised weapon. English compromise has produced the tautologous and somewhat dubious name of 'Sword-Rapier' for it, while German scholars tend to call it the '*Degen*' or '*Reitschwert*', 'knight's sword' or 'cavalry sword', which is what it is—the immediate successor of the old knightly arming-sword, a serviceable weapon 'to strike, to cut, to thruste both strong and quicke', useful in war.

And fourthly, of course, that most Romantick of weapons, the 'Rapier'.

During this period, along with the four 'families' of long sword went a host of miscellaneous short swords (among which is only one really classifiable 'family', that of the '*Landsknecht* sword'), but these must be treated on their own.

If each of these 'families' is treated separately, it is possible, to a limited extent, to make a typological classification of hilt-forms. When in *The Sword in the Age of Chivalry* I presented a typology of the medieval sword, I laid stress upon the need to classify each one in its entirety, hilt and blade as one unit; but with the sixteenth century we are faced with an almost infinite variety of far more complex hilt forms, and very many more blade-types to which any of these hilts might be allied, so any typology of swords in this period has to be confined, in a book this size, to a classification of hilts. And since to attempt such classifications in words would be like writing out a specification of the Eiffel Tower bolt by bolt—and about as interesting—I have set them out in visual form. Even so, these typologies will only offer a crude framework upon which individual hilts can be hung in some kind of order—not chronological, nor regional. Merely typological.

But before setting out to deal with this, I need to clarify two points: one, the position in which a sword is considered to be when describing it, and two, the naming of the parts of the hilt according to the nomenclature worked out by recent research, which applies terms in common English use in the seventeenth century: some of these differ from terms which have been accepted for the past hundred years or more.

DESCRIPTIVE POSITION OF SWORDS

As to the first point: modern scholars generally describe a sword as if it were being held in the hand vertically in front of the face with the point upward; yet at the same time swords are invariably shown illustrated in published works, or displayed in museums, the other way round, with the point *down*; so the unlucky student has to reverse the verbal description in his mind while examining illustration or specimen.

There is a respectable tradition in favour of describing a sword in the position in which it is exhibited in museums, hilt up and point down. Common sense suggests this position, and those prototypical swordsmen, the Vikings, always wrote of their swords in saga or poem as if they were seen this way. The names they had for the elements of the hilt, too, reinforce common sense. *Fremir hjaltit*, 'upper hilt', they called the pommel, and *efra hjaltit*, 'lower hilt', the cross. What the Vikings began in the ninth century, I continued in *The Sword in the Age of Chivalry*, so must maintain it here. Besides, when a hilt is decorated with figures or arms or naturalistic motifs, the heads or crests or tops are always towards the pommel; to describe a hilt embellished with classical figures as if the hilt were downward causes the Hercules on the pommel to stand on his head and the Leda and Swan group on the guard to assume an intriguing, though impractical, position. However, when such motifs are etched or engraved upon a *blade*, they nearly always are applied so that they are right way up when the point is uppermost! Each argument cancels the other out, but for the sake of continuity I shall go on as I began, and describe swords as they appear in my illustrations.

NAMING OF THE PARTS OF THE SWORD HILT

In setting out the terms used now for the parts of a 'swept' hilt, that convenient and time-honoured term for almost any hilt fitted to a sword of the sixteenth or seventeenth century, it will be necessary to look at one as if it were held in the right hand horizontally straight out in front of the body, with the plane of the blade vertical, the knuckles facing outward to the right and the finger-ends inward to the left. Thus the principal guards for the knuckles and the back of the hand are on the outside while those for the thumb are inside. The uppermost *quillon* will be the 'forward *quillon*', the other the 'rear *quillon*'. The elements of the hilt are the pommel, generally furnished with a button to take the riveted-over end of the tang, the grip, the *quillons*, the arms of the hilt (sometimes called the branches—this feature was dubbed the *pas d'âne* a century ago, but the correct meaning

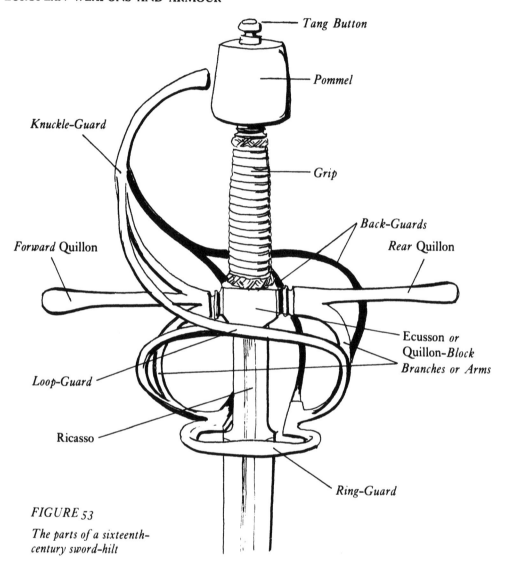

Tang Button

Pommel

Knuckle-Guard

Grip

Back-Guards

Forward Quillon

Rear Quillon

Ecusson *or*
Quillon-*Block*

Branches or Arms

Loop-Guard

Ricasso

Ring-Guard

FIGURE 53

*The parts of a sixteenth-
century sword-hilt*

of that term denotes the double shell-guards of the eighteenth-century smallsword: it is
still very widely used, though misapplied), and the knuckle-guard. On the outside of the
hilt are the outer ring-guards, the lower one of which connects the two ends of the arms
across the outside of the blade, while the upper ring springs from the outside of the
quillons. These upper rings generally spring from the *écusson* or *quillon*-block to form an
oval, but occasionally the 'ring' is bow-shaped, one end springing from a point well along
the forward *quillon* and the other from a similar point on the rear *quillon.* Sometimes the
lower ring encloses a small pierced steel plate, called appropriately a *stichblatt,* 'thrust-

leaf', in German and, somewhat misleadingly, a 'shell' in English. On the inside of the hilt are inside guards and sometimes, mostly in bastard swords and broadswords, a thumb ring (*q.v.* below). In some hilts the back-guards consist of rings similar to those on the outside, sometimes smaller. If there are extra guards linking knuckle-guard with upper ring, or upper ring with lower ring, they are loop-guards. Figure 53 will demonstrate these terms better than words can describe them.

The hilts of all these long swords can be said to stem from the hilt, with arms in addition to its plain cross, which developed in Spain late in the fifteenth century. Early in the sixteenth century, the hilts fitted to the purely military bastard sword began to differ from those fitted to the civilian *espada ropera*, which as early as about 1530 developed the form which the Victorians, not inappropriately, called 'swept' because of the sweeping lines of its guards. After about 1550 these 'swept' hilts, in bewildering variety, were fitted indiscriminately to *reitschwerte*, rapiers and broadswords, while at the same period the specialised bastard sword hilts which had developed by the 1520s began to go out of use, giving way to those forms which became so widely used all over north-west Europe on broadswords, while the specialised hilts of the *estoc* also began to develop.

THE BASTARD OR HAND-AND-A-HALF SWORD

There has always been some uncertainty as to whether the expression 'bastard sword', first in use (as far as we know) in the fifteenth century, really applied to the large weapon previously known as the 'grete war sword' or 'great sword' or *épée de guerre*. However, for lack of any indication that it ought to be applied to any other weapon, the late nineteenth century firmly used it as a label to denote the later manifestations of the great sword, and the name has stuck. It may also have been applied to little swords.

The great war sword (fully dealt with in *The Sword in the Age of Chivalry*) seems to have been in general use throughout most of western Europe, for we find it clearly shown in the art of most countries from Finland to Spain, and many specimens have been dug up. Most are of a generally German style, and Italy does not show them in art at all, nor can one say that there are any clear Italian examples surviving.

German in fashion too are all the bastard hilt-forms which emerged between about 1505 and 1550. On stylistic grounds as well as the much more positive evidence of regional distribution, most seem to have originated in southern Germany and Switzerland.

The typological diagrams (Fig. 54) show twelve distinct types and sub-types of bastard hilt-forms, though in fact there must be very many more sub-types, for almost every individual hilt forms a sub-type of its own.

These twelve types fall naturally into four main groups: those with straight (very occasionally curved) *quillons* and single side-rings on the outside and inside of the hilt; those with curved *quillons* (very occasionally straight) and guards consisting of one or two arms, a ring-guard, and a loop back-guard from the extremity of the arm to the inside of the rear *quillon*; those with *quillons*, arms and double rings; and those with these elements plus knuckle-guards and additional loop-guards of various forms producing a sort of half-basket guard for the back of the hand.

Features of these hilts are:

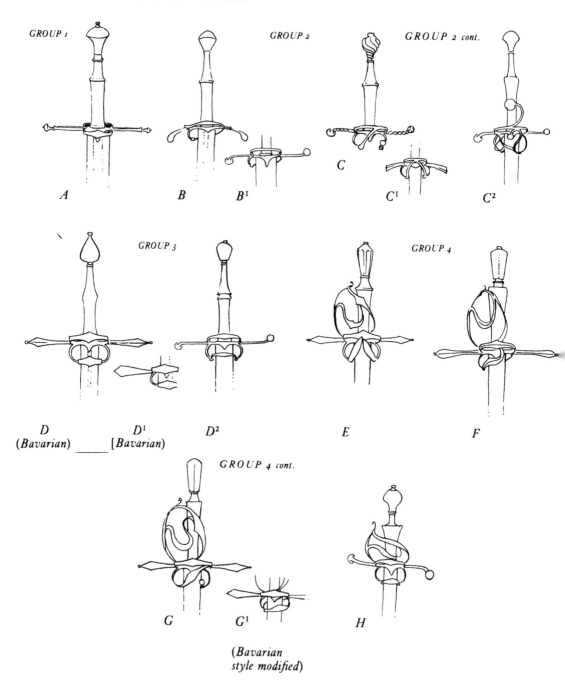

FIGURE 54   Some Bastard Sword hilt-types

A a fashion during the first quarter of the century to make use of pommels of a more or less pear-shape, grooved and twisted sideways—'writhen' is a good old English adjective much used nowadays to define this very distinctive German pommel; it was generally matched in a hilt with *quillon*-terminals of the same form.

B a South German (Bavarian) fashion for *quillons* of a flat ribbon-like section ending in spear-shaped terminals, often finished with a tiny knop on the point, and guards of the same section with a kind of angular widening in the middle.

GERMAN AND BAVARIAN STYLES

The distinctive *quillon*-form I have mentioned in point **B** above may be found as early as *c*. 1480 in a Bavarian carved wooden statuette of St George displayed in the Bavarian National Museum, Munich. In the middle years of the century this particular style of *quillon* and guard seems to have become almost exclusively Saxon; a great many of the swords and daggers dating *c*. 1540—1570 in the Historisches Museum, Dresden, (which is also the Dresden Royal Armoury) are of this kind. So are a number made for Swedish and Danish monarchs and their noblemen, and decorated by Saxon artist-craftsmen. With this form of *quillon* and guard often went a pommel as distinctive, of a shape which is difficult to describe in words. To call it pear-shaped or fig-shaped would be misleading; it is really more like a drop of some slightly viscous fluid, or the drop-shaped earrings fashionable half a century ago (Fig. 54). This pommel form was used indiscriminately either way up, as the illustrations show. A form which never seems to have been used with the ribbon-section *quillons* was the true pear-shape, either writhen or plain. If one such is found on a sword with an otherwise Bavarian hilt, it is probably a recent association. A second distinctive form of mid-century pommel usually fitted to these hilts is shaped like a tall truncated cone with a very slight taper, mounted with the broader 'base' at the top.

The use of these forms of pommel was confined to bastard sword hilts; they are not found on rapier or *reitschwert* hilts except in a very few isolated, and often suspect, cases. They are indeed the final mutations of the old 'scent-stopper' forms used on war swords during the late fourteenth and the fifteenth centuries, and had all gone out of use by 1560.

THE SWISS STYLE

The Swiss style, as distinct from the Bavarian, used the same forms of hilt as those in Group 4, but the section of guards and *quillons* was always circular or rhomboidal, never of the flat ribbon section, and pear-shaped pommels were almost always used with them. As the illustrations show (Fig. 55), the actual formation of the guards, though the same in principle, differed in technical application.

One of these Swiss forms calls for particular mention. It is characterised by a knuckle-guard and secondary knuckle-guard, generally, though not always, without any connecting loop-guards, which only reach to a point halfway up the grip, where occasionally they were held to the grip itself by a steel band (Fig. 55). Another peculiarity of these Swiss hilts is that the 'ring'-guard, where there are no arms of the hilt, is in the form of a trefoil or cinquefoil, sometimes repeated in the back-guard. This rather odd form of guard seems only to have been incorporated with these Swiss hilts (irrespective of the length of the

131

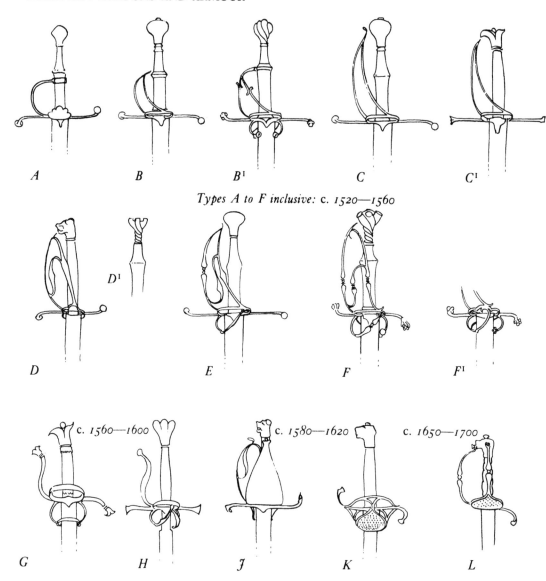

A B B¹ C C¹

Types A to F inclusive: c. 1520—1560

D D¹ E F F¹

c. 1560—1600   c. 1580—1620   c. 1650—1700

G H J K L

FIGURE 55   *Swiss Bastard Sword hilt-types*

knuckle-guards) during a period between, say, 1514 and 1540. There are fine surviving examples: one in the Wallace Collection, London (A 482), having half-length knuckle-guards; one in the Schweizerisches Landesmuseum, Zürich (LM 16218), having full-length knuckle-guards with a loop-guard; and one in the collection of Mr E. A. Christensen, Copenhagen (Number 85), having, rather unusually, arms and no knuckle-guards. This kind of hilt was also used with the long curved 'sabre' blade, originating in

Switzerland in about 1520, which in that country had almost entirely superseded the long straight bastard sword by the mid-century, and which will be discussed later (p. 155).

Round about 1560 an entirely new form of pommel had come into being, shaped like a barrel. This was used very extensively upon the hilts of *reitschwerte*, rapiers and broadswords from about 1560—1630, but there is a group of late bastard swords which also have it. The two most notable examples are in the Schweizerisches Landesmuseum, Zürich; both have barrel-shaped pommels, long, evenly-tapering grips, and straight *quillons* with arms and double ring-guards, which are repeated as back-guards on the inside of the hilt. Both are elaborately embellished with inlaid silver decoration and are datable, for both belonged to Swiss noblemen in the service of the Crown of France, Gugelberg von Moos, who died in 1616, and Rudolf von Schauenstein, whose name is etched upon the blade with the date 1614; on the pommel of his sword are portrait heads in silver of Henri IV of France and the young Louis XIII. A number of bastard swords with similar though plain blackened hilts are preserved in the armoury at Graz, though these are assumed to date some fifty years earlier than the Zürich ones.

There are two swords of similar shape but with drop-shaped pommels and gold damascened decoration of the kind often called 'Milanese' but also associated with the Spanish goldsmith Diego de Cajas who was working from about 1525—1565. One of these is in the Kunsthistorisches Museum, the other in the Odescalchi Collection, Rome, and both are presumed to date *c.* 1550 and may be of Italian origin though of German style.

THE SPANISH STYLE

In Spain the bastard sword in the form we have been considering was occasionally made rather late; but the regional derivative of the old war sword was a small two-hand sword, referred to as a *montante* or an *espadon*. The hilt had a longer grip than the bastard sword and just a plain cross in the old style, but some five inches (12·5 cm) below the cross the blade bore two lugs, forged out of each edge in the manner of the familiar two-hander (*q.v.* below, p. 146). There are a few swords, however, dating from the mid-century, which are of the same basic form as Bavarian hilts D and D¹, but the pommels, *quillons* and guards are of a very clearly defined shape which nowadays is generally accepted as being Spanish (Fig. 56). In the Vogel Collection, Zürich, is one with double ring-guards, while in the Odescalchi Collection, Rome, is another where the lower ring-guard is replaced by two prongs curving upward over the outside of the hilt, springing from each end of the arms. Surviving examples of these hilts are rare.

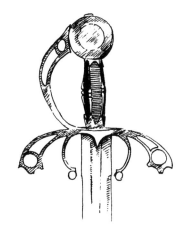

FIGURE 56   Hilt of an espada ropera, c. 1510, showing
guards of Spanish style (Collection of
Mr E. A. Christensen)

THE BOAR SWORD

Until late in the fifteenth century, it seems that large game of a dangerous kind—that is, boar and bear—was hunted with ordinary arming-swords. The famous Hunting Tapestries from Hardwick Hall, made in 1444 as a gift for the wedding of Henry VI of England with Margaret of Anjou, show scenes of boar- and bear-hunting where these animals are being attacked with ordinary swords as well as boar spears. A boar spear was a specialised kind of weapon with a short haft, some five to six feet long (1·5 to 1·8 metres), a broad leaf-shaped head and a horizontal bar, either fitted through a hole in the socket of the blade or fixed to it by a toggle. This bar was to prevent the boar's running up the spear and goring his opponent—they were ferocious and heavy animals, and would charge at high speed; even a spear going in through the mouth or throat would not stop the charge, and the point of a plain spear or sword would emerge at the farther end of the boar, to the great discomfort of the man who held it, for a boar does not die easily. The cross-bar prevented this. However, late in the fifteenth century a specialised type of sword, a cross between a plain bastard sword and a boar spear, was developed. The blade was long, of square or rectangular section for some thirty to thirty-six inches (75—90 cm); it then broadened to a spear-shaped point, with a square opening in its upper part to take the transverse bar. A few of these swords survive, notably one belonging, with a sort of inevitability, one feels, to the Emperor Maximilian. This one is in the Kunsthistorisches Museum, Vienna. Henry VIII's inventory calls them 'boar-spear' swords.

THE *ESTOC* OR TUCK

Estocs or tucks ('tuck' being simply an English way of pronouncing the French word *estoc*, meaning literally 'a thrust') were in use from the late fourteenth century, though at that date they were just long-bladed swords, generally with short grips, whose blades were very narrow and generally of a thick, flattened-hexagonal section. By the latter half of the fifteenth century they had become larger, of the size of bastard swords, and similarly hilted, with blades of an extremely stout triangular section. Until the third decade of the sixteenth century, they remained much the same, but after about 1530 the hilts tended to become much shorter, and the blade-section sometimes reverted to the flat hexagon (like the beautiful *estoc* of Henri II of France, now in the Musée de l'Armée, Paris) or became broader at the hilt and of a more conventional shape (like a most elegant sword, probably Spanish, in the Wallace Collection, London: A 517).

Late in the sixteenth century a totally new hilt-form came into being, most surviving examples being found on long tucks or short falchions; again, southern Germany seems to have been the region which produced it, for one of its more common forms has the typical spear-ended *quillons*. These hilts have no arms, only an atrophied ring below the outer *quillon* to take the end of the single back-guard with its width set at right-angles to the plane of the blade. In front of the hilt is a large triangular plate, always pierced with a series of openings in the shape of hearts. The pommel is square in plan, shaped like an angular mushroom, or a very blunt four-sided pyramid with curved edges, and the grip, always very short, is of oval section considerably wider below the pommel than above the *quillons* (Fig. 57 A). The blades of such swords were rarely excessively long, averaging about

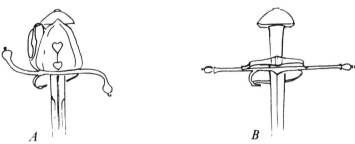

FIGURE 57   *Tuck hilts: the hilt shown in Illustration A is often found mounted with broadsword, backsword or sabre blades; the hilt shown in Illustration B is found with tuck blades only*

three feet (90 cm); they are usually of flat hexagonal section, fullered singly at the forte and with a marked *ricasso*—just, in fact, like the usual kind of rather stout *reitschwert* blade.

A parallel development in the tuck hilt, also, it seems, emanating from southern Germany, has the same form of grip and pommel (as a rule—though there *are* examples with ovoid ones) and long straight *quillons*, sometimes of typical Saxon shape, sometimes of plain circular section with knobbed terminals; but in place of the knuckle-guard and plate complex, there is a large ring-guard, often rectangular in plan, springing from the outside of the *quillons*, fitted with a flat plate which was generally decorated more or less elaborately. The back-guard is the same small loop-and-ring arrangement (Fig. 57 B). The blades of most of *these* tucks are very narrow and of the old strong triangular section—a form, incidentally, which was to reappear late in the seventeenth century in the blades of smallswords and again in the eighteenth century in bayonets.

A feature which many of these swords have is a solid sheath-cover made of metal attached to the underside of the hilt, which, when the sword was sheathed, fitted neatly over the top of the scabbard to keep rain from reaching the blade, like the old 'chappe' or rainguard of previous centuries (*S in A of C*, p. 133, Plates 22 A, 42 A, 45).

THE *REITSCHWERT* OR 'SWORD' AND THE RAPIER

Both the *reitschwert* and the rapier sprang from the same root, the mid-fifteenth-century arming-sword. During the 1460s in the Iberian peninsula this had developed a hilt more complex than the old medieval cross hilt, for at about that time Spanish fighting men had perceived that the sword was the only weapon which could be used equally well for defence and for attack. Because of this, a man with a sword could look after himself even if he wore no armour, for he could put aside all attacks on him by parrying the thrusts or strokes of other weapons with the blade of his sword. Such action, however, had its own perils. A sword held with the forefinger of the right hand passed over the outside arm of the cross can be controlled better and used more powerfully, particularly in parrying, than if the finger is safe inside the guard of the cross; but when it is beyond this protection there is a risk that the parried blade may slide down the parrying one and slice the finger off. So an extra guard, a small ring or branch, was devised just in front of the cross to protect the finger.

The earliest date which it is so far possible to give for the use of this feature is the early fourteenth century, the evidence being a sword of that date in the Armeria Reale, Turin; but it was in Spain and in Portugal in the 1460s that it seems first to have come to its full development, two branches being added in front of the cross-guard, one on either side of the blade. There is ample pictorial evidence for this in the paintings of the Portuguese Nuño Gonçalves, all dating between 1460 and *c.* 1471. Other evidence is provided by the great tapestries which were woven in 1475 to commemorate the taking of Arzila, captured from the Moors in 1471 by the King of Portugal. Some twenty or thirty years ago copies of these splendid tapestries were exhibited at Burlington House in London.

In the following classification of 'swept' hilt types I have called this hilt with a cross and two branches the 'Basic Hilt', for upon it all subsequent forms were built.

The Spaniards of the late fifteenth century, finding that they could go about armed with these swords but without armour in comparative safety, began to call such weapons *espadas roperas*, 'swords of the robe', worn with ordinary civil dress. Early in the sixteenth century, when this practice had spread across Europe, the French condensed the name and called the weapon *la rapière*, which the English further mutated to 'rapier'.

And here confusion arises, for all over Europe every sword which was not positively a bastard sword or a two-hander might be called a rapier; but it was not until the second half of the century that the true specialised rapier, a weapon suitable for thrusting only, came into being. It is a modern terminological convenience to separate the *reitschwert* (or 'Sword', to which I give a capital letter in the hope of reducing ambiguity) and the rapier into distinct and independent types, even though both had the same origin. The *reitschwert* was mainly military in its functions, but the rapier was purely civil. The first was a logical development, through the *espada ropera*, of the old-fashioned arming-sword, suitable for combat on foot or on horseback, and practical on the battlefield. Not so the rapier. It was a highly-specialised weapon, designed for the formal swordplay developed by the Italians after about 1550 from the style of fight which the Spanish masters of arms had worked out earlier in the century. It was only suitable for civil combat on foot—or, as Silver says, 'to murder poultrie'. It was utterly unsuited to any sort of use in war.

But although each type was developed for a different purpose, each was mounted with the same kind of 'swept' hilt. It is the form of the blade, not the style of the hilt, which determines the type. The true rapier, as modern terminology knows it, took its own line of development after 1560, and by the 1590s it had become the 'bird-spit' of Silver's condemnation.

The 'apish toye' despised by Silver was a blade of hexagonal or square section, rarely more than three-eighths of an inch wide (9·5 mm) and sometimes as much as fifty inches long (1·25 metres), mounted in one form or another of the classic 'swept' hilt. Whether we agree with Silver's prejudices or not, there are shortcomings, practical and aesthetic, about the rapier which cannot be attributed to the *reitschwert*, or Sword.

Some of the most elegant weapons ever to be made are *reitschwerte*. When you get a combination of a well-proportioned, restrained, well-designed hilt mounted with a graceful, practical blade which is neither feeble nor clumsy, you have something comparable with a fine work of art (Plates 9A, 9B).

If you see a group of *reitschwerte* and rapiers together in a collection, however, it will be noticed that in most cases all are labelled 'Swept-Hilt Rapier', and this is no surprise, since they all look so much alike. Some, which by definition really are rapiers, will have blades of modest length, while others, which are *reitschwerte*, will have extremely long blades. Even in their own day there was probably little rigid distinction, for most *reitschwerte*, or Swords, could be used like rapiers, *though there is no true rapier that can be used like a Sword*.

The only way in which the average rapier can be distinguished from the average Sword is by its 'look' and its feel in the hand. If you feel that you could cut off a man's arm with it, then it is a sword. If not, a rapier. The blade of a sword has to fulfil three requirements: it must have reasonable weight at the centre of percussion, or optimal striking point; at the same place it must have reasonable breadth; and its section must be *flat*. You cannot shear through flesh and bone with a thick blade with an edge at an obtuse angle. You need a blade of flat section, with a fine edge coming off at an extremely acute angle. It is the breadth of the blade and the angle of its edge that determines the weapon's use. If a blade is needed to thrust, it must be narrow, rigid, and of a thick section. It may not need an edge at all, in the true cutting sense of the word. As to length, this was a matter of personal choice dictated by the style of the owner's method of fight rather than his physical dimensions.

The true age of the rapier was not until the early seventeenth century. Silver's *bêtes noires* proliferated rapidly after 1600, and Dumas' d'Artagnan (active in real life from about 1620 until the 1660s) was the true fictional exponent of rapier-fighting.

By the 1530s, extra guards had been added to the basic form of the *espada ropera* hilt, making a simple, yet very effective, hilt which was still popular a century later, when it was often fitted to the long rapier; but after 1550 more elaborate guards came into use, the infinite complexities of which baffle description and defy classification. Even so, making allowance for the fact that almost every individual hilt is a sub-type on its own, it is possible (by the exercise perhaps of much faith and a good measure of imagination) to distinguish a number of types gathered into six groups: enough at least to give a local habitation and a name to any sword or rapier, preserving the student from the necessity of being forced to call everything a 'Swept-Hilt Rapier'. But it is very little use in pinpointing date or provenance.

It has seemed expedient in working out a typology of these hilts (Fig. 58) to group them under six headings, thus: Primary Hilt, Basic Hilt, Quarter Hilt, Half Hilt, Three-Quarter Hilt and Full Hilt. The 'Primary' hilt is the old cross-hilt upon which all subsequent patterns were based. The 'Basic' hilt is the Spanish one (p. 135) with a cross and two arms. If the lower extremities of these arms have a lower ring joining them across the outside of the blade, or a pair of short projecting prongs in lieu, it is a 'Quarter' hilt. The addition of a side-ring on the *quillons* makes a 'Half' hilt. A 'Three-Quarter' hilt has two side-rings and the forward *quillon* bent upwards and lengthened to form a knuckle-guard. A 'Full' hilt has two or more side-rings, arms, *quillons* and a knuckle-guard. Within these groupings we have sub-types according to the presence of varying loop-guards and back-guards; these can be reduced to a simple formula, as, for example, 'Full hilt B with back-guards C', or described in full, as in the *Catalogue Raisonné* of a collection.

QUARTER HILT

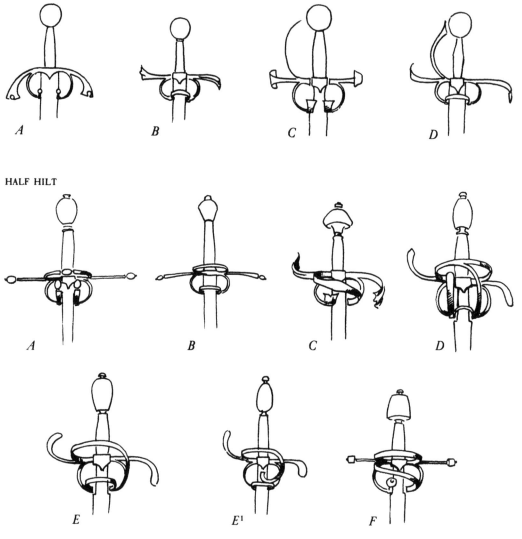

HALF HILT

Into this rough and ready framework all the variants and sub-types can be fitted; but it must be remembered that full hilts were in use by 1540, while basic hilts were still in use in 1620—indeed, in the England of James I the old primary hilt came into fashion again, probably as a manifestation of the curious social effects caused by a fashionable revival (given impetus by the Society of Antiquaries, newly founded in 1598) of interest in the Norman Conquest and a modish curiosity about medieval life and thought. There are many swords of the second or third decades of the seventeenth century which could easily be assumed to be of the last decades of the fifteenth century, while there are many others

THREE–QUARTER HILT

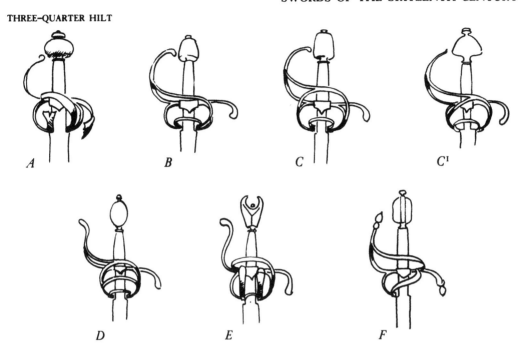

FIGURE 58 *A typological grouping of the commoner forms of 'swept' hilt on* reitschwert *and rapier* (continued overleaf)

> *QUARTER HILTS, shown on the facing page:*
> quillons, *arms, one lower ring or equivalent guard;*
> *generally with a single-loop back-guard*

> *HALF HILTS, shown on the facing page:*
> quillons, *arms, double ring or equivalent guards;*
> *generally with a double-loop back-guard*

> *THREE-QUARTER HILTS, shown above:*
> *single rear* quillon, *arms, double (sometimes treble) ring-guards,*
> *loop-guard and knuckle-guard;*
> *generally with double-loop back-guards*

dating from the 1540s and 1550s which could easily be mistaken for seventeenth-century ones. Further verbal description of these hilts is pointless; the following pages show the typology of most of the 'swept' hilts, with comment where necessary.

THE SHORT SWORD OF THE SIXTEENTH CENTURY

The many varieties of short sword in use during this period are mostly unclassifiable. Some, like the *landsknecht* sword (described below) or the Swiss sword, were military and possessed a certain classifiable uniformity; but the great mass of short swords, used for

FULL HILT

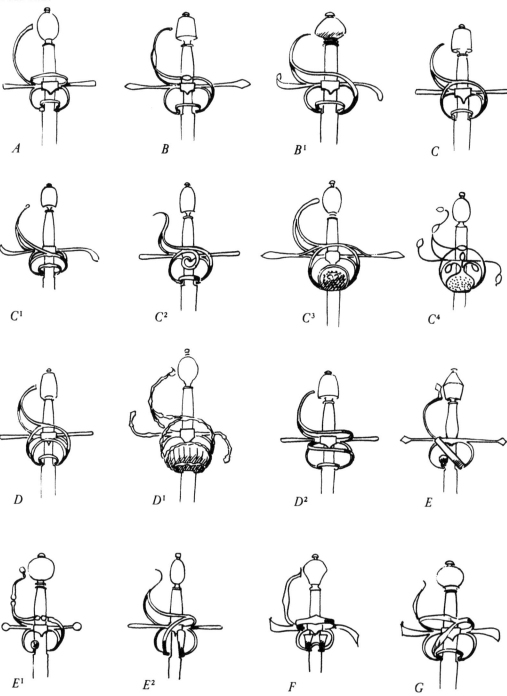

A   B   B¹   C

C¹   C²   C³   C⁴

D   D¹   D²   E

E¹   E²   F   G

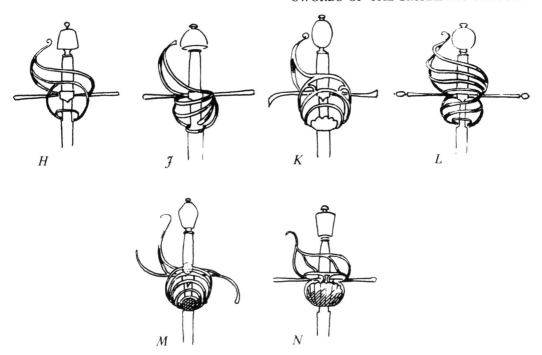

FIGURE 58   *A continuation of the typological grouping of the commoner forms of 'swept'*
hilt on reitschwert *and* rapier (begun overleaf)

FULL HILTS, shown on the facing page and above: forward and rear
quillons, arms, multiple ring-guards and loop-guards and knuckle-guard;
generally with treble-loop back-guards, though sometimes the back-guards are a
mirror-image of the forward-guards, especially after 1600

hunting or, more commonly, as handy protection against assault in city streets in the dark,
do not. Many such weapons were of the finest quality, but the majority were quite crude;
practical, but not particularly beautiful. Often an old broken blade would be sharpened up
and mounted in a simple hilt; sometimes a complete short blade of an earlier century
would be re-used; and many hilts appear almost literally to have been home-made.

There is one group of swords, however, which does have a certain uniform type of hilt.
They seem to date around the middle years of the sixteenth century, between 1535—1565,
and common to many is a curious asymmetrical pommel incorporating in its decoration a
spiral. Even in hilts otherwise totally bare of any decoration, a strong spiral is engraved on
the sides of the pommel. Elaborate examples of this pommel are formed like ram's-heads
with tight curly-spiral horns; this probably gave rise to the simple spiral on more ordinary
pommels.

FIGURE 59   A landsknecht sword c. 1540 cf Fig. 84

THE *LANDSKNECHT* SWORD

The familiar *landsknecht* sword with its characteristic grip and its figure-of-eight *quillons* had little scope for much variation. It seems first to have come into use in the opening decade of the sixteenth century, though any specific pictorial evidence for it is lacking before about 1515; but it continued to be popular as a side-arm for mercenary infantry well up into the mid-century. During the 1530s and 1540s, some *landsknecht* swords were fitted with added guards to the hilt, which actually produced what was almost the first type of basket hilt; there can be little doubt that the forms of basket hilt which began to emerge round about 1600 in England, Scandinavia and southern Germany owed as much of their development to these hilts of the 1540s (Fig. 59) as they did to the complex guards of some of the bastard swords of the same period.

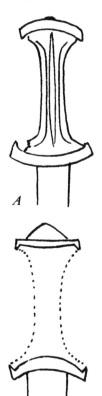

THE SWISS *HAUSWEHR*

Parallel with the *landsknecht* sword, though with a much longer ancestry (for it was in use at least by the early fifteenth century), was the short 'Swiss' sword with its rather primitive wooden hilt—a form, incidentally, found preserved upon a Frankish scramasax of the sixth century (Fig. 60). Many survive in Swiss museums, though there seem to be very few elsewhere. The Germans and Swiss, with their usual aptitude, called them *Hauswehren*, 'house-weapons'. A few long swords with such grips survive.

THE GAELIC SWORD

There were two types of cross-hilt prevalent during the sixteenth century which are quite unique in their regional development. I refer to the Irish sword and the sword used in the Highlands and Islands of Scotland—not the claymore (the Gaelic *claidheamh mòr*, 'great sword') which is a two-hander and will be discussed in its proper place, but the shorter single-handed and bastard swords of those lands, here referred to as 'Gaelic' swords. The Scottish type with its distinctive hilt was shown on many tomb slabs of

A

B

FIGURE 60   The hilt of a Swiss hauswehr and the hilt of a Frankish scramasax are here compared

FIGURE 61   *Hilt of a mid-sixteenth-century Gaelic sword*
(National Museum of Antiquities, Dublin)

the sixteenth century, but that it was in use early in the fifteenth century is proved by a slab in the now deserted graveyard at Kinkell in Aberdeenshire. This is a monument to Sir Robert de Greenlaw, who was killed in the fight at Harlaw in 1411. He is shown wearing the characteristic 'camail and jupon' armour of the International style, with one of these swords (most exactly paralleled by a surviving example in the Kienbusch Collection, Philadelphia) by his side (*A of W*, Plate 18). Another of these swords, dated in the fifteenth century, is in the National Museum of Antiquities, Edinburgh. Others have been found in Ireland: four now repose in the National Museum of Ireland, Dublin. Two of these have double-edged, single-fullered blades of a typical medieval shape, one a rather unusual blade where the fuller stops short some six inches (15 cm) from the hilt, where it is marked with a stamped lion rampant within a shield; the fourth has a four-inch (10 cm) *ricasso*. Only one retains enough of its pommel to show that it is of the form of the Kinkell grave slab and the Kienbusch sword. These pommels, which are of wheel-form with extremely tall rivet-blocks, are of frail construction, made of moulded pieces of thin bronze plate brazed together—hence the loss of most of them. One of these, brought up from the bottom of Lough Gara in County Sligo, was resting in the bottom of a dug-out canoe, together with a pole-axe head of a typically Irish/Scots form used in the sixteenth century by the mercenary Scots who fought in the endless Irish wars, the *Gallóglách* or 'Galloglasses'.

In the same museum are two other swords of the same generic form; the arms of their crosses do not, however, expand into the spoon-like forms of the others (Fig. 61). One must assume that this is a contemporary alternative style of cross. It is also necessary to mention two other fragmentary swords, for neither has any parallel. The first, of which only part of the hilt and a few inches of the blade remain, was once a fine decorated sword, by the shape of its blade with a strong *ricasso* and three fullers, dating from the first half of the sixteenth century; the one remaining arm of its cross, which sticks straight out at right-angles to the axis of the blade, is of a complex section, as of a diamond flattened on top, and ends in a quatrefoil like the Scottish claymores. The grip is narrow, of octagonal section, and is covered with a sleeve of iron over a willow-wood core. The lower part of this sleeve is formed in one with the *écusson* of the cross, a separate octagonal tube of iron providing the upper part. Between the two pieces of the sleeve are three small bronze rings, which have what appear to be settings for precious stones. Traces of incised ornament remain upon the grip. The pommel is (so far) unique, for it is double. The sides of the iron sleeve are continued upward, but are bent out either side to form a figure 8, to which are brazed the sides of the pommels. The lower one is of a deep convex section, with a gilt-bronze rosette in the centre of each side; the upper one is flat, with flat gilt-

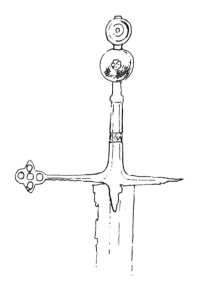

FIGURE 62   Hilt of a mid-sixteenth-century Irish
sword, found near Monastrevin

bronze plates applied to each side, decorated with
incised circles. Between the two pommels is a flat
piece of iron decorated with stylised foliage against
a hatched ground. This sword was found in County
Kildare, in the River Barrow near Monastrevin,
and similar swords (except that they do not have
double pommels) are shown on grave slabs at Kiels
on the island of Jura, at Kilmoruy in the Hebrides,
and at Kilmichael in Argyll, so it is probably of
Scots origin rather than Irish (Fig. 62).

The other fragment was found in a bog near
Ballylin, Offaly, and was once a true claymore in
respect of its size, with a mixture of Renaissance
and Celtic ornament on the bronze plates
which are riveted to the sides of the remaining arm of the cross—Renaissance foliage on one side, Celtic interlace on the other, and Renaissance spiral fluting on the
langet and on the outer edge of the arm. Unfortunately the pommel is missing, so the
principal clue to its place of origin is lacking. The end of the arm is pierced with a quatrefoil opening reminiscent of the shape of the openwork terminals of the Scottish claymore crosses, or the exactly similar openings on the ends of English crosses on swords of
the period 1275—1325 (*A of W*, p. 235, Fig. 118). This once
beautiful sword remains an enigma; one can at least say that
it is uncompromisingly British.

Three swords which are unmistakably Irish are in the same
museum. These are of a distinctive form whose origin is borne
out by a number of sixteenth-century drawings—by Dürer and
Lucas de Heere among others (Fig. 63). The pommel of this
sword-type is in the form of a hollow ring, crossed vertically
by the tang of the blade running through, while the cross-
guards, narrow near the *écusson*, broaden abruptly towards
the end into flat, bow-tie shapes, sharply recurved forwards
and backwards horizontally. A similar form of cross was in use
in Hungary from about 1400 until the seventeenth century,
combined with a very distinctive pommel shaped a little like a
shield with a central boss (Fig. 82 A, p. 184). Similar swords
seem to have been used in Venice during the period 1470—
1550 or thereabouts, to arm the guards of the Council of Ten.

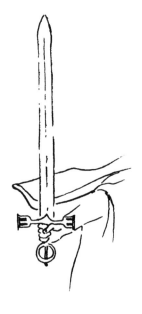

FIGURE 63   Drawing by Lucas de Heere of a Gaelic sword

BIBLIOGRAPHY

Blair, Claude, *A Royal Swordsmith and Damascener*, Met. Museum Journal, Volume 3, 1970

Castle, Egerton, *Schools and Masters of Fence*, London, 1885

Charles, R. J., *L'Epée en France au XVI Siècle*, Vaabenshistoriske Aarboge No. Xc, Copenhagen, 1961

Dufty, R., (Ed.) *European Swords and Daggers in the Tower of London*, London, 1974

Grassi, Giacomo, *His True Arte of Defence . . . Englished by I. G. (Gentleman)*, London, 1594

Hayes McCoy, G. A., *Sixteenth-Century Irish Swords in the National Museum of Ireland*, Dublin, 1959

Hayward, J. F., *Victoria and Albert Museum, Swords and Daggers*, London, 1951

Hoff, Arne, and Schepelern, H. D., and Boesen, Gudmund, *Royal Arms at Rosenborg*, Copenhagen, 1956

Orso, Filippo, *MS Book of Sword Designs, 1554*, Victoria and Albert Museum, London

Silver, George (Matthey, Cyril G. R., Ed.), *Paradoxes of Defence*, London, 1898

Wegeli, Dr Rudolf, *Inventar der Waffensammlung, Bern*, Volume II, Bern, 1929

Weyersberg, Albert, *Solinger Schwertschmiede der 16 und 17 Jahrhunderts*, Solingen, 1926

The list of material given at the end of Chapter Eleven also applies here.

CHAPTER SEVEN

THE TWO-HAND SWORD

The two-hander has great appeal to the Romantick and to small boys, but it is not a practical kind of weapon, nor has it much claim to beauty of form. Most surviving examples are downright ugly, yet a few, notably the earlier forms of the period 1500—1540, can be very handsome. Its origins were as far back as the thirteenth century; there are one or two very big swords which can be dated between 1250 and 1300 which qualify for the epithet 'Twahandswerds', but they are just ordinary warswords (Type XIII^a) writ large. The specialised two-hander, with its characteristic lugs on the blade (the Germans call them, very cogently, *parierhaken*, 'parrying-hooks') may well have had its origin in the Spanish *espadon* of the early fifteenth century. There is one in the Royal Armoury, Madrid, which has all the characteristics of a two-hander: grip and cross very long in proportion to the blade, long *ricasso* and *parierhaken*—yet it is only a little longer than a typical 'grete war sword' of the same period. Two others, rather later in date, were sold in the De Cosson sale at Sotheby's in 1929 (Lots 88 and 89), though these were more of the proportion of true two-handers. In the same sale there was a bastard sword of *c.* 1450 (Lot 96), unusual in that below the cross was a *ricasso* with two lugs below it; it is now in the Royal Ontario Museum, Toronto.

There is also a distinctive group of late-fifteenth and early-sixteenth-century 'twahandswerds' which might be said to be English. At present only five are known to me, all of which have an English provenance leading me to risk suggesting an English origin. All share the same characteristics: a grip long in proportion to the blade, which is sharply tapered and of a flattened diamond section, small (in proportion) vaguely spherical pommels, and long crosses with knobbed ends and, in two cases, well-formed and shapely *écussons*. These swords are currently located as follows: one in the British Museum, London; one at Oriel College, Oxford; one in the City Museum, York; one in the Tower of London; and one, sold at Christie's in 1977, now in a private collection in London. At least two of these seem, by the appearance of their surfaces, to have been preserved in churches: these are the British Museum sword and the one sold at Christie's. The York sword and the Tower of London sword have been so rigorously cleaned that we can no longer judge what their patination was like.

A few early two-handers are far more handsome than the familiar later ones of the second half of the century. Some of these early ones, such as two in the Wallace Collection in London (A 472 and A 473), though of true two-hander length, are very slender and graceful. Of this particular two, A 472 is Italian and A 473 is German; in this case, the

FIGURE 64   *A two-hand sword, c. 1525*
(Schweizerisches Landesmuseum,
Zürich)

German sword is the more slender—indeed, the blade is so slim that if it were not for the two small *parierhaken* it would look like an outsize rapier blade. There is a similar one in the Odescalchi Collection in Rome and another in the Kienbusch Collection in Philadelphia.

There are a good many two-handers which are shaped and hilted like outsize bastard swords. One such was sold in the Helbing Galleries in Munich in 1908 (Lot 68); it was illustrated in the catalogue. It is of a characteristic Saxon form, with an enormous 'bastard' hilt with flat ribbon-section guards, spear-ended *quillons* and a conical faceted pommel. The blade has no *parierhaken*, but there is a *ricasso*. In the Schweizerisches Landesmuseum, Zürich, there is a beautiful sword which comes halfway between these two kinds of two-hander. Its hilt is of the typical early form (Fig. 64), like the Wallace Collection ones (but more elegant than either), but the blade is plain; there is quite a short *ricasso*, and no lugs.

THE CLAIDHEAMH MÒR

The Highland Scots produced a specialised form of 'twahandit swordis' early in the sixteenth century: the *claidheamh mòr*, or 'claymore'. Unlike the Continental varieties, stemming directly from the single-handed types as shown on the Greenlaw slab (*q.v.* above, p. 143), these weapons were generally a little shorter than the Continental ones, the broad blades having *ricassos* but no lugs. The *quillons*—crosses they should be called, for they are not associated with any other kind of guard—are a definite sort of deliberate Gaelic archaism, throwbacks to the medieval war sword. They are straight, slanting downward at an angle from the *écusson*, which is furnished on either side with a long langet protruding downward over the blade. Each terminal ends in an openwork quatrefoil element forged out of the end of the arm of the cross. The grips are long, but do not have the 'shoulders' so characteristic of Continental examples, and for pommels they are furnished with odd little flimsy versions of the thirteenth-century 'wheel' pommel (*S in A of C*, Type J). There are comparatively few genuine examples of these weapons outside public collections, though there are plenty of rather unconvincing fakes; nor are there very many in museums. The largest collections are in the Museum and Art Gallery in Glasgow,

147

the Museum of Antiquities in Edinburgh, and the Armouries of the Tower of London; there is one in Mr R. T. Gwynn's Collection (once in Clontarf Castle) and one in the Kienbusch Collection in Philadelphia. The finest example is one in Glasgow, 'the Whitelaw Sword'.

THE LOWLAND SWORD

Another form of 'twahandit' sword used by the Scots was more like the Continental variety. Grip and pommel are similar to the *claidheamh mòr*, except that the pommels are generally spherical, but the crosses are long, slender, straight with sharply downturned ends, and of circular section, as are the ring-guards on either side. Blades are similar in form (*ricasso* but no lugs) to the Highland swords, but tend to be rather longer. These are generally known as 'Lowland swords', never as *claidheamh mòr*, but it is difficult to be sure that each type was only used in the regions to which it is attributed. Another form of the Lowland sword can hardly be called handsome, and examples are rare. Blade and pommel are similar to those of the commoner Lowland swords, but the guards are not. There is a downturned rear *quillon* and a longer, upturned, forward one, while on the outside of the hilt is a large, shell-shaped guard springing from the *quillon*-block and extending back over the knuckles of the forward hand (Plate 8 C).

THE USE OF THE TWO-HANDER

Swords such as these could only be used by muscular individuals fighting on foot; they had no real place in the close press of battle. In the fifteenth century, men began to use them in single-fights and in the defence of castle or town walls, and occasionally they were employed on the field of battle by picked men detailed to guard the banner. In the sixteenth century the Swiss and the *landsknechte* adopted the two-hander for this purpose, along with halberdiers, to guard the Cantonal or Company Colours. Giacomo de Grassi, late in the sixteenth century, praises it:

'One may with it, as a Galleon among many Gallies, resist many swords and other weapons; therefore in the wars it is used to be placed near unto the Ensign or Auncient for the defence thereof because being of itself able to contend with many it may better safeguard the same. And because its weight and bigness require great strength, therefore those only are allotted to the handling thereof which are mighty and big to behold, great and strong in body and of stout and valiant courage.'

In Tudor England, Colour guards who carried two-hand swords were known as 'whifflers' (an onomatopeiac word?), and their weapons were sometimes referred to as 'slaughter swords'. This comes from the German—another instance of the Teutonic aptitude at finding the *mot juste* for a weapon. They called these two-handers *schlachtschwerter*, 'battle swords'. In the English tongue, we find the word in 'slaughter', 'slaugh', 'slath' or 'slough' swords.

LATER TWO-HANDERS

The *claidheamh mòr* was carried in a scabbard slung across the back, in the manner of the Lee-Enfield rifle, but the Continental two-hander was carried at the slope over the shoulder, as many Swiss and German drawings and engravings bear witness. These swords, of the second half of the century, were totally unlike their graceful predecessors of the first half. They had a variety of pommels; some were formed as double cones, others were fig-shaped or spherical, and the swords borne by the bodyguard of the Dukes of Brunswick had large boat-shaped pommels which seem to have been peculiar to this particular body of men. The grips were long and generally had some kind of moulding in the middle—not the graceful bottle-shape or shouldered-shape of earlier days. The *quillons* were usually of a flat ribbon-like section, set in the same plane as the blade, with the ends, and sometimes even the mid-parts, tortured into curlicues; some of them were more like pieces of decorative wrought-iron work. They generally had a ring-guard on either side, and, rarely, arms. Often the *ricasso* would be considerably narrower than the blade itself, and the *parierhaken* had grown to exaggerated proportions. Many blades widened noticeably towards the point, while others were forged with wavy edges. Often the *ricasso* was covered with leather. This may have been because this part of the weapon rested on the shoulder when it was carried at the slope, but the motive was more probably to make a comfortable grip for the left hand, when this was brought forward, from its place at the pommel end of the grip, to grasp the *ricasso* when it was necessary to shorten the sword in a fight.

It is reasonable to suppose that weapons as 'fantastick' in their form were designed more to overawe common folk at festivals than to serve the practical needs of the battle-field. Indeed, the Tudor 'whiffler' had a secondary function, to keep crowds in order at procession-time. There are plenty of good, honest, two-hand swords, neat and functional, which are likely to have been what were commonly used in war up to the end of the sixteenth century.

There is in the British Museum, London, an aberrant form of the two-hand weapon which ought to be mentioned. It is hilted as a two-hand sword, in the same manner as the 'English' ones mentioned above, but instead of a sword-blade, there is a stout steel rod of circular section, some three feet long (900 cm), ending in a hammer-and-pick head like a Lucerne hammer. It looks by its form as if it should belong to the period 1480—1520, or thereabouts, but it is actually dated 1651 and has the arms of the Commonwealth on the *quillon*-block: but this of course means very little as they could easily have been added to a weapon a century earlier in date.

I believe this weapon, and others like it (though at present I have seen none), gives evidence that unusual forms of sword-like weapons did in fact exist, as, for instance, the great two-handed glaives carried by mounted, knightly figures in the Maciejowski Bible, *c.* 1250 (*A of W*, pp. 206—207, and p. 48, above). That such weapons were used cannot be doubted, for the veracity of that particular artist cannot be doubted, and evidence that similar forms of blade might be mounted in conventional sword-hilts is given by the smith's mark upon a blade of *c.* 1340, one of a group of marks showing swords or daggers in use between 1300 and 1400. Several have been recorded, all showing more or less carefully rendered swords. This particular one is obviously of the same group, but the blade shown in the mark has a short, narrow rod below the hilt, with a broad cleaver or machete-like blade springing from it.

BIBLIOGRAPHY

Dufty, R., (Ed.), *European Swords and Daggers in the Tower of London*, London, 1974

Scott, J. G., *A Hand-and-a-Half Sword from the River Clyde*, Scottish Art Review, Volume I, No. 9, 1963

Wallace, John, *Scottish Swords and Dirks*, London, 1970

CHAPTER EIGHT

THE CURVED
AND SINGLE-EDGED SWORDS
OF THE SIXTEENTH CENTURY

THE ARCHETYPAL SABRE

It might seem justifiable to assume that the western European sabre developed logically from the medieval falchion (*A of W*, pp. 235—238), but there is little evidence to suggest that it did, and a great deal which very strongly suggests that it did not. As early as the eighth century, swords were in use in eastern Europe whose blades were basically of the same shape, size and weight as English cavalry sabres of the 1796 patterns. Many of these have been found in graves in Hungary and southern Russia, dating from the eighth century to the tenth and eleventh, but the most notable, as well as the best-preserved, is the so-called 'Sword of Charlemagne' in the Treasury in Vienna. Legend has it that the Emperor Otho III, a descendant of Charles the Great, opening the tomb of his ancestor some 130 years after his death, found this sword. Certainly it has been used ceremonially at the coronations of Emperors ever since. At one time it was known as the 'Sword of Attila', an attribution dubious as to date but quite plausible as far as the place of its possible origin was concerned. Swords such as these were more than likely used by the Huns; certainly their descendants used them all over eastern Europe, southern Russia, and what is so loosely called 'the Middle East', a region which in medieval times embraced the Byzantine Empire. In the Victoria and Albert Museum, London, is a vast iron cauldron, of Turkish provenance and dating about 1170. It is decorated with figures of horsemen brandishing sabres of this kind, except that the false edge (that part of the back of the blade, its concave edge, which runs back from the point and is sharpened) is quite short. In the Charlemagne sword and many of the Hungarian ones this extends nearly halfway up the back. We find the same sort of blade in a Macedonian monastic wall-painting of the early fourteenth century, shown in Figure 65 (fully published in *Vesnik*, of Voini Muzei Jugoslavenske Narodne Armije, Belgrade, 1954), and again, four hundred years after, in pictures of Austrian and Hungarian hussars, *c*. 1725–1750.

These works of art show quite clearly where the European sabre came from. They show, too, that the hilt did not change very much, though the interesting thing is that the medieval sabre hilt, as shown on the Victoria and Albert cauldron and the Macedonian wall-painting, was adopted by the Russians, Turks and Egyptians, while the familiar stirrup hilt of the 1796 sabre originated in the West.

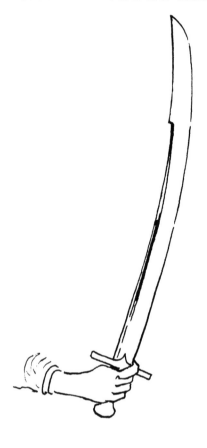

*FIGURE 65   A sabre blade, c. 1330, from a
Macedonian wall-painting*

THE FALCHION

The falchion grew quite naturally out of the Norse sax, and this line of development was covered in *The Archaeology of Weapons*, so I will take up the story late in the fifteenth century, when the falchion was outmoded and sabre-like swords were beginning to find favour. During the later Middle Ages, there were two basic forms of falchion. One form had a blade a little like a butcher's cleaver in shape. The back was straight, and the cutting edge swelled roundly outward near the point (*A of W*, p. 235, Figs 116, 117, 118). The second form had sometimes a straight and sometimes a concavely curved back and a curved cutting edge, the point-end of the back edge being cut out in a strong cusped curve. Both kinds are well represented in medieval art, but the cleaver-like form is rarely seen after about 1370 while the cusped type appears a good deal, particularly in Italian painting of the second half of the fifteenth century. One of the best examples is Pollaiuolo's engraving, 'The Battle of the Naked Men', of 1470. There are countless others too numerous to mention.

This form of blade continued into the sixteenth century in rather insignificant little weapons, but as a type it seems to have gone out of favour by about 1560, and may probably be part of that amorphous host of short anti-footpad weapons.

THE BACK-EDGED SWORD

Some time late in the fifteenth century the true sabre blade began to make its appearance in western and southern Europe, though it had been in common use farther to the East for a couple of centuries. During the mid-fifteenth century, too, a variety of back-edged sword, a kind of primitive spadroon (*q.v.* below, p. 258), had been in fairly common use in the West. Survivors are rare, possibly because they were of little account. One (which may have been found in England) is in the Armouries of the Tower of London, and there is another which was found on the site of the battle of Wakefield (1460). This was sold at Christie's on April 14 1966 (Lot L 76). Both these swords have blades which are straight on the back and slightly curved on the edge. The Tower one, illustrated in *European and American Arms*, by Claude Blair, is a short weapon but the Wakefield one is of average length, being some thirty-three inches overall (85 cm).

It should be noted here that all through the Middle Ages a few back-edged swords were

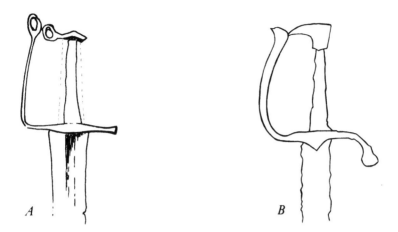

FIGURE 66   Illustration A, (left), *shows a back-edged sword found on the site of the battle of Wakefield (1460); Illustration B shows a short sword, possibly of English origin, now in the Tower of London*

in use. Some of the Norwegian long saxes had blades of the same shape as the Wakefield sword, and occasionally they were curved in the reverse direction from the customary sabre blade's curve, that is, with a convex back and a concave edge.

The interesting thing about the Wakefield sword and its kind is the shape of hilt, for one arm of the cross is bent upward to form a knuckle-guard. The rear arm of the cross of the Tower sword curves downward, but the Wakefield one sticks out straight with a slight swelling at the tip; in both we can see the shape of the eighteenth- and nineteenth-century stirrup hilt developing (Fig. 66). Similar hilts are shown in many fifteenth-century paintings and drawings, always on falchions.

An interesting medieval sword recently dug up in the Thames Embankment, near Blackfriars in London, and now in the Museum of London, has a hilt of this form, yet it looks like a conventional sword of the first half of the fifteenth century (Type XVIIIA) with one arm of its cross turned up, to form a knuckle-guard of a primitive kind. Yet this turned-up arm was forged to *be* turned up—it is half as long again as its fellow, and more slender. It must have been obvious to any medieval fighting man who had suffered a wounded hand that a turned-up cross-arm would help in preventing such a thing from happening, but extremely few hilts exist which have been so treated.

From the La Tène period of the Iron Age, it has been customary to fit swords which have curved back-edged blades with grips of the form perpetuated in the modern military sword, though best seen in the cavalry sabres of the eighteenth and nineteenth centuries. These are generally straight on the back, with a slight midway bulge on the inside and a pommel in the form of a metal cap slightly turned over towards the knuckle-guard's top. Some, particularly those used in eastern Europe in the fifteenth and sixteenth centuries, have the stylised shape of a bird's head.

EARLY SABRES

As well as the two rather crude 'spadroon' back-edged swords in London, there are a few much finer examples. In the Tower of London is a large sabre with an evenly-curved blade etched with figures of St Catherine and St Barbara and stamped with an unusual smith's mark, three double-headed eagles. The hilt is severely plain; the grip is of two plates of wood, fitted on the sandwich principle and fastened with two rivets; it is gently curved and has no pommel but broadens towards the top. The cross, however, is elegantly made with one arm up and the other down, the upcurving knuckle-guard finished with a little curl and the downturned inside arm ending in a double curve. There are etched heraldic roses on the cross, which give some ground for suggesting that the hilt may be of English origin; but there is a similar rose finely etched on the blade of a splendid fifteenth-century Italian arming-sword now in the collection of C. O. von Kienbusch in Philadelphia, so one should be considered with the other. While there is no reason to doubt that the sabre hilt (dating *c.* 1490—1510) might be English, it is doubtful that the Kienbusch sword is—certainly not its blade. However, there is no reason why an Italian-made sword should not have been owned by an Englishman, and etched with a rose after it had come into his possession. Decorative motifs or marks of a national, regional or personal heraldic character which are etched or engraved or inlaid upon arms should be treated very cautiously, for they have often been added at dates long after the actual manufacture of the piece; on the other hand, many are contemporary.

THE *GROSZE MESSER*

These weapons were often carried by noble gentlemen out hunting. Indeed, they are frequently called *jagdschwerter*, 'hunting-swords', or *hirschfänger* (though this last is more usually applied to the smaller hunting-weapons and hangers of the late-seventeenth and the eighteenth centuries). There is another group of South German swords which have been allied with those in this category, though probably on uncertain grounds. Many of them are back-edged bastard swords; some are sabre-bladed bastards, and some are quite small with either straight back-edged blades or curved sabre blades. Characteristic is a long, sandwich-formed grip of wood or horn, or in some cases elaborately-worked steel, often inlaid with small rectangular bits of ebony and mother-of-pearl. Generally, though not always, they have the top of the grip formed to a sort of hat-shaped elevation, with a projection outward towards the outside of the hilt. The most spectacular example is a pair of swords, one straight and one curved, made in 1496 for the Emperor Maximilian, now in the Kunsthistorisches Museum, Vienna. In the same museum are three similar, plainer ones. These weapons have recently been more correctly named *grosze messer*, 'great knives', which is a far better term than *jagdschwerter*, for it is doubtful if they were ever used for boar-hunting (there was a specialised weapon for that, *q.v.* above), and it seems unlikely that anyone would go after stag or hare or bear with a large bastard sword. Many such swords are shown in Hans Burgkmair's engravings in 'The Triumph of Maximilian', drawn before the Emperor's death in 1519.

Illustrations of the incomparable *grosze messer* which Hans Sumersperger of Hall in the Tyrol made for Maximilian in 1496 have been published so many times that I have chosen to illustrate a different, though very similar, sword from the Wallace Collection (A 697) in Plate 8 D. This has the same form of grip, blade and cross, but the guards are more like those on a conventional bastard sword with a ring in front of the cross having a small V-shaped guard inside it and a single-loop thumb-guard behind. The others have either small shell-guards, rectangular in shape, sticking out at right-angles in front of the cross, or, as in Maximilian's, a stout, short bar. The most striking characteristic is the shape of the grip and its decoration—the Wallace example has little plates of silver.

THE SWISS SABRE

Sabres of a purely military character seem first to have been used early in the sixteenth century in South Germany and, particularly, in Switzerland. From the 1520s onward, we can trace a distinct line of development in the Swiss sabre, running through to the end of the seventeenth century. Most of these, especially in the first part of the period, were of hand-and-a-half size, both as to the length of blade and of hilt. Blades were of true sabre form, with a gentle curve and a false edge some one-sixth of the blade's total length, and the hilts were similar to those fitted to the ordinary bastard sword, except that in the majority of cases there was not a conventional pommel but an 'off-centre' one drawn out towards the top of the knuckle-guard. Many of these were in the form of beasts' heads, lions predominating, though many more were of human form—Moors' heads (*i.e.*, Negroid), Saracens' heads (*i.e.*, Arabian), or grotesques.

In Figure 55 on page 132 I have already sketched in diagrammatic form the development of the Swiss sabre hilt, this being the same as the bastard hilt, and while these hilts seem definitely to be of Swiss origin, their use undoubtedly extended very widely.

THE GERMAN SABRE

Round about the 1540s, the German sabre's line of development diverged from that of the Swiss, and in its turn split into two distinct patterns. One seems to have been a direct evolution from the plain one-up, one-down hilts of the late fifteenth century. A large shell,

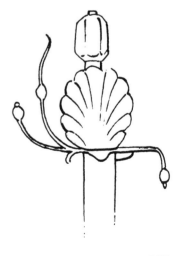

FIGURE 67   A German sabre hilt, with thumb-ring

generally of a literal scallopshell form, was added to the front of the *quillons*, curving up and back almost to the pommel to protect the back of the hand. Between this and the knuckle-guard was often an S-shaped bar, and the thumb was protected by a one-loop thumb-guard. There was frequently another loop or ring fixed at the back of the hilt, to the mid-point of the *quillons*, arching out to meet the thumb-guard at right-angles to the plane of the blade. This was to accommodate the thumb when holding the sword, thus giving a firmer grip.

The other pattern of German sabre hilt was exactly the same as that I have already described as used upon tucks. It had long *quillons*, generally straight though sometimes counter-curved, with spearpoint ends; a large triangular plate was fixed to the front of the *quillons* and curved back over the hand to the pommel, and was almost invariably pierced with two or more heart-shaped openings. Mounted in some of these hilts are very short, stout blades; a good example is in the Armouries of the Tower of London.

EXPERIMENTAL BASKET HILTS

At the turn of the century, *c.* 1600, many experimental forms of 'basket' hilt were being tried out in Germany, some mounted with sabre blades, a few with straight ones. Many are preserved in Norway, for late in the sixteenth century Christian IV of Denmark began to ship consignments of good serviceable German-made swords to Norway, then under the Danish crown, to arm the Norwegian farmers. Some of these are rather crudely made, but others are of excellent form and quality; all are well-designed, and in them we can see clearly the shapes of eighteenth- and nineteenth-century broadswords of which they, among others, were the progenitors (Fig. 68, below).

In fact, in all of the hilt-forms which had evolved by the 1570s we can trace the ancestry of those cavalry and broadsword hilts which became so widely used in the seventeenth and eighteenth centuries and which in some cases survived into the nineteenth: the *schiavona*, the English 'close' hilt so warmly advocated by George Silver, which produced the

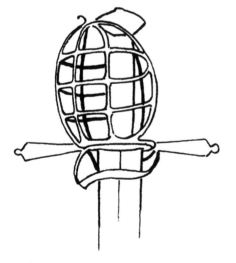

FIGURE 68   A German basket hilt,
c. 1590—1610

Highland 'claymore' hilt and some of the hilts of English dragoon swords, the so-called (erroneously) 'mortuary sword' hilt of the mid-seventeenth century, and the many types of barred hilt used all over Europe in the eighteenth and the nineteenth centuries.

BIBLIOGRAPHY

Dufty, R. (Ed.), *European Swords and Daggers in the Tower of London*, London, 1974

Wegeli, R., *Inventar der Waffensammlung, Bern, Volume II*, Bern, 1929

CHAPTER NINE

SWORD AND RAPIER IN THE SEVENTEENTH CENTURY

CHARACTERISTICS OF SEVENTEENTH-CENTURY HILT-DESIGN

With the second quarter of the seventeenth century, the sword hilt enters a new phase. In keeping with the questing, experimental spirit of the time, the makers and users of swords began to try all sorts of complexities added to the guards of the classic swept hilt, which had been little modified since its many forms had first developed, in and after the 1540s. Though the purpose of these additions was to provide increased protection for the hand against the thrusting 'uncertaine fights' which in spite of Silver and his kind had come to stay, their forms were strongly influenced by fashionable trends. These trends had in fact begun to influence the 'look' of hilts as early as the second decade of the century, for although the classic swept hilt remained in fashionable use until the 1640s, there are certain nuances, certain indefinable characteristics in their shape, proportion and decoration, which make clear distinctions between, say, a Full Hilt A of the 1580s and a similar one of the 1620s.

These nuances are best appreciated if one looks at them in conjunction with the general appearance of men of fashion, dressed, curled, booted and spurred. Let us contrast a portrait of the 1580s with one of 1623 (Plate 10). Everything about the later one is more flamboyant; the sitter's great feathered hat: his lovelocks: his fiercely-curled moustache and beard: his deep lace collar in place of the stiff ruff: his big slashed sleeves, vast breeches and boots with their wide turned-down tops, and the enormous flaps on his spur-straps. The spurs themselves are in striking contrast to the small, neat spurs of the earlier period. The buckles are big and elaborate, and the long upturned necks bear big star-shaped rowels. Now contrast two swept hilts of the same two periods (Plate 10) and it becomes plain how the sword-cutlery fits the style of the fashionable turn-out.

Early-seventeenth-century swept hilts tend to be curly; to be furnished with large decorated knops or discs or mouldings at the salient points of the guards; to have a little curl or a ring-like process at the top end of the knuckle-guard; to have excessively slender guards or very long *quillons*—always a tendency to extremes, often bordering upon the Fantastick.

PROBLEMS OF DATING HILT-TYPES

Inevitable dating problems arise during this period, although the material available as evidence is more plentiful than for any earlier period. There are countless portraits painted between about 1615 and 1660 by the most competent artists—competent, I mean, in the sense that their accurate delineation of details of costume is unsurpassed. To have available for study portraits of sword hilts by Rembrandt, Velázquez, Rubens, Van Dyck, Frans Hals, Gerard van Honthorst and many others, is of immense value. Even so, there can be no certainty in dating a hilt-type simply because it appears in a dated portrait. One must not assume that if, say, on June 1 1623 a man of thirty-seven went for a first sitting to Rubens, he had gone out on May 31, the day before, and bought himself a new sword, of the very latest pattern, to be painted with. No. He probably wore his best rapier, which he may have possessed since he was twenty in 1606. He might even have worn a sword of his father's, or a favourite uncle's—the possibilities are as endless as the ground is uncertain.

Few actual swords bear dates, and when they do they present problems more often than they offer solutions. Many swords—particularly their blades—of the first half of the seventeenth century bear obviously spurious 'dates', such as 1414, 1444, 1515, which were never intended to be anything other than groups of figures with some significance, cabalistic perhaps, to which at present we do not have the key. All that can be said of such markings is that they may fairly safely be said to date within the first half of the century.

Some, of course, have perfectly credible dates, like the big bastard sword of Rudolf von Schauenstein in the Schweizerisches Landesmuseum, Zürich, and the swords in the Musée de l'Armée, Paris, which were given to Henri IV by the City of Paris, one in 1601 and another dated 1599; or the sword given by that monarch to Ambrogio de Spinola, the Spanish Commander-in-Chief in Flanders in 1605, now in the Metropolitan Museum, New York. However, in Paris is a splendid rapier (Fig. 69) whose hilt, and the date upon whose blade, would seem to make a nonsense of some of the remarks I have just made regarding the knobbed decoration of the salient parts of hilts being a characteristic of the early seventeenth century. It has just such decorative treatment, and is dated 1570. In the Victoria and Albert Museum, London, is a sword which is even handsomer; this has a hilt so similar to the Paris one that it might have been made by the same craftsman within a month or two: yet for stylistic reasons this has been labelled as c. 1620. The particular stylistic reason in this case

FIGURE 69   *A rapier from the Musée de l'Armée, Paris, dated 1570*

159

is that its Full Hilt D has an extra ring-guard on the outside, making three rings instead of two. The earliest-dated portrait so far known which shows such a three-ring Full Hilt D is of 1599: *ergo*, it could be laid down that three-ring hilts must date after the turn of the century, and if so we would quickly find we were at sea again. A's opinion is as good as B's, and dating these weapons has to remain only a matter of opinion until a great deal more research has been done. One can carry one's scepticism further: how geniune is the date on the Paris sword? Is it a date at all? Is it perhaps an older blade remounted in a later hilt? Has it been tampered with recently?

When a blade (or hilt) is inscribed with figures such as *1660* preceded by words such as *Anno* or *Mefecit* or *Fecit*, there can be no doubt that we have a date, not a 'lucky' number or a troop or arsenal number. There is a rather useful broadsword in the Historisches Museum, Dresden, whose fine gilded Three-Quarter Hilt A, is dated 1588 but whose broad blade is inscribed:

IHUN. XPO. ENGLO. INTO. MFCT. 1557.

The last groups of letters mean *In Toledo Mefecit 1557*. Here, apart from two useful dates for a blade-type and a hilt-form—and we *assume* the 1588 is a date, because it is so consistent with the whole style of the hilt—is good evidence for the re-use of blades a generation out of date and for the hilting of broadswords with swept hilts. There is a rather similar one in the Tower of London Armouries with a typically Spanish Three-Quarter Hilt A of *c.* 1580–1600 fitted with a very broad, two-edged blade of earlier date.

SHELL-GUARDS

There were two additional elements which, with all their countless variations, made the seventeenth-century swept hilt so distinctive. These were shell-guards (or *stichblätter*, 'thrust-plates', as the Germans call them) and ring- or loop-guards. To the ordinary Full Hilt D were added, on the outside, extra rings, so that hilts appear with anything between three and nine rings. Shells, which are so-called because early in this period they were of true cockleshell shape, were first added within the rings of three-ring hilts, larger on the outside than inside, while plates were first added within the lower ring, joining the ends of the arms across the blade, towards the end of the sixteenth century. These additions, and the complexities which evolved with them, are best shown by illustration. Some examples are shown in Plate 12 C.

Around the turn of the century, hilts began to be made symmetrical: that is, the back-guards became mirror-images of the outside guards. This peculiarity cannot in any way be taken as an indication of date or place; all that can be said is that a hilt of this kind is unlikely to date before 1580—but how do we know? The answers to all such questions will probably be found in the future (indeed, the answers to many have been found but are not yet published) and one must continue to be vague. The one thing which no student of arms should do at this stage is to be positive about dating.

THE 'PAPPENHEIMER' HILT

During the second decade of the century, a new style of hilt came into fashion, probably in the Netherlands. This may have been a logical development of the three-ring hilt with

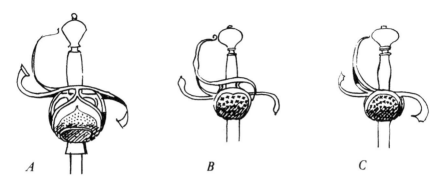

FIGURE 70   The 'Pappenheimer' hilt

Illustration A shows Pappenheimer Type 1
Illustration B shows Type 2, the Swedish Pappenheimer
Illustration C is Type 3

large shells; more probably, however, it was a style designed on its own. The basic forms might be called 'Pappenheimers 1, 2 and 3' (Fig. 70). Pappenheimer 1 could be assumed to be akin to the three-ring and shell hilt; the three rings are present, but the second one is greatly enlarged until it nearly touches the third and is completely filled with a pierced steel plate. Pappenheimer 2 is a much simpler form, where there is only one very large ring filled in with a plate. In these hilts the back-guards are the same as the front ones, except that in the Pappenheimer 2 style the back 'shell' is often a little smaller than the front one. They tend to be very big, massive hilts with an extremely flamboyant look. Many are shown in Dutch paintings of the first half of the century; the frequency of their appearance in these Dutch works of art and the rarity of their appearance anywhere else gives support to the possibility that this is a Netherlands-originated style. However, hilts of Pappenheimer 2 found much favour in Sweden. There are many survivors which belonged to Swedish officers under Gustavus II Adolphus during the Thirty Years War, now in the Livrustkammaren, Stockholm, as well as two which belonged to that monarch himself, one a Pappenheimer Type 2 encrusted with silver, which was his favourite sword, and the second a Pappenheimer 3, very plain, of gilded iron, which was in his hand when he fell at the battle of Lützen in 1632. All of these are fitted with Sword, as distinct from rapier, blades; but the hilt-type was equally popular on rapiers (Plate 12). A variant on Pappenheimer 2, which could be classified as Pappenheimer 3, has an even simpler hilt, for the upper ring is omitted and the guard consists of a large shell enclosed within a single ring.

A distinctive feature of both types is a pommel, generally faceted, of a kind of urn-shape. The hilt in Plate 12 is a good example. However, many have other kinds of pommel, such as one in the Kienbusch Collection with a vertically-ridged, barrel-shaped pommel which is typical of a generation earlier, while Gustavus's Lützen sword has a disc pommel. It is the form of the guards which distinguishes the type; if one adds the variants of pommel forms, one gets as many sub-types as there are pommels; but the urn-shape does appear to be what would be called the 'typical' Pappenheimer pommel.

While this can be said to be a Netherlandish type, there are at least two fine Pappenheimer 2 survivors which are uncompromisingly Italian. One is in the Museo Correr, Venice, and is said to have been used by the Doge Francesco Morosini (elected 1688, died 1694). Its elaborate chiselled and gold-damascened decoration is as typical of Italian work of *c.* 1620 as the unquestionably Netherlandish pierced work in the shells of most others. The second survivor is in the Palazzo Ducale there. This is absolutely Netherlandish in shape, but the chiselled decoration on the shells and pommel is positively Italian in style. This is an iron hilt plated with silver-gilt.

Why the type has been given its name, after Gottfried Heinrich, Graf zu Pappenheim, one of the most prominent cavalry leaders of the Thirty Years War, is as much a mystery as most Victorian sword-type names are; but he was certainly a contemporary of the hilt type and it is a good name, somehow appropriate to the weapon.

THE LOOP HILT

Parallel to and contemporary with the Pappenheimer hilt went a type which was its direct opposite, a hilt whose guards were cut down to the absolute minimum and consisted only of knuckle-guard, rear and forward *quillons*, and a loop-guard linking the bottom curve of the knuckle-guard with the inner part of the rear *quillon*, and often a small shell outside the *écusson* inside the loop (Fig. 71). Some of these very simple hilts were fitted with full-length rapier blades but others (the majority) were a good deal shorter. They were probably used, particularly the long ones, as dress swords, as distinct from day-to-day town swords. This possibility is rather borne out by the elaborate, and generally extremely fine, quality of their decoration. Early ones date from about 1610, but the period of this hilt's greatest popularity seems to have been the 1630s and 1640s. A particularly elaborate one in the Wallace Collection (A 683) has an extra guard in the form of a beautifully-wrought cockleshell under the loop-guard, which is inclining downwards over the top of the blade. These loop-hilt swords seem to have become military in their main usage by the middle years of the century, and although they begin as modifications of the big rapier early in the century, by the middle of it they are turning into an alternative to the smallsword.

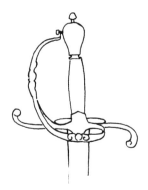

FIGURE 71   The loop hilt

At this point it will be appropriate to acknowledge the division of sword- and hilt-types into two distinct categories, one civilian and the other military. With the period of the Thirty Years War (which began in 1618 with two Bohemian councillors being flung out of a window in Prague on to a convenient dung-heap, an event ever since entitled, delightfully, 'the Defenestration of Prague'—it ended less spectacularly in 1648 with the Treaty of Munster) we reach a point where there began to be positive and noticeable distinctions between civil and military hilts.

Before the long rapier went finally out of favour, there evolved three more very distinctive types of hilt. These were based no longer upon the ring- and loop-guard system of the swept hilt but seem to have been more or less deliberate inventions, as of a cutler who sought a totally new, super-protective rapier hilt and eventually came up with a workable design. One of these designs, the earliest to appear (perhaps in the first decade of the seventeenth century), was English; the second, now called the Cavalier hilt, was an English or perhaps Netherlandish cross between this English type and a curious, short-lived, aberrant (and often ridiculous) French duelling weapon, often called the *flamberge*; and the third and last was Spanish.

THE ENGLISH HILT

There are two distinct types of the English hilt; the first (English Hilt A) is a variation upon the three-ring swept hilt. Instead of the lower ring outside and back-guard inside, there are a pair of (really shell-shaped) shell-guards. Above these (which are symmetrical) is a curved bar very like a ring-guard, parallel with the upper contour of the shell. Above this again is a second bar, not quite parallelling the contour of the first and spreading outwards to join on to the fore and rear *quillons*. These bars are joined vertically by short curved bars. There is a knuckle-guard with short connecting bars from its mid-point to the top of the second bars of the 'basket', and the pommels are ovoid.

The second (English Hilt B) is built up rather like a fire-basket of concentric bars above a small saucer-like lower guard, the whole assembly joined together by short vertical bars. The *quillons* go across the top of this cup-shaped basket and the arms are dispensed with. There is a knuckle-guard, which is joined to the upper bar of the basket by two curved bars springing from either side of a point just below the middle of the guard. Pommels of these hilts are also invariably ovoid.

In both hilt-types, the bars of the basket, the *quillons* and the knuckle-guard are usually all of a flat ribbon-like section, and the workmanship, even of finely-decorated specimens, is often rough, more like ordinary wrought-iron work than the highly-sophisticated products of Continental hilt-makers (Plate 13). There are some, however, which, while built more or less on this insular design, are of far smoother workmanship. Such is a very beautiful rapier hilt in the Tower of London.

Parallel with these 'basket'-like hilts went another, much more robust and heavy, always associated with Sword, as opposed to rapier, blades. These hilts were much more conventional, being more in the nature of variants of the old 'Full Hilt A'. They were not

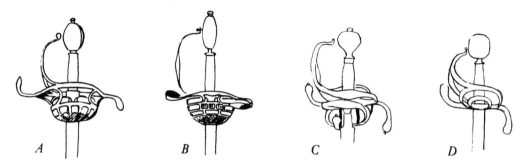

A B C D

FIGURE 72   *The English hilt*

symmetrical, having ordinary three-bar back-guards; but their pommels were very large, apple-shaped, while the guards were thick and heavy, with short, bulb-ended *quillons* curled, one up and one down, very closely against the hilt. I have dubbed the type English Hilt C (Fig. 72, Plate 13 D).

These English Hilt C hilts were paralleled with a simplified form fitted (almost invariably) to backsword blades. Here the characteristic apple-shaped pommel and the bulb-ended up-and-down *quillons* are retained, together with the thick knuckle-guard, but there is nothing below the *quillons*—no arms, no shell-, ring- or dish-guards. Instead on each side of the hilt is sometimes a pair of flat rings springing together from the *quillon*-block, inclined upward over the hand, each upper one being joined to the mid-point of the knuckle-guard by a loop (English Hilt D). Again, the guards are always of flat section. These seem very much to approximate to those 'close' hilts so much approved by George Silver. There can be no doubt that such hilts were in use, and had been in use for some time, when he wrote his *Paradoxes* in 1599. An even more enclosed 'close' hilt of English origin, absolutely parallel with these last two types of English Hilt C and English Hilt D, was developed along with them early in the seventeenth century or even—more probably—late in the sixteenth century; but since these were mounted with broadsword blades, and gave rise to the most famous military sword-type in the world, we must deal with them under the heading of military swords; as indeed we must with a simplified variant of English Hilt D which is a forerunner of a clearly developing line of purely military hilts dating between about 1610 and 1720.

These English hilts are nearly all decorated in a distinctive style which in itself is English. Some are damascened in gold and silver wire with rather insignificant floral scrolls and all the usual paraphernalia of sixteenth/seventeenth century design, similar to Diego de Cajas' work of the mid-sixteenth century, but feeble in execution by comparison. The finer English hilts, however, are decorated with designs in silver incrustation in low relief upon a ground of blackened iron. The finest example of this decoration in England is in the Wallace Collection, on the hilt of the sword of Henry, Prince of Wales, the elder son of James I, who died at the age of nineteen in 1612. This is one of those 'antique' swords to which I referred above, a plain cross-hilted sword of a kind which became very popular in England—indeed, all over Europe—from about 1600 to 1625. The large spherical or apple-shaped pommel is a typically English feature which we shall find repeated on most English military swords up to about 1680.

There are many other swords of this type in European and American collections and one was found in the coffin of the Graf zu Pappenheim when his tomb in the church at Pappenheim was opened for restoration. Hefner-Alteneck, when referring to this sword early in this century, mentioned a portrait of the Marshal zu Pappenheim wearing it. Although these swords were obviously in use all over Europe, their hilts do seem to have been of English workmanship. This group, and this decorative style, has been thoroughly dealt with by Claude Blair (some works are listed on page 145).

I am painfully aware that to attempt a work like this without specifically examining decorative styles is like cooking a Chateaubriand without any Burgundy; but severe limitations of space absolutely forbid more than passing references; however, there are many easily accessible publications which go very thoroughly into the matter of decoration. So even if this has turned out to be no more than a tolerable beef stew, I can say to my critics that from the outset I did not offer anything more elaborate.

THE DISH-HILT RAPIER OR *FLAMBERGE*

The dish-hilt rapier was probably a weapon designed entirely for fighting duels; its appearance coincides with the period of Cardinal Richelieu's repeated and stringent edicts against duelling in France, and it seems possible that the type itself originated there. Some of these are handy enough weapons, light and flexible, such as No. A 507 in the Wallace Collection which is rather like an outsize modern foil; but some are ridiculous, with stiff three-sided blades up to nearly six feet long (1·8 metres); there is one in Sweden which even has a double grip—not a two-handed grip, but a second grip and pommel placed on top of a lower one. Characteristic of the type was a very much simplified hilt—a tall,

generally ovoid pommel, short straight *quillons*, no arms or guards, protection for the hand being provided by a large dish-shaped plate set immediately below the *quillons*. This in fact exactly reproduces the old fifteenth-century *estoc* used in 'foining' play in civil judicial duels in the *champ clos*, where a long, slender, stiff sword with a cross-hilt was used 'well besagewed afore ye hiltes', *i.e.*, with a besagew or metal disc fitted under the cross-guard.

The dish-hilt rapier has been called also 'the *flamberge*'. This name was given to it late in the nineteenth century by Egerton Castle, and used in his *Schools and Masters of Fence* to differentiate it from more orthodox rapiers.

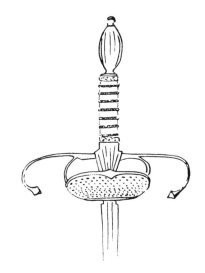

FIGURE 73   A dish-hilt rapier, or flamberge, *c. 1630 (Victoria & Albert Museum)*

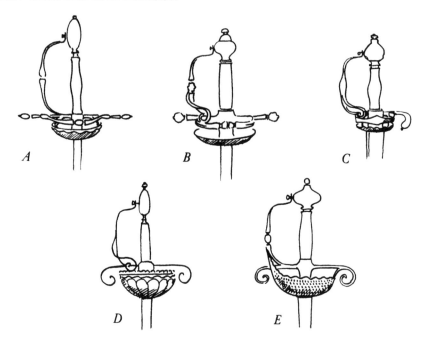

FIGURE 74   The Cavalier hilt

THE CAVALIER HILT

The rapier in Figure 73, designed for a purely thrusting style of fight, with a very simple hilt, was one of the progenitors of the smallsword which followed it some twenty years after; but before the true smallsword developed, the 1630s and 1640s saw a cross-bred hilt in popular use all over Europe, which can be said to be the very last manifestation of the many sword-types which had sprung from the *espada ropera* of the 1480s. It is clearly a type by the English hilt out of the dish hilt. Modern scholars have rather aptly called this the 'Cavalier hilt', for the period of its fashion does more or less correspond with the reign of Charles I of England before the start of the Civil War in 1641.

In Figure 74, I have drawn five of the most common forms of this hilt, the basis of which was a dish, a ring, *quillons*, a knuckle-guard and a pommel and grip. The shapes into which these elements were tortured sometimes border on the fantastic, but generally speaking they produced sensible and workmanlike hilts. Many were very ugly, but a few were handsome enough, though never did they equal the elegance of the old swept hilts they superseded nor the daintiness of the smallsword hilts which followed.

A few of the dish-hilt rapiers and some Cavalier ones had hilts with two flat oval shells instead of a dish-shaped guard, but these were the transitional predecessors of the smallsword and merit a place of their own in this sketch of the seventeenth-century sword. Figure 73 is an example.

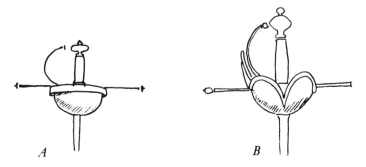

FIGURE 75   The Spanish cup hilt

THE SPANISH CUP HILT

If one were to ask the average man-in-the-street what a rapier was like, the chances are a hundred to one he would try to describe a cup-hilted rapier. This extremely practical hilt (Fig. 75), which did not come into use until the 1650s in Spain, and those parts of Europe dominated by Spain, has been favoured by actors regardless of accuracy—as indeed it still is—because of the security which the deep cup-shaped guard offers to the hand; this has probably been so from the time of its first appearance. It is strange that so eminently practical and useful a hilt-form should have enjoyed so short a life in so limited a region. Maybe it is because it came into use only when the long rapier was rapidly going out of favour elsewhere in Europe. However, in Spain and southern Italy it reigned supreme from the early 1650s until the first decade of the eighteenth century. As a weapon it was almost perfect—at least, as a rapier of the old fashion; but with its wide cup-guard, very long *quillons* and long blade, it was clumsy in wear and found no favour in fashionable circles, where emphasis was beginning to be put upon urbanity of manners and sophistication in dress. All through the second half of the sixteenth century, Spanish and Italian modes had ruled the fashionable world, but in about 1625–1650 France took the lead; and when in 1654, after the wars of the Fronde, the young Louis XIV began to take hold on the realities of power, fashion very rapidly began to discard the exaggerated flamboyancies of the earlier part of the century. While the cup-hilt rapier was at the height of its popularity in *démodé* Spanish territories, the elegant little smallsword was all the rage at Versailles, and in every corner of Europe where the styles of Versailles were emulated.

There was very little variety in these Spanish hilts, though there were noticeable distinctions between those made for Spain and those for the Kingdom of Naples. Never were they decorated as their predecessors had been with damascening of gilding or blueing. There were no silver hilts, or gilded ones. Only the best and most delicate steelwork. The finer ones had their cups or pommels exquisitely chiselled with scrolling—conventional motifs of flowers, leaves and masks; this sometimes extended to the grips as well. Less costly hilts had varying degrees of decoration, but whatever it was, it never varied from chiselled or lightly engraved work upon the surface of the steel.

In the bottom of the cup, where the blade went through its centre, there was always a flat circular plate, called the *guarda polvo*, which was nearly always chiselled even if the cup were plain. The purely Spanish hilts had cups which were vaguely semi-circular in profile, with very long, extremely slender *quillons* of circular section, often with little flat pin-head knops at the ends, semi-circular knuckle-guards and tiny, button-like pommels. There were variations (Fig. 75, Plate 12) but all kept pretty much to the regular pattern. One very noticeable feature of some of these hilts is the strongly-turned-over rim of the cup which must have been very effective in catching the point of an opposing weapon. The Italian ones, on the other hand, although their decoration was of the same nature, usually had very deep cups, well over the half-circle in profile, without turnovers; their *quillons* tended to be thicker, with bigger terminal knops, and the pommels were often ovoid or spherical. Occasionally the forward side of the cup would be swept up towards the knuckle-guard. In some cases, both Spanish and Italian cups had their upper edges scalloped.

In various collections in Europe and America are a few extremely crude swords of this pattern, hilts of the true Spanish form made by what would seem to be ordinary black-smiths, fitted with stout sword blades of very low quality. Some are said to have been used late in the seventeenth century by Covenanting Scots, and in the collection of Mr Harold Peterson of Arlington, Virginia, is one of the same kind found in the Caribbean area, presumably a relic of the buccaneers of the same period.

Parallel to, and probably contemporary with, the Spanish cup hilt is a very similar-looking hilt for which it will be convenient to use the modern collector's term of 'Bilbo'.

THE BILBO HILT

Basically the Bilbo hilt is fashioned to the same pattern as the Spanish cup hilt, except that instead of the cup the guard is formed of two very large shells, curved up and back over the *ricasso* and covering the arms of the hilt. At the sides, below and around the *quillons*, is a series of looped bars, often beautifully formed and most elegantly arranged (Plate 12). In many Bilbo hilts there is a ring-guard above the top of each shell, joining the midpoint of the knuckle-guard, which itself has a downward extension running into the outside arm of the hilt (Fig. 76).

The finer-quality examples of this kind of hilt are fitted to the same long rapier-blades as the Spanish cup hilts are, but there are many others of varying degrees of poorer

FIGURE 76   The Bilbo hilt

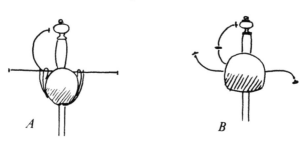

A

B

quality, always fitted with sword blades or, in some cases, broadsword blades. This is because the hilt-form continued in military use in Spain and her colonies right up into the early part of the nineteenth century. It was probably during the eighteenth century that it acquired the name Bilbo, for quantities of swords were shipped to the Spanish Americas and the Netherlands out of the port of Bilbao.

It is assumed that the Bilbo hilt and the Spanish cup hilt were contemporary, but there are grounds at least for speculation that the Bilbo form may have preceded the other by almost a quarter-century. The earliest portrait showing a Spanish hilt is in the possession of the Hispanic Society of New York. Painted by Juan Careno de Miranda and dated 1660, it shows an unnamed nobleman wearing a sword whose hilt, though partly obscured by his left hand, is unmistabably a cup hilt. At one time it was thought that this form of hilt could be dated early in the century, even to the closing years of the sixteenth, but there is no evidence at all until the 1660s and very little at that, because they are extremely rarely shown in portraits. However, there is a portrait, in private hands, of an unknown man, dated 1630 and attributed to Velazquez, which shows a cup hilt. But it has extra loop-guards, and another joining the lower curve of the knuckle-guard to the outer arm of the hilt, and so is much more likely to be a Bilbo. It has a large ovoid pommel, too, and a longer grip than the standard Spanish hilt.

Now, if the *quillons* of this painted hilt were curved, one up and one down, it would have been unhesitatingly stated that this was a Pappenheimer 2 hilt, not a Bilbo or a cup hilt. Comparison of many Bilbo hilts with Pappenheimer 2 hilts will be found to show a very marked similarity; comparison of a typical Spanish cup hilt with an English Hilt A also shows great similarity of outline (Plates 12 E, 13 C). Both Pappenheimer 2 and English Hilt A were fashionable during the 1620s and 1630s, and Spanish links both with the Netherlands and with England were strong at this time—in the Netherlands because they had been occupied by the Spanish for over half a century and were still in the process of freeing themselves from Spanish domination, and in England because of James I's policy of rapprochement with Spain. So Spanish noblemen and soldiers were in very close touch with fashion trends in weapons in both these regions; it seems logical to suppose that these northern hilts influenced the eventual design of the Bilbo and the cup hilt in the Peninsula. If, as seems reasonable, we assume the Bilbo to be a Spanish modification of the Pappenheimer 2, it is equally reasonable to suppose that it was in use before the cup hilt. We know that it survived it by some 150 years.

BIBLIOGRAPHY

Hoffmeyer, Ada Bruhn, *Die Schwertfeger Godfried Leygebe*, Tøjhusmuseums Skrifter, 1, 1945
The lists of material given at the end of Chapter Two and Chapter Six also apply.

CHAPTER TEN

THE MILITARY SWORD OF THE SEVENTEENTH CENTURY

There are five distinct types of military sword which show clear lines of development through the seventeenth century. One, to which it is hard to assign a name, plentifully surviving, is a very simple hilt based upon two flat shell-guards and a knuckle-guard. One example of it has been called the 'Walloon' sword in modern times, and seems to have been one of the earliest 'regulation' pattern swords to come into existence, for literally thousands of them, all identical, must have been made between about 1630 and 1690, judging by the numbers which survive. This, however, was only one pattern of this particular basic hilt-form. Then there is the rather similar hilt which is referred to indiscriminately as the 'Swedish', 'Netherland' or 'Sinclair' hilt, and its variants. And finally there are those three sword types which survive in such great numbers and about which so little is really known: the English 'mortuary' sword, the Venetian '*schiavona*', and the 'Scottish' sword or 'claymore'. Again, names are difficult, and we are really forced by common usage to go on using these quite misleading nineteenth-century collectors' terms, even though we now know they are inaccurate. The mortuary sword was so called because the crudely-chiselled heads on its guards were thought to be commemorative of Charles I of England, King and Martyr; and the *schiavona* got its name because it was believed to have been the exclusive weapon of the Slavonic Dalmatian troops raised by Venice in the seventeenth and eighteenth centuries. As for the 'Scottish' sword, in its earliest forms it was uncompromisingly English, and remained a standard English pattern far into the eighteenth century; only very late in the century did it become *exclusively* Scottish. Until very recently it was always, like the old 'twahandit' sword which it superseded, called the claymore; this term has a certain respectability because as far back as the days before Culloden, the Scots were calling it that themselves, and one does feel that if they, who made and used it, did not mind the inaccuracy, we should not boggle at it either. Scottish it was, even in the seventeenth century, and *exclusively* Scottish it became, but England has as good a claim to it, for it originated in that country. However, since it is always called the 'Scottish' sword (or sometimes the 'Highland' or the 'Irish' sword), it is necessary to observe the distinctions.

THE WALLOON HILT

The Walloon hilt perhaps stemmed originally from the English Hilt E. In the Armouries of the Tower of London is a sword which seems to provide a link suggesting this, for it is a typical English shape with its big apple-shaped pommel and bulb-ended *quillons*; in addition, it is decorated in the English manner with silver designs in relief on a blackened ground. This dates *c.* 1610. There is another equally undeniably English sword in Mr Harold Peterson's collection in Arlington, Virginia. Here the hilt is simpler, having no guards other than the knuckle-guard, *quillons*, and a small projection forged out of the *quillon*-block. Its back-edged blade is signed:

HOUNSLOE ME FECIT.

The next development originated perhaps in the Netherlands. The hilt was improved by the addition of a ring-guard on the outside, sometimes enclosing a shell with a corresponding smaller one on the inside, to which was added a thumb-ring. The next step was to draw the two shells forward into a sort of boat-shape sweeping upward to blend with the knuckle-guard. At some time in the 1620s, a very distinctive pommel-form came into use, flat and heart-shaped, which for some thirty years was one of the most popular forms upon the hilts of all kinds of *offizierdegen*, as most of these swords have aptly been called (Fig. 77).

About the mid-century, the forward *quillon* was abandoned, and the true Walloon hilt was produced. At the same time, this sort of hilt began to be used upon much smaller, lighter swords, often most exquisitely decorated, which look very much more like civilian transitional rapier/smallswords than military ones—which indeed they are, but in many cases they *were* true military swords used by officers in the field, and are probably what were known, from the mid-seventeenth century onwards, as 'scarf' swords, a scarf worn across the right shoulder and tied on the left hip having become an essential part of an officer's outfit in the 1630s, into the knot of which the sword was fastened. These were the loop-hilt swords of the second generation, in their turn fore-runners of the smallsword.

Towards the end of the seventeenth century, the Walloon hilt developed (probably in Germany) into a very practical double-shelled hilt with guards of a narrow circular section, embellished with spherical mouldings or discs set into the guards at right-angles to their line. These guards were extended by the addition either of a second knuckle-guard joining the top of the true knuckle-guard to the midpoint of the outside shell, or of a pair of small curved bars springing on either side from a point below the middle of the knuckle-guard to the sides of both shells.

Another variation was a sort of half-hilt where the inner shell was dispensed with altogether.

FIGURE 77 'Offizierdegen'
Note the distinctive pommel

FIGURE 78   The two types of Sinclair hilt

SINCLAIR 2

THE SINCLAIR HILT

The name 'Sinclair' has been applied to two totally different types of early-seventeenth-century hilt, so for the sake of clarity I shall call them Sinclair 1 and Sinclair 2 (Fig. 78). Sinclair 1 is the hilt already described on page 134, a South-German type fitted both to *estocs* and to sabres. It got its name in the late nineteenth century in a devious sort of way. There were many of these hilts, along with other basket-forms, among those sent into Norway by Christian IV of Denmark; and because they bear a certain resemblance to the typical Scottish or Highland sword of the seventeenth and eighteenth centuries, Victorian collectors seized upon the name of Colonel George Sinclair, the leader of a band of mercenary Scots who tried to fight their way across Norway to get to Sweden in 1612 but were wiped out in the Gudrun Valley. These swords were considered to have been relics of this force. However, the name was also given to a hilt-type which may be typically Scandinavian, and this I shall call Sinclair 2—it is this one which collectors now, in fact, always call the 'Sinclair' sword. Remarkably similar in form to the early Walloon hilts, it has a flat heart-shaped pommel instead of an apple-shaped one, and wide up-and-down *quillons* and forward ring-guard; a distinguishing feature is this large ring-guard (sometimes almost rectangular in plan), filled with a plate, generally decorated, and with a corresponding thumb-guard at the back. These are handsome weapons, mostly having quite large, broad blades, flat with several fullers at the forte, though many have more acutely pointed blades of a flattened diamond section (Plate 14).

Some which have knuckle-guards have an additional guard as well; the forward ring is drawn upward into a point, from which springs a bar, carried up over the hand to meet the pommel, where it is secured by a screw. This form of forward shell and secondary knuckle-guard is found also on the hilts of Swiss sabres dating between 1640 and 1670.

In the Livrustkammaren, Stockholm, is a sword belonging to Johan III of Sweden which dates between 1570 and 1580. It is in many ways different from the others in that the *quillons* (one of which is missing) arch towards the blade, and the flat pommel is not quite of the heart-like shape common to most of the others; however, it does seem to belong to this hilt-type. This particular hilt is of enamelled gold, by Gilius Coyet of Stockholm; some of the commoner ones are silvered or gilded, and nearly all have an all-over incised pattern of leaves and flowers, often rather crudely executed. A very fine one was recently sold at Sotheby's, London, with fine-quality silver decoration in the English manner.

There are other swords—one cannot really call them a group, because each differs considerably from the others—which seem to be a sort of cross between the Sinclair hilts and the Walloon hilts. Many have the flat heart-shaped pommel and the incised all-over decoration, but these, and the lack of any back-guards, are their only links with the Sinclair and Walloon types. These swords often take the form of modified half-hilt rapiers.

In the Livrustkammaren is a hand-and-a-half version of this kind of sword, an example of the extreme variety of the 'type'. It has been variously called the 'Swedish/Netherlands' type, or simply the 'Netherlands' type, or, more simply still, '*Offizierdegen*', a comfortable umbrella-term which can cover the whole range of these very varied hilts.

THE BASKET-HILTED BROADSWORD

Any attempt to specify prototypical patterns for the broadsword hilts of the seventeenth century would be doomed to failure, for almost all of the many basket-like forms of guard in use from about 1520 onwards influenced, or at least may have influenced, their design. There were the bastard sword guards of Switzerland and Bavaria, and the hilts of *landsknecht* swords in their later developments, and those South German hilts used upon tucks and the so-called 'Sinclair sabres', as well as Swiss sabres late in the sixteenth century. There is also a large number of extremely varied basket-hilted swords among the weapons shipped from Denmark early in the seventeenth century to arm the peasants in Norway. There is, too, a rare type which probably first appeared in about 1550 and seems to be English; this looks like the basic prototype of all the subsequent British basket hilts, English and Scottish, which in the sixteenth and seventeenth centuries were nearly always referred to as 'Irish hilts' by the English or as 'Highland hilts' by the Scots.

There are three families of broadsword in use in the seventeenth century: the English so-called 'mortuary' sword, absolutely typical of the Civil War (1644–1651) and only in use between, say, 1635 and 1680; the 'claymore' (the 'Irish' or 'Highland' sword); and the so-called '*schiavona*', probably another South German hilt-design, in use from about 1620 to 1780. Each of these requires a section to itself.

THE MORTUARY SWORD

The name 'Mortuary Sword' is, of course, another piece of nineteenth-century collectors' jargon, a fine Romantick one given to this very distinctive hilt-form; it is quite meaningless but hallowed by nearly a century of usage. Owing to the presence of crudely-chiselled, bearded heads nestling among quantities of poor and meretricious ornament in the soft iron of these hilts, they were once supposed to commemorate the martyrdom of Charles I of England. If this were truly so, these swords would have been used exclusively by exiled Royalists after 1649 (for no Parliament man would have worn one); and since they seem to have gone quite out of fashion by about 1670, they would, if truly *memento mori* for Charles the Martyr, have enjoyed only twenty-one years of popularity. However, excellent and incontrovertible evidence shows that they were used also by the Roundhead element in England: there is at least one with Commonwealth slogans on the blade, another with the name of the Great Protector on the blade and a tolerable likeness of him carved on the hilt, and a third with a head on its hilt which wears a strong look of Cromwell. There are

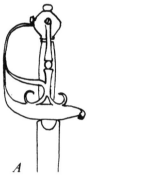
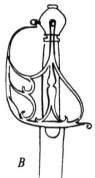

FIGURE 79 The mortuary sword

probably many more such among the numerous surviving examples, literally hundreds, of this typically English hilt.

Characteristic is a large fig-shaped pommel, generally fitted with a tang-button. The guard consists of a large plate, slightly hollowed, which sweeps up in the front of the hilt to merge into a knuckle-guard; the rear edge of the plate narrows a little and is finished off, where in other swords the rear *quillon* would be, in a narrow turned-under roll. From either side of the guard–plate, on both the inside and the outside of the hilt, secondary knuckle-guards rise; these, with the true knuckle-guard, are fastened to the pommel by means of screws. The side-guards join the plate with a scroll on either side, and one, two, or sometimes three, loop-guards on each side join the knuckle-guard to the secondary ones (Fig. 79, Plate 14 A).

Most survivors are of rather ordinary quality. The chiselled design is poorly executed, nearly always consisting of rather meaningless stylised patterns of tiny pieces of unconvincing foliage, though there are a good many hilts where the whole surface is covered with a close-set pattern of scale-like feathers. There are, however, a few hilts of superb quality; I have only ever seen two such, one in Windsor Castle, the other in a private collection (just before 1939). There is, of course, one very well-known example, now in the Kienbusch Collection, formerly in that of Edwin J. Brett. This has a magnificent blade, considerably decorated and bearing the date *1650*, the arms of England and Ireland, and the inscription:

FOR THE COMMON WEALTH OF ENGLAND

It is an enormous, very broad, back-edged blade of absolutely first quality, but the hilt, though shapely and boldly fashioned, is not particularly distinguished as to the execution of its typical patterning. It was once believed that it had belonged to the great Oliver himself, but like so many of these dubious attributions, this has now been discounted.

These hilts were generally mounted with straight blades, either back-edged or double-edged, but there are a few rare examples with curved blades. I know of one such in a private collection, with a long curved blade the size of a cavalry sabre, and another in the Armouries of the Tower of London with a short, broad blade like a cutlass. Indeed, the latter probably was for use on board ship. The hilt is rather better chiselled than most; the heads upon it are good likenesses of the Great Protector, a likeness reinforced by the words engraved upon the blade:

OLIVARUS CROMWELL ANNO DOMINI 1652

Their point of origin is obscure, but the line of development is directly through the English Cavalier hilts, with no influences from the parallel evolution of the *schiavone* and English basket hilts. One can see this quite plainly in looking, for instance, at Rembrandt's *Self-Portrait with Saskia* (*c.* 1637). The nearest parallel, perhaps, is the early Walloon hilt with its use of curved loop-guards and secondary knuckle-guards. There are two interesting swords which provide links with earlier English practice in hilt-making. In the Tøjhusmuseum, Copenhagen, is a beautiful hilt of mortuary form, with three loop-guards on either side, but instead of being decorated in the common way of mortuary hilts, it has thick-encrusted damascening of silver in the same style as the sword of Henry, Prince of Wales (page 164, above), and the basket-hilted broadsword of Sir William Twysden, now in the Metropolitan Museum, New York. The other is in a private collection in London, a Cavalier hilt similar in form to one shown in Plate 21 C, but with decoration, chiselled in soft iron, which is of outstanding (and at its period, most unusual) quality, incorporating portrait heads of Charles I of England and his queen, Henrietta Maria—unmistakable portraits, good likenesses, with crowns on their heads to dispel any possible doubt. This hilt, and maybe others like it, indisputably of loyal Royalist significance, probably were the archetypes of all the subsequent heads, good, bad and indifferent, on the mortuary hilts.

Since these hilts were only popular for a short time, it is a fairly safe generalisation to say that in most cases blades are contemporary with the hilts in which they are mounted, though there are a few examples where a good old blade, maybe half a century or more older than the hilt, has been fitted.

A contemporary form of broadsword hilt of English origin, which may have antedated the first mortuary hilts by a decade or so, is a simple one consisting of a pair of upturned shells, a single curled rear *quillon*, and a knuckle-guard, with sometimes a third shell at the base of the knuckle-guard reaching nearly halfway up to it.

THE CLAYMORE

The true claymore, of course, is the 'twahandit' sword, *claidheamh mòr*, used in the Highlands in the sixteenth century, but the familiar basket-hilted broadsword was called a 'claymore' by the Scots from early in the sixteenth century, and with such respectable contemporary usage behind it, the name may well be allowed to stick. Indeed, the word was used as a war cry at least until the '45 Rising. When the Jacobite army was in retreat from Derby in 1746, its rearguard under Lord George Murray was attacked by Cumberland's dragoons. Murray drew his broadsword, yelled 'Claymore!' and charged into them with the MacPhersons and the Glengarry MacDonalds.

The traditional hilt-pattern, so very well-known, seems to have developed during the late sixteenth century and the seventeenth, from an English-designed 'basket' hilt (Fig. 80), with very little influence from the many kinds of basket hilt evolving on the Continent, except perhaps for those South German sabre and *estoc* hilts shown in Figures 57 A and 78 (pp. 135 and 172). This English basket hilt was certainly in use as early as the

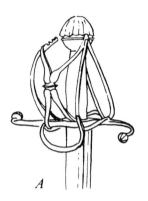 

A   *B*

FIGURE 80 English basket hilts
Type A (left) *was an ancestor of the claymore hilt,*
and of Type B (right), *a typically English style*
which continued long in use as a military pattern

1560s; a portrait at Hagley of Sir Edward Lyttelton, for example, shows him wearing one with long counter-curved *quillons*. It is likely that the earlier ones, before, say, 1580, had *quillons* as well as the two loops under the front of the basket, whereas after that date a small downturned 'back-guard', as some might call it, replaced the rear *quillon*. However, there is a hilt made in the same style as the 'beaknose' hilt of the mid-seventeenth century (Fig. 81 A), from a series of flat ribbon-like bars, which has a pair of long counter-curved *quillons*. This implies either that this form of basket is earlier than has been generally accepted, or that the use of *quillons* continued until a date later than has been allowed. This sword is in the National Museum of Antiquities, Edinburgh.

This English basket hilt was the common ancestor of the claymore hilt, as well as of a more typically English style which continued as a military pattern until about 1750–1775 (Fig. 111).

By the last years of the sixteenth century, these basket hilts had begun to become associated with the Highland Scots and the Irish. This was possibly because many of the Highland chiefs had holdings in Ulster, and in the Irish wars of Queen Elizabeth's time there were many Highland mercenaries in Ireland. Whatever the reason, these hilts became known as 'Irish hilts' in the early years of the seventeenth century. In 1622, for instance, in the wardrobe accounts of Prince Charles, a payment was recorded to Robert Southe, the royal goldsmith, for 'one Irishe hilt richly damasked with gold with a broad blade and wire handle' ('handle' being the English term, used probably since the fifteenth century, for the grip). This sword was very probably of the same form as the sword of Sir William Twysden of Royden Hall, Kent. It is plain to see how this hilt-form (of which there are a number of less handsome survivors) developed from the earlier pattern shown in Figure 80 B.

In Scotland these hilts, from at least the late sixteenth century, were called 'Highland hilts' or 'Highland guards'. The burgh records of Inverness for 1576 mention 'ane pair of Ireland hiltis with the plumet ... to be put on ane sourd bled' (the 'plumet' is the pommel). Fifteen years later, in the accounts of Alexander, Laird of Cawdor, for 1591, there is reference to an 'Ireland sword'. Unfortunately, no such hilt is shown in any painting prior to about 1680; in the National Portrait Gallery in Edinburgh there is a portrait of this date, 'Highland Chieftain' by Michael Wright, in which the sword-hilt is clearly shown. This is of a type which collectors tend to call 'beaknose', for obvious reasons; the basket is formed from a series of welded, flat, ribbon-like strips of metal and is drawn into a kind of beak in front. This is one of the earlier forms of Highland guard, though there are others of the same period, c. 1600—1680, which look much more like the familiar claymore hilts of the eighteenth century.

Three especial features distinguished the Highland hilt from the English one in the seventeenth century: a difference in the shape of the pommel, the addition of an extra pair of bars on the rear of the guards, and a small linking bar between the third and fourth bars, both on the inside and on the outside.

The English pommel remained apple-shaped all through the century, becoming bun-shaped in the eighteenth, while the Highland 'plumet' very early assumed the form of a double cone round (but just below) the centre of which a deep channel was cut to accommodate the upper ends of the base of the guard.

The English guard mostly consisted of three vertical bars on either side, as it were a knuckle-guard and a secondary one, plus a third at the rear of the hilt. The true knuckle-guard and the secondary were connected by a diagonally-crossing pair of bars with a circular plate, quite small, at the intersection (Fig. 80 B). The Highland guard developed a very much larger rectangular plate at this intersection, decorated, from the late seventeenth century onwards, sometimes with rough St Andrew's crosses cut out, more often with large heart-shaped openings among small circular ones. These heart-shaped openings are clearly derived from those large plates on the outside of the South German tuck and sabre hilts and the Sinclair hilts of the early seventeenth century.

In the English hilts, the rear bars, or tertiary knuckle-guards, sloped sharply from the pommel to the point where a rear *quillon* would be, though this was rarely present. In the Highland guards, this bar became closer to the vertical, and an extra shorter one was added to it at the back. At the same time, the small linking bar between bars 2 and 3 developed, in the Highland version, a small vertical process crossing it at right angles, spreading out above and below the intersection, like a bow-tie in some cases, while in others (a hilt in the Museum and Art Gallery, Glasgow, for instance) it is triangular with the apex upwards. Around the turn of the century, perhaps as early as 1690, this process developed into a short vertical bar with an open loop on either side, which by the nineteenth century, and in the comparatively modern Regimental hilt, has become two circles (Fig. 81, B—G).

These hilts are extremely difficult to date, even within half a century, because in the case of the earlier ones there are so few fixed points, such as portraits or signed hilts, to fix style to period; and in the case of the later ones (that is, after about 1680) they tended to be very much alike, used equally on either side of the Border. In some rare cases we are helped by hilts bearing the initials of hilt-makers of Stirling and Glasgow whose working-dates are known; it is possible because of these to define at least two quite distinct styles, Stirling and Glasgow; but beyond that, they do not help very much. One *can* say that

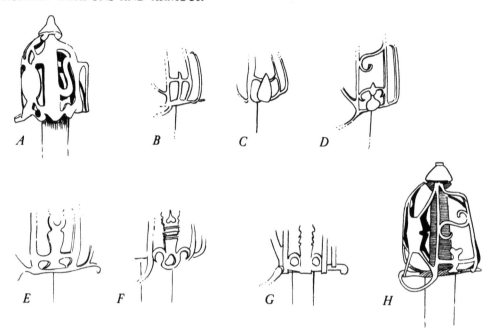

FIGURE 81   *The development of the Highland hilt, c. 1670—1900, shown diagrammatically*

between about 1725 and 1770, Stirling hilts tended to be made up of bars of circular section, rather narrow, while Glasgow ones were made of flat ribbon-like bars, rather wide.

The blades fitted to these hilts can cause confusion. Mostly they were double-edged, though back-edged ones are not uncommon especially in later English Regimental examples. The true Scots weapon tended to be broad, often with three fullers, more rarely with one wide fuller. A feature of many such, particularly after 1700, was a *ricasso* which had an extra fuller, just the length of the *ricasso*, alongside each edge of it. Nearly all Scottish blades were made in Germany, of course, and most bore the spurious name *ANDRIA* (or *ANDREA*) *FERRARA*. The Solingen smiths of the early seventeenth century had a name for the blades they made for export to Scotland, *Grösser Schotten*, 'Broad Scots'. Swords with such blades were often called 'Scots' in England at this time. As well as the spurious smith-name, they often carried loyal or encouraging slogans:

GOTT BEWAHR DIE OPRECHTE SCHOTTEN

'God protect the honest Scots'

—found on a blade mounted in a beaknose hilt of *c.* 1620, while later other slogans became popular, such as:

PROSPERITY TO SCHOTLAND AND NO UNION

with on the other side

GOD SAVE KING JAMES YE 8TH

These last dated between the Union of the Scottish and English Parliaments in 1707 and the '15 Rebellion.

Some of these hilts were mounted with old blades. For example, a very poor and battered specimen turned up at Sotheby's a few years ago with an undoubted thirteenth-century blade, and among the countless survivors there are probably others with blades dating between the thirteenth and sixteenth centuries. Occasionally one may find an old hilt fitted with a new blade, but this is probably rarer; however, there are Highland hilts used during the nineteenth, even the twentieth, centuries, which date back at least to the 1740s*.

A rare form of the claymore hilt has an S-shaped element incorporated in the guards on either side—at least, it is an S on the inside, but an S reversed on the outside of the hilt (Fig. 81 H). First found upon some early beaknose hilts, this seems to have been popular in the second half of the seventeenth century. It has been suggested that this element has meaning and purpose: S for Stuart, or S for Stirling. It has also been suggested that it has no meaning whatever, being merely an alternative to, or a predecessor of, the more usual pierced plate at either side of the hilt between the bars. There is no conclusive evidence for any of these views, and it may be left entirely to the individual to choose the academic,

---

* There must be many claymores which have seen service over a period of some 150 years. One such has a hilt made and signed by Walter Allen of Stirling; it came from the family of Keith, and by tradition belonged to Lord James Keith, Field-Marshal in the armies of Frederick the Great of Prussia. He was exiled after the '15 Rising (when he supported the Old Pretender) but was pardoned by George II *c.* 1746. Family tradition had it that he then came back to Scotland, and had the hilt made. The blade of this sword dates probably from *c.* 1550, having once been mounted in a bastard sword hilt. The sword, after Lord James's death in battle, in 1758, was kept by the family, and was used again by another Keith in the Peninsula. Then it went into honourable retirement until, in the Crimean War (1853—1856) it was used by another colourful character, a Colonel of Artillery whose name also was James Keith. For this owner, internal evidence suggests that new scabbard mounts to conform with the Regulation pattern were made, and the hilt (which retained its original grip) was secured by a screw knop on top of the pommel instead of the usual rivet. This was so that the hilt could easily be dismounted and the blade fitted with the plain cross-guard which during the nineteenth century, and to the present day, is substituted for service, as distinct from parade, wear.

A similar surviving sword with a Glasgow hilt, unsigned but probably the work of Thomas Gemmil (*c.* 1710), has a sixteenth-century blade and was adapted for Regimental wear during the Napoleonic wars. The old scabbard has new regulation mounts, the grip is of a type common in about 1790, and so is the liner of white kid covered with red felt and bound with gold thread.

A possible though vague indication of date may be given by the acutal shape of the spaces enclosed by the basket. In early examples (that is, before about 1750) the space on the outside of the grip where the knuckles go seems generally to be considerably larger than the space on the inside where the thumb goes. This disparity is paralleled by the disparate sizes of the shells of smallswords, which only become of equal size after about 1730.

prosaic or romantic explanation. The academic view, which holds that it is just part of the guard, is supported by the evidence of the many S-shaped side-guards in the South German and Swiss bastard hilts of the mid-sixteenth century which were its ancestors; the prosaic view, that S is for Stirling, is supported by the fact that it is only found (apart from beaknoses) on hilts which, on the evidence of mid-eighteenth-century examples, made by John and Walter Allen of Stirling and marked, are of a Stirling, as distinct from a Glasgow, type. The romantic view is supported by evidence which has nothing to do with Academe but much relevance to the practical swordsman (user or maker of the hilt or the blade) and for fervid supporters, now as then, of the Stuart cause. When one of these S-guards is held in the hand, the S on the outside, which is reversed, is invisible; but when one holds the hilt up, the S-shaped element facing the holder is the right way up. There before one's eyes is a clear unmistakable S. In the same way, exhortatory inscriptions such as

IN NOMINE DOMINI: O MATER DEI MEMENTO MEI: O SANCTA

and so on, upon medieval blades were only legible the right way up as the sword was lifted in the right hand; one glanced upward or sideways at it, and there was the exhortation or prayer. So perhaps with the Scots S.*

The earliest portrait that shows this S-member dates *c.* 1720, of Major James Fraser of Castle Leathers (1670–1750), but this proves nothing at all beyond the fact that Major Fraser had his portrait painted when he was about fifty years old, wearing such a sword, and that therefore swords—no, *a* sword—with the S-member was in use in 1720. It gives no clue as to the probable dating of the type's emergence, period of usage, or supersession by the more conventional types. All we can say, on internal evidence, is that there are examples (for instance, one in the Glasgow Museum) which have been dated to the period 1650—1675, and another in the National Museum of Antiquities, Edinburgh, which has been dated within the second half of that century—and, of course, Major Fraser's hilt pictured in the 1720s.

---

* That this element represents a letter at all may be called in question; its German predecessors certainly did not, nor perhaps did those on beaknose hilts. But some are unmistakably letters, as on the hilt shown in Plate 14 where the S has distinct and very well-formed serifs, leaving no doubt that here we have a letter S. Standing for what, if anything? Like those famous gold collars of SS worn round knightly necks in the late fourteenth and early fifteenth centuries. It has been suggested that those SS, found mostly on effigies of knights and barons of known Lancastrian sympathies, had some connection with John of Gaunt, Duke of Lancaster and founder of the Lancastrian line, whose motto, or one of them, was *Souvenir* or *Souvienz*, 'Remember'. The last word of Charles I on the scaffold, the signal he gave for the headsman to strike, was 'Remember!' The Scots of the late seventeenth century had strong French sympathies and much shared culture. Coincidence: Romantick nonsense? Yes, but no more so than the other theories. And one has always to remember, I think, that swords were made and used, designed and paid for, by *people*. Not scholars; ordinary, silly, romantic, sentimental people, and we ought not to dismiss as unlikely any silly, sentimental or romantic elements we may find upon them. What is more silly or sentimental than the popular inscription *No Me Saques Sin Rason, No Me Enhainez Sin Honor*, or for that matter, *God Save King James ye 8th*? There is as much, or as little evidence for one view as for the others.

Another feature of these claymore hilts is that often they were either japanned or oxidised, as gunbarrels are browned, to prevent the iron from rusting. Several survive with their black japanning intact, though this is rare; it has generally been cleaned off on the assumption that it is old Victorian varnish. The same with the dark-brown oxidised ones; too often, except were the oxidisation is in good condition, as in the S-hilt shown in Plate 14 C, it has been taken for rust and burnished off.

The leather 'liners' in these hilts sometimes give a clue to dates. Most which survive fill the entire basket, made of thin chamois covered with velvet or felt and edged with braid; these are all late, dating from about 1790 to the present day, though often added to earlier hilts. A half-filling liner of deerskin gives a date from the 1770s back to about 1730; before that, from the mid-sixteenth century on, only the very base of the basket had a lining, of very thick deerskin.

There are a few cases where one meets with two separate hilts obviously made by the same hand; a good example is a very fine sword in the collection of Mr R. T. Gwynn, said to have belonged to John Campbell, 1st Earl of Breadalbane (c. 1635—1717), and another is its fellow, recently in my care.* The actual form of the hilt basket is identical; but much more significant is the way in which the edges of the bars were decorated with very regularly cut patterns of alternating indented segments and projecting square knops, and the plates with rather roughly cut openings of St-Andrew's-Cross form with open circular holes at the end of each arm. Here are clearly two hilts, with very distinctive decorative characteristics, which must be from the same workshop. Nearly every claymore hilt has an indented pattern along the edges of the flat plates, as well as the openings in the plates themselves. Is it too much to suggest, if we accept the proposition that they were made by individual craftsmen working alone in croft or shop, that each maker identified his work by the form of its decoration, much as the Japanese bladesmiths can be identified by the forms they gave to their *Yakiba*? With marked hilts, like those of the Allens and Simpsons, one can see quite clearly the stamp of the master's hand in individual quirks of the design. If the case holds for the marked examples, it may well apply to their humbler contemporaries and predecessors.

One thing, also unsupported by evidence, is reasonably certain. The 'hammermen' who made these hilts were single craftsmen working at home; it was a cottage craft. A few years ago, someone researching into the making of knives in Sheffield in the nineteenth century, armed with the well-documented proof that many of these cutlers worked alone, maybe with an apprentice, each in a sort of little workshop in a small back-street house, as cobblers did, visited that city to find out more about them on the spot. What he found was that still, in the early 1970s, craftsmen were making knives in exactly the same way, in little one-man workshops; the only difference being that they worked by the light of fluorescent strips and anglepoise lamps—or naked electric bulbs—instead of by candles and oil-lamps.

It seems extremely probable that for centuries hilt-makers worked in this way—we know that Cellini did, and that he made hilts—and the extreme crudeness of some of the

* The former is illustrated in Claude Blair's *Weapons in Europe and America*, No. 181, and the latter in Frederick Wilkinson's *Edged Weapons*.

earlier Scottish hilts supports the theory that the Scottish hammermen worked in crofts and back-street shops before they were merged, first with larger concerns like those of the Allens and Grants of Stirling and the Gemmils and Simpsons of Glasgow, and later, of course, after 1746, with Government contractors for the Scottish Regiments.

THE *SCHIAVONA*

The ancestry of the *'schiavona'* hilt form is clear; though, like any human family, there are many progenitors. The distinctive pommel-form called by German scholars, with their unerring flair for the *mot juste* in weapon terminology, *katzenkopfknauf*, 'cat's-head pommel', is found on cross-hilted swords dating from the fourteenth century in Slavonic contexts. From these origins it came in the hands of mercenary soldiers into southern Europe, where, from the mid-fifteenth century onwards, Slavonic mercenary light-horse were employed in the armies of Spain and the Republic of Venice. In the inventory of Charles V's armoury, drawn up in 1557 and known as the *Relación de Valladolid*, are listed:

Dos espadas anche come eslavonas con pomos y guarnaciones doradas las guarnaciones revueltas de una cruz:
'Two swords like Slavonic ones with gilt pommels and hilts, the hilts cross-shaped'.

These swords can be identified with two illustrated in the *Inventario Illuminado* of this armoury, now preserved in the Royal Armoury, Madrid. One of these swords (G 26) remains in this collection; the other has migrated to the Museum für Deutsche Geschichte, Berlin. Both have rectangular pommels with raised circular bosses in the centre and crosses terminating in large rings of flat ribbon-like section; they are variations of the old fourteenth- and fifteenth-century Hungarian swords, examples of which are, for instance, in the Armoury of the Doge's Palace, Venice, in the Hermitage, Russia, in the Kienbusch Collection, Philadelphia, in the Odescalchi Collection, Rome, and in the private collection of Mr John Pocock, Devonshire, England. The swords in the *Relación* are closely akin also to swords with *katzenkopfknaufe* and horizontally recurved crosses of which there are large numbers in Venice and good examples in the Armouries of the Tower of London and in the Kienbusch, Odescalchi and Bruno Stutz collections. (This last was formerly in the De Cosson Collection, sold at Sotheby's in 1929, illustrated in the catalogue.)

The term *'Espada Eslavona'* could be applied to all of these swords, which would be *'Spada Schiavona'* in Italian, and 'Slavonic Sword' in plain English. It seems reasonable to suppose that the term was inherited by their basket-hilted successors. Evidence that the plain cross-hilted ones were used by the forces of the Republic of Venice is provided by the great numbers still surviving in the Armoury there. The leather with which their grips are covered, often gilded, is in many cases stamped with the letters CX too; standing for *Consiglio dei Dieci*, the Council of Ten which under the Doges constituted the inner governing body of the State.

There are several other swords in the Palazzo Ducale bearing this mark which provide a link between the 'old' late-medieval *espadas eslavonas* and the seventeenth-century, and later, *schiavone*; these, with similar ones in other collections, have guards which are obviously descended from some of the South German bastard-sword basket-like hilts of *c.* 1525—1550. Figure 82 shows the more significant of these hilts, illustrating progression from plain cross hilt to basket hilt, together with two semi-basket-hilted Bavarian bastard hilts of *c.* 1575. This illustrates how the hilt developed from the old Hungarian hilt (Fig. 82 A) to the late-medieval type (Fig. 82 B) and by the addition of a pair of branches and a knuckle-guard, to a more developed form, as in Figure 82 C. This particular sword is preserved in the Hermitage, Leningrad, but is very closely paralleled by Figure 82 D in the Palazzo Ducale, Venice, where the pommel is of the more conventional western European disc form; this was still extremely popular in Italy and Spain well into the third decade of the sixteenth century. A very similar hilt, inlaid in silver and gold with designs of a distinctly oriental character, probably Venetian in origin, is in the Metropolitan, New York. Then, again in Venice, there is the sword shown in Figure 82 E. Here the pommel is square and the rear *quillon* and knuckle-guard are of a distinctively Spanish nature. Another probably Venetian sword showing these characteristics is in the collection of Mr E. A. Christensen of Copenhagen, while in the Palazzo Ducale again is a similar hilt (without the typically Spanish cut-out decoration), Figure 82 F. This one has the CX stamp on its grip. Hilts in this group, Figure 82, A to F, have much in common. Three of them (and the one which is in New York) have an extremely long point growing out of the *écusson* over the blade, almost like a langet (D, E and F); and C, E, F, Figure 82, and the New York one, have knuckle-guards of a flat ribbon section broadening strongly towards the pommel. Of these, two are in Venice (one bearing the CX mark) and one by the style of its decoration seems to be of Venetian origin. An odd one, having the Venetian/Hungarian square pommel with a central recessed boss (the recess is unusual in these pommels), also in the Palazzo Ducale, is shown in Figure 82 G. It has the typical Venetian-shaped grip, covered with gilded leather and stamped with fleurs-de-lys.

Having a reasonable amount of evidence, then, that all these hilts are Venetian, it is the pommel of Figure 82 F which provides the link between the old and new *schiavona* hilts. Its curious trident-like form is not dissimilar to some of the later—much later—cat's-head pommels (shown in Plate 15 A, for instance—and remember, it is upon a CX-marked hilt). So what of Figure 82 H? Here is a sword with an exactly similar pommel but a very typically South German hilt which contains in the complexity of its basket guards elements strikingly similar to those present in one type of the later *schiavona* basket guards. This sword was sold in the Helbing Galleries, Munich, in 1908, and is, I believe, a very significant weapon. Another, perhaps even more significant in the development of the *schiavona* basket hilt, is in the collection of Dr Giorgio Bini in Rome. This is in an exceedingly bent condition; my drawing of it in Figure 83 is a straightened-out version to show how much akin it is to the later basket hilts, while being also very closely related to the earlier South German ones, as in Figures 54 E and G. Note particularly the two crossed-over, leaf-shaped bars covering the outside of the *ricasso*. However, the most significant feature of this hilt is the pommel—not a true cat's-head, but resembling the old Hungarian style, Figure 82 A. This sword has been dated by Heribert Seitz to the early sixteenth century, though I would myself think that it must belong to the second quarter.

Figure 82 J shows another South German sword, perhaps about 1570, which was also sold in Munich, the same sale as Figure 82 H. Here again, the guards have much in common

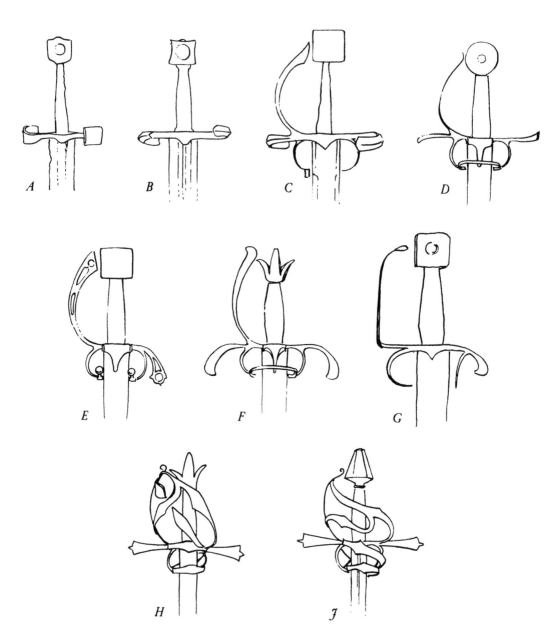

FIGURE 82   *Venetian and South German hilts, ancestors of the* schiavona *hilt*

FIGURE 83   A Venetian hilt, c. 1540
(Collection of Dr Giorgio Bini)

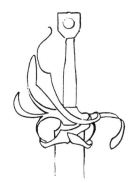

with the later *schiavona* hilts. Incidentally, these last two swords, H and J, are not broadswords but *reitschwerte*.

It is generally held that some of the late forms of *landsknecht* sword hilts had a lot to do with the development of the *schiavona* too. Figure 84 explains why.

So, then, there seems to be some evidence as to the origin and ancestry of the *schiavona*. Little of this is literary, only the two words supplied by the *Relación de Valladolid*, and—curiously—there is only one, equally tiny, piece of evidence supplied by visual art. Among all the countless hundreds of portraits of sword-wearing persons painted in the seventeenth and eighteenth centuries, and the thousands of military drawings and paintings, the only one so far noted which shows a basket-hilted *schiavona* in wear is a little drawing of a man in Turkish costume dating *c.* 1740. This might seem to suggest that the *schiavona* was a Near-Eastern weapon. Support for this view might be squeezed from the fact that in a private collection is a fine *schiavona* with a silver-gilt chape of elaborate filigree work which is uncompromisingly of Turkish design and workmanship (the chape only, not the scabbard, nor the sword). In fact, under the base of the silver-gilt pommel is a Venetian silver mark of *c.* 1770—the letters RP under a lion's head *affronté*. Actually, the Slavonic mercenary soldiers of the Republic and of Spain generally wore 'Turkish' costume, for the regions whence they came in the sixteenth, seventeenth and most of the eighteenth centuries, the Balkans and modern Yugoslavia, were all part of the Ottoman Empire. There is a passage in the *Mémoires* of Philippe de Commynes describing events in the battle across the Taro near Fornovo on July 6 1495, during Charles VIII's retreat from Naples. He writes of the mercenary light-horse employed by the Italians and called *Stradioti* (or, if they were in Spanish pay, *Estradiotas*). A large force of them had cut off a French reconnaissance patrol of forty horse, killing a man-at-arms called le Boef; they cut his head off, stuck it on a lancepoint and carried it to their captain, demanding a ducat for it—a nasty Turkish custom. He goes on:

'These Stradioti are of the same nature as the Janissaries of Turkey: they are horse and foot and dress like Turks except that they do not wear turbans. Their horses are all Turkish, and very good. They were formerly of Greek origin, from places which the Greeks control; some of them come from Naples or Romagna in the Morea, some from Albania and others from Durazzo. The Venetians employ them often in their wars and put great confidence in them.'

From 1495 to 1695—only a couple of centuries between Com-

FIGURE 84   An elaborate landsknecht *hilt, c. 1540, cf Fig. 59*

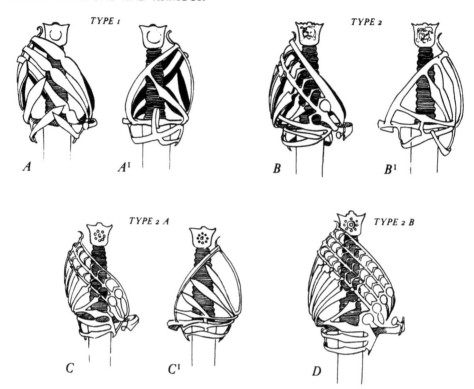

FIGURE 85   Types of the schiavona hilt
The back-guards of Type 1, shown in A, appear in A¹, the back-guards of B in
B¹, and of C in C¹

mynes' *Stradioti* and the somewhat apocryphal *Schiavoni*, who were obviously one and
the same type of mercenary.

The fully-developed *schiavona* basket hilts fall naturally into two differing types, the
second of which has two sub-types. Let us call them *Schiavona* Types 1, 2, 2 A and 2 B
(Fig. 85). Type 1 is simpler and quite different in form from the others. The guards are
always of a basic leaf-shape while the rear *quillon*, generally curved sharply round towards
the outside of the guards but occasionally left sticking straight out, is always of square
section widening a little at its end (Fig. 85 A and A¹, Plate 15). The lower part of the
'basket' in this type is always formed from two leaf-shaped elements springing from the
ends of an atrophied pair of branches and crossing over at their tips, as in the sword shown
in Figure 85 A. The back-guards (Fig. 85 B) are of a very simple form, incorporating a
thumb-ring between the lower back-guard and the grip. This hilt form seems to have no
variants, other than the way in which the guards may be bent; many examples bear the
Venice arsenal stamp of a winged lion's head *affronté* on the outermost of the forward

guards, and sometimes on the back-guards, and occasionally on both. The pommels of this type vary, but in quality and material rather than shape. A few are rather elaborate bronze ones, with various motifs in relief—a central boss, either plain or of a rose- or mask-shape, occasionally with extras in the form of wings (as in Plate 15) or smaller bosses. Some are very poor, feeble, little things of iron. Sometimes the length of the guards exceeds the length of the hilt, so the pommel almost disappears behind the upper parts of the 'basket'. In a few cases, there is a small hole pierced in the upper dexter part of the pommel, to which the little curl at the top of the knuckle-guard element of the basket is fastened. Surviving examples, if they are fastened at all, have a little piece of wire to do the job; these are mostly modern replacements, but there can be little doubt that in their original state, wire was used. The guards of these Type 1 hilts are almost always severely plain, lacking in any kind of decorative embellishment; but, as an exception to prove the rule, there is a very fine one in the armoury at Penshurst Place in Kent which has the edges of its leaf-shaped guards decorated with very restrained projections and cuspings; it also has a rear *quillon* which is absolutely typical of the *Type 2* hilts.

These Type 2 hilts are built up on a principle totally different from that of Type 1—so much so that were it not for the fact that all have the same kind of cat's-head pommel, it would be tempting to suggest that they were hilts of a different genre altogether (Figs 85 B and B¹, Plate 15), like the English basket hilts of the period 1570—1625. However, they *do* all have the typical Slavonic pommel, and so are of the *schiavona* family. The outside elements of the 'basket' are of a more complex shape than those of Type 1, splaying out quite broadly at the ends, and each end finished with a well-shaped knob (Fig. 85 B, Plate 15). This form is repeated on the single rear *quillon*, while the lower bars of the guard, like Type 1 springing from the ends of atrophied branches, are designed on quite a different principle—Figure 85 again shows this clearly. It is clear, too, that these lower guards are directly derived from the bastard hilt-style seen in Figure 54 F. The upper elements of the basket, instead of consisting of three flat bars, as in Type 1, are formed from a pair of narrow bars joining the upper part of the knuckle-guard to the inside of the rear *quillon*. These are set quite wide apart and are joined by a series of short curved bars at right-angles. Figure 85 B and Plate 15 show my meaning. The back-guards of these hilts, too (Fig. 85 B¹), are more elaborate than those of Type 1. These Type 2 hilts are treated with much more freedom than those of Type 1, for we find many variations within the basic structure.

Type 2 A is built upon exactly the same form as Type 2, except that instead of two diagonal upper bars to the 'basket' there are three, linked by a series of small bars at right-angles to form a trellis (Fig. 85 C). Type 2 B is no more than an elaboration of this, having four diagonal bars linked by small ones (Fig. 85 D). These two sub-types, which vary only in detail and according to whether they have three or four diagonal bars, seem to have been to some extent a 'regulation' pattern, for only minimal variations have been observed, while several silver-marks on pommels or scabbard-mounts have given dates within the period 1750—1800. Some of these 2 A and 2 B hilts have curious little star-like excrescences forged into one of the bars of the back-guards; it is hard to resist a temptation to believe that this is some kind of identification or distinguishing mark, though there seems little chance of ever being able to discover what.

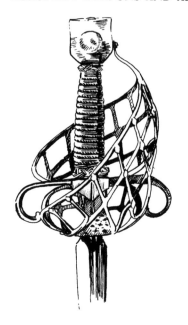

FIGURE 86   Rapier, c. 1630, with hilt of schiavona form
(Museum of Fine Arts, Boston)

In the Museum of Fine Arts, Boston, is a rapier (Fig. 86) with a narrow blade—a true rapier, not a *reitschwert*—but its hilt is a cross between a *schiavona* Type 2 and a Cavalier rapier's hilt. It has the *schiavona's* cat's-head pommel, a basket guard like an adaptation of Type 2 A, long, slender, down-curled *quillons*, branches and an oval outer shell and a triangular inner one, fitting into the back of the basket which, uncharacteristically, is almost a mirror-image of the front. The forward shell is an oval ring filled with a thin steel plate elegantly pierced with a pattern of circular and star-shaped holes. The triangular insert in the back-guard is filled with a similarly decorated plate. These plates, this kind of pierced decoration, these curled *quillons*, are all absolutely typical of rapier and *reitschwert* hilts of the period from about 1625 to 1645, mostly of Netherlands origin.

This hilt seems to supply some fairly hard evidence that *schiavona* Type 2, or even 2 A, hilts must have been in use as early as the second quarter of the seventeenth century. Thus, as it seems reasonable to assume that Type 1 preceded them, we are left wondering by how long? Were they in fact in use late in the sixteenth century, as was once believed? Until further evidence appears, we can only speculate; for one thing, there is no adequate reason for assuming that Type 1 *did* precede Type 2. They could equally well have evolved—or been designed—in different areas simultaneously. There is evidence which can be made to support either theory: first, the Type 1 hilts do bear a very marked structural resemblance to hilts which are absolutely indisputably of mid-sixteenth-century date; if they are a direct development of these, and Type 2 hilts developed from *them*, then *ipso facto*, they must have come first. But, the second piece of evidence: many Type 1 guards bear the Venetian arsenal mark; so, they are of Venetian origin. Type 2 hilts, however, do not; and the variations of detail in their design, and the frequency with which decorated examples occur (unlike the Type 1 hilts, which are only decorated at all in exceptional cases) as well as the fact that examples are found all over Europe while none (of Type 2) are in Venice, does suggest that here was a less regional form of the hilt, in widespread use all over Europe. A Type 2 guard, for instance, now in the National Museum of Wales, Cardiff, was dug out of the tidal mud of the River Taff, perhaps a relic of the Civil War.

Hence it could be argued that Types 1 and 2 are contemporary, but of different origin. However, that Sub-Types 2 A and 2 B are of definitely Venetian origin, there can be no doubt at all, any more than that they date, broadly speaking, between about 1740 and 1780. There is still a certain amount of decorative treatment, to the edges of the bars which form the basket, for instance, in 2 A examples; but 2 B seems to have been, as nearly as anything in the later eighteenth century can be, a regulation pattern; variations are minimal and decoration, if any, is confined to the chapes of scabbards.

Some interesting (and most confusing) evidence as to dating is to be found in the hilts of these 2 A and 2 B *schiavone*. For instance, the silver-mark I have just mentioned, the letters RP under a lion's mask, has been identified as the stamp of a Venetian silversmith working in the 1770s. The same mark appears on one of the scabbard-mounts of a 2 B in the Klingenmuseum, Solingen. This sword also has the numerals *1909* roughly incised upon the back-guard. In Britain are two 2 B examples, both of the same pattern as this Solingen one; one, the *schiavona* in the Armouries of the Tower of London, has the numerals *1781* incised on the back-guard, while the other, in the Royal Scottish Museum, Edinburgh, bears the figures *1780*. Another of the same pattern, sold at Christie's on April 14 1966 (Lot 152), has *1561* incised on the back-guard. But that is not all. The Tower of London example has, as well as the figures *1781*, the letters M.C. on its guard. So has the one sold at Christie's. So here we have two identical swords (or as nearly identical as two swords of the same pattern can be) with the same letters, M.C., on them, but one carrying the figures *1780* and the other the figures *1561*. In the collection of the *Cavaliere* Luigi Marzoli in Brescia there is yet another, with the letters M.C. but no figures.

It has long been accepted that the figures on the Edinburgh and Tower of London examples, *1780* and *1781*, represent dates—dates not at all inconsistent with the silver-marks. How then does one reconcile a 'date' of *1561* for a similar hilt? I believe the Solingen example gives us the reply—one does not. No *schiavona* was ever made in 1909. Another 2 A hilt was sold in a London saleroom in 1970 with a long inscription crudely cut on the back-guard in characters which might be Russian (Fig. 87) and this, if translated, might give another clue to the dates of these hilts.

The quality of all these hilts varies. Most of the *schiavona* hilts are quite plain (though the Penshurst one suggests that there were exceptions) but in the quality of their pommels and blades they vary greatly. Some pommels are poorly-shaped, feeble, flat iron things, whereas others are splendid bronze ones which by themselves would qualify as works of art for the excellence of the lion masks, ferocious whiskered faces, *putti* or roses which form the central boss; a few are of silver. Where the pommel is of iron (or of the same feeble form in bronze), the blade is broad, not as a rule more than thirty inches (77·5 cm) in length, with a short, rather nondescript, broad fuller at the forte; but if the pommel is good, then as a rule the blade is of excellent quality, often being a century or more earlier in date than the hilt. One which was once in my collection (Plate 15 A) has a magnificent back-edged blade some thirty-six inches long (91 cm), with a panel of excellently drawn floral scrolls, so typical of Italian work of the period *c.* 1490—1510, etched (and once gilt) on the forte; the sword at Penshurst has an admirable thirteenth-century blade, from a sword of a type which I have classified as Type 12. It seems

FIGURE 87   Inscription on the back-guard of a
Schiavona 2 A hilt

probable that the commoner swords were Regimental issue weapons, whereas the better ones were not.

With the Type 2 and 2 A hilts, however, things are different; most of the guards are of good quality, well-proportioned, while none (that I have seen, that is) has an iron pommel. Many have severely plain, but well-shaped, cat's-head pommels of bronze or silver (Plate 15 B), others have more elaborate ones with masks and so on (Plate 15 C). Many have elaborately-decorated guards: one in the Marzoli Collection has a hilt of browned and blued iron, with a line of silver inlaid just inside each edge of each element of the 'basket'. Another, in the Odescalchi Collection, has a quantity of little gilt rosettes all over the guard; while a third (Type 2 A) in the Christensen Collection has the edges of its bars filed to a graceful wave-like pattern. A Type 2 hilt formerly in the Peter Dale Collection (Plate 15 B) has its iron guard thickly gilded with an incised line just inside the edge of each element of the guards. The blade of this sword is of magnificent quality, with a very broad fuller etched and gilded from hilt to point with trophies and various floral motifs and the insignia and name of the Emperor Charles VI (ruled 1711—1740), which gives the sword a date in the first half of the eighteenth century, a good hundred years later than the Type 2 hilt style of the Boston rapier and of another Type 2 (seen in Plate 15 B) whose double fullers bear the figures *1414* four times repeated. Blades inscribed with figures of this kind—*1414, 1415, 1444, 1515*—all date within the first half of the seventeenth century. So here are two hilts almost exactly the same in design though they may be a century apart in date.

The only conclusion with regard to dating which can be drawn from all this is that the general *schiavona* pattern of hilt was in use between about 1610 and 1770. Maybe the Type 1 pattern was earlier than Type 2, maybe it was a Venetian as against a South German style; and maybe both were in use by 1600. That Type 2 A was in 'regulation' use along with its variant 2 B in the second half of the eighteenth century is suggested by the silver-marks and by the fact that many are still preserved in the Palazzo Ducale, Venice; and if all of these were to be examined, no doubt further troop or arsenal numbers would be found on their guards.

The reader will have observed, probably with irritation, that in all the foregoing comments upon swords, there is only very scanty mention of blades. The reason is that any close discussion of sword-blades in the sixteenth and seventeenth centuries would require a large volume to itself, so great is their number and so varied their styles and the work of the bladesmiths who forged them. Since it has been necessary for the basic purpose of this work to include at least some mention of all kinds of edged weapon in use during so long a period—an impossible task anyway with less than encyclopaedic scope!—as well as a reasonably careful sketch of the development and decline of armour, deeper study of blades has been ruled out. However, may I draw attention to the books listed below and at the end of Chapter Two and Chapter Six.

NOTE

Since the manuscript of this book was sent to the printer's, a sword has come up in a London saleroom (and is now in a private collection in the U.S.A.) which may set back the dating of the fully-developed 'Highland' hilt by nearly half a century. It came from the collection at Apethorpe Hall, Peterborough, in Northamptonshire, most of which was assembled for practical purposes during the Civil War (1642—1651) and has not been disturbed since then. It is a small, typical 'claymore' hilt fitted with a good back-edged blade of a kind commonly found in the hilts of mortuary-type swords; and though the bars and plates have neither piercings or decorated edges, and the back-guard (like so many) has been removed, it is still of precisely the same form as the fully-developed hilt hitherto considered to be little earlier than *c.* 1700.

This find does seem to suggest that the developed form was in use at least as early as 1650, probably before; and also that the 'beaknose' hilts considered to be fore-runners of the developed form were in fact contemporary. Their distinctive shape and the crudeness of their execution probably indicates a local regional origin rather than an earlier date.

BIBLIOGRAPHY

Blair, Claude, *A Schiavona Rapier*, Journal of the Arms and Armour Society, Vol. V, No. 12, 1967

Scott, J. G., *Basket-Hilted Swords of Glasgow Make*, Scottish Art Review, Vol. IX, No. 1, 1963

Whitelaw, Charles E., ed. Barton, Sarah, *Scottish Arms Makers*, Arms and Armour Press, 1977

The lists of material given at the end of Chapter Two and Chapter Six also apply.

CHAPTER ELEVEN

ARMOUR IN DECLINE

On February 25 1525, François I of France was defeated and made a prisoner of war by the Emperor Charles V in a desperate confused battle fought in the half-light of a winter dawn among the plantations and gardens of a nobleman's park outside Pavia. One of the turning-points in political history, it was also a watershed in the history of armour, for by eleven o'clock on that Friday morning, the Imperial arquebusiers had finally made it plain that no force of armoured chivalry could any longer be effective against the power of the bullet. Two centuries earlier, the disasters of Morgarten (1315) and Crécy (1346) had convinced the military thinkers of Europe that better defences than the old reinforced mail were needed against the halberd and the longbow. These battles above all others gave the decisive impetus to the development of the full harness of plate; and in 1525, Pavia brought home the realisation that this would at last have to be abandoned.

The outcome of Pavia was determined by the action of infantry and lightly-armoured cavalry. After some success in the early minutes of the battle, the heavily-armoured *gens d'armes* of François' *Compagnies d'Ordonnance*, the flower of old-style chivalry, were shot down by Charles's arquebusiers; and after François' Swiss had been driven off the field by the Emperor's *landsknechte*, his knights were totally destroyed; killed or captured to a man. The slaughter of France's nobility in this battle was only equalled by that of Agincourt. The whole affair, ending with the King of France in a Spanish prison, was highly dramatic, as theatrical as François' alleged *cri de coeur* in his letter to his mother after the battle, 'All is lost, save honour.' What he actually wrote was:

'Madame, to let you know the state of my misfortune, not a thing remains to me but my honour and my life, which is secure. And since in your trouble this news may be a little comfort to you, I have begged to be let write this letter, which has been freely accorded. I implore you not to take it too hard, using your customary sagacity, for I have confidence that in the end God will not desert me . . .

And with this humbly commending himself to your good grace, your very humble and very obedient son, François.'

It was his reporters who afterwards turned his sentence to the dramatic saying, worthy of a Viking.

Here we take leave of the monarch with whose birth we began in 1494, and with his eclipse (only temporary, as it happened) we fully enter another era in the story of armour.

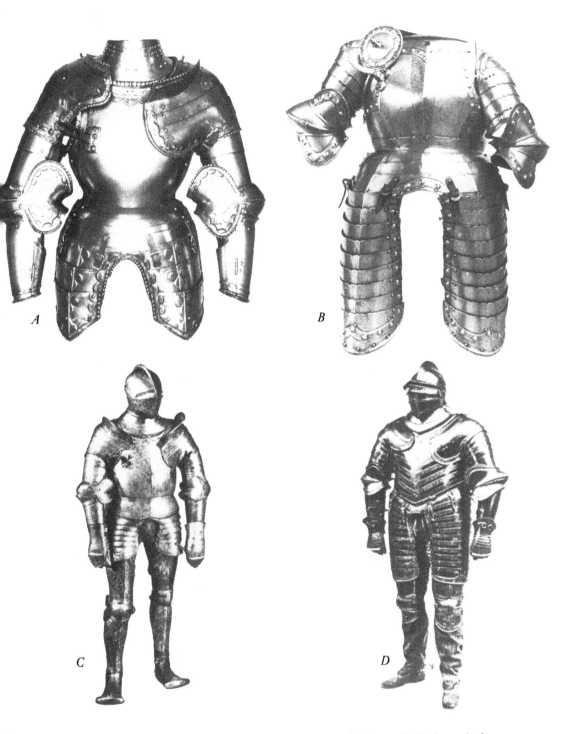

Plate 17   A   Part armour, German (Augsburg), *c.* 1515–1520: unmarked but probably the work of
Koloman Helmschmied; similar in workmanship to the 'KD' armour of Charles V

          B   Part of an armour, German (Brunswick), *c.* 1540: '*Tapulbrust*' breastplate; the long tassets
suggest that it was meant to be worn without legharness

          C   Armour of Galiot de Genouilhac (1465–1546), *Maître de l'Artillerie* to François I

          D   Armour of Anne de Montmorency, Constable of France (1493–1567): but see page 207

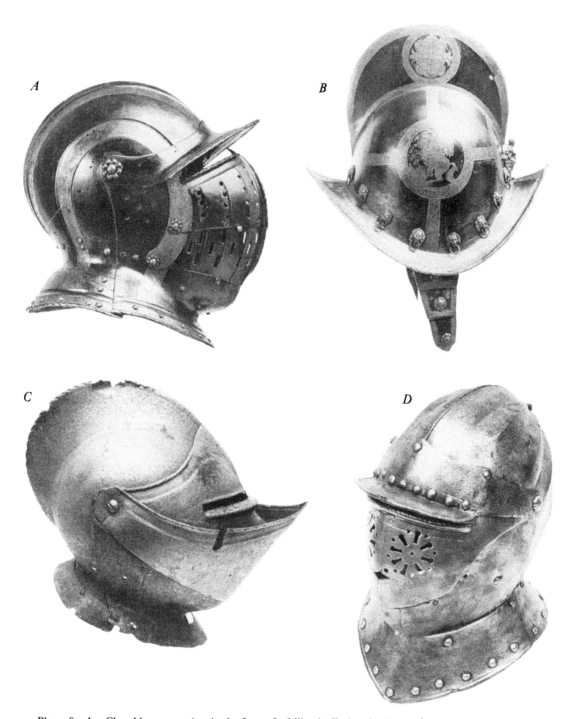

Plate 18   A   Closed burgonet: visor in the form of a falling buffe, but forming an integral part of the
bevor which is pivoted above the ears in the manner of a close helmet: *c.* 1540
          B   Morion, German (Nuremberg), *c.* 1580: chin-straps formed of three plates on either
side secured by rosette-headed gilt rivets: made for the Guard of the Electors of Saxony
          C   Close helmet, Italian, *c.* 1550–1560
          D   '*Todenkopf*' close helmet, German (?), *c.* 1630

Plate 19 A *Landsknecht* dagger and sheath, German, *c.* 1530–1550
     B Holbein dagger and sheath, Swiss, 1571
     C Dagger, English, *c.* 1630: similar in style to the inscribed Scottish dudgeons
     D *Maingauche* dagger, Spanish, *c.* 1660
     E Silver-mounted dirk, with sheath (and knife and fork): baluster hilt: Edinburgh
       hallmarks, 1796–1797

Plate 20

A   Rapier of *'flamberge'* type, *c.* 1650
B   Scarf-sword, English, *c.* 1630: unusually
    slender for a scarf-sword

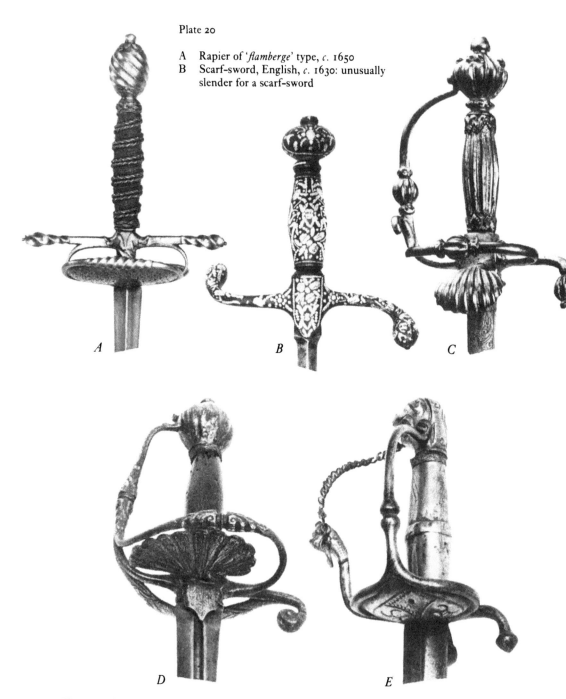

A   B   C

D   E

Plate 20   C   Loop hilt, South German, *c.* 1640: one loop only, downward shell lying parallel with
(*cont.*)   plane of blade (*cf* D, below)
           D   Loop hilt sword, German/Netherlands, *c.* 1640: chiselled steel decoration: shell fits flat
               within the outside loop guard
           E   Sword with dog's-head pommel, Netherlands, *c.* 1650–1660: *cf* Rotius' painting, 'The
               Banner of Capt. Jan Simonsz Jongemasts', Town Guard of Hoorn (1652)

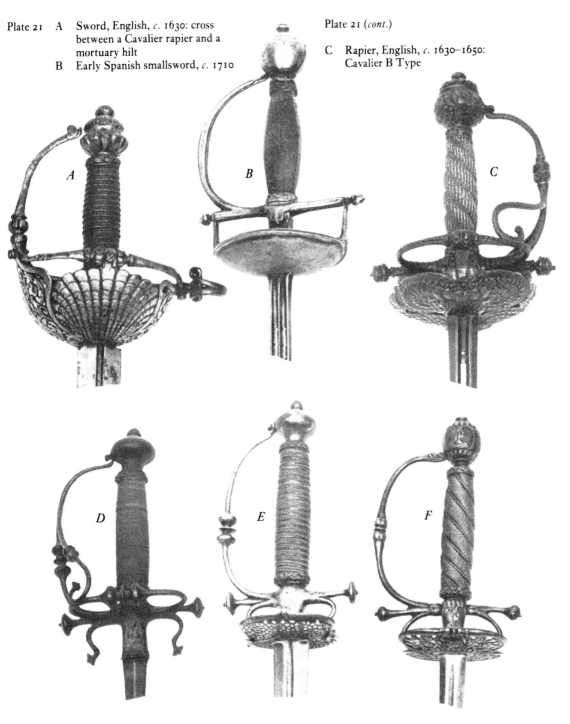

Plate 21   A   Sword, English, *c.* 1630: cross
                between a Cavalier rapier and a
                mortuary hilt
           B   Early Spanish smallsword, *c.* 1710

Plate 21 (*cont.*)

           C   Rapier, English, *c.* 1630–1650:
                Cavalier B Type

Plate 21   Three swords of North German/Netherlands origin, *c.* 1640–1710, showing the transition
(*cont.*)   from the late forms of Cavalier hilt to the true smallsword form:
           D   *c.* 1630–1640: note the disc-like terminals to the *quillons* (shells missing)
           E   *c.* 1640–1650: in form, a true smallsword
           F   *c.* 1680–1700: a true smallsword except that it retains the forward *quillon*

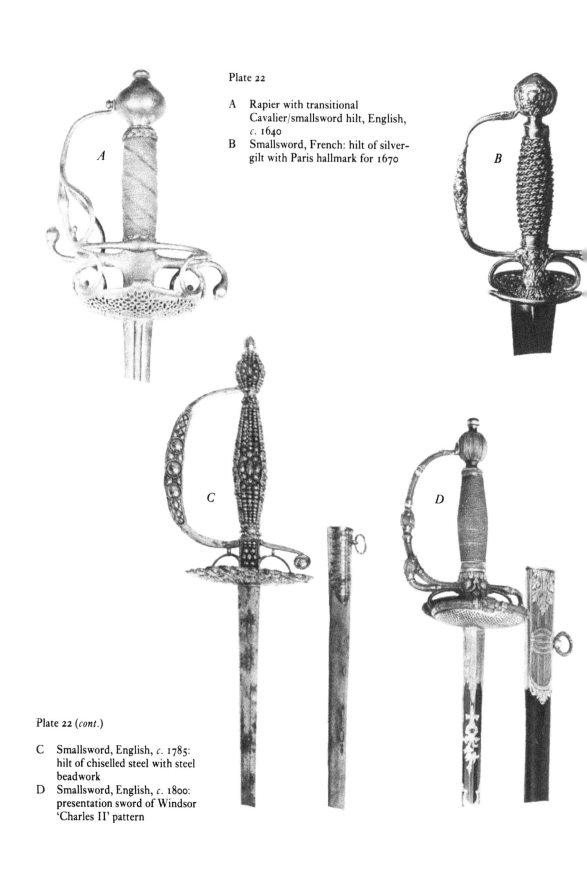

Plate 22

A   Rapier with transitional
Cavalier/smallsword hilt, English,
c. 1640

B   Smallsword, French: hilt of silver-
gilt with Paris hallmark for 1670

Plate 22 (*cont.*)

C   Smallsword, English, *c.* 1785:
hilt of chiselled steel with steel
beadwork

D   Smallsword, English, *c.* 1800:
presentation sword of Windsor
'Charles II' pattern

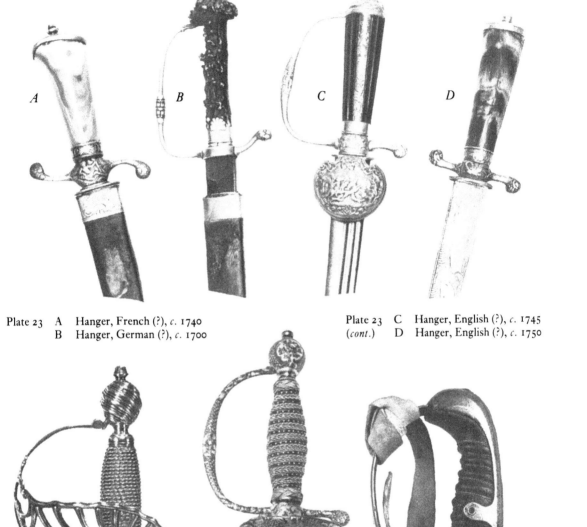

Plate 23   A   Hanger, French (?), *c.* 1740
          B   Hanger, German (?), *c.* 1700

Plate 23   C   Hanger, English (?), *c.* 1745
(*cont.*)   D   Hanger, English (?), *c.* 1750

Plate 23   E   English Dragoon officer's sword, *c.* 1760: silver hilt
(*cont.*)   F   Smallsword, French, *c.* 1760: hilt delicately engraved with a trellis pattern enclosing
               cartouches, each containing a rose, against a gold ground: scabbard-mounts *en suite*
          G   Heavy Dragoon officer's sword, English, of the 1796 pattern: back-edged blade etched,
               gilded and blued at the *forte*: hilt retains original buff-leather liner, as well as sword-
               knot of pipeclay buff-leather

Plate 24   Armour for the *Gestech*, German, *c.* 1490

For the rest of the century, the battlefields of Europe would be dominated by 'shot': arquebusiers on foot, pistoleers on horseback, arquebusiers mounted for mobility but fighting on foot (dragoons they would be called in the next century), and lightly-armoured cavalry. It will be appropriate at this point to go back a little in time, to the early part of the century, and discuss the various kinds of armour provided for these troops.

BODY DEFENCES

The basis of all armour has always been defence for the trunk and the head. Whatever other parts of 'full' armour may have been discarded, a cuirass and a helmet have been an essential protective nucleus right up to the present day. In this sense 'cuirass' does not necessarily mean a breastplate and backplate of steel. From the time of the Pharaohs, there have been many kinds of body defence in use made from natural materials—horn scales, crocodile skin, leather, quilted fabric—and many which incorporated small plates of metal, bronze or brass or iron, together with fabric. This kind of armour lasted all through the Middle Ages and became more popular than ever during the sixteenth century, only to be finally superseded by the 'buff coat', a full-skirted long-sleeved coat of thick deerskin, in the 1620s.

One is tempted to regard these defences—brigandines, jacks, eyelet doublets, penny-plate coats, and so on—as only fit for military riff-raff or poor men. In fact, they were so comfortable, and in their limited way so effective, that they were much worn by the noblest of Europe's knighthood. In the fourteenth and fifteenth centuries, a brigandine or a jack might be worn with full vambraces, pauldrons and legharness, instead of a steel cuirass.

Of the combination garments of iron and fabric, and the all-fabric or leather ones like the eyelet doublet and the buff coat, there were many varieties. They might have long sleeves, or short sleeves, or none; they might have skirt-like flaps or not (in the case of buff coats, they might be like short jackets or like frock-coats); and there were various ways of opening them—down the front or the back or even at the side.

THE BRIGANDINE

The brigandine was a time-honoured garment made in the same way as the old coat of plates of the thirteenth and fourteenth centuries (*A of W*, pp. 286—287), upon the principle of small plates of iron fastened by rivets to the inside of a fabric cover. In the case of the brigandine, the plates were all very much smaller; whereas the old coat of plates might contain as many as twenty plates, or as few as six, a brigandine might contain hundreds, working over each other and producing a very flexible defence. Some idea of the appearance of a brigandine can be gained from an entry in the inventory of the effects of Thomas, Duke of Gloucester, in 1397:

'j peir briganters coverez de rouge velvet garnisez dargent endorrez ove j peir maunches de plate . . .

'j peir briganters coverez de blu baudekyn garnisez dargent ove les manches sanz plate . . .

'j peir briganters dont le pys & le dos blanc et de bas coverez de blu velvet.'

A brigandine covered with red velvet, garnished with silver-gilt, and having plate sleeves, and another covered in blue baudekin garnished with silver and having fabric sleeves, must have been very handsome, and probably gave the same outward appearance as a tight-fitting jupon covering a mail hauberk or a plate cuirass. The other, with a 'white' back and breast (*i.e.*, plain polished steel), but a skirt covered in blue velvet, is a near approach to the 'alwyte' harness which became universally popular a couple of decades after. Philippe de Commynes, in his *Mémoires*, writing of the Siege of Paris by the Lords of the League of the Public Weal in 1465, in telling of the array of the Lords as their forces marched on the city, says:

'The Count of Charolais [Charles the Rash, later Duke of Burgundy] and the Duke of Calabria took great care to command and keep order in their armies. They rode fully-armed and seemed willing to fulfil their duties well. The Dukes of Berri and Bretagne rode at their ease on small palfreys, wearing lightly-armed brigandines. Some said that they only had little gilded nails sewn onto satin so they weighed less, but I do not know the truth about this.'

THE JACK

The jack is a humbler garment altogether, made of hundreds of small plates of iron or horn sandwiched between two layers of fabric and secured by a criss-cross trellis of stitching. Even these were often covered with rich stuff; when the peasant rebels of 1381 stormed John of Gaunt's palace of the Savoy in London, they got hold of one of his jacks—maybe it had his arms, England and France quarterly with his cadency mark of a label of four points—and stuck it up on a pole in the Strand to shoot arrows at.

THE PENNYPLATE COAT

Both the brigandine and the jack were very widely used by archers, pikemen, arquebusiers and musketeers from the fifteenth century until about 1620. Another, even cheaper garment was the pennyplate coat, a jack-like garment made up of many small discs of iron or horn each secured by a rivet to a canvas backing.

THE EYELET DOUBLET

There was also the eyelet doublet, a short jacket made of canvas (fustian) covered with little round holes, each sewn round with a buttonhole stitch. Sir John Smythe, in one of his literary works called *Instructions, Observations and Orders Militarie* (written by 1591, not published until 1594) says that:

'. . . archers should either wear Ilet holed doublets that will resist the thrust of a sword, or dagger, and covered with some trim and gallant kinde of coloured cloth to the liking of the Captains, with their sleeves striped within, with certen narrow stripes of serecloth or maile, to resist the cut of a sword, or else Jackes of maile quilted upon fustian.'

SILK ARMOUR

There was another sort of fabric armour which came briefly to life, probably only in England, late in the seventeenth century. This was silk armour. Some pieces are preserved in the Pitt-Rivers Museum, Oxford. It there consists of wadding secured upon a backing of stiff stuff—leather or canvas—and held in place by quilting under a cover of salmon-coloured silk. It was supposed to be pistol-proof, and was made in the form current in everyday armour of its period: pot helmet, cuirass and long bridle-gauntlet for the left hand. Roger North wrote in *Examen* (posthumously published, 1740) that anyone wearing it 'was as safe as in an House, for it was impossible anyone could go to strike him for laughing'.

THE BUFF COAT

The buff coat probably first came into use late in the sixteenth century. One is tempted to suppose that its origin was the old arming-doublet, for since the 1530s armour had often been worn over a doublet of plain deerskin or hide. This was probably found to be as effective against sword-cut or pike-thrust if it was worn *without* the steel cuirass which was meant to cover it as the Roundhead troopers later found their buff coats to be in the Civil War. (The garment which is understood by the term 'buff coat' is, of course, a long-sleeved coat with full and wide skirts which covered the thigh almost to the knee when the wearer was mounted.)

MUNITION HALF-ARMOUR FOR INFANTRY

From the end of the fifteenth century the foot soldier had tended to use a sort of part-armour—indeed, he had undoubtedly done so from ancient times, but it was not really until the rise of the disciplined Swiss in the second half of the fifteenth century, followed by their (slightly less disciplined) imitators and rivals, the *landsknechte*, that infantry was supplied with armour specifically designed for it. Previously, infantry had been pretty generally despised; necessary and expendable, armed with what it could get. But with the rise of large, mercenary, semi-permanent forces of effective infantry, and the 'munition armour' mass-produced to satisfy the needs of the hard-headed businessmen who 'ran' these forces, a new kind of harness appeared. At its least expensive, it consisted of a breastplate, worn without a backplate but secured by straps crossed behind, and a light open helmet (*q.v.* below). More elaborately, it had a backplate, a steel collar and short vambraces made in the form of long spaudlers reaching almost to the elbow (Fig. 88). In

FIGURE 88   An 'Almain collar', c. 1530

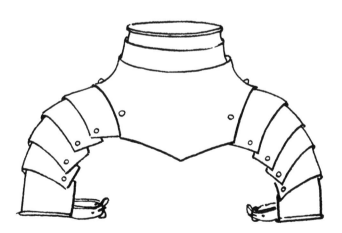

England this arrangement was called an 'Almain collar'. The next stage upward comprised a cuirass, collar, skirt and tassets, and these same long spaudlers, which have been called occasionally 'monnions', a very rare seventeenth-century term (from the French *mognion*). A better arm-defence produced in enormous quantities during the period 1480—1530 or thereabouts, known in England as 'splints', consisted of vambraces very similar to the early-fifteenth-century German ones; there was a small spaudler of three or four lames, fastened by sliding rivets to a half-upper-cannon, which in turn was fixed to the upper edge of a shallow saucer-like couter either by sliding rivets or by internal leathers; below this was a gutter-shaped half-lower-cannon, fixed in the same way to the lower edge of the couter, ending in laminated extensions over the backs of the hands instead of gauntlets.

Such armours were what the English called 'corslets' or 'Almain rivets'. In 1512, Guido Portinari, a merchant of Florence, supplied to Henry VIII:

'2,000 complete harness called Almayne ryvettes ... accounting always a salet, a gorjet, a breastplate, a backplate and a pair of splints for every complete harness at 16s a set' [*Letters and Papers of Henry VIII*, 1, 415, 1862].

Much of this half-armour was made in the 'Maximilian' fluted style. There are some extremely fine examples, dating from quite early in the century, in Bologna, in the Swiss National Museum, Zürich, and in the Wallace Collection (A 210, by Koloman Helmschmied, etched by Daniel Hopfer). A style which came into fashion a little later, mostly in conjunction with breasts of the ridged or peaked forms (*q.v.* below), was the famous black-and-white armour which collectors have tended to dub '*landsknecht* armour'; the plates are edged with broad bands sunk fractionally (about 1 mm) below the level of the rest of the plate; these bands are left white, while the main areas of the plates are blackened. Most breastplates of this fashion had three bands of 'white' across them or, instead, designs such as fleurs-de-lys. Many of them had the 'white' areas beautifully etched.

These light armours could also be fitted with complete vambraces and large pauldrons; a few even had lance-rests and the right pauldron's front plates recessed upwards to accommodate the couched lance. There are many—countless—plain ones, some of poor quality, but also many superb 'half-armours' and 'three-quarter-armours' made by the great masters for the Princes of Europe. This kind of armour seems to have been worn mostly with tassets a good deal longer than those in use with complete armour. For infantry use, the tassets were either of mid-thigh length or reached down to the knee, the curving lower edge of the lowest lame just covering the top of the kneecap. In some illustrations these tassets are shown hanging free—as in Dosso Dossi's portrait of Alfonso d'Este (Fig. 26, above) but in other cases they were secured by a tape or a thong tied round the leg.

The factors which in these light armours differentiated those for use on foot from those for mounted wear are found in the pauldrons (if any) and the tassets. An infantry armour has symmetrical front plates to the pauldrons, a cavalry one has the lower edge of the right pauldron cut higher than the left one to allow a lance to be couched under the arm; and cavalry tassets tended to be, as it were, combination tasset-with-poleyns so that the knee, always vulnerable on horseback, was properly protected. However, it should not be taken for granted that an armour with a long tasset was only for mounted use, or the other way round; judging by the numerous engravings of all kinds of sixteenth-century soldiery which survive, it seems that the light armours were used freely by horse and foot alike.

Among the finest of these armours are two in London made *c.* 1540 for the court of Brunswick. One, in the Wallace Collection (A 32), is of bright steel with etched decoration, while the other, in the Tower, is a black-and-white armour, similarly decorated (11, 29). The main difference between these two is that the Wallace armour has (or had— the pauldrons and lower cannons and gauntlets are lost) complete vambraces, whereas the Tower one has only an Almain collar and gauntlets.

Armour such as this was very occasionally worn over legharness, usually with very short cuishes, or worn sometimes over detached poleyns. An armour which Hans Ringler of Nuremberg made in 1532 for Otto Heinrich, Count Palatine of the Rhine, has long tassets suggesting an infantry armour, but they are worn over complete legharness, and the whole harness is mounted upon a horse with a matching bard (Wallace Collection, A 52). But this is a composite armour, like so many others.

Many of these tasset-cuish-poleyn combinations were made to come apart, so that by undoing a turning-pin or a hook or a buckle, one could have long, medium or short tassets.

The infantry men who wore these armours were either pikemen or 'shot', arquebusiers or (later in the century) musketeers. The question of helmets will be treated separately, in Chapter Twelve, but it should be noted here that the infantry rarely used close helmets. The various successors of the sallet and *barbuta*—light open helmets such as the developed burgonet, the morion, the cabasset or Spanish morion, or the plain wide-brimmed pot, legitimate descendant of the old kettle hat and ancestor of the tin hat, were always worn. The 'shot' often dispensed with any kind of helmet, for the cheekplates or chinstraps and the brims tended to get in the way when taking aim.

CAVALRY ARMOUR

The cavalry could be divided into two main groups, heavy and light. The heavy cavalry, which up to Pavia wore full armour and fought with the heavy lance, began to change its tactical character in the 1530s and 1540s. The French continued to use the long lance right up to the end of the Wars of Religion at the close of the century; so, to a rather lesser degree, did the Spanish. The English developed the demi-lance, a lighter shorter weapon like a modern (that is, a nineteenth/early-twentieth-century) lance, which was not necessarily couched under the arm but could be wielded freely at the righthand side of the horse's head. The German mercenary cavalry took very early to the pistol, and became a sort of halfway force between heavy and light cavalry. They got the name of *schwarzreiter*, 'black riders', because they nearly always seem to have worn black-and-white armour. This soon got shortened to *reiter*, and as *reiter* they were known for the rest of the century, along with their secondary name, 'pistoleers'. The pistoleer was a logical development of the mounted arquebusier who was essentially an infantryman mounted for mobility. The arquebus was a difficult thing to use on horseback, but the mounted pistoleer *could* use a pistol. A few lancers remained among the main bodies of *reiter*, but the vast majority used pistol and sword: three pistols (wheel-locks), two being in holsters in front of the saddle, and another in the sash or the right boot-top, and a sword—at first a bastard sword, later a *reitschwert* or a tuck. In their heyday they used a tactical approach to their enemy which was clumsy, inefficient and downright dangerous—to the columns of *reiter*, not to their foes. They called it the 'Caracole'. They rode in column, some twenty men across, and perhaps ten to fifteen ranks deep, and approached the enemy at a trot or a canter, riding up by successive ranks to fire. The first rank cantered to within a few yards of its opponents, and fired; then one half of the riders wheeled away to the left and the others to the right, and trotted round to the back of the column to re-form and reload, or to change pistols if there was no time for reloading. Meanwhile the successive ranks were supposed to be doing the same thing—except that at this stage in the proceedings the column would be halted. Even highly-trained and rigidly-disciplined men could rarely perform the caracole effectively. The tendency was always to fire too soon; often men in the inner ranks fired before their comrades in front had wheeled away, with dire results; rear-rank men (always the scruffiest, least-experienced, poorest-armed and worst-mounted) too often fired into the air. And the innate common sense of the average horse defeated the pistoleer; when a horse is wheeled away from his bristling enemy, he trots off in the direction of home with relief, and tends to keep going in spite of his rider. When rear-rank men saw their front-rank comrades riding off the field, however unwillingly, they had a good excuse to follow.

The heavy cavalry have generally been termed 'cuirassiers' by modern writers, though the term itself did not come into use until the 1620s. The three-quarter-armour is nearly always called a cuirassier armour, even if it dates from the mid-sixteenth century. In 1632, one Captain Cruso produced a treatise, *Militarie Instructions for the Cavallrie*, in which he said that the cuirassier should be 'armed at all points', which probably meant only to the knees at this date, and should be 'accoated with a buffe coat under his arms like the Launce':

'His horse not inferior in stature and strength, though not so swift. He must have 2 cases with good firelock pistols hanging at his saddle ... a good sword stiffe and sharp pointed like the Lancier [this would be the specialised tuck for cavalry use]. This sort of Cavallrie is of late invention, namely by the Germans; for when the Lanciers proved hard to be gotten, first by reason of their horses, which must be very good and exceedingly well excersised: secondly by reason their paye was abated through scarcitie of money: thirdly and principally, because of the scarcitie of such as were practiced and excersised to use the lance, it being a thing of much labour and industry to learn: the Cuirassier was invented onely by discharging the Lancier of his lance.'

The Germans, quick as ever to come up with appropriate names for armaments, called such half- and three-quarter-armours *harnasch* and *trabharnisch* to differentiate them from the full harness known as *harnische* or *küriss*.

BASIC ARMOUR STYLES: 1525—1600

During the period 1525—1600 there were four basic styles of body armour in use. In considering the previous age, the fifteenth and early-sixteenth centuries, it was feasible to name armour-styles by the names of original owners, but once we get beyond the first quarter of the sixteenth century, this becomes impossible because there are so many surviving armours whose owners are known to us: it is thus necessary to define the styles by their forms. The earliest, which followed the SS and Maximilian styles, was the Ridged; this was followed by the Peaked, the Long-Bellied, and the extension of the latter which, at the end of the century, developed that extraordinary pointed hump at the base, and which in Elizabethan England was called a 'Peascod Doublet'.

This was the period above all others in the history of arms when the influence of a few royal and princely patrons, with the most excellent taste and most exacting standards, upon a small number of master-craftsmen and artists, produced armour of a quality and grace which cannot be matched, in spite of the fact that it was no longer regarded as essential wear upon the battlefield. Maybe that is why it has such grace, for the superb armour made for these potentates was meant primarily for show, not to sustain hard knocks—at least, only such as might be got in the tiltyard under the eyes of admiring ladies. These armours are pre-eminent as works of art because the goldsmiths and engravers who decorated them had endless scope for the most delicate work, yet never lost sight of the sculptural quality which the armourer had built into the plates themselves; they achieved an harmonious blend of the major art of sculpture with the minor arts of decoration.

Certain family likenesses can be detected in their work, too; the princes for whom they wrought their masterpieces were, many of them, closely related by blood or dynastic ties, and nearly all of them shared a fashionable taste—really, more a passion than a mere taste at this time—for fine armour. Many of them emptied their countries' treasuries in the pursuit of it, too. The armourers also had a great deal in common; young scions of Innsbruck armourers' families, for instance, worked as apprentices in the shops of the Helmschmieds in Augsburg, and vice versa—all over Germany this kind of cross-fertilisation was going on.

THE HAPSBURG ARMOURIES

The present age owes the preservation of so much fine armour to the interest shown by the sixteenth-century Hapsburg princes. All of them except Rudolf II (Emperor from 1578–1612) were avid collectors of armour and patrons of armourers. The great collection now housed in the Neue Burg, Vienna, was started in 1436 by the Emperor Frederick III who in that year obtained from his uncle all the armour which had belonged to his father, 'Ernest The Lion'. Much of it he obviously wanted as war equipment, but he seems to have regarded it also as a memorial to his ancestors. On his death in 1493, his son Maximilian I inherited the collection and added to it the armours already made for him by Lorenz Kolman of Augsburg and others. In 1496 his father's cousin, Archduke Sigismund of the Tyrol, died and left him all his armour, and ten years later, in 1506, his own son, 'Philip The Handsome', King of Spain and Duke of Burgundy, died; and he aquired armour from him as well. At the same time his patronage and active participation in the reorganisation of Sigismund's armouries at Innsbruck under Konrad Seusenhofer created a greatly-increased output. Between them, Chairman and Managing Director of a Company, as it were, they remodelled the Innsbruck workshops on the lines of the Milan factories of the great Italian firm of Missaglia. From Seusenhofer Maximilian had much armour for himself and his family and friends; indeed, he seems to have collected armour from the leading masters of the craft as a man today might collect pictures or sculpture from contemporary artists. He was at pains, too, to make rich presents of armour to his allies and rivals among the crowned heads of Europe, setting a tradition which his successors followed.

His grandson Charles, son of Philip the Handsome and Juana of Castile, inherited the crown of Spain and the duchy of Burgundy upon the death of Philip in 1506; when Maximilian died he became Emperor as well, as Charles V; but of necessity he based himself upon his Spanish kingdom. Hence his collection of armour, which outshone his grandfather's, was housed in Madrid where it—or much of it—remains.

However, his younger brother Ferdinand, Archduke of the Tyrol, and later Emperor as Ferdinand I, was an equally fervent patron of the armourers of Germany, and it was he who set in motion the events which were to concentrate so much of their best work in Vienna. On his death in 1564 his collection was divided between his sons, Maximilian, who became Emperor as Maximilian II, and Ferdinand, who was in his turn Archduke of the Tyrol. Maximilian kept his armoury in Vienna, while Ferdinand's share went to his castle of Ambras, near Innsbruck. Here he immediately began to enlarge his collection. He added to it all the arms and costumes, field, tournament and parade armours which he had used in his capacity of Governor of Bohemia and ruler of the Tyrol, as well as a good deal of armour given to him by princely guests. Then, from 1577 onwards, he began his real work of assembling armours of emperors, kings and captains, alive or dead, of the fifteenth and sixteenth centuries, together with portraits of them. This was the nucleus of his aim to create a great private museum. He had agents buying for him all over Europe and the enormous amount of correspondence and cataloguing which this entailed was undertaken by his secretary, Konrad Schrenk von Notzing. This industrious nobleman compiled a folio volume of engravings of the armour at Ambras, the first illustrated *catalogue raissoné* of its kind ever to be printed. He called it *Armentarium Heroicum*. From Schrenk's time until 1877 there is an unbroken series of inventories of this collection.

In 1606 the Ambras collection came back into the possession of the senior branch of the family, being purchased by Ferdinand's nephew, the Emperor Rudolf II. From that time onward until Franz Josef I (1830—1916), each successive Emperor except the peace-loving Rudolf (and he added much hunting equipment), added some militaria to the collection.

In 1805, the troops of Bonaparte looted Ambras and removed some of the valuable armour, which is now in the Musée de l'Armée, Paris. The following year all the rest of the collection was moved to Vienna for safety, but in spite of this it was rifled again by the French in 1809. In 1889, Franz Josef united the two collections, which had existed separately in Vienna for eighty years, in his new Kunsthistorisches Museum, and in 1936, all the armour was moved again to its present home in the Neue Burg.

So we have for study an unrivalled collection of armour, mostly of German make, but a good deal Italian, of the finest quality. In nearly every case, the date, the name of the armourer, and the name of the owner are known; a good deal of the correspondence relating to the ordering of many of the armours survives, as well as entries in accounts and inventories; and much of it can be compared with paintings in which it sets off the majesty of its regal wearers. If England had had a prince with the tastes of Ferdinand of the Tyrol, she too would have had a magnificent collection of royal armours. Her great collector monarch, Charles I, was not really interested in armour, though few people realise how much is owed to him in the national collections of pictures in London, Windsor and Hampton Court; and by the time George, Prince of Wales, later George IV, began collecting works of art and such fine arms as he could get, a national heritage of armour had, most of it, been 'throwne appon Hepes' and was lost. Much of the splendid national collection of France is Napoleonic booty, and the collections of Italy are the result of the individual efforts of nineteenth- and twentieth-century private collectors; only in Spain can the Vienna collection be rivalled, but much of the Spanish material was severely damaged in the Civil War, and since then the Spanish Royal Armoury has suffered much neglect, many of its pieces being scattered up and down the Peninsula in various provincial museums.

It is partly owing to these factors that we have more German armour to study than in the preceding periods; but it is also true that after Charles V's victory at Pavia in 1525, the armourers of Milan who had been supplying François I's forces for so long were suppressed by the Emperor for a time, and so Italian armour suffered a sharp decline in quality, as well as in the quantity produced. The great Missaglia consortium had faded away after about 1515, and though much armour continued to be made in Italy, it could not compete with the products of Augsburg, Innsbruck, Nuremburg and Landshut. However, a new style of armour, politically and militarily harmless, arose in Italy in the late 1520s. This was embossed parade armour made in a romanticised classical style, the body armour based upon antique Roman models where the musculature of the torso and back are naturalistically modelled in the steel. The most notable of these armours is one made by Bartolomeo Campi of Pesaro in 1546 as a gift to the Emperor from Guidobaldo II of Urbino. Campi is recorded as having completed the work in two months, all the intricate goldsmith's work of the decoration as well as the basic armour. This astonishing piece of fancy dress is in the Royal Armoury, Madrid.

THE RIDGED STYLE

And so to the armour styles of the period 1525—1600. In order to come to terms with the 'Ridged style', shown in Figure 89 A, we must go back to its origins in the Italian styles of the turn of the century. In its mature form, this style appears to be the result of a cross between the short, high-waisted, low-necked breastplate of the German Schott-Sonnenberg style and the ridged, rather flat breast of the Italian Giovanni Fregoso style (pp. 89—99, Fig. 24 D, E, H). The link between them is probably to be found in the Flemish armour of the second decade of the century, exemplified by many representations in art from tomb effigies to tapestries; there is, for instance, the part-armour of Italo-Flemish origin in the Hungarian National Museum (p. 98).

The true prototype of the ridged style is a garniture in the Spanish Royal Armoury, Madrid, made for Charles V before his accession to the Imperial throne in 1519. He was at this time Archduke of Austria and Duke of Burgundy, and the armour is very fine; it is known as the *KD* garniture because those initials are etched upon the haute-piece on the left pauldron. It resembles in many ways the armours of Nicolo de Silva in the Musée de l'Armée (G 7 and G 10) and the silvered armour of Henry VIII in the Tower of London, but it is neither Italian nor Flemish, being one of the finest works of Koloman Colman

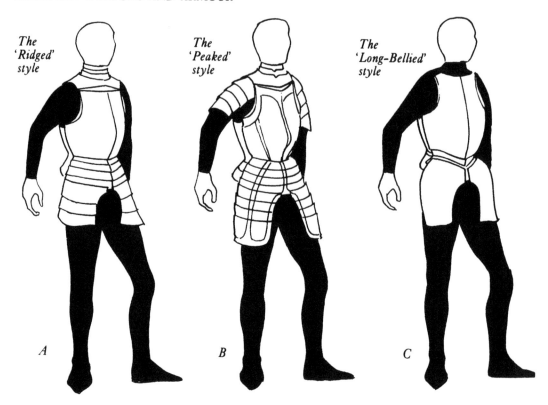

The 'Ridged' style

The 'Peaked' style

The 'Long-Bellied' style

A

B

C

FIGURE 89   Armour styles, 1525—1600

Illustration A (above), *shows the 'Ridged' style*
Illustration B (above), *shows the 'Peaked' style*
Illustration C (above), *shows the 'Long-Bellied' style*

(who at about this time took the name of Helmschmied) of Augsburg. The garniture comprises thirty-six pieces for field and tournament use, based upon two complete *cap-à-pie* armours, the field armour being the one we are concerned with. It is quite unlike any other armours made at that time in Germany (as far as we know), but in the Wallace Collection is the upper half of a very similar armour (A 30) which, although no part carries Koloman Helmschmied's mark of a helm surmounted by a star, or the pine-cone stamp of the Augsburg armourers' guild, yet bears all the unmistakable characteristics of Helmschmied's craftsmanship. It is so rich, so similar in detail and dimension to the *KD* armour, that one is tempted to suppose that it also may have been made for Charles. Whether it was he or not, one of the princes must have been its owner (Plate 17). The lefthand greave and sabaton belonging to it are in the Armouries of the Tower of London, much the worse for wear and over-cleaning, while the righthand ones are known to be in the Bargello, Florence. The cuishes are lost track of, though they probably survive somewhere in private collections.

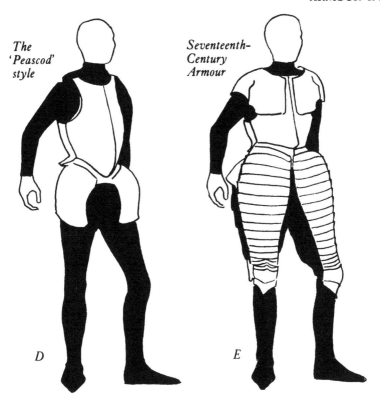

The
'Peascod'
style

Seventeenth-
Century
Armour

D

E

FIGURE 89   Armour styles, continued

Illustration D (above), *shows the 'Peascod' style*
Illustration E (above), *shows seventeenth-century armour*

The *KD* armour of Charles V and its cousin in the Wallace Collection preceded the general introduction to Europe of the ridged style by a decade; in the north, the 1520s and the early 1530s were still dominated by the globose-breastplate German style of the earlier part of the century, but by the mid-thirties the ridged style seems to have been well established. Two armours made by Hans Ringler of Nuremberg in 1532 and 1533 for Otto Heinrich, Count Palatine of the Rhine, show that both styles were in fashion at that time. One, in the Wallace Collection (A 52), has a globose breast with very long tassets; the other, in the Musée de l'Armée, has a ridged breast and much shorter tassets.

One of the best-known armours in the Tower of London is of this style, the so-called 'Giant' armour, a North German harness of *c.* 1540 made for a man six feet nine inches tall (2·05 metres). Once known as John of Gaunt's armour, for many years in the early nineteenth century it featured in the Lord Mayor's Show in London. When this armour was paraded through the streets in the procession, it became customary for the spectators to pelt it with all manner of missiles, in consequence of which it became badly battered;

the many scars it bears are not the romantic stigmata of honourable combat but the dents left by the brickbats of Londoners having fun. Another large Brunswick armour of this date is in the Kienbusch Collection, Philadelphia. It has no marks but clearly belongs to a series of armours made for the court of the Duke of Brunswick by Peter von Speyer, the court armourer of the Elector of Saxony. This one seems to have been made for the Duke himself. It is an immense armour—Duke Julius stood six feet four tall (1·9 metres) and was big in proportion (a striking man)—but it is particularly interesting for its quality and adaptability; it has long knee-length tassets and full legharness and sabatons as well. The greaves are articulated with seven little lames at the ankle, and the straight up-and-down shape of them suggests that they were meant to be worn over long soft boots. The armour is black, with fine sunk borders of polished steel outlining the plates. On the breast is a silvered medallion finely etched with Daniel and a pair of lions in a rocky landscape, with an angel accompanying a woman carrying a loaf of bread and a tall jar. Around this:

> *ACH GOTT BEWAR NICH MER DAN LEEB SIEL GUT UND ERE*
> 'O God, protect no more than body, soul, property and honour'

One is tempted to wonder what she had left *to* protect. Among the letters are cherubs' heads, and below are the initials *HI* for *Herzog Iulius*.

In Vienna three other armours, all in the Brunswick fashion and possibly from Peter von Speyer's workshop, show the ridged style of breastplate in an extreme form which is very nearly of the style described below, the 'Peaked'. These are the armour of Philip, Landgrave of Hesse (1504—1567), and the three-quarter light armours of two members of a Holstein family, Johan and Heinrich von Rantzau. Johan (1492—1565) was one of the most famous war heroes of his time, for which reason his armour (A 691, Vienna) got into Ferdinand of the Tyrol's Valhalla at Ambras; Heinrich (1526—1599) was one of Charles V's most famous captains and served both succeeding Emperors. He gave this armour to Ferdinand and is known to have written a poem for him about his Heroes' Armoury. All three of these armours seem to be to some extent influenced by Nuremberg technical styles, though it is not at present known where they come from. Other well-known armours in this style are a garniture made in 1537 by Jörg Seusenhofer for Ferdinand I of the Tyrol (later Emperor) and, at Churburg, a magnificent armour from the same source, made in about 1540 for Jakob VII von Trapp.

In many armours of this period, very prominent codpieces are often present. In fashionable wear, an outstanding codpiece had become *de rigueur* during the early part of the century, and with the introduction of infantry armours, this feature was included as one of the parts of such an armour. For obvious reasons, codpieces of steel were not worn on horseback, partly because the high front plate of the saddle came too close to the front of the body to allow room for a codpiece; the high saddle-steel, anyway, performed a far better protective office than a codpiece could. However, in infantry armour it was different, and it is upon such armours that in these days we find codpieces mounted. The foot-combat armour made *c*. 1520 at Greenwich for Henry VIII, now in the Tower of London, is a case in point; the foot-combat part of his garniture of 1537 is also fitted with one. In the Armouries of the Tower early in the nineteenth century several of the 'suits' in the famous 'line of Kings' were set up with codpieces; one in particular was ingeniously rigged up with a mechanical system by means of which, upon the spectator's paying a small fee to an attendant, a jet of water could be made to shoot out. This unfortunately was played by some wag when the then Bishop of London was examining the armour; a few days later, by request of the Bishop, the device was dismantled and all the codpieces removed, never to reappear until the more free-thinking days of the 1950s.

THE PEAKED STYLE

The strange peak which began to appear in breastplates during the 1540s, and which gives its name to the 'Peaked style', can have had nothing to do with fashionable trends in male dress, and it served no military purpose; and yet it lasted for a couple of decades until the Italian long-bellied style finally ousted it in the 1560s. There are not many complete armours with this style of breastplate surviving, though one of the most complete and amazing harnesses of all has it. This is a matching field armour and bard made by Kunz Lochner of Nuremberg in about 1555 for Sigismund II Augustus of Poland, which is in the Livrustkammaren, Stockholm (2603). The name of the artist who decorated this armour is not recorded, but it is an astonishing piece of work. The whole surface was etched with interlacing ribbon-like patterns of a distinctly near-Eastern character (like Persian carpets). The surface was gilded, and these patterns were coloured in black, white and red varnish, a sort of cold enamel technique. This king's brother-in-law, Prince Nicholas IV Radziwill ('Nicholas The Black') had a garniture made for himself in the same style and with a very similar pattern. The half-armour from this garniture is now preserved in Vienna, but bits of it are in Paris and New York. An interesting thing about the Radziwill armour is that the breast, instead of having the peak sticking out in the middle, almost foreshadows the peascod shape of the 1570s and 1580s; the waistline dips sharply below the navel and the ridge comes to a peak in the dip.

An extreme example of the peaked breast is a cuirass made by Paul Meitinger of Innsbruck, probably between 1554 and 1558; another good Innsbruck example is a *harnasch* made in 1555 for Kaspar von Montani by Sebastian Katzmair. It is a black-and-white three-quarter armour with great bold patterns of leafy sprays spread all over the black surface, like a wallpaper design.

Meyrick called this peak a 'tapul'. The term appears in *Hall's Chronicle*, written by the Englishman Edward Hall (*c.* 1498—1547), first published in 1542, but nowhere does the chronicler indicate what it means. Adopted by Meyrick, it has been applied to this feature ever since, though in England it has been out of use since the late 1930s. German scholars still call such a breastplate a *tapulbrust*.

THE LONG-BELLIED STYLE

During the 1530s, probably because of the Austro-Spanish occupation of Italy, the fashionable world of Europe began to be dominated by Italian modes of dress. It was at this time, too, that the new Italian methods of sword-fighting so much despised by George Silver began to influence that same fashionable world. Maybe this is one of the reasons why the Italianate long-bellied doublet began to be imitated in steel by the revivified armourers' firms of Milan and Brescia in the mid-1530s, a fashion very rapidly followed by the German masters too: hence the 'Long-Bellied style'.

An interesting transitional armour is one made for Charles V in 1538 by Desiderius Kolman Helmschmied, son of Konrad who died in that year. The breast is of the ridged style, but dips considerably below the waist and overlaps a deep waistplate. It is on a light field armour with long articulated tassets and a codpiece, together with legharness with extremely short cuishes—obviously a foot-armour and optional legharness. This is called the armour *De Fajas Espesas*. Another of Charles's garnitures in Madrid, made in 1539, is definitely of the long-bellied style. Made by the Negroli family of Milan (relatives-in-law and successors of the Missaglia family), its breastplate is made with a series of horizontal channels across it in imitation of a new form of articulated breastplate called an 'anime', where the breast is made up of a series of overlapping horizontal lames fastened together by internal leathers and sliding rivets. This is decorated on helmet, pauldrons, couters and poleyns with grotesque masks, and is called the garniture *De Los Mascarónes*.

It may be appropriate at this point to mention the names which have been borne by various garnitures in Madrid and Vienna almost from the time they were built. Nearly all of these garnitures have among the decorative motifs which adorn them some particular image by which they can be identified. In Madrid are the two garnitures just mentioned, Charles V's *De Fajas Espesas* and *De Los Mascarónes*. Belonging to his son, Philip II of Spain, are the 'Burgundy Cross' (that is, the St Andrew's Cross of the Duchy of Burgundy), *De Ondes o De Nubes* ('Waves and Clouds'), and the 'Flower' garniture. In Vienna are the *Adlergarnitur* of Ferdinand I with the eagles of Old Austria, the *Rosenblatt* garniture, decorated with rose-leaves, of Maximilian II, and the lovely 'Firesteel' armour of Philip II of Spain, dating from before he became king in 1558 (Plate 16), named from the firesteel insignia of the Order of the Golden Fleece embossed upon the couters. Such names are useful in identifying pieces, often widely scattered, but can be confusing to the layman unless they are to some extent explained.

With the introduction of the long-bellied breast, European armour more or less reached another 'International' style, for the armourers of Germany, Italy and England, as well as the so-far unidentified armourers working in France and the Low Countries, used the style indiscriminately. The easiest—indeed, the only—way to distinguish an Italian armour of this style from a German one at a glance is by the form of the tassets (which were nearly always quite long): in German armours the edges were parallel, but Italian ones were made wider at the bottom so that they spread out to enclose more of the inside of the thigh, a form producing a sort of keyhole-shaped aperture at the fork, often filled with a codpiece. However, this can be no hard-and-fast rule, for Desiderius Helmschmied's *De Fajas Espesas* field armour has very Italian-shaped tassets—indeed, the whole armour, though of German make, clearly reflects Italo-Spanish taste.

Piccadills

It was at about this time that the pauldrons and tassets of armour began to be embellished with 'piccadills'. These were scalloped borders of fabric, fastened (with lining rivets) to the inside of the edges of the pauldrons where they overlapped the breastplate and the backplate, and of tassets. This was partly decorative, partly functional: a soft fabric lining introduced between the plates of pauldrons and cuirass, and of tassets and cuishes, would prevent the slight tap and rattle which these parts make when metal touches metal. (The old fairytale of the heavy clanking of armour is, of course, as absurd as the crane-and-shirehorse fantasies.)

The word 'piccadill' is first noted in 1607: 'The several divisions or peeces fastened together about the brimme of a collar of a doublet.' It is a diminutive, *piccadilles*, of the Spanish *picado*, 'pricked' or 'pierced' or 'slashed', and in seventeenth-century England was generally applied to the bordering of collars or the stiffening of ruffs. It seems to have been very widely used upon armour during the second half of the sixteenth century—for as long as armour continued to be used, in fact.

Not much original piccadill remains, though a very fine Italian long-bellied armour in the Musée de l'Armée, Paris, has it more or less intact, and it is present on two very late half-armours in the Tower of London, made for two small boys in about 1610; these are from the Armoury of the Duke of Saxe-Altenburg (and lest any should believe that such armours for boys of eight or ten years old were merely for show, the close helmets and pauldrons of these little harnesses show numerous dents and cuts, testifying to the well-known fact that nobly-born boys were severely trained in the use of arms at a tender age, even as late as the early seventeenth century). Another outstanding example is an Italian cuirassier armour, *c.* 1610, of one of the Barberini family; this is in the Metropolitan, New York, and has its piccadills under the pauldrons, the entire length of the long tassets-with-poleyns, and in the cuffs of its gauntlets (Z 6 210). Other surviving piccadills may be seen in Florence's Museo Stibbert on part of an armour of *c.* 1560, and on the very elaborate Italian parade armour of the Emperor Ferdinand II in Vienna (A 785), though the most notable survivor is Ferdinand I's *Adlergarnitur* in Vienna (A 530), dating 1547.

Piccadills are, of course, to be seen in nearly all armoured portraits after *c.* 1550, as well as upon tomb effigies and sculptures. One of the best-known streets in Europe, Piccadilly in London, got its name from the makers and vendors of piccadill, who originally occupied its length.

Returning to the long-bellied style, we note that the breast was nearly always fitted with one or more lames at the bottom, connecting it with a waistplate, to which was attached a vestigial skirt of only one lame. Sometimes these waistplates overlapped the lower edge of the breast, but more often the waistplate was overlapped by it. This is in contrast to the last style of the sixteenth century, the 'Peascod', which had no waistplate.

One of the most striking of long-bellied Italian armours of the 1540s is a very massive three-quarter armour in the Metropolitan, New York, long believed to have belonged to Anne, Duke of Montmorency, Constable of France, who died of his wounds after the battle of St Denis in 1567. Recent research, however, suggests that it may have belonged to Henry VIII, and it seems to have had considerable influence upon armours subsequently built in his royal workshops at Greenwich. He must have acquired it in about 1540; it is a very handsome harness (part of a garniture, in fact, but most of the extra pieces are lost) with long tassets and separate poleyns, without cuishes, worn over long boots (Plate 17). The massive breastplate is an 'anime' and the open helmet, a burgonet closed by a buffe (to be dealt with later).

More evidence, if any were needed, that the long-bellied style was in use during the 1540s is given by a fine, light field armour in New York, made in 1549 in Nuremberg (though unfortunately it bears no armourer's mark, only the city guild mark of the arms of Bavaria and a Gothic *N* within a pearled border). There is also an extant garniture which Ferdinand I intended to give to François of France in 1539. This was made by Jörg Seusenhofer of Innsbruck, but only the field armour seems to have been delivered. The pieces for the tilt are now in Vienna, and probably never left Austria since François was at war with Ferdinand and his brother Charles V very soon after the first parts of the garniture were delivered to him. They are now in the Musée de l'Armée, Paris. Another very striking royal armour in the same collection is the light field armour of François' second son, the Dauphin Henri, later Henri II, which was made in about 1540, probably by Filippo and Francesco Negroli of Milan. Perhaps the best armour to illustrate the style is the incomparable 'Firesteel' field harness from the garniture made by Desiderius Helmschmied in 1546 (Plate 16), which is typical of the most popular European style from the late 1530s until the 1570s.

THE PEASCOD STYLE

It is plain that during the 1540s nearly every style of the sixteenth century was in use—the early globose forms lasted on, and the ridged, peaked and long-bellied styles were in use together. Only the exaggerated 'Peascod style' (Fig. 89 D) was absent, though this, both in the civilian doublet and in the steel breastplate, was coming into fashion in the 1560s. By 1570 it had reached a full development from the long-bellied style (Fig. 89 C). The waist dipped even more sharply towards the fork, and that curious humped projection at the base became prominent. There was very rarely a waistplate, and even the one-lame skirt had been dispensed with; instead, big swelling tassets were fastened directly to the flange at the bottom of the breastplate. Some of these tassets swelled out sharply at the waist to an inordinate width to accommodate the huge, stuffed trunk-hose of the Italian fashion; armours which were made to be worn over the tighter, knee-length breeches of the German style did not have such an exaggerated form.

It is clear from many portraits of armoured noblemen that by the 1550s and 1560s only the upper half of a field armour was generally worn, even tassets often being dispensed with. No doubt the trunk-hose, stuffed as they were with wool or tow (or even, like a pair of breeches belonging to James I of England and VI of Scotland, now in the Victoria and Albert Museum, London, with bran), would have provided pretty adequate protection even against pistol balls; and long, thigh-length leather boots had for some time been worn instead of legharness. There are enormous quantities of portraits of noblemen and princes painted between 1550 and 1600 which show the complete armour, including gorget, pauldrons and vambraces, being worn while close helmet and gauntlets lie on a table near by, but the legs are only clad in stockings and soft, very light slippers or socks—the wearers being evidently all ready to have the long boots put on. In similar portraits after about 1610, the artists (or the sitters) seem to have had less concern with portraying an elegant pair of legs, their owners being always shown booted and spurred. This very probably was because the armour itself had become so ugly and clumsy that a pair of slender stockinged legs appearing below the huge swelling tassets would have looked ludicrous, whereas the boots do provide a kind of balance.

SEVENTEENTH-CENTURY ARMOUR

By the end of the sixteenth century, complete armour was hardly worn in war except by heavy cavalry, who were more or less forced to wear 'armour of proofe' whether they wanted to or not. 'Armour of proofe' meant armour thick enough to withstand the force of bullets; cuirasses were tested (by firing a shot at close range from the appropriate firearm) as 'pistol-proof' or 'musket-proof', in the same way as in the fifteenth century armour was tested by shooting crossbow bolts at it. Needless to say, musket-proof, or even pistol-proof, armour was heavy. And at the end of the sixteenth century, all the aesthetic quality went out of armour, as if the craftsmen who made it had lost heart; as indeed they probably had in view of the dislike and scorn with which it had come to be regarded. Also, of course, its form continued to follow fashion; and the necessity to make armour conform with the short, high-waisted, huge-sleeved doublet and the colossal baggy breeches which followed the later-sixteenth-century styles of dress must have been enough to make any self-respecting master armourer throw in the towel, for the armour which they had to make can, in many cases, only be called ludicrous. Maybe merely ugly, shapeless forms would not have been too bad; but the stuff was actually comical (Fig. 89 E). Unfortunately, there are more of such armours on display throughout the western world than any other kind, often very badly set up. And it is from these pathetic and *louche* relics that the modern tourist gets his idea of armour. It is small wonder that to the average twentieth-century man, armour is a joke. To add to this impression, this early-seventeenth-century stuff is the last kind of armour which was actually *seen* in use, so it is that particular style which has got into the folk-memory; and of course it was armour of this kind upon which seventeenth-century writers, from James I of England onwards, sharpened their wits.

It might be appropriate at this point to tabulate the various forms of soldiery which comprised the armies of Europe, together with the types of armour they wore, between about 1550 and 1625. I am using English terminology, though the same kinds of soldier fought in all the continental armies.

1 Heavy cavalry, after about 1620 called cuirassiers, wore three-quarter armour, close helmets and long boots.

2 Medium cavalry were similar, but wore open burgonets, and often long spaudlers instead of vambraces and long tassets instead of tasset-cuish-poleyn combinations.

3 Light cavalry wore what was called 'harquebus armour'—cuirass, collar and spaudlers, an open helmet and an elbow-length gauntlet on the left hand, called a bridle-gauntlet, or a mail shirt, gauntlets and burgonet.

4 'Shot' before 1600 usually wore jacks, but after that more usually wore short buff coats; open helmets—morions or 'Spanish morions'—until about 1620, after which they generally made do with hats.

5 'Armed Pikes' (that is, the 'heavy' infantry put in the front ranks of pike-columns) wore cuirass, collar, pauldrons, sometimes vambraces and tassets with open helmets.

6 'Dry Pikes', rear-rank men, wore jacks with mail sleeves and open helmets or nothing.

The cuirassier was prominent in the Thirty Years War and to some extent in the early part of the English Civil War. There is an interesting example of an English gentleman's feeling about armour in a letter written in 1639 by Sir Edmund Verney of Claydon in Buckinghamshire. He was summoned by Charles I to serve against the Scots, and instructed to come to the muster armed 'as a cuirassier in russett armes with gilded studs or nayles'. Verney wrote:

'It will kill a man to serve in a whole cuirass. I am resolved to use nothing but back, brest and gauntlett. If I had a pott for the hedd that were pistol-proofe, it may be I would use it, if it were light, but my whole helmett will bee of noe use to mee at all.'

Such a minimum of armour as Sir Edmund specifies, worn over a buff coat, was in fact the more or less regular armament of all the cavalry on both sides during the Civil War, except for a regiment of heavy horse raised, for Parliament, by Sir Arthur Haselrig. Known always as 'Haselrig's Lobsters', they wore the full cuirassier armour; and some evidence that it was effective may be found in an account written after the battle of Roundway Down near Devizes in 1643, when the Royalist cavalry under Lord Byron scattered the Lobsters in one of those dashing charges for which Byron, no less than Prince Rupert, was famous. The Lobsters rode off as best they could down the steep chalky slope, Sir Arthur Haselrig himself being hotly pursued by a Royalist captain who tried in vain with pistol and sword to penetrate his armour. This produced one of the few jests, perhaps the only one, Charles I was ever heard to utter: 'If Sir Arthur,' he said, 'had been victualled as well as fortified, he might have endured a siege!'

THE ROYAL 'ALMAIN' ARMOURIES AT GREENWICH

The Royal 'Almain' Armouries, set up in about 1525 by Henry VIII at Greenwich near London, are so important that the armour produced in them deserves a section to itself, for not only was it almost the equal of the best that came out of Germany, but a distinctive national style arose in it. Its genesis was in Henry's desire to have, for himself and his Court, armour made on his native soil, with which he could match the products of the workshops patronised by his brother-monarchs and rivals in Europe. There can be no doubt that when he recognised this desire—or need—early in his reign, there were no native-born armourers who could make anything of the quality he demanded—after all, he was going to pit his armourers against the Helmschmieds and Seusenhofers. At first, in 1511, he imported Italian armourers to work for him in London, possibly at Southwark. Maybe Filippo de Grampis and Giovanni Angelo de Littis, who built the engraved and silvered armour for him, were among these. A probable production of these craftsmen, too, is the great bascinet of Sir Giles Capel now in the Metropolitan, New York. However, nothing much seems to have come of this venture, and at some time round about 1515 he brought in a group of armourers from Germany and the Netherlands. The foot-combat armour in the Tower of London is probably one of their products. They were finally established at Greenwich between 1520 and 1525 under the administrative direction of Martin van Royne, a mixed group of master craftsmen from Milan, Augsburg, Landshut, Nuremberg, Cologne, Brunswick and the Low Countries, who settled down to produce armour of very high quality and of a distinctive style, though to call it 'English' is to stretch credibility, for probably the only native-born English were brought in as an unskilled labour force.

Henry VIII's foot-combat armour in the Tower of London (11.6), although it was not from the Greenwich workshops, does already show many of those distinctive details of form and construction which characterised the work of the Greenwich group from about 1525 until the last armours made before the closure in 1637. A footnote to its quality and completeness is given by the interest taken in it during the 1950s by the National Aero-Space Agency of the United States, when the matter came up of designing space-suits for outdoor wear on the moon.

The diversity of the armour-making centres from which Henry's craftsmen came is reflected in the technology of the armour they produced. The shape of the Greenwich cuirass from the very start followed the Italian styles, whereas helmets were nearly always armets—right up to about 1610—of the German fashion, rotating upon the top of the collar. The juxtaposition of long tassets and short cuishes is in the tradition of the Nuremberg and Low German armourers; the exquisite engineering and precision owes much to Augsburg; the fastening of the cuirass with iron hinged straps engaging over turning- or spring-loaded pins at waist and shoulder is Italian; while the decoration throughout is almost always of French fashion. The English contribution in all this was probably the iron, presumably from Sussex, the charcoal to heat the forges from the woodlands to the south of London (in the sixteenth century the regions around Croydon abounded in charcoal-burners), and the labour to blow for the furnaces and bring round the ale.

Distinctive forms visible from a distance are the large, hunched pauldrons which upon close inspection can be seen to be made of a series of upward-lapping lames of even width fastened by internal leathers (not the usual series of three upper lames overlapping downwards, then a large rounded plate over the point of the shoulder with a series of upward-lapping lames below it, fixed with sliding rivets as well as leathers); and the markedly concave profiles of the upper bevors of the helmets (*q.v.* below) and the ridged, long-bellied or, later, peascod breastplates in the Italian manner.

Another thing which characterised the workshops of Greenwich was their particular interpretation of the concept of the 'great garniture'. The German masters of the first half of the century with their *wechselgarnituren* and *reihengarnituren* (p. 76, above) needed some eighty to a hundred extra pieces to complete the set, but the Italians devised a 'small garniture' which consisted simply of an infantry armour as a basis, upon which the addition of a close helmet, a heavy reinforcing breastplate with a lance-rest, and leg-harness, formed an equestrian field harness. Henry VIII, wishing to emulate the garnitures, great and small, of Charles V, ordered great garnitures from Greenwich, and van Royne's team produced a new and simple form of this whereby they achieved, with some forty extra pieces based upon a field harness, garnitures of a kind for which the Germans needed a very large number.

The second surviving Greenwich armour in date is a plain harness in Paris of *c.* 1520, but far and away the most important early one is the so-called 'Genouilhac Armour' of 1527 in New York (19.131.1). Since the early part of this century it has been believed that this armour was made for Galiot de Genouilhac, *Grand Maître de l'Artillerie* and *Grand*

Ecuyer du Roi to Louis XII and François I. It is so rich and splendid, all that remains of a garniture, that it is difficult to see why, at a period when England and France were not on particularly good terms, an exceptionally rich product of this exclusive workshop should have been made, either as a gift or under licence, for a high-ranking French officer. The entire surface is silvered and gilt, engraved all over with designs of foliage enclosing *putti*, monsters, mermaids and animals, with a series of the labours of Hercules. This engraving, as well as the design, is of Italian style, and may have been produced by the Florentine artist, Giovanni de Maiano. The only other extant armour which can match it, and even that is not so fine or so rich, is the silvered armour of Henry VIII. It is perhaps a coincidence that the actual dimensions of the Genouilhac armour are the same as those of Henry himself.

This armour also has a feature only found elsewhere on Henry's garniture of 1540 in the Tower of London: an extra, inner breastplate, quite small and made up of three narrow rectangular plates overlapping downwards. It is attached to the inside of the backplate with straps. The backplate was put on, and then this inner breastplate was firmly fastened in front, holding the back secure. Then the true breastplate was put on above it. A long threaded bolt protruding from the inner plate passed through a hole in the outer one to be secured by a nut. An extra reinforcing breastplate could be fastened over the same bolt, as well as a grand guard over the whole lot if needed. As well as this, there are other features in the Genouilhac armour which are rare. The breastplate and backplate are each made up of three vertically placed plates, and the skirt consists of one deep lame, curving at its bottom edge but slightly arched over the fork, and *overlapping* the tassets, which are attached below it. Each tasset consists of six lames, overlapping downwards, instead of upwards as in all others.

Martin van Royne was succeeded in 1536 by Erasmus Kirkenar, who must have been in control when the Great Garniture of Henry VIII, which still graces the Tower of London, was made *c.* 1538—1540. This now bright-polished armour was once blued, but only the gilded borders of the plates, probably etched by François Queblaunche to designs by Hans Holbein, retain their original colour. In Windsor Castle is another armour made for the king in 1537.

At some time around 1540, Henry acquired the Italian garniture of which the field harness is in New York. Armours built subsequently under Kirkenar's direction during the reigns of Edward VI and Mary I seem to have been influenced by this, for a number were made using the 'anime' form of articulated breast, as well as the decoration of gilded edging upon a russeted surface. The breast-and-tassets for a boy's armour in the Tower of London (11 178), perhaps made for Edward VI, is of this form, as is a similar, almost complete garniture, made *c.* 1556 for William Herbert, second Earl of Pembroke. This, in the Museum and Art Gallery, Glasgow, has its matching horse armour still with it, though all the other pieces except an open burgonet are lost.

It will not be possible to mention by name all the Greenwich armours which survive in Britain and America; let it suffice to say that the style followed fashion in England, as it did elsewhere. A group made for noblemen of Elizabeth I's court in the 1570s are distinguished by having very wide-spreading tassets; in Glasgow is one made for the second Earl of Pembroke which has the widest-spreading tassets in existence, to contain a pair of trunk-hose of truly heroic proportions. These perhaps are some of the silliest-looking armours surviving. Another in New York, made for George Clifford, third Earl of Cumberland, in 1590, is very much more restrained in shape, and is distinctive because it retains its beautiful purple-blue colour upon which the decoration in bright gilt stands out very handsomely.

An armour made in Augsburg but augmented into a small garniture and decorated at Greenwich is in the Tower of London (II.84). It was brought home by Sir John Smythe when he returned to England after twenty years of service under the Hapsburgs, on Maximilian II's death in 1576. This is a good example of a light *reiter* armour—cuirass, close helmet, almain collar and mail sleeves, with long articulated tassets with poleyns.

John Kelte succeeded Kirkenar in 1567, to be followed by Jakob Halder, the son of an Augsburg goldsmith, who had been working in the Armoury since the mid-fifties. He has left as a memorial, besides many fine armours, a large folio album of coloured drawings showing most of the armours made at Greenwich since about 1540, together with the names of their owners. (It is now in the Victoria and Albert Museum, London.) This has been of invaluable help to modern scholarship in identifying existing armours and isolated pieces. Halder was succeeded in 1607 by the last of the 'Managers', William Pickering—an Englishman after nearly a century!

BIBLIOGRAPHY

Blair, Claude, *A Cuirassier Armour in the Scott Collection, Glasgow*, Scottish Art Review, Volume XII, No. 2, Glasgow, 1969

Boccia, C. G., and Coelho, E. T., *L'Arte dell'Armatura in Italia*, Milan, 1967

    and also   *Armi Bianchi Italiane*, Milan, 1975

The list of material given at the end of Chapter Four also applies.

CHAPTER TWELVE

HELMETS IN THE SIXTEENTH AND SEVENTEENTH CENTURIES

There were four main types of helmet in use during the period 1525—1600: the burgonet, the morion, the close helmet and the armet.

THE BURGONET

The helmet most widely used in the field, both for infantry and light horse, was the burgonet. This was an open helmet, an alternative to the sallet rather than a direct descendant of it. When it was in use it was called generally a 'Burgundian Sallet'—*Salade à la Bourgogne* or *Celada Borgonona*; the shape of its skull, closely formed to the head with a short out-turned 'brim' over the back of the neck, was very similar in its development to that of the contemporary close helmet. It was a mutation of the burgonets of the early sixteenth century which were discussed in Chapter Five. The peak ('fall' in England), sometimes fixed and sometimes pivoted above the ears, remained the most prominent feature. After about 1525 the small earflaps which some of the early ones had—three or four narrow lames attached to leathers which were tied under the chin with a lace—became greatly enlarged as cheekpieces of a rectangular shape hinged against the skull just above and behind the ears. These too were laced together under the chin, except in a few rare cases where they were brought forward to overlap in front and fasten with a catch like the cheekpieces of an armet. Some German and Flemish burgonets of the last quarter of the century have cheekpieces completely covering the face except for rounded cut-outs in front of the eyes; sometimes these were extended to expose the nose and mouth, which were then protected by a narrow bar passing through a slot in the fall and secured through a staple on the brow by a wing-nut, forming an adjustable nasal. This is a purely eastern kind of face-guard which was adopted in the West largely owing to the confrontations between the Turks and the nations of eastern Europe during the sixteenth century.

In common with the close helmet which developed alongside it, the burgonet by the middle of the century had developed a tall keel-like comb across the top of the skull. A few burgonets in the 1540s and 1550s had three combs, lower and less pronounced. From the 1520s this form of burgonet was often fitted with a tall bevor ('buffe') sometimes made up of several horizontal lames overlapping upward and pivoted at the sides so that if necessary the whole of the buffe could be lowered without taking it off. In England this was known

FIGURE 90   Variations of the burgonet
(continued on pages 216 and 217)

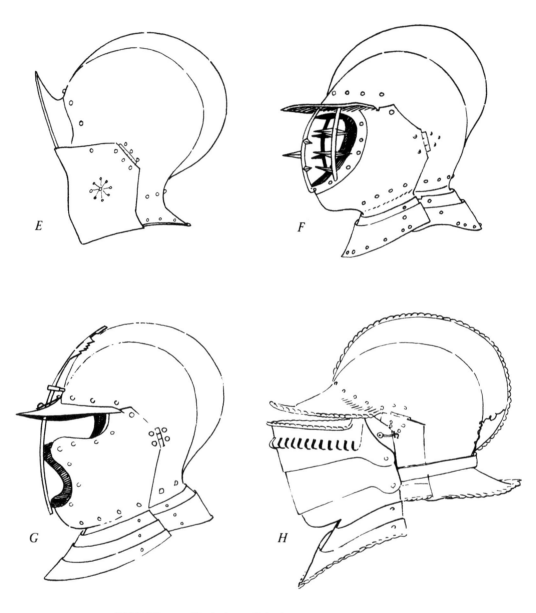

FIGURE 90   *Variations of the burgonet*
(cont.)   (begun overleaf, continued on facing page)

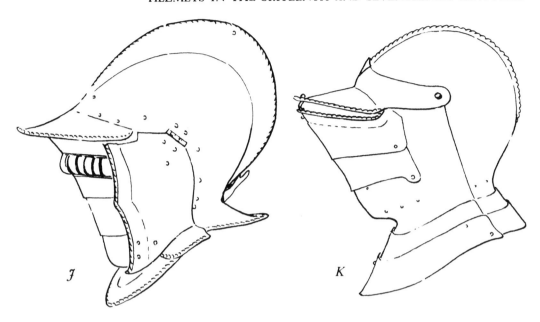

FIGURE 90   Variations of the burgonet
(cont.)   (begun on pages 215 and 216)

as a 'falling buffe'. Sight was provided either by a pair of horizontal slots cut in the upper part, if it reached right up to the underside of the fall, or—more usually—by a gap which was left between the upper edge of the buffe and the fall. It was attached by means of a strap passing round the lower part of the skull. The lowest plate of the buffe carried two or three gorgetplates to protect the throat.

There are too many variations of detail in the form of these burgonets and buffes to be able to describe or illustrate all of them; Figure 90 shows the most common of these variations. There is one group of particularly fine examples, best shown perhaps by the burgonet of the Augsburg armour which Sir John Smythe brought home with him for Jakob Halder to transform into a garniture. Of this style is the burgonet of Henry VIII's armour in New York (Fig. 90 H). This one and Sir John's have their buffes fitting over the outside of the cheekpieces, and their profiles look bold and aggressive. Another burgonet, though, of this style, once the property of the mercenary soldier Valerio Corvino Zacchei and now in the Armeria Reale, Turin, has its (very similar) buffe fitted much closer to the face and inside the cheekpieces. This, combined with a slight concavity in the line of the buffe, gives the helmet an effete, though very aristocratic, appearance (Fig. 90 J). The Greenwich burgonet in Glasgow of William Herbert, the second Earl of Pembroke, has an even stranger look. There is no comb to the skull but the shape of the buffe and the fall makes it look like a hen's head (Fig. 90 K). Incidentally, in some of these burgonets the fall is in fact a pointed peak forged in one with the skull.

A second basic form of burgonet was of a neo–classical style (Fig. 90 D). Most survivors

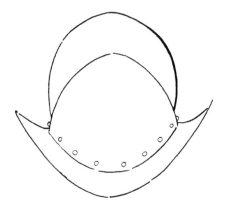

FIGURE 91   The basic form of the morion

of this form are in fact embossed with classical motifs *à l'antique*, for wear with the sort of classical fancy-dress armour so popular in the first half of the sixteenth century, but there are many which are perfectly plain, obviously workaday, helmets which nevertheless have a distinctive and extremely graceful form.

THE MORION AND THE CABASSET OR SPANISH MORION

The other styles of open helmet so popular in this period were the various types of morion. This is a helmet directly stemming from the old Spanish *cabacete* (*q.v.*, above, p. 113 and Fig. 40), and both kinds are very distinctive. The morion proper (Fig. 91) is characterised by its very large comb and a narrow, downturned brim which rises fore and aft into an acute peak. Often these helmets were of the richest workmanship, and all the decorative techniques in use were lavished upon them. Many were made by the great armourers for the princes of Europe (as indeed were burgonets), for their own wear and for the arming of their personal guards, while town and city guards too were equipped with them. Almost equal in popularity was the other form, the Spanish morion or cabasset, with its tall half-almond-shaped skull, often ending in a little back-turned stalk, and its narrow, generally flat brim (Fig. 92). These too were often richly wrought, though the majority of the countless surviving specimens are plain. Such were the munition pots supplied for the militia in the English countryside in 1588 under Philip II of Spain's threat of invasion; until the 1930s stacks of them could be found piled one inside another like hats in a hatter's shop and immovably rusted together, in many a country church in the south of England.

The close helmets and armets of the first quarter of the century began in the 1520s to give place to a

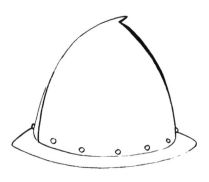

FIGURE 92   The basic form of the cabasset, or Spanish morion

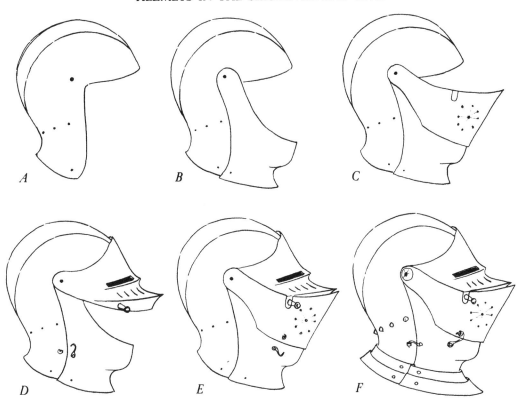

FIGURE 93   The construction of the close helmet, c. 1550, in diagrammatic form

new type. The one-piece visors of the sparrow's-beak, bellows and monkey-face forms were superseded by a more complex system of opening the face that very soon became, except for small differences of constructional detail, international and universally used. This constructional change was brought about by, as it were, cutting the visor horizontally in two just below the eye-slits; the lower part, now called the 'ventail' (but by most modern students the 'upper bevor') became almost flat-sided and shaped in the front like the prow of a ship, while the visor proper fitted down within the space at the top of it. Now the bevor (which remained the same shape as in the earlier close helmets), upper bevor and visor were all pivoted from the same point. This pivot was made by means of a threaded bolt secured by a nut inside—though in a few cases the bolt was pierced for a lynch-pin. Figure 93 shows this construction in diagrammatic form. The same principle was used for the visors of armets. The bevor (cheekpieces), still hinged in the German manner to the wide back part of the skull, was fastened by a catch in front of the chin; but the upper bevor and visor were pivoted at the sides as in a close helmet. The old hinge-and-pin attachments used upon the visor-pivots of Italian armets up to the 1520s had been abandoned almost completely by 1525. In some cases the visor proper has large piercings

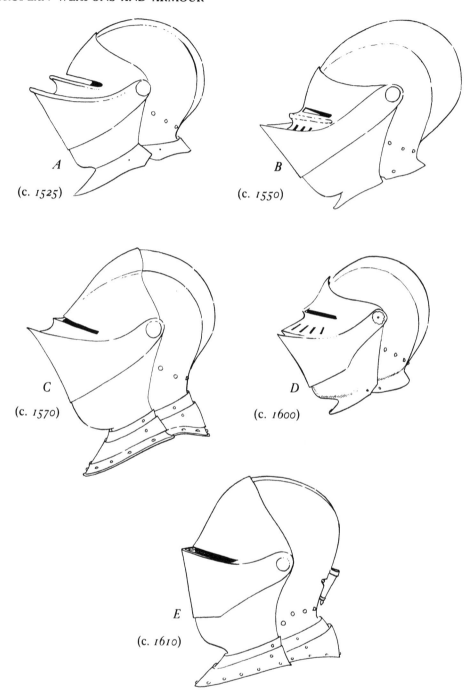

A

(c. *1525*)

B

(c. *1550*)

C

(c. *1570*)

D

(c. *1600*)

E

(c. *1610*)

FIGURE 94   *Variations in the profile of the close helmet*

below the sight, covered by a second reinforcing visor, and the upper bevor is pierced with breath-holes and always has a notch in its upper edge on the righthand side to accommodate a lifting-peg fixed to the visor. At the same time, in the 1520s, except in helmets which rotated on the top of the collar, laminated gorgetplates were fixed to the rear of the skull and the base of the bevor. Before 1570 or thereabouts, the profile of this upper bevor sloped sharply forward and outward, but after that date the angle became progressively nearer to the vertical. Another feature which developed after about 1560 was the comb, particularly upon Italian helmets; it had increased in size from the low, roped combs of the early close helmets to attain a considerable height by the 1550s, but soon after that it became enormously enlarged, producing a curiously hydrocephalic shape to the skull (Fig. 94 B). Helmets from Greenwich retained the armet construction right up to the 1620s; though there were quite a number of close helmets made there. A feature of both kinds was that right up to the end the profile-line of the upper bevor always slanted boldly outward, and was always in a concave curve.

POTS: THE *ZISCHAGGE* AND THE PIKEMAN'S POT

The seventeenth century saw the abandonment of the burgonet in favour of an eastern-European type of helmet called the '*zischagge*'. Some, from Poland and Hungary, are very handsomely made, though no one could call their shape elegant. The form consisted of a hemispherical bowl (the skull) with a large fall or peak in front, triangular earflaps at the side and a broad, spreading tail of four or five (sometimes more) lames sweeping out over the back of the neck (Fig. 95 A). Apart from the true Polish/Hungarian *zischagge*, there were two basic forms in use in Europe: the German and a typical English adaptation of it. The Eastern and German types had a face-protection in the shape of a single nasal-bar (Fig. 95 B), but the English form generally favoured a sort of visor of three bars (Fig. 95 C).

At the same time as the *zischagge* was adopted for cavalry use, the Spanish morion developed into an equally graceless form generally referred to now as a 'pikeman's pot'. In the seventeenth century both these helmets were universally called simply 'pots'. Indeed they were unworthy of a better name.

THE SAVOY HELMET (*TODENKOPF*)

There was a curious hybrid in use for a while early in the seventeenth century, a cross between a burgonet and a close helmet; there is an example in the Odescalchi Collection in Rome. This has a pivoted fall, and a high falling-buffe fitting close up under the fall, but the cheekpieces are made like the rear half of the bevor of a close helmet, the buffe fitting snugly into the opening between them. This, however, was a rare type, not so much used as the last and ugliest closed helmet ever to have been devised: *Todenkopf*, 'death's-head', the Germans call it, with their invariable flair for the *mot juste*; but it is also more politely known as a Savoy helmet. Most of the survivors are of the crudest make, their surfaces black and rough from the hammer; to call them ugly is inaccurate. They are brutish, horrible in the way the black iron masks of torturers are (Fig. 96). There is a specimen in

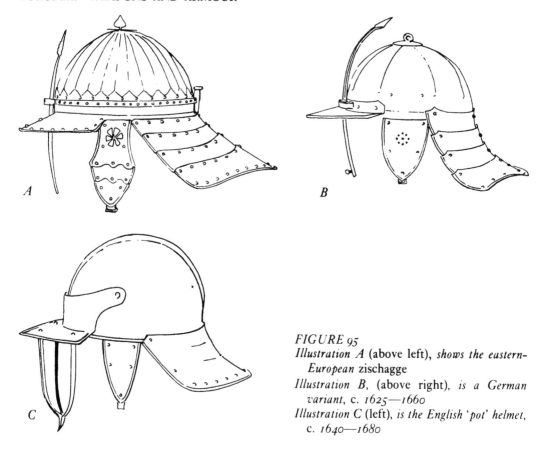

FIGURE 95
Illustration A (above left), *shows the eastern-European* zischagge
Illustration B, (above right), *is a German variant, c. 1625—1660*
Illustration C (left), *is the English 'pot' helmet, c. 1640—1680*

the Armeria Reale in Turin which, rather more elaborate than most, carries away the palm for crude beastliness. These, and the bulbous, robot-like armour which went with them, are what the seventeenth century laughed to scorn, and left as a memory to us in the twentieth century.

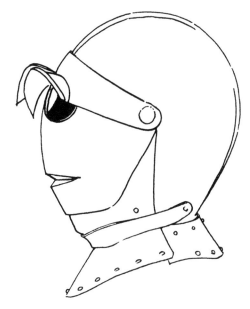

FIGURE 96   *The 'death's-head' helmet*

Such were the depths to which the craft of the armourer had descended by the end of the Thirty Years War in Europe (1648) and the Civil War in England (1651). The lower literary efforts of the times were filled with funny or merely bawdy tales about, for instance, the way in which the vast balloon-like breeches, fashionable in Germany early in the seventeenth century, were used for stowing away victuals or loot—not that there was anything but sober fact in the reality behind the satire. A fitting tailpiece to this section which ends the era of pike and musket and leads into the more sordid age of bayonet and cannon is to quote a few couplets from the political satire *Hudibras* written in 1662—1664 by Samuel Butler; it is a double-edged send-up of the old Romance of Chivalry and of the Cavaliers and Roundheads of the Civil War. Some of it is relevant here:

> *Then did Sir Knight abandon dwelling*
> *And out he rode a-colonelling . . .*
> *His back, or rather burthen, showed*
> *As if it stooped with its own load*

223

EUROPEAN WEAPONS AND ARMOUR

For as Aeneas bore his sire
Upon his shoulders thro' the fire
Our Knight did bear no less a pack
Of his own buttocks on his back.
To poise this equally, he bore
A paunch of the same bulk before....
When of his hose we come to treat,
The cup-board where he kept his meet,
His doublet was of sturdy Buff
And though not sword yet cudgel-proof;
His breeches were of rugged woollen
And had been at the Siege of Bullen
To old King Harry so well known,
Some writers held they were his own.
Though they were lined with many a piece
Of ammunition bread-and-cheese
And fat black-puddings, proper food
For warriors that delight in blood:
For, as we said, he always chose
To carry vittle in his hose....

CHAPTER THIRTEEN

THE DAGGER: 1500—1650

His puissant sword unto his side
Near his undaunted heart was ty'd . . .
This sword a dagger had t' his page
That was but little for his age . . .
It was a serviceable dudgeon
Either for fighting or for drudging.
When it had stabb'd, or broke a head,
It would scrape trenchers, or chip bread,
Toast cheese or bacon. Though it were
To bait a mouse-trap, 'twould not care;
'Twould make clean shoes, and in the earth
Set leeks and onions, and so forth.

(Samuel Butler, *Hudibras*, 1662—1664)

However much Samuel Butler was sending up the social *mores* of his time, what he wrote about the uses to which his hero put his dagger was no more than a simple statement of accepted fact, even to the leeks and onions. The dagger was never a noble weapon, however exquisite individual specimens may have been; but as a handy multi-purpose tool or an excellent weapon to use in a close-packed *mêlée*, it was incomparable, and of course with the introduction of the Italian and Spanish methods of rapier-fighting it soon became the essential defensive partner to the long sword.

Any attempt to classify daggers, even as crudely as I have classified sword hilts, would be a waste of space and temper, for with the exception of three specific styles every dagger was a 'one-off job' or paired with its companion sword hilt. However, most of them did follow certain more or less constant constructional principles.

From about 1500 to about 1525, a hotch-potch of dagger styles left over from the previous century was in use all over Europe alongside a host of individuals, some beautiful, some fantastic, thrown off by the seething creativity of the Renaissance craftsmen. From the fifteenth century the rondel, ballock and ear-dagger continued to be fashionable; the cinquedea, though never quite a dagger or quite a sword, survived into the second decade of the century. These types were sketched in the previous volume (*A of W*, pp. 337—340, Plates 21—22) and so are not relevant here.

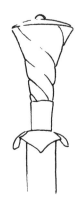

FIGURE 97   *Transitional form of the rondel/*landsknecht *dagger*

THE *LANDSKNECHT* DAGGER

One highly distinctive form of dagger, which does indeed constitute a class of its own, is the so-called '*landsknecht* dagger' which appeared at some unspecified time early in the century, an obvious product of that same fashion trend which evolved the fantastically puffed and slashed *landsknecht* costumes. Not only does the form match the style: the hilts and scabbards of many of these daggers are themselves embellished with puffs and slashes of wire. There are a great many examples from which I can only illustrate one, from the Wallace Collection, London (A 752: Plate 19). Similar ones are in the Metropolitan Museum, New York, the Odescalchi Collection, Rome (Number 298), and—a late example, *c.* 1585—one made for Christian IV of Denmark, now in the National Museum, Copenhagen.

The *landsknecht* dagger of the 1520s (Fig. 97) seems a logical development of the rondel dagger of the 1480s, though it is far more likely to be a deliberate design. It is hard to say when this style first appeared, for lack of any precisely dated material, though there are German drawings of the 1540s which show it clearly, particularly the illustrations to Count Solms's *Treatise on War* of 1545, illustrated by an artist who signs himself simply *HD*. As they are so clearly linked with the *landsknecht* fashion which came into being even before 1500, it is difficult not to assume that this dagger-design did not more nearly correspond with it. This assumption is strengthened by the fact that in Hans Burgkmair's engravings for his *Triumph of Maximilian* at least three clearly-shown daggers are of this form, while most of the others are late kinds of rondel daggers. The *Triumph* was completed before—or at least work upon it ceased at—Maximilian's death in January, 1519, so it does seem that the type must have been developing in the 1520s. The clearest is shown on Fol. 62, while on Fol. 61 and Fol. 59 are daggers which have the very distinctive downturned guards typical of the *landsknecht* dagger, and on Fol. 110 is one which has the typical conical grip and pommel-cap as well as the trilobate guard. A curious thing about these engravings is that among the many *landsknechte* shown, only two wear daggers at all—rondel daggers at that. All the other daggers, mostly rondels, and one ballock knife, are worn by knightly figures.

The late rondel daggers tended to have conical grips, narrower at the bottom and flaring out at the top into the usual flat disc set at right-angles to the weapon's axis. When the lower rondel guard, a corresponding disc, was changed to a trilobate form consisting of a pair of leaf-shaped *quillons* turned sharply down over the blade with a similar leaf-shaped guard at the front of the hilt, the *landsknecht* form was basically complete, only needing the dome-shaped cap to the grip and the puffed and slashed rings on grip and scabbard to complete the thing in its full-blown form. The engravings in the *Triumph* suggest that these daggers were in use by the 1520s, but there is small

FIGURE 98   *A* landsknecht *dagger, dating*
c. *1585*

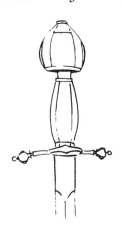

doubt that most surviving specimens have to be dated on stylistic grounds to the 1550s onwards.

The later ones abandoned the conical grip and used a pommel shaped like the pod of a Cape gooseberry (Fig. 98), together with a baluster-shaped grip—or in more common examples, a narrow barrel-shaped one—and short knob-ended *quillons.* Such are Numbers 300 and 301 in the Odescalchi Collection, Rome, and the one made for Christian IV of Denmark in 1585, now in Copenhagen—though this has the trilobate guard, the lobes being, however, more like down-turned prongs.

The scabbards of these daggers are usually of metal, frequently richly ornamented, girdled with bold rings, often made in puffs and slashes of wire, set in groups in twos and threes, sometimes with a series of five or more to form a kind of chape at the bottom, which is generally finished off with a bold bulb.

Landsknecht dagger blades tended to be broad, of a flattened diamond section with a strong *ricasso*, though in the Odescalchi Collection is one with a back-edged knife-blade. (The hilt of this is almost that of a rondel dagger, and could be taken as a transitional form.) As a general rule, the earlier a dagger is, the broader its blade. The later ones—that is, after about 1570—have blades of the same form and dimensions as those of the contemporary lefthand daggers (*q.v.*, below). The *landsknecht* daggers were probably intended for use as weapons on their own, not to be paired with rapiers as lefthand defences. It was an essentially German design, though it was in use all over north-west Europe.

THE HOLBEIN DAGGER

As typically of Swiss origin as the *landsknecht* dagger was of German, and as widely used, was the so-called 'Holbein dagger'. This, its essential form based upon the fourteenth- and fifteenth-century Swiss short sword known as the *hauswehr*, with its hilt shaped like a cuttlefish-bone (Plate 19), was a sort of elitist weapon, worn as a piece of personal jewellery by the upper classes of society, while more ordinary folk carried a similarly shaped but undecorated dagger descended from the same common ancestor. The blades of these daggers were broad and almost leaf-shaped, double-edged and of diamond section, generally some ten inches long (25·5 cm); most had *ricassos*, though not all. The reason for their nineteenth-century name of 'Holbein' daggers was that the elaborate openwork decoration in copper, or silver-gilt, over a wooden sheath (often first covered with leather or velvet) was in many cases strictly based upon Hans Holbein the Younger's drawing for a dagger sheath, now in the Basel Museum, with its design of the Dance of Death. This was a favourite design for 'Holbein' dagger sheaths, as was the legend of William Tell.

One could, I believe, say that the Holbein dagger was the immediate successor, as a piece of dresswear, of the cinquedea, though it never attained the massive dimensions of that strange weapon. It would certainly never have been put to domestic trencher-scraping or shoe-cleaning uses. It appears in many mid-century portraits, being shown, for instance, in a stained-glass window in the Historisches Museum, Basel, which depicts a group of men eating at a circular table (Number 1870, 1284); here it is worn at the same angle, in the small of the back, as was the cinquedea.

THE BALLOCK DAGGER: THE DUDGEON

The ballock dagger, first shown in art in manuscript pictures and sculptured effigies late in the thirteenth century, had always strong regional links with England and the Low Countries and, later, with the areas of Burgundian influence. By the mid-sixteenth century, it had become almost exclusively a British weapon, changing slightly in form between 1500 and 1550. In the fourteenth and fifteenth centuries, it had been quite deliberately phallic, both in the form of its hilt and in the way it was worn—carried at the mid-point of the low-slung hip-belt, grip upright, as may be seen in many paintings, particularly those of the period 1400—1450 (for instance, the *Très Riches Heures* of the Duke of Berri). At Christie's, London, in 1956, from the F. C. Lucas Collection, there was sold a ballock dagger to end all ballock daggers, the hilt being carved in pink stone into a very literal representation of the entire male apparatus in a fully extended condition. It is, however, possible that this was not a genuine late-fifteenth-century hilt but a Victorian restoration, one of those exuberant flights of fancy that age was inclined to take. In sixteenth-century England, while it retained vestiges of the two lobes at the base of the grip, it became an altogether less provocative-looking object. By the end of the sixteenth century, and until it became *démodé* in the 1640s, it was generally known as a dudgeon, or a dudgeon dagger. Shakespeare often used the term, and as we have seen, Butler later did so in *Hudibras*. The origin of the word is obscure, but it meant any dagger or knife with a wooden hilt—box, briar-root, heather-root, dogwood— and the last of these probably provides a clue. This small tree, *Cornea Sanguinea*, with its hard, horny, red-coloured wood, was called in the vernacular 'dogwood' or 'dagger wood' and reportedly, in some regional dialect, though I myself have been unable to trace it, 'dudgeon'.

THE SCOTTISH DUDGEON

I said that the ballock dagger became British, not English, for a close analysis of forty-one fine-quality examples has shown pretty conclusively that they were, in fact, Scottish in the main, a few being probably of Northumbrian origin. The specimens so examined all date *c.* 1590—1630, and all have blades of similar form decorated in a more or less uniform manner with panels of etched conventional foliage, 'staggered' up each face of the diamond-section blade and incorporating mottoes in Lowland Scots or in English. These mottoes are of three basic forms:

Used once: *GOD GYDE THE HAND THAT I INSTAND*

Used five times, with variations:

MY HOPE AND TREIST IS IN YE LORD

Used three times with variations:

BE MY DEFENS GOD ME DEFEND FOREVER MORE

Used once: *ASK ME NOT FOR SCHAME DRINK LIS AND BY ANE*

Used once, being a Latin version of the second motto:

UNICA SPES MEA CHRISTUS

Used once:

QUHA VIL PERSEV I VIL DEFEND
MY LYF AND HONOUR TO YE END

The first of these mottoes, which does not look particularly Scottish, is to be seen on the barrel of a very Scottish gun, *c.* 1600, in the Tullie House Museum, Carlisle. The second is found, with a bewildering variety of spelling, carved upon the lintels of doors and on stones set in walls, in the Old Town of Edinburgh. The third seems to be a phrase taken from a piece of doggerel very popular in Scotland early in the sixteenth century and all through the decades until the seventeenth century, when it became a motto of the House of Stuart: *In my defens God us defend.* The fourth motto is of an entirely frivolous nature—'Don't ask me, for shame: Drink less and buy one yourself.' Versions of this appear on two powder-horns of the late seventeenth century and on a brass tobacco-box as late as 1756. The fifth motto is just a Latin version of the second, while the sixth has no known parallels, though its spelling of 'who' as 'quha' is guid Scots, and its *ricasso* bears the initials *I. R. 6* (*Jacobus Rex*, for James VI King of Scots who became also James I King of England). It might look as if these blades, all so similar in size, about ten and a half inches long (26·5 cm), and similar too in proportion and in style of decoration—for those without mottoes are decorated—must have come from the same workshop; but though most of the blades bear makers' stamps, all are different (Plate 19 C).

These forty-one surviving daggers are all of top quality; there are countless lesser ones which are the ordinary English/Scots dudgeons of the period 1550—1660.

THE LEFTHAND DAGGER

The daggers described above were all just daggers, weapons on their own, but from the 1540s we find the 'companion' dagger coming more and more into use. This, although each one was made to match a sword hilt, was always of a similar form, a simple cross-hilted little dagger with a ten-inch blade (25·5 cm), sometimes having a ring-guard in front of the *quillons*, with as many varieties of pommel as there were sword-pommels, and simple cross-guards which were made to match in section and terminals the swords to which the daggers belonged. Some *quillons* were straight, some downcurved, some curved one up and one down, and some curved one forward and one back. A good many, particularly those matching Dresden sword hilts, had downcurved *quillons* set at an angle of forty-five degrees to the axis of the blade in a forward position, with a small ring-guard on the front of the *quillon*-block. Though these daggers, called 'lefthand' or *maingauche* daggers, were meant to partner rapiers, many were made *en suite* with swords, *reitschwerte*, such as the Dresden pair in the Victoria and Albert Museum, London.

Few pairs are still together. In the Wallace Collection, London, is a dagger (A 790) to match a sword in the Musée de l'Armée, Paris, the pair having been presented in 1600 to Henri IV of France by the citizens of Paris on the occasion of his marriage to Marie de' Medici; and similar divorced couples must abound. I had a rapier, *c.* 1620, whose companion dagger is in the Dalpozzo Collection. One of the finest couples still together dwells safely in the Waffensammlung, Vienna, a particularly fine pair of chiselled steel dating *c.* 1560, while another pair, even richer though not so handsome, is in the Historisches Museum, Dresden (among many others), dating about ten years earlier. Here the dagger has very short, ribbon-section *quillons* like a little bow-tie.

Some ingenious ways were devised to enable one to catch an opponent's sword blade and with a strong turn of the wrist, snap it off or wrench it out of his grasp. The forward-angled *quillons* provided a mechanical means of achieving this, if properly used; but some bladesmiths formed their blades like a comb or a rake, with some twenty horizontal teeth between which a blade could be trapped with far greater ease; while another pure piece of machinery was a neat device whereby, at the pressing of a spring-catch, the blade sprang asunder, a long piece on either side shooting outward to form a trident.

This simple cross-hilted lefthand dagger style lasted well into the seventeenth century, until by the 1630s it had gone out of fashion everywhere except in Spain and southern Italy, where in the 1650s it developed into a highly specialised and very distinctive weapon which went on being used until almost the middle of the eighteenth century: the Spanish *maingauche* dagger.

THE SPANISH *MAINGAUCHE* DAGGER

Spanish *maingauche* daggers are, not without reason, greatly prized and sought after by collectors, for not only are they nearly always decorated in the same manner and style of fine chiselled steelwork as the cup-hilted rapiers to which they were paired, but the shape in itself is aesthetically satisfying (Plate 19). Like their companion rapiers, they did not come into fashion until the mid-seventeenth century, though in Spain, and in the Spanish kingdom of Naples, they survived into the eighteenth. For practical purposes, these rapier-and-dagger pairs were the most effective ever designed for the rapier-and-dagger style of fighting: so much so that one feels they must have been designed by a practical swordsman rather than being one of those 'natural' developments or evolutions of one style out of another. The reason, of course, why they were not adopted and used elsewhere in Europe was that by the time they appeared in the 1650s the 'Cavalier' rapier was *de rigueur* in Britain, Scandinavia, Germany, the Netherlands and France, and the use of the

FIGURE 99   The Italian stiletto, c. 1640

lefthand dagger had lapsed. Indeed, the development of the Spanish weapons coincided almost exactly with the evolution of the smallsword in the Netherlands and France.

THE STILETTO

No chapter dealing with the dagger in its final forms up to 1700, however sketchily, would be complete without mention of the beautiful, horrible, little Italian stilettos of the close of the period, with their steel chiselled hilts which often look as if they had been turned on a lathe. These vary in size from some twelve to thirteen inches long (30·5—33 cm) down to tiny weapons with blades like big needles, only some five to six inches long (12·5—15·25 cm). A few were made (and these are probably the earlier ones) with hilts like miniature versions of the *maingauches* of the early seventeenth century, but most of the distinctive form shown in Figure 99. As for the purposes for which they were devised, and the manner in which they were used, there is no need to be explicit. They were not exactly honourable weapons. There is, however, one notable exception: the 'Gunner's Stiletto'.

THE *FUSETTO* OR GUNNER'S STILETTO

Carried by chief cannoneers as a kind of compendium tool-weapon, the 'Gunner's Stiletto' was of the same general form as the more common assassin's—or ladies'—*pugnale*, but its blade was always of the section of an isosceles triangle with perfectly flat faces, and on the broader base was engraved a numbered scale. In individual specimens the scales differ widely and seem to indicate varied units of measurement. Since it was strictly illegal for persons other than cannoneers to carry stilettos, it had been suggested that some are in fact ordinary *pugnali* mocked up to look like *stiletti degli bombardieri*, so that the owner, if caught, could claim to be a gunner, particularly after 1661 when in Venice the Council of Ten granted to *bona fide bombardieri* the right to wear them.

These *fusetti*, to give them their correct name, could be used in at least seven specific and valuable ways by a cannoneer: to measure the bore of a gun or to measure, roughly, the calibre of a ball; to tear open the cloth or paper cartridges in which at this time the propellant charges were generally contained (as they still were until very recently in naval guns); to open the cartridge through the touch-hole so that the priming charge could fire it; to clean out the touch-hole; to spike it if the gun had to be abandoned; and to block it during loading. And, of course, the *fusetto* would be useful in a hand-to-hand struggle if the *bombardiere's* gun were over-run. An engaging notion once enjoyed by amateurs of arms was that the purpose of the numbered scale was to prove to the clients of hired assassins, by the blood-marks up the scale, that their victims had been properly attended to.

THE HIGHLAND DIRK

The Scottish dirk was a descendant of the old ballock dagger in the same way as the dudgeon, but it was essentially a Highland weapon, and until it became, early in the nineteenth century, simply an adjunct to Highland dress or uniform, it was always rather a large weapon, very much the size and shape of the Roman legionary's *gladius*. Possibly the earliest document to indicate a dirk is an effigy, in Ardchattan Priory, of a

FIGURE 100   *The development of the Scottish dirk*

Illustration A, c. 1550—1600
Illustration B, early seventeenth century
Illustration C, early eighteenth century
Illustration D, c. 1790
Illustration E, c. 1810—1880

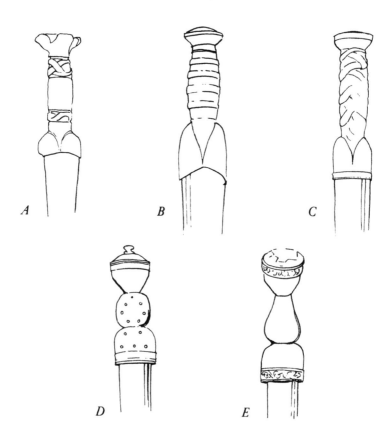

knight wearing a dagger with all the characteristics of a dirk. This was carved in 1502. It is 'traditional' in form, too, for in its scabbard is a 'by-knife' whose handle protrudes from a pocket. Similar by-knives had of course been common in the sheaths of ballock and rondel daggers from the end of the fourteenth century, but they became quite a prominent feature with the Highland dirk. There are frequent mentions of dirks, variously spelt, in Burgh and Court records of brawls and affrays. The earliest is from the Inverness Burgh records for 1557:

'Mans McGillmichael is jugit in amerciament for the wrang use drawin of ane dowrk to Andro Dempster, and briking of the dowrk at the said Androis head.'

The next recorded appearances are the Michael Wright 'Portrait' in the National Portrait Gallery, referred to on page 177, dated *c.* 1680, and the comment of a Yorkshire visitor to Inverness, Thomas Kirk, who in 1677 wrote of a habit of the Highlanders:

'On their right side they wear a dagger, about a foot or half-a-yard long, the back filed like a saw, and several kinnes [*sgians*, 'by-knives'] stuck in the sheath of it.'

From these early dirks there was little change in the form, shown chronologically in Figure 100, until the end of the eighteenth century. Until the dirk became at about that time, a dress accessory, it was severely plain, its only ornament a restrained use of the ancient Celtic (and Norse) strap-interlace work; only after about 1740 did silver pommel-caps and 'ferrules' at the base of hilts become common, and not until after about 1800 were cairngorms mounted in the pommels of the dirks themselves and of their accessory by-knives, which by the mid-eighteenth century had become a small knife-and-fork set.

I should mention here the small *sgian dubh*, the little knife worn in the top of the stocking with full Highland dress. The Gaelic name means simply 'black knife'; the hilt was generally made of bog-oak and conformed in shape to the dirk's hilt, except that instead of a disc-shaped pommel set at right angles to the plane of the blade it had a flat pommel to lie smoothly against the leg. It is interesting that Chaucer mentions a knife worn like this, though not, of course, by a Highlander.

The blades of the earlier dirks, 'filed like a saw', were broad at the hilt, single-edged with a short false edge up the back. The saw on the back was probably originally for the same purpose as the saw-edged back of many hunting knives and hangers—to saw through the bones of game; or, by the same token, like the saw-backs of many nineteenth- and early-twentieth-century bayonets, to make an efficient weapon double up as a useful tool. These saw-backs in the later dirks became simply decoration, more a series of semi-circular dimples along part of the back. Many surviving dirks of the period 1620—1740 are fitted with old cut-down sword-blades.

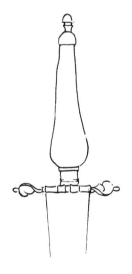

FIGURE 101   The plug bayonet, c. 1690

When after the suppression of the 1745 rebellion the carrying of arms by clansmen was punishable by death and the wearing of tartan, kilt or plaid was banned, suspected men were forced to swear upon the holy iron of a dirk that they were not concealing weapons in their crofts. This is very much in keeping with the ancient traditions going back into the mists of time that made the Highland warrior of the eighteenth century, like the Zulu of the nineteenth, so much a maintainer of the prehistoric awe in which iron weapons were once held. It is about the only instance too of any form of dagger which held this awesome mystique.

THE BAYONET

The bayonet originated in a type of dagger, whose precise form is unknown, made at Bayonne in southern France. In the mid-seventeenth century, some such daggers, elaborately decorated with motifs which were almost exclusively sporting, were stuck into the muzzles of sporting-guns to turn them into boar-spears; it was immediately obvious that by doing this, the musketeer, who had hitherto needed the services of pikemen to keep off hostile cavalry while he re-loaded, could now, to some extent, convert his discharged musket into a spear. These early plug-bayonets (Fig. 101), in fairly widespread military use from the 1660s onward, had the disadvantage that they bunged up the barrel of the gun, so that it could not be reloaded. So a new form was devised with two rings on the side of the hilt to slip over the end of the barrel. Now the gun could be loaded, fired and reloaded with the bayonet in position. Unfortunately the rings did not really hold it firm enough; it either swung round or fell off. Late in the seventeenth century, a much better form was devised, the socket-bayonet which fitted over the end of the gunbarrel, invented by Lieutenant-Colonel Jean Martinet, *Inspecteur de l'Infantarie* in the army of Louis XIV. The blade was of the same section as a smallsword blade, a triangle with concave sides, about fifteen to eighteen inches long (38—45 cm), joined to the tubular socket by a curved bar (Fig. 102). This had been adopted by all European armies by the early eighteenth century, and remained in use until late in the nineteenth. It was almost the only type in use (except perhaps in Spain where the plug-bayonet continued to be popular, for hunting

FIGURE 102   The socket bayonet, c. 1720—1900

at least, until well into the nineteenth century) until the early 1800s when various experimental methods of attachment to the side of the barrel were worked out. The story of the bayonet's later development has no place here, but much extremely detailed work has been done, as listed below.

NOTE
Yet another fascinating, if irrelevant, comment is that early dirk hilts (particularly as shown in Figure 100 B) have an extraordinarily close resemblance to the hilts of Scandinavian bronze swords of *c.* 1000 B.C. (*A of W*, pp. 30—36, *Plates 1 a, b, c*).

BIBLIOGRAPHY

Blair, Claude, and Wallace, John, *Scots—Or Still English? An Introductory Survey of a Distinctive Group of 17th-Century Ballock Daggers*, Scottish Art Review, Volume II, No. 1, 1963

Dean, B., *The Metropolitan Museum of Art, Catalogue of Daggers*, New York, 1929

Hayward, J. F., *Victoria and Albert Museum, Swords and Daggers*, London, 1951

Latham, R. J. W., *British Military Bayonets*, London, 1967

Wallace, John, *Scottish Swords and Dirks*, London, 1970

Whitelaw, C. E., *The Origin and Development of the Highland Dirk*, Trans. Glasgow Arch. Soc., Volume IV, 11, 1902

CHAPTER FOURTEEN

THE SMALLSWORD

'. . . And coming back [wrote Sam Pepys in his diary on January 10, 1660] drank a pint of wine at the Star in Cheapside. So to Westminster, overtaking Capt. Okeshott in his silk cloak, whose sword got hold of many people in walking. Thence to the coffee-house . . .'

This comment highlights a trend, already well-established on the Continent, which after the Restoration of Charles II, a few months later, would rapidly gain ground in England. The sword of 'Capt. Okeshott' had two obvious characteristics, both un-social in crowded streets. It was big in the hilt and probably in the blade, and an infernal nuisance to passers-by. Who this seemingly dandified forbear of mine was is not known; neither Pepys nor anyone else ever mentions him again. Irrelevant he may be, but his sword is not. London at the turn of the year, 1659/1660, teemed with military officers. Pepys's specific mention of the silk cloak suggests that the Captain was not in military gear but in civil dress, so his sword would not have been (like Hudibras's) a big mortuary-style broadsword, but one of the large Cavalier rapiers so popular in the 1640s and 1650s.

Such weapons on the Continent, and particularly in the Netherlands, had as early as the 1630s begun to be replaced by swords with much smaller, neater hilts and shorter blades. When Charles II and his brother and their followers returned from their long exile in Holland and France, they brought the fashion for these 'town swords' with them. The English, who still called their military swords by the old medieval term of 'great swords', immediately dubbed these dainty weapons 'smallswords' and the name has stuck, though it is no more appropriate than that of 'town sword'. In a Swedish inventory of 1665 such swords were equally appropriately called 'walking-swords'. A portrait of the Swedish poet Georg Stiernhielm, painted in 1663 by D. K. Ehrenstahl, shows him wearing one of these *promenierdegen* and carrying a walking-cane. The nuisance caused by a big-hilted sword in the narrow crowded streets of London between Cheapside and Westminster was considered to be worthy of notice by Pepys, that acute observer of men and manners, and goes far to explain why smallswords which sat much closer to their wearers' bodies were first called 'town swords'.

ANCESTRY OF THE SMALLSWORD:
FLAMBERGE AND TOWN SWORD

The whole concept of such a weapon, the social idea that a gentleman's sword hilt ought not to be a public nuisance, had its first practical expression very early in the seventeenth

FIGURE 103 *The rapier of Johann de Mont, c. 1625*
(Schweizerisches
Landesmuseum, Zürich)

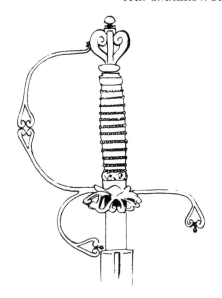

century—that period of the most flamboyant and immense 'swept' hilts—with a revival (in a sense) of a hilt pattern of nearly a century before, where the guards consisted merely of a rear *quillon*, knuckle-guard and one branch on the outside of the blade, with the addition, sometimes, of a small ornamental shell-guard projecting at a sharp downward angle from the outside of the *quillon*-block, and no back-guards. One of the best surviving examples of this is in the Schweizerisches Landesmuseum in Zürich (Fig. 103). This supremely elegant rapier—its blade is as long as all but the most extravagant contemporary ones—belonged to Johann de Mont, who in 1621 was Captain of a company of Swiss Guards in the service of Louis XIII of France, and who died in 1635. A few similar hilts are shown in portraits during this period, but most, though simplified from the traditional swept forms, are still more complex than the de Mont one—for instance, a portrait in the Maurits-huis at The Hague of Count Jan of Nassau, painted in 1611 by J. A. van Ravenstijn. A near-similar hilt is in the Wallace Collection, London (A 672), dating *c.* 1600, but even this has a large ring-guard on the outside of the hilt; both of these, however, have no back-guards, and so sit close to the wearer's side. A rather similar sword, though it has two branches joined by a ring-guard, and a small ring-guard at the back turned up at right-angles to the lie of the forward ring to allow a close set against the body, was made in 1610 for Christian II, Elector of Saxony, as a present for his brother Johann Georg. It is remarkable for having a watch (a timepiece would be a more accurate word for it) set in its exquisite gold-inlaid pommel.

Swords like this were a practical expression of a social idea, but I believe that in a technical sense too they were the archetypes of the smallsword. If we were to take as an analogy the manyfold descendants of Queen Victoria, with the de Mont 'town rapier' as the Queen Matriarch of this smallsword family, we would find as many branches and collaterals flourishing all over Europe as in 1921 there were grandchildren and great-grand-children of the Queen; the 'true' smallsword hilt-type could be compared with Edward VII, whose line, like that of the smallsword, survives. To carry the analogy a step farther, we might say that if the de Mont rapier is the Victoria of this family, then the so-called 'dish-hilt rapier' was its Prince Albert, for it was from a marriage of the two that all the town swords and smallswords sprang.

It will be as well to examine carefully the very large number of transitional types of hilt which were developed *c.* 1625—1650; and I shall do this in greater detail than for the true smallsword hilts which have already had much more attention given to them, particularly in the publications listed on page 253.

Be all this as it may, the smallsword's origins were not based only upon an increase in the social importance of urbanity and good manners, or the growth of urban populations. If the Netherlanders developed the townsword for walking, the French had got in first by developing a light rapier for duelling, along with further refinements upon the Italian modes of doing it.

The Escrime Française

In 1567, an *Académie d'Armes* had been founded in Paris, and early in the seventeenth century its Masters began to perfect the *Escrime Française* which was given expression in 1605 by M. le Perche de Coudray in his book *L'Exercice des Armes ou le Maniement du Fleuret*, reprinted in 1676 and even in 1750. He emphasised a more flexible way of holding the sword, for a start, by allowing the thumb and forefinger to lie on either side of the lower part of the hilt, absolutely forbidding that the forefinger be put through the outside branch of the hilt. This gave much more subtlety of movement to the weapon, and we can see clearly how it influenced the form of the hilt in north-west Europe; now that the branches had lost their prime function, they could be dispensed with, and the *quillons* could lie a lot closer to the dish- or shell-guard. Some of the Cavalier rapiers, and many of the *flamberges*, dispensed with branches, while those retaining this feature had the branches too small to be functional, though they acted as a support and reinforcement between the shells and the *quillons*. Probably it was the technological value of this which caused them to be retained even until the early nineteenth century. In Spain and Italy, where the *Escrime Française* found no favour, the branches became much larger, as we shall see.

The light rapier to which I have already referred (page 165) has in modern times been named the '*flamberge*'. Because there was no term by which it could be defined when Egerton Castle produced his book *Schools and Masters of Fence* in 1885, he took the name of '*flamberge*' and applied it to supply the lack. The original *Flamberge* was, of course, Roland's Durandal, an alternative name which the poet of the *Chanson de Roland* occasionally used for this epic sword. This, however, was not where Egerton Castle got it from, but from Molière, who satirically used the expression *mettre flamberge au vent* to describe the act of drawing a courtly little sword with a flourish, as if it were the immortal *Flamberge* itself. So the term was by no means inappropriately used, and does very well.

There are many surviving examples of the *flamberge*, two particularly good ones being in London, one in the Victoria and Albert Museum (M 2755—1931) and the other in the Wallace Collection (A 507). Both date *c.* 1630, and both have hilts which are almost true smallsword hilts, lacking only a knuckle-guard, for the guards consist of a pair of unequal-sized oval shells (the smaller on the inside), rather shallow branches, and a pair of *quillons*, long and downturned in the Victoria and Albert example, (Fig. 73, above), and straight in the Wallace one. The main difference from the very similar early smallswords of two decades later is that in size these are still virtually rapiers. Many such hilts are shown in the engravings of Abraham Bosse (1602—1676), particularly one in his *Le Jardin de la Noblesse Françoise* of 1629, which, except that there are no branches, is almost identical with the Wallace sword.

SCARF SWORDS

The essence of the new French styles of fence was speed in defence as well as attack, and it seems that even the *flamberge* was not light enough to meet this need. In civilian portraits of the 1640s we begin to find that the sitters are wearing very simple-hilted little swords, having no guards other than a pair of short, stubby, knobbed *quillons*. Until recently these (on quite untenable grounds) were called 'pillow swords', it being supposed that they were hung at the bed-head, or put under the pillow, in case of midnight burglary, assassination, rape and so forth; but there seems little doubt that the contemporary name was 'scarf swords'. In the *Lexicon Tetraglotton* by James Howell produced in 1659—1660 is a reference to 'a short or scarf sword: *Spada corta, o spada da banda*'; a name appropriately acquired, since they were often worn on the waist- or shoulder-scarf which was so prominent a feature of the mid-seventeenth-century military costume for officers. A most beautiful example of such a scarf once belonging to Charles I of England is preserved in the Victoria and Albert Museum, London. They can also be seen, scarf and sword together, in portraits, such as one by Jacob Frans van der Merck of Claes Hendriksz de Mett painted *c.* 1660. Some of these hilts are very rich; two, for instance, in the Waffensammlung, Vienna, one with a hilt of crystal and a blade dated 1647, and another, dated 1664, with a hilt of onyx and enamel. An equally fine one is in the Victoria and Albert Museum with a hilt of pink, cream and white agate, elegantly mounted with silver.

However, these are rare and beautiful examples; most of them were of more or less plain steel, occasionally chiselled or inlaid with silver. This type of scarf sword was popular from the 1640s to the 1670s, but there was a heavier, rather longer version of it, more likely for military use than the smaller one. This had a ring on the outside of the *quillons*, a blade some three or four inches longer (7½ to 10 cm), a longer grip and a slightly bigger pommel to balance the blade (Fig. 104). Sometimes the ring was filled with a pierced plate. These were very practical weapons, so much so that one must really think that the simpler, smaller ones were town swords or walking-swords, while their larger contemporaries were a type of the more military scarf sword. There is a portrait in Ham House, Chiswick, near London, of a Colonel Russell, painted by Michael Wright and dated 1659, which shows a sword of this type, almost identical with one made in Denmark in 1648 for Frederick III, now preserved among the Royal arms at Rosenborg Castle.

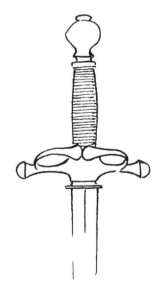

FIGURE 104   A scarf sword, c. 1640

THE NON-MILITARY LOOP HILT

A type of town sword which seems to be a smaller adaptation of the style of the big de Mont rapier developed in Germany and the Netherlands during the 1640s and 1650s at the same time as the French were developing the *flamberge*, and the Dutch (and maybe the Danes and the Swedes) were making the scarf sword fashionable. Early examples to which I referred earlier (p. 237) in the Wallace Collection (A 672) and in the portrait of Count Jan of Nassau, were followed by a neater smaller version of the same hilt, which was built upon exactly the same principles as the military Walloon hilt (p. 171, and Fig. 78, above). There is a group of particularly fine ones in the Wallace Collection, Numbers A 671, 672, 673, 681, 682 and 683. Number A 672, shown in Plate 20 C, has a hilt chiselled by Caspar Spät, who succeeded Daniel Sadeler (whose work upon the swept-hilts of the previous generation is so well-known) as steel-chiseller to the Bavarian Court. These, and the many others like them in public and private collections, have as their only guards a knuckle-guard and a loop springing from its base to join a rear *quillon*; but a few are more elaborate. Caspar Spät's hilt in the Wallace Collection, for instance, has a small curl springing outward from the lower curve of the knuckle-guard; and Number A 673 in the same collection, and an example dated 1646 in the church at Flisby in Smaland, Sweden, have a small downturned shell under the loop-guard, as in the de Mont hilt. Number A 683 in the Wallace Collection has this feature, further elaborated by a forward *quillon* with a single branch below it, which is purely decorative because it comes so close to the shell that no forefinger could go through it. It is an extravagantly handsome sword—and it *is* a sword, with a big double-edged blade of flattened diamond section—but uncomfortable to hold.

THE MODIFIED *FLAMBERGE*

By the late 1640s and the early 1650s, the French had adapted their *flamberge* into more of an approximation of a modified kind of scarf sword. With a lighter blade, smaller shells not curved upward over the hand, shorter and rather stumpy *quillons* with knobbed terminals, and a pommel in the shape of a flattened sphere rather than a duck's egg, they had a light manoeuvrable weapon which satisfied the requirements of the *Escrime Française*. They had in fact produced the true smallsword hilt. When Charles X Gustavus of Sweden was crowned in 1654, he was given a French sword of this type, which is preserved in the Livrustkammaren, Stockholm; there is a very similar sword in the Royal Collection at Windsor, said to have been given to John Churchill, 1st Duke of Marlborough, and there are very many others of the same kind—for instance, at Skokloster, Veste Coburg, Rosenborg—with good specimens in the Tower of London, the Arsenal at Colombier in Switzerland, and the Marzoli Collection at Brescia. A portrait painted in 1653 by Philippe de Champaigne of the young Charles II of England during his exile, now in the Museum of Art in Cleveland, Ohio, shows a simple unadorned hilt of this form, while a similar one appears at the side of a citizen-soldier of the north Netherland town of Hoorn, in one of the big group paintings of the Town Guard of Hoorn, painted in 1655 by Jan Albertz Rotius.

THE GROUP PAINTINGS OF THE TOWN GUARD OF HOORN

The group paintings of the Town Guard of Hoorn, four of them, dated 1649, 1651, 1655, and again 1655, in the Westfries Museum, Hoorn, are particularly interesting because they show in excellent detail several of the town sword types in use at this period. The paintings are in the same tradition and style as those better-known Town Guard groups by Rembrandt, Frans Hals and Bartholomeus van der Helst: but whereas these nearly all show swords of the Pappenheimer or later swept-hilt types, Rotius's are of town swords.

It seems probable that the northern Netherlands had more to do with the development of the true smallsword than is generally believed, credit for this having been given almost exclusively to the French. The swords in these pictures, as well as the countless surviving specimens of transitional sword hilts of obvious Netherland or West German origin, give very strong support. As in most other cases in arms and armour, the fully-fledged small-sword hilt of the eighteenth century was the offspring of a marriage between two 'nationals', the all-French *flamberge* and the Netherlandish town sword.

The first of Rotius's paintings, 'The Banner of Captain Seyne Conink' (the inference in these titles, 'The Banner of So-and-So', etc., is that these were portraits of members of a particular Captain's Company), shows the captain seated in the foreground with a long-bladed loop-hilt sword of the same style as Number A 683 in the Wallace Collection. Next to him sits his lieutenant, Pieter Willemsz van Neck, with a town sword—a scarf sword, really—similar to one illustrated in Plate 20 B.

The next picture, three years later (1651), 'The Banner of Captain Jan Vreericks Abbekirk', shows him with a long sword which has an interesting hilt, with a lion's-head pommel and a long grip like a Swiss sabre, up-and-down *quillons*, and a neat downturned shell, of true cockleshell form, on the outside, no other guards, while his lieutenant sits holding a great Pappenheimer between his knees. Behind stands a musketeer, holding matchlock, musket-rest and match, with a great bandolier across his chest and a sword hilt which might be of smallsword shape; but the important part, the *quillon* and the guards, is hidden behind the lieutenant's hat. Above Captain Abbekirk's right shoulder is the beautiful little silver-gilt hilt of a town sword, worn by Sergeant Josyas Wybo; the grip of this typically baroque hilt is formed of two nude figures, back to back, emerging from scrolls. A hilt of similar form is in the Rijksmuseum, Amsterdam, made by the silversmith Michael van Esselbeck, who became Master of the Amsterdam guild in 1642; I shall refer to this hilt again.

In the next picture, 'The Banner of Captain Jan Simonsz Jongemaets', 1655, the artist has placed himself, Sergeant Jan Albertz Rotius, in the foreground; and at his side is a most unusual little sword. The pommel is formed as a dog's head (like the Swiss lion's-head pommels) and the knuckle-guard, also like a Swiss one, reaches just about halfway up the grip and then turns outward, and is also finished with a dog's head, a smaller one this time. This is attached to the lower lip of the pommel head by a chain. The shell-guard, which extends a little at the back of the grip, is curved up in front over the hand. This hilt can be matched, almost exactly, by a similar sword in a private collection (Plate 20 E); the only difference is that the front shell does not extend behind the grip, and there is a secondary knuckle-guard rising from the point of the upturned shell, fixed into the side of the pommel by a screw. The dog's head on the pommel of this actual sword has an array of clenched teeth which the one in the painting lacks; otherwise, the two are so similar that one has to suspect that both came from the same workshop. The actual sword's hilt is made of a mixture of brass (once gilt) and iron. The *quillon*-knuckle-guard-ring unit (enclosing the shell) and the secondary knuckle-guard are of steel, while the doggy extremities of *quillon* and knuckle-guard are of brass, as is the embossed shell enclosed by the forward ring. The grip is rather crudely covered by a sheet of brass hammered round, but there are wire Turks' heads surviving at the top and bottom of the grip, which suggests a wire binding replaced, probably, by the look of it, while the sword was still in use. That so unusual a hilt in a little-known painting should be so closely matched by a surviving specimen is quite remarkable.

The last of the series, 'The Banner of Captain Claes Willemsz Jager', shows the captain wearing a sword which in many ways is exactly like a number of survivors, such as the fine steel-hilted sword in Plate 20 D. The best parallel, however, is a hilt preserved in the church of Kungs-Husby in Uppland, Sweden, illustrated by Heribert Seitz in *Blankwaffen II* (p. 98, Fig. 107) which, though Seitz dates it *c.* 1670—1680, could be a contemporary of Captain Jager's. The lieutenant, Willem van Sander, wears a French-style mini-*flamberge*. Behind, Sergeant Groot de Jonghe's hilt is another elaborate silver one, a scarf sword with baroque beast's-head *quillon*-ends and a lion pommel, with a forward ring.

All these swords, even Lieutenant van Neck's Pappenheimer, are painted as if they were of brass or bronze-gilt, except the obvious silver-gilt ones, which poses a very interesting question: were they made at Hoorn? The town had a very flourishing bronze foundry, engaged until the Treaty of Munster (1648) in casting cannon. After the end of the Thirty Years War, it turned over to making domestic things, mortars and candlesticks and tablewear; and very probably sword hilts too. There is in the same museum as the paintings a fine Pappenheimer with a bronze hilt known to have been made in Hoorn and belonging to Vice-Admiral Pieter Florisz, who died in 1659.

ANATOMICAL DESIGNS

Sergeant Wybo's beautiful hilt, and its parallel by van Esselbeck in the Rijksmuseum, show a fashion trend which was particularly rife in Amsterdam and northern Holland *c.* 1625—1650: a fashion for making use of the human form as a part of baroque ornament —a fashion, of course, by no means confined to these rapiers, or to this time, but which, in Amsterdam, had peculiar manifestations. Wybo's hilt has human bodies on it; so does van Esselbeck's—but it does not show the body from the outside. The whole, beautiful, masterly design is built up from the more intimate internal parts of the human frame. Upon each side of the grip, two brains lie side by side, linked to an unidentifiable organ, which might be a very freely represented human heart, by a scrolling pattern of viscera. On the front of the forward ring are two colons, similarly linked to the *quillons* by an intestinal design; the *quillon*-ends might at a glance be taken to represent crouching devils, but they are foetusés; the pommel, itself of an organic (though unidentifiable) shape, is covered with scrollwork based upon muscles—muscles after the outer covering of skin has been removed. Altogether a remarkable hilt, and as remarkably beautiful, for aesthetically it cannot be faulted, though it is not entirely acceptable to modern taste.

This Dutch interest in anatomical detail is probably a result of the granting in 1557 to the city of Amsterdam of the privilege of having, once a year, the corpse of a condemned criminal, for dissection and experiment; this was followed in 1624 by the opening of the *Theatrum Anatomicum*. Rembrandt's painting, 'The Anatomy Lesson', is another manifestation of a fashionable interest in the workings of the human body. Indeed, most of these lectures were attended by audiences of hundreds, and dissections were carried out in a very full blaze of publicity.

Though some of the citizens in Rotius's pictures wear scarf swords, and all wear scarves, none of the swords shown is attached in any way to a scarf, most of them being carried on broad, elaborately-embroidered baldrics (one is reminded of Porthos) worn over the right shoulder—though Lieutenant van Sander's mini-*flamberge* is worn on a waist-belt and Lieutenant van Neck's scarf sword has no visible means of support at all. The scarves here are all worn round—or rather above—the waist, with a large fall of material over the left rump where the scarf is tied. The fashion for wearing the scarf over the right shoulder and knotted on the left hip seems to have prevailed, if we are to judge on the evidence of portraits, from about 1630 to about 1645. The sword of Charles X Gustavus of Sweden, of 1654, is carried on a baldric similar to those shown in Rotius's pictures, except that it is nearly twice as broad.

THE FLEMISH TOWN SWORD STYLES

The transition which took place in France from the swept hilt to the *flamberge* and thence to the French-styled early smallsword without knuckle-guard is well-known. Perhaps not so familiar is the parallel development which took place farther north at the same time, in Germany and in Scandinavia but particularly in the Netherlands. These hilts, which it will be convenient, though not pedantically accurate, to call Flemish, showed a lot more individuality in design than did the *flamberges*. A few seem so eccentric that no link with any other is apparent, but this is brought about by a combination of two research factors: one, that often only one specimen is known to survive; and two, that no such hilt has been observed in a portrait. A good example of this is the little dog-headed sword shown in Plate 20 and its parallel in Rotius's self-portrait. Another example, and one that seems to be unique, is a hilt which combines elements of the English hilt, the Spanish cup hilt, and the mortuary hilt; but a painted hilt very similarly formed is shown in wonderful detail in the foreground of Rembrandt's portrait of himself and Saskia, painted *c.* 1635. The painted sword is clearly of the town sword genre, while the actual specimen looks and feels like a very practical fighting sword; but it is small and neat, of town sword proportions.

However, these two, obviously of a type with few survivors, are not in the direct line of descent of the true smallsword. In the Flemish style this development was simply a shrinking in size, first of the ordinary swept hilt, and then, drastically, in the number of its guards. Plate 22 shows a small Cavalier hilt which in the arrangement and section of its guards is very similar to some English/Flemish full-hilt rapiers of a kind well-portrayed in Van Dyck's painting, *c.* 1635, of Charles I hunting. If, as is shown in Figure 105, the outside ring-guard, the

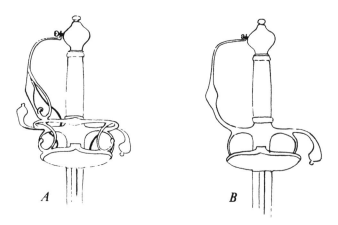

FIGURE 105 A   shows a small Cavalier rapier,
possibly English, dating c. 1650

B   shows how the same hilt, if the
ring-guards and loop-guards are in
imagination removed, becomes a true
smallsword hilt

small loop-guards and the forward *quillon* of this small hilt are removed, we are left with a true smallsword hilt.

The same phenomenon may be observed in three other hilts of the same period of the 1630s and 1640s. Two of these, in the Victoria and Albert Museum, are English and would be classed as late examples of the Cavalier rapier; one has a hilt (extremely ornate) of silver which carries an English mark, the letters *TH* within a shield, and the other is of iron ornamented with numerous small dots of applied silver, a typical English style of the mid-century. Both of these have the basic smallsword form overlaid with forward *quillon* and extra guards. The third hilt, in the Musée de l'Armée, Paris, in silhouette could be taken to be a smallsword one, except that its single rear *quillon* is missing; but instead of a pair of shells, the guard is a deep 'dish'.

Two other hilts, probably of north German origin, are shown in Plate 21 D and E. The disc-like mouldings incorporated in the knuckle-guards and forming the ends of the *quillons* put hilt 21 D in style among those early Walloon hilts so popular in north-west Europe during the Thirty Years War. It is of pure smallsword form, though an unusual feature is that the end of each branch turns sharply outward away from the *ricasso*, protruding through the space between the shells (which in the second sword shown are missing), and each of these ends is finished, like the *quillons*, with a small disc with a tiny nipple-like point in its centre. The style of the beautifully-cut, pierced design of the shells is similar in technique to that of the sword in Plate 21 E. Its blade is long, narrowing sharply (like a colichemarde blade, *q.v.*, below) some twelve inches (30 cm) below the hilt. It is a pure smallsword in design, but a rapier in intent.

A piece of entirely useless information which I offer because it fascinates me is that the actual design of the pierced shells on this hilt is uncannily similar to the design on the gold-and-garnet *cloisonné* decoration of the shoulder-buckles found, among other jewellery, in the seventh-century ship-burial at Sutton Hoo, Suffolk. How does one account for this similarity of design on two items of military hardware separated by a thousand years?

There were a great many diverse designs of this hilt, far too many to enumerate or illustrate; but all were of true smallsword form, always with knuckle-guards and often with a forward as well as a rear *quillon*. Upon the basic shape, infinite variation of detail was possible, but one constant feature of these early Netherlandish hilts (*i.e.*, *c.* 1645—1665) is that the principal guards consist of an outside and an inside ring-guard, each ring filled with a thin steel plate pierced in various ways, forming a pair of shells. Some of these pierced plates are of high quality, both in design and execution, but others are crudely made with many small uneven holes bored in them.

Perhaps the first type of smallsword hilt to be made with shells cast in one piece appeared in the 1650s, probably in the Netherlands. This was a distinct type on its own, of true smallsword form without a forward *quillon*; the hilt was generously proportioned, made of cast iron, which was then intricately worked up with the chisel. This chiselled decoration consisted of groups of war-like figures: on the shells were scenes of mounted combat, those on the underside being worked up in such high relief that in some cases the little horsemen stood clear, almost freed from the iron; on the inside the relief was very low. The *quillon*-end usually showed a figure, sometimes on horseback but often just a nude form. The centre of the *quillon*-block and the swelling mid-point of the knuckle-guard were also chiselled in high relief, the figure on the knuckle-guard being generally cut *à jour*. Pommels, generally spherical or fig-shaped, showed more horsemen in high relief. These hilts range in quality from superb works of art through all the grades of craftsmanship down to crudely-worked, ill-proportioned and meretricious copies of the better ones. But all are of the same construction and follow the same designs upon the same theme. Most of them were mounted with rapier-blades of modest mid-seventeenth-century dimensions, some thirty-two inches long (about 80 cm).

THE SMALLSWORD IN ITALY AND SPAIN

While the 'Flemish'-style swords and their French and Germanic predecessors were fashionable in the north, in Italy and Spain—where the *Escrime Française* was held in contempt—the final forms of the long rapier, the very quintessence of the weapon, had only just come into use. It was the final and most efficient type of rapier, designed to improve the Italo-Spanish style of fence as the smallsword was designed to match the needs of the *Escrime Française*. It is an interesting fact that both, so different in size and shape, came into prominence during the same decade. However, in the last twenty years of the century the French- and Netherlands-style hilt was taken up in Spain, though never to the detriment of the cup-hilt rapier which, as we have seen, lasted well into the eighteenth century. The Spanish adaptation of the Low Countries hilt made no concessions to French modes in fencing, for they were big hilts with very deep branches and long narrow

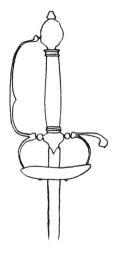

FIGURE 106 A Spanish smallsword hilt, c. 1700

blades of the same pattern as those fitted to the native hilts. Not many of these Spanish smallswords survive, but such as do are worth noting. There is a good one in the private collection of Mr Steven V. Granesay in New York (Fig. 106) and a very similar one in an English private collection. Of a different and even rarer form, an unsightly design which seems to be unique, are three long rapiers in England. Two are in the Museum and Art Gallery at Cheltenham, Gloucestershire, and one is in a private collection in London. The hilts are big and plain, with large double shells; rather short, narrow, straight *quillons*; and branches which are merely narrow bars falling vertically from the undersides of the *quillons* to join the apex of the indentation between the lobes of the shells. The one in London has a plain steel hilt and a superb blade, with pierced patterns in the fullers; one almost identical in shape at Cheltenham has a silver hilt but not nearly such a good blade, while the other Cheltenham sword has a cut-steel hilt of a kind which, if similar work were found on the mounts of a pistol, would be called Brescian.

A few late Spanish rapiers were made with, instead of cups on their hilts, pairs of enormous shells. Some, like an example dating *c.* 1710 in the Tower of London, are a form of Bilbo, but an example in the Royal Armoury, Madrid (G 64), has two huge shells, almost flat, below the long straight *quillons*, knuckle-guard and pommel, all modified from the traditional shape into more robust forms with chiselled embellishment, producing a clumsy design without the elegance and grace which characterises the cup-hilt rapier. A rich sword, of beautiful workmanship, but in every sense except the one applied to swords, a bastard.

THE TRUE SMALLSWORD

By the early 1660s, as we now have proof, the fully developed—or rather, fully simplified—smallsword hilt was in widespread use in a form which would persist for some ninety years before any fundamental change was made in its design. Egerton Castle, in his authoritative *Schools and Masters of Fence*, published in 1885, followed by the writers of several works on the smallsword published since, stated categorically that the true smallsword hilt, as distinct from the *flamberge* and the transitional types, was not in use until the 1680s, at the earliest. Research carried out in the past twenty years has shown that this is not so; there is no doubt that the true smallsword, alongside some older types, was by no means uncommon by 1660, and had entirely ousted other styles by the 1670s. Proof of this is found in portraits and dated swords, and in surviving swords in Stockholm, Copenhagen and Paris. In the Musée de l'Armée is a fine bronze-gilt (ormolu) hilt cast and chiselled with standard baroque ornament, made for Louis XIV in 1664; a silver-gilt hilt (Plate 22) which is so similar in form and ornament that it must emanate from the same workshop, has Paris hallmarks for 1670; and another ormolu hilt very similar to these two, though differing a little in details of ornament, is in the Victoria and Albert Museum—where there is also an exquisite little Dutch sword of gold and enamel with an Amsterdam mark, *c.* 1668—1670: and so on.

DEVELOPMENTS: 1660—1800

It is pointless to try to describe in words all the *minutiae* of the changes which affected this hilt-form between, say, 1660 and 1800 (to set arbitrary dates to the period), but there are certain well-defined variations upon the basic form which were pan-European and can best be summarised in fifteen-year periods, with drawings, and on the understanding that there must inevitably be a good deal of overlap. In some cases (mostly personal) and some places (mostly provincial) old styles lasted longer than the *haut monde* demanded. But allowing for this and for some generalisation, these styles varied as set out below.

1660—1675: Fig. 107 A
Pommels tended to retain the old elongated oval form or to be of a flattened spherical shape; a few were fig-shaped, and many were vertically fluted. Grips were long, narrow, and of a rectangular—nearly square—section, with only a very slight swell in the middle. Knuckle-guards had a rectangular profile, often being set closer to the grip at the top than at the base, sloping outward and down at an angle to turn sharply at the bottom. Branches were large, and the single rear *quillon* quite long, ending in a swelling which was often chiselled into the shape of a beast's head and turning outward and down. Shells were not symmetrical, the inner being noticeably smaller than the outer, and the moulded-on rims were thick. These rims and the knuckle-guards just below the midpoint were often decorated with a pair of drop-shaped swellings *affronté*—a feature first seen on some of the Swiss bastard hilts of the 1530s; Figure 55 E and F, for example.

1675—1690: Fig. 107 B
Pommels were nearly always spherical or tub-shaped; hilts became shorter, knuckle-guards more evenly curved, grips oval in section and a little thicker. Branches and shells remained the same.

1690—1715: Fig. 107 C
Very little change, but the grip became shorter still and began to acquire a rounded swelling in the middle, like a barrel. The branches became smaller, the *quillon* shrank inwards a little and the rims around the shells became less thick. Some pommels (particularly on silver hilts) became pear-shaped, and occasionally the space inside the curl of the branches was filled with a small decorative element curving up from the branches' ends.

1715—1730: Fig. 107 D
Pommels tended to become smaller, reverting once more to an ovoid shape. At the start of the period the drop-shaped mouldings on shells and knuckle-guard had disappeared, and the shells became almost symmetrical.

1730—1745
The most noticeable change is that the rims to the shells were abandoned; this apart, there is no change in the form. However, many smallswords began to be made, particularly in

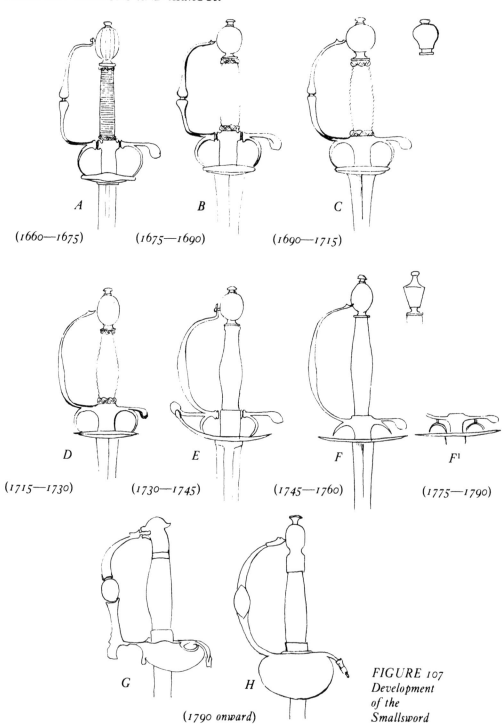

A
(1660—1675)

B
(1675—1690)

C
(1690—1715)

D
(1715—1730)

E
(1730—1745)

F
(1745—1760)

F¹
(1775—1790)

G

H
(1790 onward)

FIGURE 107
Development
of the
Smallsword

Germany, with even simpler hilts which were, in fact, reversions to the old loop-hilts of a century before. Many such swords had beautiful grips of Meissen porcelain; in a few cases, such grips may be found upon conventional hilts too.

1745—1760: Fig. 107 E

While the conventional hilt remained the most popular, two developments took place affecting the form of the shell, one at the beginning of the period and one at its end. In the mid-1740s, a form of single shell which had been used sometimes in the late seventeenth century was revived. For the double-shell was substituted a single one of oval shape, rather deeply hollowed, the forward end of which was turned abruptly upward and bifurcated to allow a forward *quillon* to pass through. At the same time, the top end of the knuckle-guard, instead of having a short projecting tongue which slotted into a hole in the side of the pommel, was finished with a flat, rather broad piece turned upward at a right-angle and secured to the side of the pommel with a screw—again, a reversion to seventeenth-century practice. The grips of these hilts, which were always ornamented in a rococo manner, were of solid metal which was decorated *en suite* with the rest of the hilt. Some hilts of this form are of silver, many of ormolu and a few of brass. Steel seems very rarely to have been used. In England they were, throughout the second half of the eighteenth century, more or less standard weapons for naval officers, while the 1796 regulations prescribed a simplified, undecorated form of brass-gilt for heavy cavalry officers' wear on certain dismounted duties. It was adopted too by general officers, and the 1822 dress regulations prescribe it for full dress, as did those of 1834 in more detail: 'Gilt guard, pommel and boat-shell.' The grips of these regulation swords were bound with twisted gilt wire over a wood core.

A second innovation of the mid-1750s was the introduction of a supremely elegant hilt; the shell is a single, very shallow, oval plate, and the branches have dwindled to a pair of little claws under the *quillon* and knuckle-guard. The knuckle-guard, swelling a little in the middle, forms a regular, symmetrical curve to a rather tall, ovoid pommel (Fig. 107 F).

The grips of these hilts were generally made of solid metal, but there are a number of cases where they are bound in one of the many intricate ways in use from the 1660s. Some of these hilts had no branches at all, others had a pair of little arches rising from the shell below the *quillon* and knuckle-guard, joined to them by small balls or cubes of steel. Steel was very frequently used for hilts of this kind. Some were completely plain, burnished bright or blued; others were decorated on grip and pommel by restrained faceting, while still others, in the later years of the century, were elaborately decorated with delicate openwork of cut-steel adorned with beadwork, or by beadwork alone (Plate 22).

1760—1775

Apart from fashionable changes in decorative treatment for which I have no space, there was neither change nor innovation.

1775—1790: Fig. 107 F[1]

The old conventional hilt began to be unfashionable, while the cut-steel single-shell sword was very much *à la mode*. During these years, silver-gilt or ormolu began to be popular for this kind of hilt. Under the influence of neo-classical taste, pommels became urn-shaped.

1790 onward: Fig. 107 H

In Revolutionary France a totally new form developed, built upon the principles of some of the early town swords. The knuckle-guard became angular at the base, like the stirrup hilts of sabres (*q.v.*, below), while the pommel generally consisted of a cap to the grip turned outward over the knuckle-guard, also like military sabre hilts. There was neither shell nor branches, but a large plate, often of a kind of cockleshell form but more usually delta-shaped, springing from the *quillon*-block and turned sharply down over the blade, parallel to its surface, while at the back was a very small lappet turned similarly upward. Originally, it seems, intended as a full-dress weapon for military and diplomatic officers in France (the earliest-dated one I know of bears a Paris silver-mark for 1793), it became standard full-dress wear in continental Europe for diplomats and all kinds of civil and ceremonial officers. In England, the Gentlemen of the Bedchamber, from the reigns of William IV to Edward VII, seem to have worn it, and even today it is part of the uniform of the Royal Bodyguard of Scottish Archers. The more usual Court sword in England, however, was (and is) of the urn-pommel, oval shell, cut-steel type with a chain, often made of elaborate cut-steel beadwork, in place of a knuckle-guard.

PRESENTATION SMALLSWORDS FROM WINDSOR

There is a group of late smallswords of extreme interest which must yet be noted. I only know of four of these, though there must be more; one is in the Museum of London, one in a private collection, one was briefly in my collection; there is also a fourth in a private collection in London. At first glance one would say that these were cast-bronze gilt hilts of a late transitional, rather typically English, form, *c.* 1650—1660, with two *quillons* and large, perforated shells fitted into ring-guards (Plate 22 D). The first three were clearly from the same mould, though by different degrees of bending and distortion of the *quillons* they look to be slightly different shapes; each pommel, however, is different. The Museum of London one is shaped like a rugby-ball, the second is rather small and spherical; the one I had myself, though still spherical, was a bit bigger. The grip of the second sword is bound with wire (which may be of silver or copper-gilt), with collars instead of Turks' heads at top and bottom, while mine had a silver-wire grip of the same form. (The grip of the Museum of London sword was restored in 1949.) Each has a totally different form of blade, and each blade clearly dates from the very end of the eighteenth century or the beginning of the nineteenth. The Museum of London one has a strong shoulder like a *ricasso* and a hexagonal blade, blued and gilt and etched with devices and designs typical of the period; the second has a fine, triangular, very narrow blade decorated in the same way; mine had a broad, flat blade with a strong mid-rib on each face, and its decoration consisted solely of a very delicate pattern of narrow, horizontal, waved lines across the faces of the blade, alternating blue and gilt. A similar blade is in a naval sword of *c.* 1810 in the National Maritime Museum, Greenwich.

Among the archives at Windsor Castle relating to the arms there, is an entry referring to swords of 'Charles II type' with copper-gilt hilts which appear to have been made as gifts for the monarch to present to unspecified persons. The swords are of extremely fine form, most accurate to the period they are supposed to represent, and the temptation is strong to believe that the mould from which they were cast was taken from an actual sword which had belonged to Charles II and which has since disappeared.

* * * * *

These smallsword hilts came to their final development at the height of the Baroque period of art, and their decoration followed the fashionable styles of ornamentation as applied to furniture and interior decoration. It passed, as all else did, from this to the Rococo. Perhaps the most notable examples of this lovely style with its emphasis upon assymetry are the boat-shell hilts of the mid-century. After about 1760 Neo-Classicism began to prevail, until it was ousted, particularly on the Continent, by the Aegypto-Classical style of the First Empire and the Regency. The question of decoration, as in the case of armour and of earlier sword-hilts, has to be omitted here for lack of space, but it has been covered in the publications listed on page 253.

BLADES

The forms of blades changed over the period 1660—1800 as subtly as hilts did. At the start, shorter versions of conventional rapier blades, generally of hexagonal section and fullered at the forte, were used. A few of them had blades of this kind which were quite broad at the forte and which then narrowed abruptly where the fullers ended. Some appear to have been forged like this, others to have been deliberately ground down to this shape. After the turn of the century, this form of blade (which had become very popular, either in a hexagonal section or in the newer, hollow, triangular section) began to be called a 'Colichemarde'.

Tradition, that hard-working handmaid of nineteenth-century studies, has attributed the actual invention of this blade-form to the noble Swedish soldier of fortune, Philipp Christoph, Count of Königsmark, 'colichemarde' supposedly being a French rendition of his name (in the same way as *hakenbüchse* became 'arquebus'). The fact that so many blades of this form seem to have been in use for a decade or so before his birth, in 1665, rather tarnishes the traditional view. The French probably had a perfectly good reason of their own for dubbing such blades *colichemardes*.

The hollow triangular blade was in use by the 1670s; examples between the 1660s and about 1720 tend to be extremely broad at the shoulder, tapering sharply with a marked concavity at the edges. The flat underside of these blades—the base of the triangle—is often inlaid with large, indeterminately geometrical patterns in brass. After about 1720, however, most blades became narrower, losing the handsome flare towards the hilt. The great period of the colichemarde's popularity was between about 1690 and 1750, though one occasionally finds an example mounted in a hilt of the 1770s or even the 1780s. As the eighteenth century wore on, blades became even narrower, until by 1800 they had attained the feeble and flimsy proportions they have today.

Blades of hexagonal section, though without fullers and often with a strong built-up shoulder almost like a *ricasso*, continued to be popular, particularly in Germany and the Netherlands. Boat-shell hilts, Continental or English, almost always had them, as did the post-1793 French Court swords, which seem rarely to have been fitted with triangular blades. A rather feeble-looking version of these hexagonal blades made its appearance around the mid-eighteenth century, of a flat convex section. The English regulation boat-shell hilts were fitted with long, narrow, back-edged blades. The Italian smallsword, mostly retaining its fine cut-steel hilt (such as the sword shown in Plate 22) continued to be fitted with a fullered rapier blade, only now reduced to the modest length of the northern smallsword.

HANGERS AND CUTTOS

Mr Pepys makes several mentions of swords: on February 3 1661 he bought a sword in Fleet Street, and on April 30 1669 he seems to have had quite a field day—he bought his man Tom a sword (for twelve shillings), himself an embroidered sword-belt for fifty-five shillings, and 'set my silver-hilt sword a-gilding at the cutler's'. He nowhere mentions the names of any of the sword-cutlers he patronised, but among his papers in the Pepysian Collection at Magdalen College, Cambridge, there is a volume he compiled in 1700 which contains a number of trade-cards of London shops. One of these is the card of Nicholas Croucher:

> At ye Flaming Sword
> In St Paul's Churchyard ye corner of ye Booksellers Row
> Fronting Cheapside liveth
> NICHOLAS CROUCHER, SWORD CUTLER,
> that maketh and selleth all sorts of Swords, Hang^{rs} Bayonets
> and Corslets, with all manner of Belts for Swords, and also
> new Forbisheth old Swords and Hangers &tc. at Reasonable Rates

The 'hangers' mentioned are the short weapons sometimes called hunting-swords, or *hirschfänger* or *couteaux-de-chasse* which, anglicised, turned to 'cuttos'. We find during the eighteenth century that many hatters and gold-lace-men dealt in swords and cuttos, so before leaving the smallsword, we should consider its partner, the hanger. Some of these are as exquisite in workmanship and as elegant in form as the smallswords to which they were, in a manner of speaking, out-of-door companions. They were intended either as part of formal hunting-dress, or as handy anti-footpad weapons to wear when walking abroad at night; varieties of them also were much favoured, particularly in the 1660—1720 period, by naval officers for active service, forerunners of the little ceremonial midship-man's dirk. The blades could be either straight or curved, and the form of their hilts fol-lowed as clear a line of development from the 1640s as smallsword hilts, though the form was fully developed by *c.* 1550 (Fig. 108 A). Earlier ones were often quite crudely made, with large shell-guards, knuckle-guard and flat pommel-cap. Some were chiselled in the manner of contemporary Cavalier or mortuary hilts, but many were more delicately ornamented with a profusion of small silver dots. These hilts, like their more urbane companions, became smaller by the mid-1760s, and were often made of silver; shells became smaller, or were dispensed with altogether. By the end of the century, many were made with no more than a pair of *quillons*, very short, and grips, tapering upward, made of bone, staghorn, ivory (sometimes plain but often elaborately and exquisitely carved) or various kinds of stone, such as agate or jasper. A form very popular in the period from about 1725 to 1770 had a large, turned-down shell on the outside, a short rear *quillon*, a knuckle-guard, and a cap upon the top of a grip which tapered

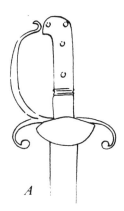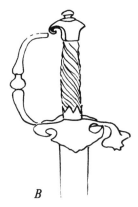

A   *B*

FIGURE 108   *Illustration A shows an early form of the hanger,*
dating from the second half of the eighteenth
century;
Illustration B shows a hanger hilt, c. 1670

upward (Plate 23 C). Many of these were of silver, beautifully ornamented with cast and chiselled-up rococo designs, while less expensive ones had the same form of decoration but were made of brass, either plain or gilded. Some, both of silver and of brass, were hardly decorated at all.

The gentlemanly practice of wearing a sword was rapidly dying out by 1770—indeed, Sheridan said in 1774 that in Bath, under the regime of Beau Nash, 'a sword seen in the streets would create as much alarm as a mad dog'. The hanger, worn upon the reeking decks of a man-of-war or in the robust conditions of the hunting-field, held its own a little longer, but by about 1775, in any but a military capacity, it was relegated entirely to Court or ceremonial occasions.

BIBLIOGRAPHY

Angelo, Domenico, *L'Ecole des Armes*, London 1765

Aylward, J. D., *The Small-Sword in England*, London, 1960

   and also .. *The English Master of Arms*, London, 1956

Dean, B., *The Metropolitan Museum of Art, Catalogue of European Court and Hunting Swords*, New York, 1929

Gay, John, *Trivia*, or *The Art of Walking the Streets of London*, London, 1715

EUROPEAN WEAPONS AND ARMOUR

Hope, Sir William, *The Scots Fencing Master*, Edinburgh, 1687

Hutton, Alfred, *Old Sword Play*, London, 1892

Labat, *L'Art en Fait d'Armes*, Toulouse, 1696, *see* Mahon, Andrew

Mahon, Andrew, *The Art of Fencing* (translation of L'Art en Fait d'Armes by Labat), London, 1735

May, W. E., *The 5-ball Type of Sword Hilt*, Journal of the Arms and Armour Society, London, 1963

Norman, A. V. B., *Some Eighteenth-Century Civilian Swords*, Scottish Art Review, Vol. XII, No. 2, Glasgow, 1969

. . . . *Smallswords and Military Swords*, London, 1967

. . . . *Notes on some Scottish Infantry Swords in the Scottish United Services Museum*, Journal of the Arms and Armour Society, London, 1965

Pierce, Major P. Carrington-, *A Handbook of Court and Hunting Swords*, London, 1936

Setiz, H., *Quelques Armes Exquises de la Manufacture de Versailles*, Armes Anciennes No. 10, 1958

Ward, Ned, *The London Spy*, 1695—1703, reprinted London, 1927

The Gentleman's Tutor for the Small Sword, London, 1737

Geschichte der Solinger Klingen Industrie, Dresden, 1885

L'Art du Coutelier, Fougeroux de Bourderon, Paris, 1726

The lists of material given at the end of Chapter Two and Chapter Six also apply.

CONCLUSION

At the time when the sword ceases to be an indispensable part of a gentleman's everyday dress, we reach an archaeological terminus. In this book and its predecessor, *The Archaeology of Weapons*, we have followed Man's armaments, particularly the sword to which he accorded so much mystical significance, from those very first Bronze Age weapons, the long rapiers of Ireland, right up to their latest successors, the very similarly bladed smallswords of the seventeenth and eighteenth centuries. Beyond these we are in the Age of Industry, of mass-produced armaments—even mass-produced swords—and have reached the last phase of the military era of bayonet and cannon wherein the individual soldier's part in the business of waging war was to become ever more squalid.

After about 1690, leaving aside the infantryman's bayonet, a few ceremonial staff-weapons, and the inevitable and nasty all-purpose knives, the sword remained the only edged weapon in ordinary military use. The military swords of the eighteenth and nineteenth centuries, in all their bewildering variety, have been covered almost as thoroughly as firearms have been, in many comprehensive and authoritative books. I, as a student of the archaeology of weapons, have no brief here to deal with them again. However, it would leave this whole work of mine too open-ended were I to finish it without a mention of some of the trends which affected the military sword in Europe up to the Congress of Vienna, after Napoleon's defeat in 1815, and beyond it into the Age of Steam and the Industrial Revolution.

In the first half of the eighteenth century, the sword-types which had become established in the closing decade of the seventeenth century continued in use in all the nations of Europe. There seems nowhere to have been any system of standardisation, so the variants upon these forms are infinite; however, early in the century a new pattern of hilt evolved in Austria and was to be the common ancestor of a great many of the styles used by the vast armies of the Napoleonic period. This was a simple, practical hilt which had its origins in the fifteenth century: a marriage with the Turkish–Egyptian–Persian cross-hilted sabre-style which had been ubiquitous in eastern Europe from the second half of the sixteenth century produced the so-called 'Stirrup hilt' (Figs. 109 A, B, C). Its genesis, as the hilt of the cavalry sword *par excellence*, can be clearly seen in Rembrandt's 'The Polish Rider', painted *c.* 1655. There are two sabres, one of them on the rider's left hip, the other under his right knee, carried under the saddle-flap. The latter is apparently of silver, and its pistol-shaped grip is very Persian in style, but the hilt on the hip is the clear ancestor of

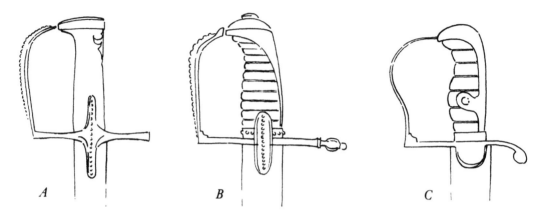

FIGURE *109*   *The development of the 'Stirrup' hilt*

Illustration A, Austrian, c. 1700
Illustration B, Austrian, c. 1750
Illustration C, English, 1796 pattern

the Austro-Hungarian sabres. There is no knuckle-guard, only a pair of short straight *quillons*; the grip is of wood covered with leather, of very much the shape of most subsequent cavalry sabres, and it is surmounted by an angular pommel-cap projecting forward and being carried a little way down the back like an embryonic back-strap. A number of such sabres of this date survive (notably that of István [Stephen] Bathory, *c.* 1580, now in the Wojska Polskiego Museum, Warsaw). A very similar one was sold in London on January 25 1971 (Elliott & Snowdon, Lot 136). This is shown in Figure 110.

The stirrup hilt, fully developed, was in use by the Austro-Hungarian cavalry from about 1700 onwards, generally mounted with a sabre blade but sometimes also with a long, straight, back-edged blade called in Hungary a *pallasch*. Many of these sabres, whose hilts were of bronze gilded, were the weapons of *prima plana* men, 'Front page' men, a survival from the old *landsknecht* companies where the aristocratic enlisted men were entered on the front pages of the Company registers. By the eighteenth century this term had come to apply to all those who did not fall in with the Companies—officers' sergeants and musicians.

By the time of the wars of Frederick the Great of Prussia in the mid-century, this hilt-form had spread to the armies of Russia, Prussia and France. England was slow to adopt it, continuing to use variants of the Scots–English basket hilt for her cavalry (Fig. 111). Some of the hilts used by

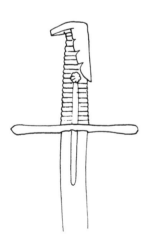

FIGURE *110*   *The hilt of a Polish sabre*

FIGURE 111   An English Dragoon hilt, c. 1750

Dragoon officers were very handsome (Plate 23 E), but many were very ordinary, particularly the swords of troopers. In the 1770s and 1780s, both the British and the French brought out variants of their own on the basket hilt (perhaps a mutation of the *schiavona*); both of these were handsomer than their predecessors, but the French version was by far the more elegant. Examples are now unfortunately very rare.

With the pan-European wars at the close of the eighteenth century came the need—or the desire—for standardisation of sword-types by the principal contestants. Following Austria's lead, both Russia and Prussia, and to a lesser degree Saxony and Bavaria, adopted very similar sword-patterns, each nation's hilts differing mainly in detail, but it was not until 1788 that Britain began to standardise, and then only in a very half-hearted way. In 1796, however, a complete and effective standardised group of swords of regulation pattern was introduced, the few patterns of 1788 being scrapped. There were really only three basic styles, one for light cavalry, one for heavy cavalry, and one for infantry officers and sergeants. These designs were approved by the monarch, the commander-in-chief, and the War Office. Since at that time the 'monarch' was in effect the Prince of Wales, then acting for the first time as Regent, and the C-in-C was his brother the Duke of York, it is possible that Prinny's impeccable good taste may have affected the designs of these swords, which were among the most beautiful weapons ever to be made during the long lapse of the centuries: their fine proportions, their elegance and simplicity made them akin to the most beautiful cross-hilted swords of the mid-fifteenth century. These swords were, of course, subject to much variation of detail, but the basic designs were fundamental to officers and troopers alike. The blades of officers' swords were often decorated, in the upper half, with etched designs, gilded upon a blued ground. The majority of these decorations were motifs—floral arabesques, trophies of arms, the Royal monogram; often used was the figure of a mounted, sabre-brandishing cavalryman; all too rarely used were Regimental insignia. These designs were generally of a very high artistic and technical quality, but a few blades made for parade swords, or presentation ones, can be said to be equal in achievement with the work of the Italian and German etchers in the great days of the sixteenth century. Such weapons are true collectors' pieces: works of art as well as arms.

The hilts of these regulation swords were of gilded bronze (officers) or plain steel (other ranks) if the Regimental facings were of gold braid; if the facings were silver, the hilts to match them were of bright steel or blued steel or, in a few rich and rare cases, of silver. The light cavalry swords generally had curved back-edged blades with a very broad and shallow fuller running to within some six inches (15.25 cm) of the point; the back edge was sharpened to this distance from the point as well. The curvature varied a great deal, as did the weight and width of the blade. Many of these sword blades broadened perceptibly towards the point. There were many light cavalry blades, however, which had perfectly flat sections and very strong curvature—there was scope for an infinite variation.

The 'heavies' generally used the *pallasch*—a long, straight, back-edged blade, broad and shallowly fullered, with a curious D-shaped 'point' like the *kissaki* of a Japanese *katana*. The hilts of the troopers' swords of this pattern were quite hideous, but the officers' version was handsome enough. Individual cutlers, of course, making the same regulation hilt, nevertheless produced a great number of different-looking hilts; all a matter of proportion. Common to all the officers' hilts was an adaptation in the guard (which was, it appears, itself an adaptation of the old mortuary hilt) of the Ancient Greek *anthemion*, or honeysuckle, motif. Most of the blades of surviving officers' swords of this pattern have etched and gilded decoration, but no blueing. These swords (some, incidentally, being made, hilt and scabbard, of brass) look very ponderous; it is always quite a surprise on handling one of them to find how exceedingly light and well-balanced they are.

The pattern for infantry officers and sergeants was a kind of reversion to the double-shelled swords of the late seventeenth century, except that the design was far more elegant, usually reflecting the decorative style, as applied to furniture and interiors, of the Adam brothers. (In the same way, some of the English and Irish smallsword hilts of the early eighteenth century reflected the styles of William Kent.) These swords generally had straight, back-edged blades of a kind which had been popular all through the period 1750—1800 on plain-hilted infantry officers' swords, known by the name 'spadroons'. Very occasionally, though, they had double-edged blades of a flat diamond section, and in a few cases old (that is, sixteenth- or seventeenth-century) blades fitted to them. This, indeed, was quite often done; there is a fine English sword of the 1834 2nd Life-Guards pattern, which was sold recently, fitted to which was the blade out of an Indian *firangi*; and another with a modified hilt of the 1822 English pattern, dating probably *c.* 1860, which had a good early-seventeenth-century blade. These were no modern replacements, but had obviously been married together during their working life for some perfectly good, even possibly romantic, reason. There are too many examples of the re-using of old blades for me to recount them all here, but I should perhaps mention again that fine seventh-century 'pattern-welded' blade mounted in a *landsknecht* hilt of *c.* 1510 which is now in the Schweizerisches Landesmuseum, Zürich, and a fine boat-shelled officer's dress sword of the 1796 pattern mounted with an 'Andrea Ferrara' blade out of a claymore.

I have said that there were only three basic styles in the 1796 patterns; this, of course, referred to campaign swords, as opposed to dress swords (the latter being dealt with in the preceding chapter). However, mention should be made of the naval swords of this period. They were in the main adaptations of the light cavalry stirrup hilt, mounted as a rule with straight 'spadroon' blades, though many are to all intents and purposes indistinguishable from light cavalry sabres—unless there are naval motifs etched on the blade, such as tridents, dolphins, etc., or, on the langets on the hilt, fouled anchors. In many cases the knuckle-guards do not have the extra bowed curve in the upper part, which instead is made very broad and stout to act as a guard; naval officers, unlike the military (who were specifically forbidden to engage in hand-to-hand combat) were always in the thick of the fray when boarding an enemy ship—Nelson and his officers of *HMS Captain*, for instance, when they took the *San Josef* at the battle of Cape St Vincent. Naval swords always had gilt-bronze hilts, which would not be ruined by salt water; for officers above

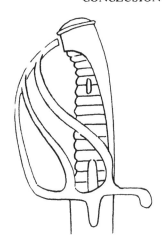

FIGURE 112   A French light cavalry sabre hilt, 1811 pattern

the rank of lieutenant, there were ivory grips, while lieutenants and warrant-officers had grips of black sharkskin.

A new set of patterns, being mainly modifications of the 1796 ones, was produced in 1803, the only totally new design being a hilt for the officers of infantry flank companies. They used the light cavalry sabre blade but the hilt, though basically still of the stirrup form, instead of *quillons* had an openwork plate of a very narrow oval shape and a knuckle-guard which broadened at the base where it was cast as an openwork design incorporating either a Regimental badge, like the bugle-horn of the Light Infantry, or the Royal cypher, crowned. The pommel-cap on the top of the back-strap was formed as a lion's head, the end of the knuckle-guard fitting into its mouth. The grips were of pale grey shagreen or ivory bound with gilt wire, unlike the cavalry swords of the earlier pattern which (except for individual aberrations) were covered in black leather, bound with silver wire on a steel hilt or gilt wire on a gilded or brass one. These 1803 infantry sabres always had copper-gilt hilts.

The French, having adopted the Austrian-style sabre hilt earlier in the century, began to standardise in the 1790s with a series of hilts which had loop-guards on the outside, looking rather like some of the late-seventeenth-century hilts but with a whiff about them of the *Schiavona I* hilt (Fig. 112). Those for infantry NCOs and light cavalry had two loop-guards; most of the hilts were of brass, and the curved back-edged blades were much narrower than the British or Austrian or German ones. For heavy cavalry they had a hilt generally with three loop-guards, in a few cases incorporating the graceful shell in the front of the hilt which they used in their Dragoon swords of the 1780s. There were at least two 'regulation' dates, 1800 (An XI according to the Revolutionary dating, which began from July 14 1789) and 1811 (by which time they had more or less returned to the form of dating used everywhere else in Europe—probably very necessary, as by that date almost all Europe was under French domination).

Characteristic of these French swords were the narrow blades and the lack of a backstrap on the grip. Instead they favoured a tall pommel-cap, angled towards the front of the hilt with a broad flap-like extension at the back falling about a third of the way down the back of the grip. General officers seem as a rule to have had swords

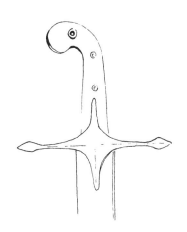

FIGURE 113   A Turkish/Egyptian sabre hilt

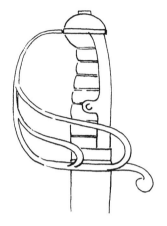

FIGURE 114   An English hilt, 1822 pattern

of regulation pattern according to their various ranks, as, for instance, Generals of Brigade and of Division. These were variants of the Austrian hilts used in earlier years but after Napoleon's campaign in Egypt and in Palestine, 1798—1802, a new fashion appeared. This was purely eastern, the typical Turkish *Kilij* or Persian *Shamshir* hilt (Fig. 113). Many of these were mounted with rare old Turkish or Egyptian blades, dating back as far as the fifteenth century in some cases; some hilts were made in Cairo or Damascus in true mid-eastern style, some were taken just as they were from defeated Emirs or given as tokens of esteem by friendly ones. Many others, such as the swords of Massena and Bernadotte in the Livrustkammaren, Stockholm, had hilts made by Nicholas Noel Boutet and other French masters of *orfevrerie*, with beautiful old oriental blades mounted in them.

This style was almost instantly adopted in Britain, first by high-ranking officers, then by quite ordinary cavalry officers. The 'Mameluke hilt', as it was called, lasted almost unchallenged by any other style for Field-Marshals and lesser, but still high-ranking, general officers, and for diplomats, all through the nineteenth century, and it remains as the sword for military, as distinct from Court, dress wear, to this day.

In 1822 the British army evolved another set of regulation patterns, the principal one of which seems, with its oval plate guard, knuckle-guard, and two loop-guards, to have been influenced by the French patterns (Fig. 114). It was used by light cavalry, artillery and infantry officers and by NCOs, with some modifications made from time to time throughout the century. A variation of it, much favoured by naval officers, and called for some reason the 'Gothic hilt', was of a similar general shape but with the front lower part of the guards filled in, often solid but in many cases cast in openwork with a cartouche incorporating the Royal cypher—we find *GR IV, WR IV* and *VR*. Naval versions tended to have fouled anchors instead. This pattern is still used in the Royal Navy for full-dress wear. All these swords of the 1822 patterns, and their subsequent modifications, had narrower, less sharply curved blades than their predecessors—indeed, they barely curved at all. Most were back-edged and fullered, but for a time in the 1820s and 1830s they tended to have 'pipe-back' blades of a flat section with a strong rib, circular in section, running along the back and merging into the back of the point.

The Life-Guards retained their long straight swords until near the end of the century, when the modern, lightly curved pattern came into use, while the heavy, rather elaborate hilt gave way to the modern type, which is a kind of modification of the 1796 Dragoon officers pattern.

The foregoing paragraphs do not set themselves up as a chapter on the swords of the 'modern' centuries, not even as a synopsis of one. They are meant merely to be a frail bridge between what I have set down in two volumes (this book and its predecessor, *The Archaeology of Weapons*) and in some 250,000 words, and the quantity of excellent books, many in English, scholarly, authoritative and lavishly illustrated, which deal in depth and in detail with these weapons. Like the noble statesman, I do not itch to interfere in matters which I do not understand. As I have done throughout this book, I append a list of some of these publications at the foot of this last page.

So, as it were, I have corked up the bottle which has been so long in filling, hoping that what it contains may mature well, give pleasure to the experienced palate, stimulate the rather less experienced, and arouse a great thirst for more in the inexperienced one. These are rare and fine vintages that I have listed: may you find in them the same delight and inspiration as I have done.

BIBLIOGRAPHY

Almayer, J. P., *American Presentation Swords*, Mobile, Alabama, 1958

May, W. E., and Annis, P. G. W., *Swords for Sea Service*, London, 1970

Neumann, Geo. C., *Swords and Blades of the American Revolution*, Newton Abbot, 1973

Peterson, H. L., *Arms and Armor in Colonial America, 1526—1783*, Harrisburg, 1956

and also ... *American Knives*, New York, 1958

Robson, Brian, *Swords of the British Army*, London, 1975

Wagner, Eduard, *Cut and Thrust Weapons*, London, 1967

TOURNAMENT ARMOUR

Special pieces for jousting had been in use, in a limited way, from the second half of the thirteenth century, as noted above and in *The Archaeology of Weapons*, but during the second half of the fifteenth century, these developed quite rapidly into extremely specialised complete armours. Most of our knowledge (which is disappointingly scanty) of the various forms for the tournament and the joust is confined to the styles affected by the German nations after about 1480, which were much influenced and encouraged by the inevitable Maximilian I. However, two very notable developments are clearly attributable to the Italians and the French.

At some time in the 1420s, along with international forms of much stricter rules governing jousts and tournaments, the Italians introduced an important safety device. This was a long barrier set up along the length of the course to be run, one contestant riding on either side. It was a great help in preventing the opposing horses from colliding. At first, the barrier seems to have been simply a light wooden framework about six feet high (1·80 metres), covered with cloth or canvas, which became known in England as the 'tilt', the same word being used for the canvas covering of carts and wagons (as it was until the middle years of this century). Later, and in Germany, when joust armour—'tilting' armour it is often called, for the name given to the barrier was soon applied to the sport itself—became much heavier, the tilt was made of solid planks of wood. The Germans called the courses which were run with a barrier '*über die Planken*'.

It is to the French that modern scholars owe the earliest-written description of the armour worn for jousting. This is to be found in an anonymous manuscript of 1446. The armour comprised a cuirass, or a brigandine, fitted with a lance-rest, having a series of buckles for the attachment of the helm and various other pieces; a *main de fer* (called a 'manifer' in English) for the left hand, 'made of one piece', to guard 'the hand and the arm up to three or four fingers above the elbow'; a small one-piece pauldron for the left shoulder (the left, or bridle, arm may be kept almost immobile when jousting); and a small gauntlet for the right hand which in this manuscript is called a *gagnepain*, 'breadwinner', perhaps for obvious reasons considering how many 'professional' jousters made a living out of ransoms. This glove was often made of leather, for the large steel vamplate of the lance protected the hand. Worn above the glove on the right forearm was a piece of armour which the French, with an almost Teutonic aptness, called an *épaule de mouton*, 'shoulder of mutton', for its shape was indeed reminiscent of that particular joint of meat.

A lower cannon flared out at the inner bend of the elbow to cover the outside of the elbow itself, curved in at the bend of the joint, and then curved out again to protect the lower half of the upper arm; when the wearer's arm was bent, holding the lance couched, this effectively protected the upper arm as well as the bend of the elbow. The English rendered the French name in their inimitable and entirely modern phonetic way as 'polder mitten', or, sometimes, just as 'moton'. Above this was a small, laminated pauldron with a large besagew in front, and hanging over the left side of the chest, a pear-shaped object made of wood or leather (called a *poire*) which made a buffer for the small, rectangular, wooden shield, faced with squares of horn, which was also hung by a cord from the shoulder. The author of this passage goes on to say that in France legharness was usually worn, suggesting perhaps that elsewhere it was not. This may have been because of the use of the tilt, and the large leg-defences which were fitted to the front of the saddle.

This form of armour continued, with modifications regional or chronological, to be used for the joust all over Europe until about 1530 for every kind of course with lances which was not run in field armour, and in Germany for the course known as the *Gestech*. Originally they applied this term to the ordinary joust fought with lances, but late in the fourteenth century a special form developed which they called the *Hohenzeuggestech*. In this the object was to shatter the lances rather than unseat either opponent, but its distinctive feature was the use of a diabolical form of saddle. This had the seat raised at least ten inches (25 cm) above the horse's back, so that the jouster stood. In front, it was shaped like a large wooden shield, forked to accommodate the horse's back. This very sensibly protected the rider from his feet to his waist; but for some unimaginable reason, two wooden bars just below hip-level extended to the high back of the saddle, to prevent (presumably) his being unseated. How many broken thighs or pelvises or spines this produced is nowhere recorded. It went out of fashion by about 1450, though Maximilian revived a modified form of it. Ordinary field harness, less legharness, seems to have been worn, but with a frog-mouthed joust helm instead of an armet or a bascinet.

These joust helms, a logical development of the old fourteenth-century 'great helms', such as those of the Black Prince in Canterbury, and, later, Henry V in Westminster, came into use late in the fourteenth century. They differed greatly in shape from the war helm, for the upper plate was very nearly flat, and the sight aperture was a horizontal slit (shaped like a frog's mouth) formed by a gap between the front faceplate and the flat browplate (Plate 24). When the head is held up, no vision is possible, but when the wearer hunches his shoulders and lowers his head to the jousting position, vision is excellent; and since the lower plate, concavely curved and ridged in front like a ship's prow, considerably overlaps the upper, there is very little danger of a lancepoint entering the eye-slit.

By about 1480, the shields in front of the saddle for the *gestech* were generally dispensed with, a curious, padded bumper being attached to the horse's chest and withers instead, called a *stechsack*. This not only protected the horse's shoulders if it should collide with the barrier, but protected the rider's legs too.

A considerable number of late-fifteenth and early-sixteenth-century armours for the *Gestech* survive, particularly in Vienna, and in the Germanisches Museum, Nuremberg. There is a fine one in the Wallace Collection, London (A 23), and one that is mounted, *stechsack*, lance and all, in the Metropolitan Museum, New York. The form of these armours is much as described in the French manuscript of 1446, except that they are (presumably) more massive, and the great frog-mouthed *stechhelm* is fastened with a screw or a bolt and not with a strap and buckle. The breastplate is very short and very heavy, the right side boxed and flattened for the lance-rest, and a great flat bar of steel bolted on, extending back behind the right shoulder, where it is hooked over outwards to accommodate the butt-end of the lance, thus transferring much of the weight from the jouster's arm to his breastplate. Below the skirt and tassets there is a stout plate, arched over the fork and resting upon the top of the thigh, riveted under the lower edge of the breast. Round the edge of this plate are broad flaps of leather which can be laced to corresponding flaps on the culet behind. There are straps and buckles round the inside of the thighs too. The back-plate, joined to the breast by hinged metal hasps at the sides and shoulders, is very light, often only an X-shaped frame with a little culet below. The shoulders are protected by small laminated pauldrons, with large besagews, usually on the right side only, with short laminated extensions down the outside of the arm to the elbow. A polder mitten protects the right forearm, a *main-de-fer* the left, and the small rectangular shield (*stechtartsche*) hangs over its pear on the left side of the breast. On the points of the shoulders often appear little stalks, about three to four inches long (7·5 to 10 cm), with knobs on top. It has been suggested that these were intended to spread out and fasten the mantling of the crest, but it is much more probable that the stalks were designed to prevent the heavy lance from rolling off the hard, rounded surface of the pauldron when it was carried over the shoulder.

This form of armour for the *Gestech* lasted until the 1530s, but was subject to minor variations to suit special versions of the course. The tilt was not introduced into Germany until the second decade of the sixteenth century. Then the course became known as the *Welschgestech über die Planken* or *Plankengestech*.

The other specialised form of joust devised at this time was called *Scharfrennen*, its main object being to unhorse the opponent, though points were gained for lance-splintering too. The earliest mention of it is in an inventory of the armour of the Archduke Friedrich, later the Emperor Frederick III and father of Maximilian I, which was taken in 1436. Before the 1480s, this course was run in light half-armour with sallet and bevor and often only a brigandine, with a rectangular shield on the left shoulder. By 1480, however, a special armour had been devised, many examples surviving in Vienna and one in the Tower of London. It was generally without legharness, vambraces, pauldrons or gauntlets, the large vamplate, much bigger than in lances for the *gestech*, and the *renntartsche*, a shield covering all the left arm, side and even the chin (in a special little beard-like extension supplied at the top edge), being quite adequate. The vamplate was of steel, in the form of a large semi-disc, cut off straight on the left where it met the shield, which was of wood covered with layers of glue and leather and screwed to the cuirass. This was similar to that used for the *gestech*, but the tassets tended to be heavier and, shaped to fit over the thighs, reached almost to the knees. On the head was worn a large, heavy, one-piece sallet, called a *rennhut*, with a vision slit cut in it, and a deep bevor fastened by screws to the breast. To the brow were attached two small steel wings, fixed by means of pins and a pivoted bar; these flew off when they were struck. The legs were protected by heavy boots and large metal plates, generally disc-shaped, called *dilgen*, 'tilting-sockets', one hanging on either side of the saddle. This form of armour lasted into the 1550s, though there were many variations. The most ingenious—no need to speculate on who devised it!—was the *mechanisches rennen*, and its variants. Basic to it was the idea that the breast was fitted with a spring-operated mechanism covered by a metal shield made in several parts. When this was struck, the whole thing blew up and flew off in all directions.

For the rest, field armour was worn with various extra pieces (*q.v.*, above) to suit it to the joust, tourney or foot combat. In Germany, the old tournament, a general *mêlée* called the *Freiturnier*, was fought in reinforced field armour, often with rebated weapons, occasionally with clubs (*kolbenturnier*). In foot combats over barriers, half-armour was sometimes worn, with a great bascinet or a reinforced armet fastened to the cuirass by buckles or bolts. The specialised foot-combat armours of Henry VIII, and the tonnlet armours worn at the Courts of Maximilian and his successors, have already been described in Chapter Four.

By the latter part of the sixteenth century, the main features of jousting armour were a specially heavy and reinforced form of the fashionable close helmet, a *main-de-fer*, and a large plate, not unlike the *renntartsche*, covering the left side of the body and flaring out forward over the bridle-hand and a plate called a grandguard which was a sort of exaggerated haute-piece to protect the left side of the neck and head. This was called a tilting-targe (*manteau d'armes, targetta*). Often its surface was covered with a trellis of applied steel strips; one wonders why. To reinforce and stiffen the large plate, or to give a lodgment to an opposing lance, tipped not with a point but a cronel? These late joust armours look, at first sight, as if they were no more than reinforced field armours, as, indeed, most in use were. But those made especially for monarchs like Philip II of Spain or Henri II of France are of simpler and more rigid form than field armours; the whole of the breast is covered by an extra piece, almost a second breastplate, the tassets tend to be single plates, as do the pauldrons, and the helmets, though heavier than those for field use, have large reinforcing wrappers as well.

AMERICAN SWORDS IN THE NINETEENTH CENTURY

The first swords to be made in a distinctively national style in America were only produced in any quantity after the close of the period with which I have been dealing. Up to and during the War of Independence (1774—1783), all swords used by American troops were of 'foreign' styles—English, French and German, with a predominance of the French types.

There are, however, one or two American swords, for instance those made by Nathan Starr and Son of Middletown, Connecticut, which antedate 1800; these are so similar in form to German swords of the period that no national style is apparent. One, however, dating perhaps as early as 1800, has its pommel-cap formed as an eagle's head. This apart, the only thing which seems to distinguish these American swords is a very feeble-looking hilt-design, and poor-quality blades. After about 1800, the incorporation of an eagle's-head pommel-cap became fairly common and did give a positively 'American' style to the swords thus adorned. It should be said that all through the first half of the nineteenth century, the blades of all types of American sword, which in the main followed contemporary European patterns of light cavalry sabre, heavy cavalry *pallasch*, and infantry spadroon, were made in Europe—mostly in Germany, at Solingen and Klingenthal, but also in France.

It could be said that during the first quarter of the nineteenth century, a period which embraces the war with England in 1812—1814, all swords made in America for enlisted men followed German styles, while the dress swords of officers were of an exclusively French pattern—those late smallswords which appeared in the 1790s (Fig. 107, above). However, in the midst of this following of French and German styles, the swords of militia officers showed a much more enterprising and distinctive American bias. It is upon these weapons, mostly, that the eagle's-head pommel-caps are to be found.

Between about 1825 and 1840, this general trend continued, with a few English models thrown in; but in the succeeding twenty years, from about 1840 to 1860, the matter was taken in hand more effectively, and a completely new series of patterns, all of them based upon French designs, was adopted. These continued in use until the end of the century.

Notable manufacturers of swords in America from about 1790 until the close of the nineteenth century, were Nathan Starr and Son. The elder Starr was authorised to make swords for the U.S. army in 1798, and he and his son produced many of the weapons used in the War of 1812, after which they made a number of presentation swords. Later, the

N. P. Ames Manufacturing Company of Springfield, Massachusetts, became the major producer of swords, at Cabotville, and from 1834 until the end of the American Civil War this firm produced large numbers of military and naval swords. Another notable manufacturer, William H. Horstmann of Philadelphia, started life in Germany, emigrating to the United States in 1816. He set up in Philadelphia as a dealer in textiles, which led him on to develop a business in uniforms and military equipment generally. At some time around 1830, he bought up a sword-making business which was being carried on in the city by a German cutler and armourer named Widtmann. The firm of Horstmann continued, like N. P. Ames, to produce swords until the early years of the twentieth century.

Photographic Acknowledgements

The Author and the Publishers express their gratitude to those who have granted permission for the use of copyright photographs or for the photographing of weapons and armour which are in their possession. They wish particularly to thank the following:

Peter Dale Ltd, London, for	Plate 1 B and C; Plate 4 B, C and D; Plate 5 B and C; Plate 7 C; Plate 8 C; Plate 10 C; Plate 11 A and B; Plate 12 E, F and G; Plate 13 B, E and F; Plate 14 A, B, C, D, E and F; Plate 15 A, B and C; Plate 18 C and D; Plate 19 D; Plate 20 B, D and E; Plate 21 A, B, C, D, E and F; Plate 22 A, C and D; Plate 23 A, B, C, D, F and G
The Kunsthistorisches Museum, for	Plate 6 B and C; Plate 7 B; Plate 16
The Metropolitan Museum of Art, for	Plate 12 A (Rogers Fund, 1932); Plate 17 C (Rogers Fund, 1919); Plate 17 D (Harris Brisbane Dick Fund, 1932)
National Museum of Antiquities of Scotland, for	Plate 19 E
National Portrait Gallery, for	Plate 10 A and B
The Trustees of the Wallace Collection, for	Plate 1 A and D; Plate 2 A, B, C, D and E; Plate 3 A, B, C and D; Plate 4 A; Plate 5 A; Plate 6 A and D; Plate 7 A and D; Plate 8 A, B and D; Plate 12 B; Plate 17 A and B; Plate 18 A and B; Plate 19 A and B; Plate 20 A and C; Plate 24
The owners of private collections, for	Plate 9 A, B, C and D; Plate 10 D; Plate 12 C and D; Plate 13 C and D; Plate 19 C; Plate 22 B; Plate 23 E

Plate 13 A is Crown Copyright and is reproduced with permission of the Controller of Her Majesty's Stationery Office.

Time Chart

DATE	MILITARY & POLITICAL EVENTS	HEADS OF STATE	IMPORTANT PERSONS	ARTISTS	CRAFTSMEN OF ARMS & ARMOUR	WRITERS	MUSICIANS
1450		Henry VI of Lancaster K. of England since 1422	Richard of York with rival claim to English crown	Donatello 1386–1466	*Milan* 'Missaglia Company'	François Villon 1431–c.85	John Dunstable d. c.1453
		Charles VII K. of France since 1422	Charles of Charolais, heir to Burgundy 'Le Téméraire'	Paolo Uccello 1397–1475	Bellino and Ambrogio Coria	Antoine de la Salle c.1388–1462	
		Philip 'Le Bon' D. of Burgundy		Filippo Lippi 1406–69	Giovanni da Caravalle		
1452		Francesco Sforza seizes Milan		Hugo van der Goes c.1440–82			
		Frederick III becomes Holy Roman Emperor					
1453	End of Hundred Years War		Richard Neville, E. of Warwick 'Kingmaker'	Piero della Francesca c.1420–92	Damiano Missaglia	Enguerrand de Monstrelet c.1400–53	Guillaume Dufay c.1400–74
1455	Wars of Roses begin				Domenico Negroli	Olivier de la Marche	
1460	Battle of Wakefield: Richard of York killed		Edward of March Yorkist heir			Sir Thomas Malory d.1470	
1461	Battles of St Albans, Mortimer's Cross, Towton	Henry VI deposed: Edward of York rules as Edward IV		Andrea del Verrocchio 1435–88			
		Louis XI now K. of France		Gentile Bellini 1430–1516			
				Sandro Botticelli 1444–1510			
1464 –65	Wars of League of Public Weal in France: Battle of Monthéry	Charles of Charolais regent of Burg. 1465–67, then succeeds his father					
1469		Isabella of Castile marries Ferdinand of Aragon		Martin Schongauer c.1445–91			Joannes Okeghem d. c.1495
1470 –71	Resurgence of Lancastrians as Warwick changes sides quashed by Yorkist victs. of Barnet and, conclusively, Tewkesbury	Edward IV exiled in 1470: makes triumphant return 1471: Henry VI prisoner in Tower, dies there		Benozzo Gozzoli 1420–97		Luigi Pulci 1432–84	
						Angelo Ambro. Politian 1454–94	

DATE	MILITARY & POLITICAL EVENTS	HEADS OF STATE	IMPORTANT PERSONS	ARTISTS	CRAFTSMEN OF ARMS & ARMOUR	WRITERS	MUSICIANS
1476 –77	Swiss Confederation defeats Charles of Burgundy. Battles of Grandson, Morat, Nancy	Charles of Burg. dies Nancy: dau. Marie inherits: weds Maximilian, son of Emp. Frederick III	Medici family: Lorenzo 'Il Magnifico' 1449–92	Andrea Mantegna 1431–1506	*Innsbruck* Caspar Rieder *fl.*1475–1500	Giov. Pico della Mirandola 1463–94	
1483		Edward IV dies: young son Edward V deposed by uncle Richard III / Charles VIII suc. Louis XI as K. of France	William Caxton		*Innsbruck* Jörg Wagner *fl.*1485 / Treytz family *fl.*1460–1536		
1485	Henry of Richmond, Lancastrian claimant, invades England: Battle of Bosworth	Richard III killed at Bosworth: Henry of Richmond becomes Henry VII (Tudor), marries Elizabeth of York					
1492	Columbus discovers W. Indies			Hans Memling *c.*1430–94	*Hull* Hans Sumersperger *cutler*	Philippe de Commynes *c.*1447–1511	William Cornyshe 'Elder' *c.*1502
1493		Maximilian I becomes Holy Roman Emperor		Vit. Carpaccio *c.*1460–1525/6	*Augsburg* Lorenz and Koloman Colman 'Helmschmied' 1467–1516 & 1470–1532		
1494 –95	French invade Italy: capture Naples: retreat: Battle of Fornovo		Ludovico Sforza D. of Milan since 1479	Hieronymus Bosch *c.* 1450–1516		Girolamo Savonarola 1452–98 Desiderius Erasmus 1466–1536	
1496		Maximilian's son Philip of Burg. weds Juana of Spain		Luca Signorelli *c.*1445–1523	*Milan* Giovan Marco Meraviglia		
1497 –98	Voyages of John Cabot and of Vasco da Gama			Leonardo da Vinci 1452–1519	Paulus Negroli Nicola de Silva		
1499		Charles VIII dies: suc. by Louis XII	Borgia family: Alexander VI, Pope 1492–1503: son Cesare 1475/6–1507; dau. Lucrezia 1480–1519	Michelangelo 1475–1564	*Arbois* Francesco Merate	Nicolo Machiavelli 1469–1527	
1500 –10	Portuguese settlements in India			Raphael 1483–1520 Albrecht Dürer 1471–1528	*Innsbruck* Hans Prunner Hans Müllner		

Year	Events	Statesmen	Artists	Armourers	Writers	Musicians
1504	Isabella of Castile dies					
1509	Henry VII dies: suc. by son Henry VIII					William Cornyshe 'Younger' d.1523
1513	Battle of Flodden: Scots defeated		Hans Holbein 'Younger' 1497/8–1543	*Augsburg* Helmschmied family	John Skelton ?1460–1529	
1514	François of Angoulême weds Claude of France: is K. within a year	Cardinal Wolsey c.1473–1530	Dosso Dossi 1479–1542	*Innsbruck* Hans Rabeiler fl.1501–19	John Colet ?1467–1519	
1515	Battle of Marignano		Hans Burgkmair 1473–1531	*Brussels* Filippo de Grampis	Thomas More 1478–1535	
1516	Ferdinand of Aragon and Philip of Spain and Burg. die: Charles of Burg. now also Charles I of Spain		Hans Baldung Grien 1484/5–1545	*Brussels* Gio. Angelo de Littis · *Innsbruck* Hans Maystetter fl.1510–53	Ludovico Ariosto · Martin Luther 1474–1546	
1519	Maxim. I dies: suc. by g'son Charles of Burg. & Spain as Emperor Charles V		Jean Clouet 1485–1540	*Brussels/London* Paul van Vrelant · *Greenwich* Martin van Royne	Francesco Guicciardini 1483–1540 · François Rabelais c.1495–1553	
1520	Field of Cloth of Gold; Suleiman I, Sultan of Turkey		Lorenzo Lotto 1490–1541	*Milan* Filippo Negroli	Pietro Aretino 1492–1556 · Matt. Bandello 1485–1561	Thomas Tallis c.1505–85
1525	Battle of Pavia; François I imprisoned			*Innsbruck* Seusenhofer fam., fl.1470–1555 · *Augsburg* Hans Ringler / Daniel Hopfer 1470–1536	John Calvin 1509–64	
1526	Battle of Panipat; Babur founding Mogul Empire in India		Benvenuto Cellini 1500–71 · Antonio Correggio 1489–1534	*Greenwich* Erasmus Kirkenar	John Knox 1505–72	
1529–30	Fall of Wolsey: English Reformation: dissolution of monasteries	Thomas Cromwell c.1485–1540		*Augsburg* Matthäus Frauenpreiss fl.1530–49		
1534	Henry VIII 'Supreme Head of Church in England'			*Nuremberg* Kunz Lochner 1510–67 · Seb. Katzmair fl.1558		
1547	Henry VIII dies: suc. by young son Edw. VI under Protectorship of mat. uncle, Edw. Seymour · François I dies: suc. by Henri II, son	Seymour family: Edw. D. of Somerset *exec.* 1552; Thomas Baron Sudeley *exec.* 1549	Pieter Brueghel c.1525–69 · Lucas Cranach 1472–1553	*Landshut / Solingen* Grosschedel fam. Amb. Gemlich *bladesmith* · *Milan* Antonio Picinino fl.1550		Giovanni Pier-Luigi da Palestrina c.1524–94

DATE	MILITARY & POLITICAL EVENTS	HEADS OF STATE	IMPORTANT PERSONS	ARTISTS	CRAFTSMEN OF ARMS & ARMOUR	WRITERS	MUSICIANS
1553		Edw. VI dies: suc. by Mary I, half-sister, Catholic Queen		Titian 1488/9-1576 Agnolo Bronzino 1503-72			
1554	Persecution of English Protestants	Mary I marries Philip of Spain, son of Emp. Charles V	Catherine de Medici, w. of Henri II				
1556	Akbar expands the Mogul Empire	Emp. Charles V abdicates emp. in favour of bro. Ferdinand and crown of Spain in favour of son, Philip II	Duc Claude de Guise, 1496-1550; Card. Jean, bro., 1498-1550; Duc François, son, 1519-63; Marie, w. of K. of Scots, dau., Duc Henri, g'son 1550-88	Jacopo Tintoretto 1518/9-94	*Spain & France & England* Diego de Caias *damasc.*		
1558	England loses Calais to France	Mary Tudor dies; suc. by half-sister, Elizabeth I					
1559		Henri II of France dies: eldest son François II now K. (husb. of Mary Q of Scots)			*Milan* Daniele di Saravalle *bladesmith*		
1560		François II dies: Charles IX now King	Henri of Navarre Prot. cousin of French king	Paolo Veronese 1528-88	*Augsburg* Jorg Sorg *engraver fl.*1560		
1562	French religious wars intermittent until 1598		Louis I de Bourbon Huguenot Prince de Condé		*Italy* Filippo Orro *designer of ornament*		
1564		Emp. Ferdinand I dies; suc. by son Maximilian II	William Cecil Lord Burghley 1520-98		*Antwerp* Eliseus Libaerts *dec. work fl.* 1562	Pierre de Ronsard 1524-85	Orlando de Lassus 1532-94
1565 -67		Mary Q of Scots marries Henry Lord Darnley; after his murder marries suspect, E. of Bothwell; Scots rebel; Mary forced to abdicate in favour of baby son James VI; flees to England; imprisoned	Henry Stuart Lord Darnley 1545-67; gt-g'son of Henry VII / James Hepburn Earl of Bothwell c.1536-78		*Munich* Melchior Diefstetter *bladesmith* / *Toledo* Sahagun family: Alonso de, 'Elder'; Alonso de, 'Younger'; Luis de *bladesmiths*		

1571	Battle of Lepanto: Turkish fleet destroyed		Don Juan of Austria	
1572	St Bartholomew's Day: Huguenots massacred	Henri of Navarre marries Marguerite de Valois sister of Charles IX	John Hawkins mariner 1532–95	
1574		Charles IX dies; suc. by Henri III, bro.		
1576	Henri of Navarre, leading Huguenot, escapes Court	Emp. Maxim. II dies: suc. by Rudolf II, son	Francis Drake c.1543–96	
1577	Drake circumnavigates globe. War of Liberation as Prot. Dutch rise against Catholic Spanish overlords	William 'the Silent', Prince of Orange, leads Dutch against Span. occupying forces	Robert Dudley E. of Leicester 1532/3–88	
1584		William the Silent assassinated	François Duc d'Alençon	
1585–86	English army sent to aid Dutch: battle of Zutphen – Sidney killed		Sir Philip Sidney	
1587		Mary Q. of Scots executed by English	Walter Raleigh c.1552–1618	
1588	Defeat of Spanish Armada			
1589–90		Henri III assassinated: Henri of Navarre begins ten-year struggle to claim throne as Henri IV; turns Catholic 1593		El Greco 1541–1614; Nich. Hilliard 1547–1619
1596	Drake dies at sea: Eng. fleet under Howard and Essex sacks Cadiz	Philip II of Spain dies; suc. by Philip III, son	Robert Devereux E. of Essex c.1566–1601	
1598	Edict of Nantes ends relig. wars in France			

Arms and armour centres:

Dresden	Othmar Wetter *cutler*
Greenwich	John Kelte *fl.*1567–76; Jacob Halder
Munich	Kaspar Spät; Daniel Sadeler
Augsburg	Anton Peffenhauser
Milan	Andrea Ferara 1555–93; Pietro Caino
Toledo	*Bladesmiths:* Sebastian Hernandez; Tomas de Ayala; Aquirre family
Nuremberg	Peter Danner *gunsmith*
Holland	Adolf Bosch *gunsmith*; Herold family *gunsmiths*
Dresden	
Munich	Stantler family: Christoph & Wolfgang *bladesmiths*
Solingen	Berns family; Clemens Horn *bladesmith*; Weyersberg fam. *bladesmiths fl.*1488–1638; Paullus & Clemens Willems

Writers: Christopher Marlowe 1564–93; Edmund Spenser ?1552–99

Music: Wm. Byrd 1543–1623

DATE	MILITARY & POLITICAL EVENTS	HEADS OF STATE	IMPORTANT PERSONS	ARTISTS	CRAFTSMEN OF ARMS & ARMOUR	WRITERS	MUSICIANS
1601	Essex rebellion; leaders imprisoned, Essex exec.				*Lisieux* Jean Le Bourgeois *gunsmith*	William Shakespeare 1564–1616	Tomás Luis de Victoria 1584–1611
					Figeac R. Cisteron *gunsmith*		
1603		Elizabeth I dies; suc. by cousin James VI of Scots (I of England)			*Greenwich* Wm Pickering Thomas Stevens *armourer*		
1608	Samuel de Champlain founds Quebec		Michelangelo da Caravaggio 1573–1610		Nich. Sherman *armourer*	Ben Jonson 1572–1637	John Dowland 1563–1626
	Virginia Co.'s first permanent settlement				*Solingen* Tesche family *fl.*1518–1700	Miguel de Cervantes 1547–1616	
					Friedrich & Peter Munch *fl.*1595–1660	John Donne 1571/2–1631	
					Kreisser family *fl. until* 1840		
1610	Settlement of Ulster by Eng. and Scots begins	Henri IV assassinated: suc. by Louis XIII	Henry Prince of Wales d.1612				
1618	Execution of Raleigh		Geo. Villiers D. of Buckingham 1592–1628				
	Oppression of Prots. in Bohemia leads to Thirty Years War						
1619		Emp. Matthias dies; suc. by Ferdinand III		Frans Hals c.1583–1666			
1620	Pilgrim Fathers land in New England			Diego Rodriguez de Silva Velásquez 1599–1660			
1625		James VI and I dies; suc. by Charles I, son	Cardinal Richelieu 1585–1642				
1627	Buckingham's abortive La Rochelle exped.	Gustavus Adolphus of Sweden at height of struggle with Poland and Germany		Anth. van Dyke 1599–1641	*Toledo* Pedro de Toro		
1628	Buckingham assassinated		Albrecht von Wallenstein 1583–1664	Peter Paul Rubens 1577–1640	*Milan* Federigo Picinino	René Descartes 1596–1650	
	Fall of La Rochelle		Johann Count Tilly 1559–1632		*Brescia* Gunsmiths: Lazzarino Comminazzo		

Year	Events	Events	People	Artists	Bladesmiths	Writers
1632	Battle of Lutzen: Gust. Adolphus killed	Christina child queen of Sweden	Gottfried Hein. von Pappenheim 1594–1632		Giovanni Battista Francino	
1637	'Ship Money' dispute in Parliament				Giovanni Antonio Gavaccioli	
1638	Wars of Covenant in Scotland			Gerrit van Honthorst 1590–1656		
1641	Execution of Stafford		John Hampden 1594–1643	Rembrandt van Rijn 1606–69		
1642		Charles I raises standard at Nottingham: Civil War begins: Louis XIII dies: suc. by Louis XIV, son		Nich. Poussin 1594–1665		
1643				Giovanni Lorenzo Bernini 1598–1680		
1645	Battle of Naseby finishes Royalist hopes		Oliver Cromwell 1599–1658	Claude Lorraine 1600–82	*Solingen* Johannes Hoppe	
1647	Scots hand over Charles I to Eng. Parl, which imprisons him		Elizabeth of Bohemia and sons, Rupert (1619–82) and Maurice			
1648	Wars of the Fronde / Treaty of Münster and Peace of Westphalia end Thirty Years War		Cardinal Mazarin 1602–61			
1649	Cromwellian massacres of Drogheda & Wexford	Execution of Charles I: Charles II King in exile				
1650	Charles II and Scots army defeated at Worcester: King flees abroad again			Philips de Koninck 1619–88		
1653	Cromwell Lord Protector		Admiral Blake 1599–1657	Jacob van Ruisdael 1628/9–82	*Solingen* Wundes family *bladesmiths*	John Milton 1608–74
1658	Cromwell dies, son Richard succeeds him for ineffectual year		Richard Cromwell 'Tumbledown Dick'	Jan Albertz Rotius	*Hounslow* 'Factory' of *bladesmiths* fl.1620–80	Thomas Hobbes 1588–1679
1660	Restoration of Charles II (to his kingdom)		General Monk 1608–70	Geraert Terborch	*Greenwich* Johan Hoppie *bladesmith*	

DATE	MILITARY & POLITICAL EVENTS	HEADS OF STATE	IMPORTANT PERSONS	ARTISTS	CRAFTSMEN OF ARMS & ARMOUR	WRITERS	MUSICIANS
1664	Anglo-Dutch naval wars: English capture New Amsterdam, rename it New York		James D. of York, bro. of Charles II	Sir Peter Lely 1618–80 Meindert Hobbema 1638–1709	Maastricht Jan Hermans gunsmith	John Evelyn 1620–1706 Samuel Pepys 1633–1703	
1665	Battle off Lowestoft: Dutch defeated Great Plague of London			Cuyp family: Aelbert, 1605–91			
1666	Great Fire of London					Benedictus de Spinoza 1632–77 Molière 1622–73	
1667	Dutch raid on Medway					Jean Racine 1639–99	Jean Bapt. Lully 1632–87
1678	'The Popish Plot'		Titus Oates	Willem I van der Velde 1611–93	Brescia Filippo Moretti gunsmith		
1683		Charles II dies, leaving no legit. child: suc. by Catholic bro., James II	James D. of Monmouth illeg son of Charles II	Willem II van der Velde 1633–1707	Filippo Malschetti gunsmith		
1685	Monmouth Rebellion: Battle of Sedgemoor	Monmouth executed, followers hanged and transported			Aqua Fresca 1651–1738	Isaac Newton 1642–1727 John Locke 1632–1704	Henry Purcell 1659–95
1688	'The Glorious Revolution'	James II deposed and exiled: Prot. son-in-law & dau. suc., William III & Mary	Anthony Ashley Cooper, E. of Shaftesbury 1671–1713				
1694		Mary II dies: Wm rules alone					
1700	Kingdom of Prussia founded Russia begins struggle with Baltic powers for hegemony of the north	Elector of Brandenburg made 1st King of Prussia Charles II of Spain dies childless, naming Philippe of Anjou, grandson of Louis XIV, as heir Peter the Great, Tsar of Russia	John Churchill D. of Marlborough 1650–1722				

Year	History and Politics	Rulers and Succession	Prominent People	Art	Literature	Music
1702	War of Spanish Succession: France v England, Holland and Austria	William III, widower of Mary II, dies; suc. by sister-in-law, Q. Anne				François Couperin 1688–1733 / Antonio Vivaldi 1675–1741
1704	British and Dutch capture Gibraltar / Battle of Blenheim: French army defeated		Eugene of Savoy 1663–1736			
1705		Emp. Leopold I dies: suc. by Joseph I, son	James D. of Berwick illeg. son of James II 1670–1734		Jos. Addison 1672–1719 / Rich. Steele 1672–1729	
1706	Battle of Ramillies: French army routed					
1707	Union of Scotland and England					
1708	Battle of Oudenarde: French army defeated					
1709	Battle of Malplaquet: French army retreats					
1711		Emp. Joseph I dies: suc. by Charles VI, brother	James Edward Stuart, 'Old Pretender', son of James II (1688–1766)			
1713	Treaty of Utrecht ends War of Spanish Suc.: Philip V conf. as king of Spain: England takes Gib, Austria takes Span. Neth.	Frederick of Prussia dies: suc. by Fred. Wm I, son / Charles XII of Sweden struggling against Peter of Russia				
1714	'Pragmatic Sanction' issued by Charles VI to secure Empire for his unborn heirs	Queen Anne dies: suc. by distant Prot. cousin, Elector of Hanover, as George I	Sir Robert Walpole first Prime Minister	Jean Antoine Watteau 1684–1721		
1715	First Jacobite Rising: Old Pretender defeated	Louis XIV dies: suc. by child king Louis XV			Jon. Swift 1667–1720 / Dan. Defoe ? 1660–1731	
1721 –22		Charles VI settles Emp. on dau. Maria Theresa (born 1717)				
1727		George I dies: suc. by George II, son				George Fredk. Handel 1685–1759

DATE	MILITARY & POLITICAL EVENTS	HEADS OF STATE	IMPORTANT PERSONS	ARTISTS	CRAFTSMEN OF ARMS & ARMOUR	WRITERS	MUSICIANS
1727 –29	Spain besieging Gibraltar: Brit. rights ratified by Treaty of Seville			William Hogarth 1697–1764		Samuel Richardson 1689–1761	J. S. Bach 1685–1750
1740 –60	Gradual collapse of Mogul Empire in India				*Spain* Juan Santos *fl.*1740–60		Domenico Scarlatti 1685–1757
1740 –48	War of Austrian Succession	Frederick Wm of Prussia dies: suc. by son, 'Frederick the Great'; Emp. Charles VI dies: heir, dau. Maria Theresa, Q. of Hungary		Canaletto 1697–1768	*Regens- burg* Johannes And. Keuchenreuter *gunsmith*	Voltaire 1694–1778	
	Battles of Mollwitz (1741), Dettingen (1743), Fontenoy (1745), Peace of Aix (1748)	Prussia seizes Silesia (event. retains by Peace of Aix); Maria Theresa's husband, Francis of Lorraine, elected Emp. (1745)		François Boucher 1703–70	*Paris* Jean Bapt. La Roche *gunsmith*		
1745	Second Jacobite Rising led by 'Young Pretender' at head of Scots army		Charles Ed. Stuart 'Young Pretender' 1720–88			Henry Fielding 1707–54	
1746	Battle of Culloden: Scots routed, destroyed		Wm of Cumberland son of George II				
1751	Battle of Arcot: Clive defeats French in India	Philip V of Spain dies: suc. by Ferdinand VI, son	Robert Clive, 'Clive of India' 1725–74	Jean Bapt. Chardin 1699–1770	*Heiders- bach* J. C. Stockmar *gunsmith*	*Philosophes & Encyclopédistes*: Diderot, d'Alembert *et al.*	
1756	Seven Years War: Aust., France, v. Eng., Prussia			Giovanni Batt. Tiepolo 1696–1770	*Paris* Mazellier *gunsmith*		
1757	Nawab of Bengal seizes Calcutta: 'Black Hole'				*Madrid* Francisco Lopez *gunsmith*		
	Clive retakes Calcutta, defeats Nawab at Plassey: made Gov. of Bengal (1757–60)						
1758	British capture Louisburg & Fort Duquesne in America from French		James Wolfe 'Wolfe of Quebec' 1727–59				

Year	Events	Rulers	Statesmen	Painters		Writers	Musicians
1759–60	Wolfe captures Quebec: all Canada taken and held by Britain	Ferdinand of Spain dies: suc. by Charles III / George II dies: suc. by grandson, George III	William Pitt 'the Elder', E. of Chatham 1708–78	Jean Bapt. Greuze 1725–1805 / Guardi bros.		Benjamin Franklin 1706–90 / Jean Jacques Rousseau 1712–28	Franz. Jos. Haydn 1732–1809 / Christoph Willibald Gluck 1714–87
1763	Peace of Hubertusburg: *status quo ante bellum*	Catherine the Great rules Russia 1762–96		Jean Honoré Fragonard 1732–1806		Sam. Johnson 1709–84	
1765	Despite colonies' protests, Parl. passes Stamp Act						
1767	Townshend Acts to tax American imports			John Singleton Copley 1738–1815		Laurence Sterne 1713–68 / Tobias Smollett 1721–71 / Beaumarchais 1732–99	
1773	Riots in New England: 'Boston Tea Party'		Warren Hastings 1st Gov.-Gen. Brit. India 1732–1818	Sir Joshua Reynolds 1723–92 / Thomas Gainsborough 1727–88			
1774		Louis XV dies: suc. by Louis XVI, grandson					
1775	War of American Indep.: Battles of Lexington & Bunker Hill; U.S. invade Canada		George Washington 1732–99 / Thomas Jefferson 1743–1826 / Ben. Arnold 1741–1801	Angelica Kauffmann 1741–1807		Johann Wolf. von Goethe 1749–1832 / Immanuel Kant 1724–1807	Wolfgang Amadeus Mozart 1759–91
1776	Declaration of Indep.			George Stubbs 1724–1806			
1779–83	Spain besieging Gib.						
1780		Maria Theresa dies: suc. by Joseph II		George Morland 1763–1804			
1781	Cornwallis surrenders at Yorktown		William Pitt 'Younger' 1759–1806	George Romney 1734–1802	*Anghiari*	Giuseppe Guardiani *gunsmith* / Edw. Gibbon 1737–94	
1783	War of Indep. ends: Britain recognises the United States						
1786	Treaty of Versailles: Gibraltar confirmed to Britain	Frederick the Great dies	Charles James Fox 1749–1806	Fran. Goya 1746–1828			

DATE	MILITARY & POLITICAL EVENTS	HEADS OF STATE	IMPORTANT PERSONS	ARTISTS	CRAFTSMEN OF ARMS & ARMOUR	WRITERS	MUSICIANS
1788		Charles III of Spain dies			*Birm'ham* Thomas Gill *bladesmith*		
1789	Fall of Bastille: French Revolution begins	Washington inaug. as 1st Pres. of U.S.		Jacques-Louis David 1748–1825			
1791	Britain grants Canada self-government			Wm Blake 1757–1827	*Sweden* Johan Adolf Grecke *gunsmith*	James Boswell 1740–95	
1792	Paris mob storms Tuileries: royal family imprisoned by Paris commune			Thomas Girtin 1775–1802			
1793	France at war with 1st coalition of allied powers: Committee of Public Safety: Reign of Terror: Sept. Massacres	Louis XVI deposed Louis XVI executed		Chas. Willson Peale 1741–1827			
1794	Robespierre's dictatorship: falls from power, executed (preceded by fall and exec. of Danton)	Marie Antoinette executed		Gilbert Stuart 1755–1828 John Trumbull 1756–1843 James Gillray 1757–1815			
1795 –99	Directory governs France: Nap. Bonaparte puts down Paris insurrection: appt. to army of Alps & Italy, string of spectac. victs.: campaign in Egypt, Battle of Nile ('98), Syrian campaign ('99): return to France, *coup d'état*	John Adams as 2nd Pres. of U.S. (1796)	Josephine Beauharnais marries Napoleon (1796)		*Paris* Nich. Noel Bontet *gunsmith cutler craftsman*	Johann Chr. Fried. von Schiller 1759–1805	
1800	The Napoleonic Wars: vict. of Marengo makes him master of Italy: vict. of Hohenlinden compels Austria to sue for peace	Napoleon elected First Consul	Horatio Nelson destroyer of French fleet 1758–1805	John Crome 'Old Crome' 1768–1821	*Lepage gunsmith*	William Wordsworth 1770–1850 Samuel Taylor Coleridge 1772–1834	Ludwig van Beethoven 1770–1827
1801	Britain defeats French in Egypt	Thomas Jefferson 3rd Pres. of U.S.		Sir Thomas Lawrence 1769–1830			

Year	Events	Politics	People	Painters		Writers	Composers
			John Quincy Adams: senator (later Pres.) 1767–1848				Franz Peter Schubert 1797–1828
						Jane Austen 1775–1817	
						George Gordon Lord Byron 1788–1824	
						Sir Walter Scott 1771–1832	
					London Joseph Manton *gunsmith* ?1766–1835		
1802	Treaty of Amiens: brief truce between Britain & Napoleonic France						
1803	Renewal of war: threat of French invasion · Nap. sells Louisiana (coerced from Spain in 1800) to U.S.						
1804		Napoleon crowned Emperor of the French					
1805	Battle of Ulm: Austria surrenders · Battle of Trafalgar: French routed · Battle of Austerlitz: Russia defeated		Bonaparte family aggrandised: Joseph K. of Naples, K. of Spain · Elisa Dss of Tuscany				
1806	After defeating Prussia at Jena, Napoleon turns on Russia to secure conquest		Louis K. of Holland · Pauline Dss of Guastalla				
1807	Pact of Tilsit with Russia: Nap. invades Portugal, instals bro. in Spain		Jerome K. of Westphalia · Caroline Q. of Naples				
1808	Spain & Portugal occup. by Frnch: Brit. exped. force: Peninsular Wars		Sir Arthur Wellesley, later D. of Wellington 1769–1852	Thomas Rowlandson 1756–1827			
1809 –11	Austria re-enters war: defeats of Essling, Wagram	George III ill: P. of Wales acts as Regent (1811)		J. M. W. Turner 1775–1851			
1812	America declares war on Britain, attacks Canada · Nap. invades Russia, burns Moscow; 'The Retreat'			Jean Aug. Ingres 1781–1867			
1813	Battle of Leipzig: Nap. defeated, loses Germany			Jean Louis Gericault 1791–1824			
1814	Allies invade France: Napoleon abdicates: exiled to Elba	Louis XVIII established in Paris					
1815	Napoleon's escape from Elba: 'The 100 Days' · Battle of Waterloo · The second exile – St Helena · Congress of Vienna re-arranges Europe	Napoleon dies in exile (1821)					

INDEX
by Michael Hobbs

Illustration references are in italics. Numbers given in brackets after Figure references are those of pages.

Monarchs are indexed by their Christian names.

Weapons and armour are indexed by major groupings, 'armet' being under 'helmet(s)', 'bayonet' under 'dagger(s)', 'rapier' under 'sword(s)', etc.

INDEX

www.ingramcontent.com/pod-product-compliance
Ingram Content Group UK Ltd.
Pitfield, Milton Keynes, MK11 3LW, UK
UKHW050010220225
455427UK00008B/112